Refo500 Academic Studies

Herausgegeben von
Herman J. Selderhuis

In Zusammenarbeit mit
Christopher B. Brown (Boston), Günter Frank (Bretten),
Barbara Mahlmann-Bauer (Bern), Tarald Rasmussen (Oslo),
Violet Soen (Leuven), Zsombor Tóth (Budapest),
Günther Wassilowsky (Berlin), Siegrid Westphal (Osnabrück).

Band 93

Günter Frank / Volker Leppin /
Herman J. Selderhuis / Klaus Unterburger (Hg.)

Totus noster?

Augustinus zwischen den Konfessionen

Vandenhoeck & Ruprecht

Bibliografische Information der Deutschen Bibliothek:
Die Deutsche Nationalbibliothek verzeichnet diese Publikation in der
Deutschen Nationalbibliografie; detaillierte bibliografische Daten sind
im Internet über https://dnb.de abrufbar.

© 2023 Vandenhoeck & Ruprecht, Theaterstraße 13, D-37073 Göttingen,
ein Imprint der Brill-Gruppe
(Koninklijke Brill NV, Leiden, Niederlande; Brill USA Inc., Boston MA, USA;
Brill Asia Pte Ltd, Singapore; Brill Deutschland GmbH, Paderborn, Deutschland;
Brill Österreich GmbH, Wien, Österreich)
Koninklijke Brill NV umfasst die Imprints Brill, Brill Nijhoff, Brill Hotei, Brill Schöningh,
Brill Fink, Brill mentis, Vandenhoeck & Ruprecht, Böhlau, V&R unipress und
Wageningen Academic.

Alle Rechte vorbehalten. Das Werk und seine Teile sind urheberrechtlich geschützt.
Jede Verwertung in anderen als den gesetzlich zugelassenen Fällen bedarf der vorherigen
schriftlichen Einwilligung des Verlages.

Umschlaggestaltung: SchwabScantechnik, Göttingen
Satz: le-tex publishing services GmbH, Leipzig
Druck und Bindung: Hubert & Co. BuchPartner, Göttingen
Printed in the EU

Vandenhoeck & Ruprecht Verlage | www.vandenhoeck-ruprecht-verlage.com

ISSN 2198-3089
ISBN 978-3-525-57352-5

Inhaltsverzeichnis

Vorwort 7

Martin Wernisch
Augustinus in den Hussitischen Debatten 9

Volker Leppin
Augustin zwischen Wittenberg, Zürich und Löwen. Die frühen
Kontroversen der Reformationszeit 25

Stefania Salvadori
The Reception of Augustine in Karlstadt's Writings from 1517 to 1521 43

Mark W. Elliott
Melanchthon und Augustinus. Brüche in der Soteriologie mit
besonderem Bezug zu den Römerbriefen. 61

Amy Nelson Burnett
Reading Augustine in the Early Eucharistic Controversy 77

Christoph Strohm
Augustin als Autorität bei Martin Bucer und in den
Auseinandersetzungen um die Kölner Reformation 97

Willem van Vlastuin
Calvin's un-Augustinian concept of Catholicity 115

Herman J. Selderhuis
Augustine in Reformed tradition: an impetus for further research 135

Mathijs Lamberigts
Augustine and/in Trent's Decree on Justification 153

Wim François
Augustinus und die Löwener Kontroversen über Prädestination,
Gnade und freien Willen 189

Jakub Koryl
Common Bond of Thinking. Saint Augustine and the Socinian
Metaphysics of Presence 217

Hartmut Rudolph
Der Rekurs auf Augustinus in G. W. Leibniz' ökumenischer Argumentation .. 247

Register 271

Vorwort

Mit Augustinus steht der wohl gewichtigste Kirchenvater der frühen Kirche im Zentrum des Interesses. Keine Gestalt hatte eine solche Autorität über das ganze Mittelalter, aber auch in der Neuzeit. Dies gilt in solchen für die Theologie höchst wichtigen sakraments- und gnadentheologischen, geschichtstheologischen, ekklesiologischen und anthropologischen Fragen. Kein ernst zu nehmender Theologe konnte scheinbar an ihm vorbei. Dies gilt umso mehr für die Auseinandersetzungen in der Zeit der Reformation. Zugespitzt kann man sagen: Ohne Augustinus gäbe es die Theologien der Reformationszeit vermutlich nicht. Jeder Theologe bezog sich irgendwie auf ihn – und doch führte dies mitunter zu verschiedenen theologischen Perspektiven.

Das Augustinus-Thema, das in diesem Sammelband dokumentiert und diskutiert wird, steht jedoch in einem umfangreicheren Kontext, wozu eine Gruppe von Gelehrten, u. a. der viel zu früh verstorbene Peter Walter, schon seit längerer Zeit Überlegungen angestellt haben. Diese Überlegungen gingen und gehen von der kaum bestreitbaren Beobachtung aus, dass die Erforschung der frühneuzeitlichen Theologiegeschichtsschreibung noch immer durch die konfessionellen Interessen und Perspektiven der Forschenden geprägt ist. Dieser Umstand kontrastiert freilich mit der Tatsache, dass sich nicht nur in allen konfessionellen theologischen Wissenskulturen ähnliche Debatten und parallele Entwicklungen ereignet haben, sondern auch damit, dass es vielfach zu Wechselwirkungen bzw. gegenseitigen Beeinflussungen gekommen ist. Daher verspricht ein trans- und interkonfessioneller Ansatz, der diese Interferenzen explizit in den Blick nimmt, methodischen Fortschritt und neue inhaltliche Einsichten. Diese transkonfessionelle Perspektive ist deshalb der Ansatz, zu dem die "Europäische Melanchthon-Akademie" Referenten zu dem Symposium "Totus noster? Augustinus zwischen den Konfessionen" vom 9.–11. September 2020 in die Melanchthonstadt nach Bretten eingeladen hatte.

Den Autoren, deren Beiträge in diesem Band dokumentiert sind, ist zunächst für Ihre Bereitschaft zu danken, sich auf dieses transkonfessionelle Wagnis eingelassen zu haben. Daneben danken die Herausgeber Herrn Niels Stouten (Theologische Universität Apeldoorn), der die Lektorierung der Beiträge sorgfältig begleitet hat. Schließlich ist der Fritz Thyssen Stiftung zu danken für ihre großzügige Förderung dieses Projekts.

Günter Frank, Volker Leppin, Herman Selderhuis und Klaus Unterburger

Martin Wernisch

Augustinus in den Hussitischen Debatten

Einführung

Augustinus in der Hussitischen Debatte – zu Beginn muss eine präzisierende Einschränkung vorgenommen werden: Dem Titel gemäß sollten verschiedene Vertreter jener Gedankenrichtung analysiert werden, die wir das Hussitentum nennen. Dabei wäre zu zeigen, dass sie mit den augustinischen Inspirationen jeweils auf unterschiedliche Weisen arbeiteten, manchmal auch im Gegensatz zueinander. Doch wie schon viele vor mir, bleibe ich in diesem Beitrag bei jener Gestalt stecken, die der ganzen Bewegung ihren Namen gegeben hat und deren Impulsen sie verbunden blieb, ohne doch bei ihm stehen zu bleiben.

Doch trotz dieser Beschränkung ist es kein Leichtes, die bisherige Forschung einfach zusammenzufassen und ein gesichertes, klar umrissenes Bild zu entwerfen. Die wichtigsten Gründe hierfür liegen in einer gegenläufigen Richtung: Einerseits können wir nur auf wenige einschlägige Spezialstudien zurückgreifen,[1] ja selbst die – umfangreiche – Quellengrundlage steht uns nicht vollständig zur Verfügung. Selbst die kritische Gesamtausgabe der Schriften von Jan Hus ist bis heute nicht abgeschlossen.[2] Diese geht auch deshalb so langsam voran, weil sie mit hohen editorischen Standards durchgeführt wird; so sind bis heute mühsame Vorarbeiten erfolgt. Analog ist die Lage in Bezug auf die weiteren hussitischen Autoren. Über eine Karte, die ausgesprochen voll ist von weißen Flecken, lässt sich kaum sprechen. Einige Beobachtungen will ich dennoch mutig vortragen, auch wenn selbst diese eingeschränkten Perspektiven ein gewisses Wagnis darstellen.

---

1 Aus den namhafteren Ausnahmen seien hier wenigstens die Arbeiten des belgischen Benediktiners Paul de Vooght erwähnt.
2 Magistri Iohannis Hus Opera omnia, sub auspiciis Academiae scientiarum rei publicae Bohemorum vulgata, seit 1959 in Prag, danach seit 2004 in Turnhout, im Rahmen der Reihe Corpus Christianorum – Continuatio mediaevalis. Unten wird leider nicht immer und einheitlich auf diese Ausgabe hingewiesen, auch bei den Texten, die bereits darin erschienen sind, da der Verfasser wegen der pandemischen Notlage am Zugang zu den neueren Bänden gehindert wurde.

1. Augustins Präsenz

Eine allgemeine, wenig überraschende Charakteristik teilt die hussistische Kontroverse mit allem Strömungen und Gruppierungen, die in diesem Band behandelt werden: Augustinus ist in diesen Debatten fast allgegenwärtig. Am häufigsten bezieht man sich zwar auf die Hl. Schrift, aber unter den nachbiblischen Autoritäten hat Augustin keine wirkliche Konkurrenz. Dies gilt bezüglich der altkirchlichen Väter, und noch weniger können die *moderni* sich mit ihm messen. Selbst John Wyclif nicht, trotz all seiner Popularität in der ersten Phase der Bewegung. Auch später, als die einheimischen Gründergestalten selbst zu Bezugspersonen wurden, änderte sich die Lage nur wenig – stärker erst mit dem Antritt der europäischen Reformatoren mit Martin Luther an der Spitze im 16. Jahrhundert. Dann beginnt freilich eine neue Epoche, die auf ein eigenes Blatt gehört; dennoch beziehe ich die Reformation als Vergleichspunkt mit ein. Dies ist durch die Tatsache legitimiert, dass das Hussitentum sich in den Protestantismus eingefügt hat und seine selbständige Existenz somit vergleichsweise kurz geblieben ist und einen auffallenden Übergangscharakter trägt.

Die epochale Wende, welche den Aufstieg der europäischen Reformation von der Entstehung des Hussitentums trennt, ist nichtsdestoweniger im Sinn zu behalten. Hier stellt die Einführung des Buchdrucks einen grundlegenden Einschnitt dar. Obgleich die Hussiten ihm zeitlich relativ nahestanden, waren sie selbst doch noch ganz und gar auf Handschriften angewiesen. Ihr Zugang zum Werk des Augustinus war dadurch auf charakteristische Weise limitiert.

Im Vergleich mit den Universitätsgelehrten des beginnenden 16. Jahrhunderts, die bereits über mehr oder weniger vollständige Ausgaben verfügten,[3] konnten die Kenntnisse ihrer Vorgänger hundert Jahre früher nur lückenhaft, wenn nicht geradezu fragmentarisch sein. Vielfach kannten diese die einzelnen Schriften nicht vollständig; sie mussten sich mit Zitaten und Anthologien zufriedengeben. In welchem Maß, das lässt sich allerdings keineswegs genau bestimmen. Eine Antwort auf die Frage, welche Schriften des Augustins Hus in ihrer ursprünglichen Gestalt zu Verfügung standen, ist nicht leicht zu geben.[4] Etliche mussten es gewesen sein; auch in den Böhmischen Ländern ist eine Reihe von entsprechenden Handschriften erhalten. Wahrscheinlich kursierten sie jedoch eher vereinzelt, als dass einzelne Personen größere Sammlungen besessen hätten. Ihre Spuren zu erkennen erschwert die Tatsache, dass man für Zitate aus solchen Texten öfters doch wieder die "Rüstkammern alles mittelalterlichen Wissens" benützte, die man gerade griffbereit hatte.[5]

---

3 Im Fall Augustinus' seit der Basler Ausgabe von Johannes Amerbach, die 1506 abgeschlossen wurde.
4 Zu Versuchen einer Rekonstruierung der Handbibliothek von Hus und den Problemen, die solchen im Wege stehen, siehe Hlaváček (1997).
5 Novotný: 1919, 13.

Bedenken wir all dies, müssen wir auch die einleitende Erklärung über die am häufigsten zitierte Autorität nach der Bibel noch korrigieren: sie stimmt, wenn man lediglich einzelne Denker zählt, aber sie beginnt zu wackeln, falls man Florilegien und Sammlungen ähnlicher Art in Erwägung zieht. Für Hus gilt dann die Feststellung, dass es das Dekret Gratians war, das ihm "nach der Schrift als die überhaupt häufigste Stütze" diente, "und zwar auch in den tschechischen Schriften".[6] Ursprünglich also eigentlich ein Handbuch des kanonischen Rechts – doch es ist zu betonen, dass diese seine Beschaffenheit bei Hus und seinen Nachfolgern, einschließlich der Gründer der Brüderunität, in einer auffälligen Umwandlung begriffen war. Sie behandelten es nämlich nicht mehr mit der juristischen Logik, sondern souverän theologisch, es wurde ihnen zu einem Mittel des Eindringens in das Denken der alten Kirche.

Es versteht sich freilich, dass ein solches Verfahren an seine Grenzen stößt. Aus den besagten Einschränkungen ergaben sich weitere, z. B. hinsichtlich der Möglichkeiten, die Authentizität einer Autorschaft zu prüfen. Immerhin gilt, dass das kritische Rüstzeug im Vergleich zu vorherigen Jahrhunderten zunahm. Der Buchdruck brachte dann einen deutlichen Einschnitt, der eine Zeit vorher von einer nachher schied. Andere Determinanten, der Frühhumanismus und die spätmittelalterliche Vertiefung des Augustinismus, wurden ebenfalls durch den Buchdruck befördert, entwickelten sich aber eher graduell und hatten auch in Böhmen Einfluss. Insgesamt war es mühsam, die Mängel der Textbasis zu überwinden; die Folgen werden noch sichtbar werden.

2. Hus und das Denken Augustins

Nach diesen Präliminarien ist die Frage zu behandeln, wie Hus mit dem Denken des Augustinus umging. Zunächst sollen jene Momente betrachtet werden, die sich mit den Tendenzen des "neuen Augustinismus" in Einklang finden und zum Teil schon auf den reformatorisch ausgeprägten Augustinismus verweisen.

Wie viele andere auch rechnete Hus den Bischof von Hippo nicht nur zu den großen Lehrern und Zeugen, sondern er gab ihm unter diesen eine Vorzugsstellung: "ymmo habeo sanctum Augustinum, Bernhardum et Benedictum pro magnis sanctis et specialiter beatum Augustinum pro magno et sancto doctore ecclesie".[7] Benedikt von Nursia ist in dieser Dreiergruppe eher zufällig aufgetaucht, denn Hus wies hier eine Klage zurück, er hätte die Genannten verketzert – aber die beiden anderen spielen in seinem Werk tatsächlich eine wesentliche Rolle. Die

---

6 Kejř: 1966, 89.
7 Sedlák: 1915, 310*.

Vorrangstellung des Augustinus erklärt vor allem die Charakteristik, dass dieser "der hervorragendste Ausleger der Schrift" war.[8] Auch diese Präzisierung ist nicht außergewöhnlich, sie entspricht im Gegenteil der bekannten Beschreibung Heiko A. Obermans, der über "den neuen Versuch" gesprochen hat, seit dem 14. Jahrhundert "Augustin nicht mehr nur als einen der vier Kirchenlehrer, sondern als qualifizierten Interpreten des Evangeliums zur Geltung kommen zu lassen."[9] Im Kontext der hussitischen Debatten gewinnt diese Ausrichtung neue und folgenschwere Akzente. So hören wir bei Hus:

> Daher besteht kein Zweifel, dass der selige Augustinus der Kirche nützlicher war als viele Päpste und in der Lehre vielleicht mehr als alle Kardinäle, angefangen bei den ersten bis zu den jetzigen. In Bezug auf kirchenleitendes Handeln kannte er nämlich die Schrift Christi besser, erklärte aus ihr den katholischen Glauben und entfernte die ketzerischen Irrtümer aus der Kirche und berichtigte sie.[10]

Obwohl er also kein Papst war, diente er als Vikar Christi, und zwar besser, als die offiziellen Träger des Magisteriums in kurialen Ämtern. Die Formulierung ist positiv, dennoch deutet sie an: sollte es geschehen, dass die anerkannten Größen der bisherigen christlichen Überlieferung in Konflikt geraten, sind wir bereit, uns für Augustinus und die Schrift zu entscheiden, für die *viva vox evangelii* und ihren Tradenten, auch gegen die Hierarchie, wollte diese jene Stimme mundtot machen.

Bekanntlich ging an diesem Punkt das Szenario in die Realität über: die Hussiten nahmen eine Dissonanz der Autoritäten wahr, sie machten auf diese aufmerksam, und als ihnen eine Antwort in der Gestalt von gerichtlichen Klagen und Entscheidungen zuteilwurde, lehnten sie diese als unannehmbar ab und verharrten im Widerstand. Die Methode des Streites wurde ihnen selbst zum Streitgegenstand: die formale Gerichtsgewalt, die sich aus dem Besitz eines Amtes ergibt und sich anmaßt, eine inhaltliche Diskussion durch ein Strafverfahren zu unterdrücken, stand hier gegen die Forderung, Probleme der Glaubenslehre theologisch zu lösen, also "disputative", argumentativ, gestützt auf die Hl. Schrift und die schriftgemäße Lehre, mit Hilfe der anerkannten Autoritäten, dem Weisheitsschatz der Kirche. Für die Gegner war freilich auch diese Verfahrensforderung einer der Anklagepunkte, die Hus' Irrglauben bestätigen sollten – dieweil er bei seiner Verteidigung sich auf Augustinus berief: eine Ketzerei solle man ihm nachweisen, er müsse derselben "durch Schrift oder Vernunft" überführt werden.[11] Vergeblich; kein geringer als Jean Ger-

---

8 Hus: 1958, 62; dt. nach 2017, 409, 21f.
9 Oberman: 1979, 282.
10 Hus: 1958, 121; 2017, 460, 31–37.
11 Palacký: 1869, 231f; Hus: 2017, 671, 11.

son verlangte eine Verurteilung noch vor seiner Ankunft in Konstanz und ermahnte den Prager Erzbischof, über die Thesen Hus' nicht zu diskutieren, sondern diese durch Gewalt ("Feuer und Schwert") auszurotten.[12] Dazu ließ er sich durch sein Erschrecken vor dem Artikel Wyclifs hinreißen, dessen Übernahme Hus vermutlich am meisten belastete: "Nullus est dominus […] dum est in peccato mortali."[13] Hus wollte mithilfe dieses Grundsatzes die heute leicht einsehbare Notwendigkeit ausdrücken, die Legitimität der Ordnung durch gerechten Regierungsvollzug instand zu halten – aber das Beispiel Gersons zeigt, dass auch seine intelligentesten Gegner die These in einem anarchischen Sinne begreifen konnten. Dieses Missverständnis war äußerst gefährlich, Hus wollte es jedoch nicht durch Widerruf räumen, um nicht den "sensum verum" zu leugnen, den "ista proposicio habet" "iuxta sanctorum sentenciam Augustini" und anderer Kirchenlehrer.[14]

Aber Augustinus war ihm als Zeuge bei einer anderen These noch wichtiger, die eine zentrale Bedeutung weniger für Gerson, als eben für Hus selbst hatte, da sie in seinen eigenen Augen den Kern, ja auch den Ursprung des Konfliktes betraf, in welchem er so weit zu gehen wagte: "Jedem, der ein Priester wird, ist das Predigeramt anbefohlen (praedicantis officium de mandato accipit)"; dies sei ein Ausspruch vieler Heiliger mit Augustinus an der Spitze.[15] "Evangelizare" war ihm die Grundlage und das Wesen des geistlichen Dienstes, nicht nur eine sekundäre, zusätzliche Funktion des Priestertums, die durch den Bischof eventuell aufgetragen, aber dann wiederum auch verboten werden durfte, je nach dessen Gutdünken und Willen.[16] Hier gerieten freilich gegensätzliche Prinzipien aneinander und es ist deutlich, dass die Hussiten auf diesem Gebiet einen ausgesprochen proto-reformatorischen Weg gingen, an welchen dann der ganze Protestantismus angeknüpft hat.

Wer hätte sich übrigens bereits bei der Forderung, durch "Schrift oder Vernunft" überzeugt zu werden, nicht an Luther in Worms erinnert?[17] Dort wurde sie zwar nicht auf Augustinus gestützt, der im Lichte des Schriftprinzips selbst zur sekundären Autorität wurde. Doch dasselbe galt auch schon für die Hussiten, und die späteren Reformatoren haben wiederum mit diesen die Überzeugung geteilt, die

---

12 Palacký: 1869, 528.
13 Hus: 1966, 205(–230); 2017, 257(–281). Zuletzt der 30. der verdammten "Irrtümer Jan Hus" (Denzinger-Hünermann Nr. 1230).
14 Sedlák: 1915, 307*.
15 Palacký: 1869, 228.
16 Gegenüber dem Prager Erzbischof verteidigte Hus diesen Standpunkt polemisch bereits 1408, als es sich noch nicht um seine eigene Person handelte, und setzte so seine bis dahin guten Beziehungen mit dem Vorgesetzten aufs Spiel: "O pater, que pietas est, prohibere ewangelizare, quod precepit Christus suis discipulis principaliter"; Novotný: 1920, 29. Bereits auch in eigener Sache sprach er dann 1410 unentwegt den Grundsatz aus: "De prohibicione ewangelisacionis manifestum est, quod non sapit viam Iesu Cristi, qui precepit in universo mundo predicare"; Hus: 1966, 48, 22 f.
17 WA 7, 838, 4.

beiden im Widerstand half, dass sie nämlich trotz des Widerspruchs zu Papst und Konzil in Übereinstimmung mit der katholischen Überlieferung bleiben, insofern diese auf der Schrift beruht.

Entsprechend bekannte der Konstanzer Märtyrer sich zu dieser Tradition noch am letzten Tag vor seinem Feuertod in seiner eigentlich nur noch hypothetischen Verteidigung vor den Richtern, weil er damals bloß seinen Freunden mitteilen konnte, was zu sagen sein würde, falls er noch eine Gelegenheit dazu bekäme. Da erklärte er ausdrücklich: "Ich, Johannes Hus, in der Hoffnung Priester Jesu Christi, will nicht bekennen, dass jeder aus meinen Büchern ausgewählte Artikel irrig sei, damit ich nicht die Meinung der heiligen Lehrer und besonders des heiligen Augustinus verdamme."[18] Tags darauf, als man ihm schon die Rede verwehrte, berief er sich lediglich auf Christus.

3. Der hussitische Augustinismus

Im Hus' endgültigem Sichergeben an Christus den Heiland sah Luther begründeterweise einen Akt des rechtfertigenden Glaubens. In der Lehre des Prager Magisters ist die Lage bekanntlich weniger durchsichtig. Können wir unter dem Gesichtspunkt des sog. "formalen Prinzips" der Reformation offenkundige Übereinstimmungen feststellen, bei dem "materialen Prinzip" ist es komplizierter. Die Untersuchung des hussitischen Augustinismus bestätigt diesen Befund.

Zugleich zeigt sich allerdings, dass gerade in diesem Punkt die "technischen" Bedingungen eine keineswegs geringe Rolle spielten. Wenn nämlich der erschwerte Zugang zu den Schriften des Augustinus eine ganze Themengruppe betraf, dann waren es gerade diejenigen, die sich gegen die Pelagianer richtete – also dieselben, die für die Reformation so wichtig waren, dass sie den Wittenberger Studenten an erster Stelle empfohlen wurden. Selbstverständlich "post sacras literas", doch "elige tibi Magistrum hunc S. Augustinum, maxime ubi contra Pelagianos, Donatistas et Manicheos pugnat."[19] Diese Forderung konnte Hus noch nicht erfüllen. Unter den sporadischen, zerstreuten Spuren nach der antipelagianischen Polemik Augustins, die wir bei ihm finden, fehlt "das mit Abstand wichtigste" Werk, "für alle Reformatoren",[20] d. h. *De spiritu et littera*, nahezu vollständig.[21] Damit korrespondiert natürlich, dass Hus das ganze Problem des Pelagianismus ziemlich dürftig

---

18 Novotný: 1920, 334; Hus: 2017, 632, 15–18.
19 WA. B 12, 388, 35 f.
20 Delius: 1984, 171.
21 In Hus: 1903–1905, 170, 8–11, wird es ausdrücklich nach Petrus Lombardus zitiert.

erörtert; korrekt, ohne semipelagianische Tendenzen, aber auch ohne besonderen Nachdruck, ohne eine spürbare Ergriffenheit.[22]

Das Ausmaß der Vernebelung des Bewußtseins über die antipelagianische Schriften verdeutlicht die gelegentliche Unsicherheit bei der Attribuierung der Autorschaft einzelner Texte aus dem Umkreis der ursprünglichen Polemik. In dieser Hinsicht drohte zwar keine große Verzeichnung, wenn Hus öfters das Kompedium *De fide ad Petrum* des Fulgentius von Ruspe dem Bischof von Hippo zurechnete. Es konnte sogar denjenigen bedenklich erscheinen, die einen "exzessiven" Augustinismus befürchteten, welcher ihrer Meinung nach in der Reformation belebt wurde.[23] Umso mehr verblüfft jedoch der – wenn auch vereinzelte – Fehlgriff, durch den Hus den Brief *Ad Demetriadem* in denselben Bereich einreihte, der traditionell dem Kirchenvater Hieronymus zugeschrieben wurde, tatsächlich jedoch von niemand anderem als von Pelagius selbst stammt. Und dennoch nannte Hus, sogar der späte Hus, an betreffender Stelle nicht bloß den "gloriosum Slawum"[24] Hieronymus, sondern gerade den "Doctor gratiae" als Verfasser![25]

Nicht einmal eine so frappante Einzelheit darf man freilich interpretativ überstrapazieren. Man muss mit ihrer Zufälligkeit rechnen, zumal der zitierte Satz keine offensichtliche Irrlehre beinhaltet. In der pelagianischen Argumentationskette ist er häretisch ausgerichtet, aber nicht im Gedankengang Hus', der in seiner Quästion "quid sit virtus" unbeirrbar zum Schluss kam, "nunquam [...] est vera humilitas sine gracia, nec vera iusticia aut alia quecunque virtus moralis".[26] Das Problem lag also mehr in der Unkenntnis des ursprünglichen Kontextes als in einer Beeinflussung durch die verborgenen Intentionen des Verfassers. Trotzdem können wir der Frage nicht ausweichen, inwieweit sich aus ähnlichen Verwechslungen Konsequenzen auch für die theologische Urteilsbildung ergeben haben. Auf jeden Fall sagen sie etwas aus über das Maß der Konzentration auf die Fragestellung, was ein Vergleich mit Luther erfolgreich verdeutlichen könnte.[27]

Aber nicht nur mit diesem; hier taucht vor uns ein neues Rätsel auf, das nicht ganz einfach zu lösen ist. Dass die wahre Urheberschaft des Briefes an Demetrias noch lange nach Hus unbekannt sein konnte, belegt eine Episode aus der Leipziger

---

22 Cf. Hus: 1903–1905, 310 ff.
23 Cf. wieder WA. B 12, 387, 11–20, aber ebenso bereits die erste These der Disputatio contra scholasticam Theologiam, in WA 1, 224, 7 f.; bzw. denselben Text in: LuStA 1, 165, mit den editorischen Belegen von Helmar Junghans, die auch die eventuelle Verwechslung von Fulgentius mit Augustinus betreffen.
24 Hus: 1948, 142, 6 f.
25 Hus: 1966, 384, 25.
26 Hus: 1903–1905, 305, 41 f.
27 Konkret mit der frühen Erkenntnis des Reformators, dass die Schrift *De vera et falsa poenitentia*, in die Edition Amerbachs noch eingeschlossen, Augustinus nicht zugerechnet werden darf; siehe WA. B 1, 65, 24–35.

Disputation, als Johann Eck durch seine Berufung auf diesen Text Andreas Karlstadt zunächst in Verlegenheit brachte.[28] Trotzdem stimmt es nicht, dass es unmöglich gewesen ist, den richtigen Tatbestand auch schon lange vor Hus zu erkennen. Bereits die Protagonisten des spätmittelalterlichen Augustinismus warfen ja den Fehdehandschuh dem "modernen Pelagianismus" zu und die geschärfte Aufmerksamkeit gegenüber dem glaubensmäßigen Kern der Sache ging bei ihnen Hand in Hand mit der Fähigkeit, die Verwechslung der Autoren aufzudecken. Gregor von Rimini und Thomas Bradwardine erkannten sie unabhängig voneinander.[29] Der Nominalist Gregor zog zwar die realistischen Protagonisten des Hussitentums nicht an, aber warum widmeten diese nur ein beschränktes Interesse dem *Doctori profundo*, der in seiner *Causa Dei contra Pelagium* gerade die Ockhamisten aufs Korn nahm? Die Antwort ist bei den Anhängern des Oxforder Schülers Bradwardines, John Wyclif, der das Meisterwerk seines Lehrers "unzählige Male zitierte",[30] nicht nahe liegend.

Teilweise ist es immerhin möglich, die Gründe hierfür aus der Überlieferungskette zu entnehmen, denn deren Entwicklungslogik ist noch relativ ersichtlich: das Ringen Bradwardines hatte bereits für Wyclif nicht mehr dieselbe existentielle Bedeutung, weil er den Kampf weitgehend als inzwischen gewonnen wahrnahm "and the problem of the nature and efficacy of divine grace was no longer an acute issue. In Wyclif's theology it has a secondary, if still important, part."[31] Auch seine Gegner provozierten Hus auf diesem Gebiet weniger als durch ihre maßlosen Ansprüche, durch die Identifizierung der Kirche mit der päpstlichen Kurie, also mit den Inhabern der Verwaltungsämter, welchen sie volles *regitivum* an Christi Statt zusprachen.[32]

Diesen gegenüber nahm Hus eine ausgeprägt polemische Einstellung ein und führte seine eigene *causa Dei*, auch wenn er in der Minderheit war. Ansonsten war er nach seiner Veranlagung im Grunde ein maßvoller Mensch, der klassische Vorbilder respektierte – und klassische Ausdrücke, in Übereinstimmung mit der Überzeugung des Augustinus, Theologen sollen in dieser Hinsicht disziplinierter als Philosophen sein.[33] Und hier könnte vielleicht auch ein weiterer Teilaspekt der Antwort auf die gestellte Frage liegen.

Angedeutet wird dies an einer der seltenen Stellen, in denen sich Hus ausdrücklich mit Bradwardine als dem Theologen auseinandergesetzt hat (denn der Professor

---

28 Seitz: 1903, 15 f; ein stärkerer Gegenschlag folgt erst 41. Den Fall untersuchte näher Grane: 1999, 42 ff.
29 Zu Gregor: Grane: 1999, 44; bei Bradwardine: 1618, 312C–313B.
30 Robson: 1961, 36.
31 Robson: 1961, 207.
32 Ekklesiologische Traktate von Stephan Páleč und Stanislaus von Znaim, mit denen Hus sich auseinandersetzte, edierte Sedlák (1915) im Quellenanhang und Polc (1996).
33 *De civ.* x. 23.

war zugleich auch als Mathematiker berühmt[34]); zwar nur in einem Detail, aber auf eine verhältnismäßig sprechende Weise: Eine Äußerung des Oxforder Meisters über die Problematik der Willensentscheidung bezeichnete Hus freundlich als "pulcra [...] sentencia et ymaginacio", nichtsdestoweniger nahm er seinen Vorschlag, die gewöhnliche Reihenfolge der Wörter *liberum* und *arbitrium* umzukehren, nicht an und gab dem Usus den Vorzug, der "cum b[eato] *Augustino* et omnibus aliis" geteilt wird, "cum in vi vocis non sit multa intricacio ponenda".[35] Der wahrgenommenen positiven Absicht zum Trotz kam ihm die Möglichkeit, die Bradwardine eröffnet hatte (um sich dann übrigens selbst doch an der Überlieferung zu halten), als eine zu "wortklauberische" Lösung vor,[36] die als solche zum Trend nach "novellis terminis" passe, welche Wyclif bereits scharf abgelehnt hatte, da sie vom Wortlaut der Schrift samt ihrer inneren Wahrheit immer weiter wegführe.[37]

Wyclif tat dies im Kontext der Streitigkeiten zwischen den Realisten, die verlangten, sich mehr mit Wirklichkeiten als mit Wörtern zu befassen, und den Nominalisten, die sich mit den Begriffen vorzugsweise auseinandersetzten[38] – und Hus teilte diese Frontstellung bekanntlich im Grunde. Aber wie wir an der besagten Stelle bemerken, kam die hier entscheidende Einstellung logisch vor dem Universalienstreit, und daher konnte sie gleichfalls gegen einen Anhänger der *viae antiquae* gewendet werden (dessen ungeachtet, dass seine Neuerergeste ältere, mittlerweile verblasste augustinische Einsichten zu beleben beabsichtigte[39] – was allerdings Hus, der allem Anschein nach den vollen Kontext der behandelten Notiz nicht kannte, überhaupt nicht wahrnehmen musste).

Die augustinischen Warnungen vor nutzlosen Wortgezänken sprachen übrigens ebenso den Zögling der Nominalisten Luther an, spätestens als Sententiarius,[40] und mit der Zeit nahm er eine ähnliche Distanz, nicht völlig ablehnend, aber sicherlich reserviert, zum "spitzen Vigleph" selbst ein, der für den Reformator auch an Stellen noch zu stark philosophierte, wo er schon theologisieren sollte.[41] Dies hin-

---

34 Siehe Hus: 1948, 105, 11.
35 Hus: 1903–1905, 294, 1ff. Hervorhebung im Original.
36 Cf. Kybal: 1931, 95.
37 Wyclif: 1905, 309; cf. auch 214 f. An dieser Schrift Wyclifs fand Hus ein besonderes Gefallen.
38 Cf. Seeberg: 1953, 750.
39 Dazu Flasch: 1986, 60 f: "Wenn Bradwardine zu Augustins Gnadenlehre zurückwollte, mußte er Innovationskraft beweisen. [...] Die Originalität Bradwardines bestand nicht in der Repetition des dogmatischen Standpunktes Augustins, sondern in seiner philosophischen Rekonstruktion und in seiner polemischen Aktualisierung."
40 Als er zu *de civ.* ix. 4 am Rande bemerkte, wie Philosophen "in nudis verborum novitatibus et aequivocationibus certant"; WA 9, 24, 25 f.
41 WA 26, 443, 8; In der Frage der Gegenwart Christi in den eucharistischen Elementen, um die es an dieser Stelle ging, stand Hus übrigens Luther näher als Wyclif, da er auch eher in "konsubstantialen" Kategorien dachte und keine bloße "Remanenz" vertrat.

derte Luther mitnichten, Schranken versteifter Konventionen zu überschreiten und zum Ursprung gerade im Bereich der Rechtfertigungslehre zu gelangen, aber Hus wollte auf diesem Gebiet eher eine gemäßigte Mittelströmung vertreten als zum Vorkämpfer werden.[42] Folglich beschwor er auf diesem Gebiet keine so heftigen Reaktionen herauf, aber er entwickelte auf ihm auch keine außerordentliche Durchschlagskraft. Seine Gnadenlehre lässt sich einfacher in den Kontext der Annäherung an Paulus und Augustin im Rahmen der spätmittelalterlichen Belebung des Thomismus einordnen, als in die Koordinaten der spezifisch reformatorischen Fortführung dieser Inspirationen.

4. Hus und die antidonatistischen Texte Augustins

Doch bei dieser Feststellung können wir nicht stehenbleiben. Wenn es auch gilt, dass es in Bezug auf das "materiale Prinzip" der Reformation schwieriger als auf das "formale" ist, bei den frühen Hussiten bereits die reformatorischen Prinzipien zu finden, bedeutet es nicht, dass es sie gar nicht gibt. Bei Hus gelangen wir zu ihnen gewissermaßen auf einem Umweg.

Hatte Hus nicht die Studienempfehlungen Luthers befolgen können, was die Traktate gegen die Pelagianer betraf, eine andere Gruppe der antihäretischen Werken Augustinus' war ihm merklich zugänglicher – nämlich die Schriften gegen die Donatisten. Auch sie bis zu einem gewissen Grad nur vermittelt; augenscheinlich spielte hier eine gewisse Rolle, dass Auszüge aus diesen stärker in das Kirchenrecht eingegangen waren. Aber die Weise, wie Hus und seine Nachfolger diese anwandten, ist bedeutsam.

Die Tatsache, wie bereitwillig die Hussiten aus den antidonatistischen Texten schöpften, mag überraschen, denn sie kontrastiert mit dem hartnäckigen Verdacht, sie selbst verträten die entsprechende Ketzerei. Bereits Hus wurde entsprechend geklagt,[43] was dem Blickwinkel entspricht, unter dem Gerson die oben zitierte These über die Bedingtheit der Herrschaft wahrnahm. Doch ist diese Anklage falsch und zeigt sein Unverständnis für die Gedankenwelt von Hus.[44] Bei den Gegner enstprach der Vorwurf des Donatismus meistens dem Hang zum entgegengesetzten Extrem, der Neigung, einen Mangel an Wahrhaftigkeit und Würdigkeit im geistlichen Dienst überhaupt für kein echtes Problem zu halten. Aus der unzureichenden Unterscheidung der beiden Problemfelder ging ein Anspruch auf Entscheidungsautorität der

---

42 Cf. Hus: 1942, 13: "Sed nos illis dimissis erroribus mediam teneamus secundum Apostolum".
43 Cf. Palacký: 1869, 231; Hus: 2017, 670, 30 ff.
44 Ebenda konnte der Angeklagte sich mit der lakonischen Antwort zufriedengeben: "Non est verum; nam praedicavi oppositum." Unter den "Irrtümern Jan Hus" figuriert die ihm untergeschobene Behauptung nicht mehr.

Unwürdigen hervor, welche sich grundsätzlich jeder Kontrolle und jeder Kritik seitens der christlichen Öffentlichkeit entziehen wollte, sei diese auch berechtigt und normativ begründet.

Die hierarchische bzw. priesterliche Eigenmächtigkeit, die Vorstellung, dass die Träger der kanonischen Ämter selber über göttliche Macht verfügen, nicht diese als Diener durch das Wort Gottes vermitteln, das dabei frei und souverän bleiben soll, wurde zu einem der Hauptziele der Polemik Jan Hus'. Uns gibt das die Gelegenheit, sich dessen bewusst zu werden, dass sein Kampf sich weithin auf das ekklesiologische Gebiet konzentrierte, aus äußeren und inneren Gründen, doch dass er dabei nicht nur die Glaubenslehre ziemlich intensiv tangierte, besonders jene Frage, die im Rahmen der pelagianischen Streitigkeiten im soteriologischen Kontext exponiert worden war; nämlich ob die Gnade den menschlichen Taten zuvorkommt oder ihnen nachfolgt bzw. ob die guten Taten des Menschen die Begnadigung begründen oder umgekehrt. Hier wird klar, dass Hus immerhin in der Linie des klassischen Christentums stand, die von Augustin zur europäischen Reformation führt, und dass seine *causa Dei* auch einen soteriologischen Kern gehabt hat.

In diesem Kontext sollte man zuerst der Schrift Hus' gegen sechs Irrlehren Aufmerksamkeit schenken, die in seinen Augen die Freiheit und Souveränität Gottes bedrohten. Er verfasste sie, als der Konflikt eskalierte, und ihre programmatische Bedeutung wurde dadurch höchst anschaulich gemacht, dass er die ursprüngliche, knappere lateinische Fassung, eine stichwortartige Aufzählung von Streitpunkten und Argumente der Autoritäten zu ihrer Lösung bestehend, an die Wände der Bethlehemer Kapelle schreiben ließ.[45] Augustinus war in allen Unterpunkten vertreten, fünfmal gleich an erster Stelle. Bei dem letzten Artikel, der die Simonie betraf, erscheint der Bischof von Hippo erst etwa in der Mitte, aber signifikant: der Grundsatz, in der Schrift *De baptismo* ausgesprochen, dass die Wahrheit schwerer als der Brauch wiegt, korrespondierte mit dem "formalen Prinzip" der Reformation.[46] Luther berief sich darauf später ebenso explizit, wobei er sogar die Stelle nach dem *Decretum Gratiani* zitierte.[47]

Beachtenswert ist der dritte Unterpunkt, nach welchem die Priester nach der Überzeugung Hus' die Sündenvergebung verkünden, die den Glaubenden jedoch von Gott selbst gewährt wird. Daraus ergibt sich, dass die Priester diese weder eigenmächtig zubilligen noch eigenwillig verweigern dürfen. Von den zwei Aussprüchen des Augustinus, die diese These begründen sollen, ist besonders der zweite wichtig:

---

45 Ryba: 1951, 39–63; Hus: 2017, 311–344, ist eine Übersetzung der veränderten tschechischsprachigen Version (zu den Wandinschriften siehe hier 313, 1 ff.).
46 Ibid., 58, 552–559; 340, 12–18.
47 Delius: 1984, 167.

"Non tollit peccata nisi solus Cristus, qui est agnus tollens peccata mundi".[48] Diese Sentenz liefert zugleich das markanteste Beispiel einer Schlussfolgerung, die aus einer der antipelagianischen Schriften genommen, in der Gestalt eines Zitates zu Hus gelangte. Dass er dieser großes Gewicht zumaß, ergibt sich aus der Tatsache, dass der Satz zu einem beliebten Bestandteil seines Argumentationsschatzes wurde. Auch in diesem Fall war es wieder einmal das *Decretum*, das zuerst (noch vor der Verfassung des Irrlehren-Katalogs) als Fundgrube nützte – wobei es aber bezeichnend ist, dass der Grundsatz dort aus dem Kontext gerissen ist und die Primärquelle falsch bezeichnet. Umso bemerkenswerter ist es freilich, dass Hus, von dieser Aussage lebhaft eingenommen, ihre Herkunft offenbar überprüfte und schließlich doch imstande war, sie als Zitat aus *Opus imperfectus contra Iulianum* zu bestimmen.[49]

Unter den Stellen, bei denen Hus die Maxime dann verwendete, dürfte das fünfte Kapitel seiner polemischen Erwiderung auf einen Angriff etlicher seiner Universitätskollegen wohl theologisch am meisten durchgearbeitet sein. Hier setzte er sich mit dem Vorwurf auseinander, er stelle den Glauben in Zweifel, "quod papa possit dare indulgenciam et remissionem plenam omnium peccatorum".[50] Einen solchen Anspruch wies Hus als irrig und unevangelisch zurück.[51] Und er stützte sich dabei auf seine Unterscheidung der Grade der Vollmacht zur Vergebung von Sünden: in authentischer Form kommt sie Gott allein zu, eine subauthentische erlangte Christus als Mensch durch die hypostatische Union, und eine dienstliche (*ministerialis*) geschieht durch den Dienst an Wort und Sakrament, die Seelsorge und das Gebet.[52] Kurzum: auch für Hus wurde der Ablass zu einem zwar konkreten, aber bloß äußerlichen, eigentlich eher zufälligen Gegenstand seines Kampfes, dessen Wurzel in tieferen Schichten lagen.

Somit sollte der spätere Eindruck Ecks bei der Leipziger Disputation nicht Verwunderung auslösen, dass sein Opponent sich gleich in der Eingangspredigt sich "ganz böhmisch" äußere[53] – als Luther es "in wenigen Sätzen gelungen [ist], die Rechtfertigung als das Wesentliche herauszustellen, demgegenüber das kirchliche Amt lediglich funktionale Bedeutung hat."[54]

---

48 Ryba: 1951, 43, 73–76; Hus: 2017, 320, 30 f.
49 Siehe die editorische Notiz von Daňhelka in Hus: 1985, 547 f.
50 Hus: 1966, 400, 8 ff.
51 Hus: 1966, 407, 19–21.
52 Hus: 1966, 401, 18–403, 14 (und weiter); hier auch der Ausspruch Augustins, 402, 2 1f.
53 Ein Sermon gepredigt zu Leipzig auf dem Schloß am Tage Petri und Pauli, in: WA. B 1, 427, Anm. 44.
54 Brecht: 1990, 304. Luther selbst postulierte in seinem Sermon: "Das ewangelium begreift alle materien der gantzen disputation, dan es von tzweyerley materien furnemlich redt: Zum ersten von der gnaden gottis und unserm freyen willen, Zum andernn von der gewalt sanct Peters und der schlussell"; WA 2, 246, 23–26.

Der Reformator legte damals übrigens den *locus classicus* aus dem 16. Kapitel des Matthäusevangeliums über Petrus und den Felsen aus – und mit ihm ist der allerdeutlichste Beleg einer direkten augustinischen Inspiration verbunden, die Hus und Luther übereinstimmend verarbeiteten (auf eine Weise, die dann in der reformatorischen Theologie zum Gemeingut geworden ist). Beide machten eine Umwandlung der Perspektive durch, die Augustinus in seinen *Retractationes* schildert, wo er bekennt, dass er selber anfangs gemeint habe, wie "cantatur ore multorum", als ob die Kirche auf dem Apostel Petrus gegründet wäre; erst später, als er den Text aufmerksamer überlegte, begriff er, dass "Petrus ab hac petra appellatus personam Ecclesiae figuraret, quae super hanc petram aedificatur", so dass der Fels Christus selbst sei.[55] "Non enim a Petro petra, sed Petrus a petra; sicut non Christus a christiano, sed christianus a Christo vocatur".[56]

Beachtenswert ist es, dass Hus sich diese Erkenntnis ziemlich bald aneignete. Bereits in den frühen Jahren seiner Predigertätigkeit an der Bethlehemkapelle begegnet man folgender Doppelthese: "primum in solum Cristum credere debemus, secundo quod sine papa salvari possumus".[57] Zu Recht dürfen wir fragen, ob sich nicht gerade hier der Kristallisationskern seiner Gedankenentwicklung in Richtung auf die künftigen reformatorischen Grundsätzen zeigt. Obwohl er nicht über genügend Quellen verfügte, um diese Grundsätze noch während seines Lebens mit wünschenswerter Deutlichkeit herausarbeiten zu können, die Tendenzen hierzu fehlen nicht und sind keineswegs nebensächlich.

Mithin sollte uns die Meinung Ecks nicht befremden, dazu auch die Tatsache, dass Luther diese akzeptierte. Anfangs, noch in Leipzig, wo er den inneren Zusammenhang eines der verurteilten Artikel des Hus, über die "Zweiteilung menschlicher Handlungen", mit der Position des Gregor von Rimini bemerkte.[58] Wie durfte das Konzil eine Lehre verwerfen, die "a sancto Paulo et Augustino asseritur, deinde per Gregorium Ariminensem"?[59] Eck kam diese Verbindung an den Haaren herbeigezogen vor, weil er die Verschiedenheit des Kontextes registrierte: Hus begründete ja eine Bedingtheit und Begrenztheit der Gehorsamspflicht den kirchlichen Vorgesetzten gegenüber und stellte damit die heilbringende Autorität der römischen Kirche

---

55 *Retr.* i. 21.
56 *Io. ev. tr.* cxxiv. 5.
57 Hus: 1988, 164, 109f; ein Hinweis auf die Sentenz aus *Io. ev. tr.* folgt 164, 118 – 165, 119.
58 16. der "Irrtümer Jan Hus" (Denzinger-Hünermann Nr. 1216); er stammt aus Hus: 1958, 176; 2017, 512, 8–15. Bei der Disputatio inter Ioannem Eccium et Martinum Lutherum behandelt ab WA 59, 478, 1430–1437, bzw. Seitz: 1903, 98; hier auf Gregor vorerst nur angespielt, erneut mit Namen angeführt wird er ebenda 490, 1777, bzw. 109. Auch diesem Motiv schenkte seine Aufmerksamkeit Grane (1999, 45–50).
59 WA 59, 507, 2304 f.; Seitz: 1903, 126.

in Frage (worüber man edisputierte),[60] während Gregor das Verhältnis zwischen der Gnade, der Willensentscheidung und den menschlichen Taten erläuterte (was bereits vorher mit Karlstadt disputiert wurde). Doch die Beobachtung Luthers, mag sie auch nur intuitiv gewesen sein, hatte ebenso ihre Gültigkeit. Auch für Hus war das Behauptete nicht nur im unmittelbaren ekklesiologischen Kontext wichtig; namentlich die Fiktion von an sich indifferenten Taten der Menschen vor Gott lehnte er bereits als Sententiar mit auffallender Vehemenz ab: "relinquatur *Scotus* et acceptetur *Christus*"![61]

Er gehörte also tatsächlich nicht zu jenen verborgenen Pelagianern, die nicht einmal ahnen, "dass Gott die Gottlosen auch in ihren guten Werken sündigen lässt."[62] Umso stärker identifizierte sich Luther dann mit der Streitsache Hus', als er den Traktat *De ecclesia* im vollen Zusammenhang las und darauf mit jenem scheinbar so übertriebenen Aphorismus reagierte: "sumus omnes Hussitae ignorantes. Denique Paulus et Augustinus ad verbum sunt Hussitae."[63]

Quellen und Literatur

Quellen

Bradwardin, Thomas (1618), De Causa Dei, Contra Pelagium, London: Norton, nachgedruckt Frankfurt a. M. 1964.

Hus, Jan (1903–1905), Super IV. Sententiarum, Wenzel Flajšhans/Marie Komínková (ed.), Prag o. J.: Verlag von Jarosl. Bursík.

Hus, Jan (1942), Sermones in capella Bethlehem, vol. 5, Václav Flajšhans (ed.), Praha: Královská česká společnost nauk.

Hus, Jan (1948), Quodlibet. Disputationis de Quolibet Pragae in Facultate Artium Mense Ianuario Anni 1411 habitae Enchiridion, Bohumil Ryba (ed.), Prag: Orbis.

Hus, Jan (1958), Tractatus de ecclesia, S. Harrison Thomson (ed.), Praha: Komenského evangelická fakulta bohoslovecká.

Hus, Jan (1966), Polemica, OO 22, Jaroslav Eršil (ed.), Prag: Academia.

Hus, Jan (1985), Drobné spisy české, OO 4, Jiří Daňhelka (ed.), Praha: Academia.

Hus, Jan (1988), Leccionarium bipartitum – Pars hiemalis, OO 9, Anežka Vidmanová-Schmidtová (ed.), Praha: Academia.

---

60 Ibid., 511, 2409–2417; 129.
61 Hus: 1903–1905, 356, 17f. Hervorhebung im Original.
62 WA 56, 502, 24f; deutsch nach Luther: 1957, 436.
63 WA. B 2, 42, 24f; Zur späteren Entwicklung der Einstellung Luthers gegenüber Hus, die zwar differenzierter, aber kaum distanzierter wurde, siehe Wernisch (2014) bzw. (2015).

Hus, Jan (2017), Johannes Hus Deutsch, Armin Kohnle/Thomas Krzenck (ed.), Leipzig: Evangelische Verlagsanstalt.

Luther, Martin (1957), Vorlesung über den Römerbrief 1515/1516, Georg Merz (ed.), München: Christian Kaiser Verlag.

Novotný, Václav (ed.) (1920): M. Jana Husi korespondence a dokumenty, Praha: Komise pro Vydávání Pramenů Náboženského Hnutí Českého.

Palacký, Franciscus (ed.) (1869), Documenta Mag. Ioannis Hus vitam, doctrinam, causam, in Constantiensi concilio actam et controversias de religione in Bohemia annis 1403–1418 motas illustrantia, Prag.

Polc, Jaroslav V./Přibyl, Stanislav (ed.) (1996), Miscellanea husitica Ioannis Sedlák, Praha: Katolická teologická fakulta Univerzity Karlovy : Karolinum.

Ryba, Bohumil (ed.) (1951), Betlemské texty, Praha: Orbis.

Seitz, Otto (ed.) (1903), Der authentische Text der Leipziger Disputation (1519), Berlin: C.A. Schwetschke.

Wyclif, John (1905), De Veritate Sacrae Scripturae, vol. 1, Rudolf Buddensieg (ed.), London: Wyclif Society.

Forschungsliteratur

Brecht, Martin (1990), Martin Luther, vol. 1: Sein Weg zur Reformation 1483–1521, 3rd ed., Stuttgart: Calwer Verlag.

Delius, Hans-Ulrich (1984), Augustin als Quelle Luthers, Eine Materialsammlung, Berlin: Evangelische Verlagsanstalt.

Flasch, Kurt (1986), Das philosophische Denken im Mittelalter, Von Augustin zu Machiavelli, Stuttgart: Philipp Reclam jan. GmbH & Co.

Grane, Leif (1999), Gregor von Rimini und Luthers Leipziger Disputation, in: Reformationsstudien, Beiträge zu Luther und zur dänischen Reformation, Mainz: von Zabern, 37–56.

Hlaváček, Ivan (1997), Hussens Bücher, Einige Überlegungen zu Hussens Bibliothek und Bücherbenutzung, in: F. Seibt (ed.), Jan Hus – Zwischen Zeiten, Völkern, Konfessionen, München: Oldenbourg, 113–119.

Kejř, Jiří (1966), Právo a právní prameny v Husově díle, in: R. Říčan,/M. Flegl, (ed.): Husův sborník, Praha: Komenského evangelická fakulta bohoslovecká, 84–94.

Kybal, Vlastimil (1931), M. Jan Hus, Učení, vol. 3, Praha: Laichter.

Novotný, Václav (1919), M. Jan Hus, Život a dílo, vol. 1, Praha: Laichter.

Oberman, Heiko Augustinus (1979), Werden und Wertung der Reformation, Von Wegestreit zum Glaubenskampf; Spätscholastik und Reformation, 2nd ed., Tübingen: Mohr.

Robson, J.A. (1961), Wyclif and the Oxford Schools, The Relation of the "Summa de Ente" to Scholastic Debates at Oxford in the Later Fourteenth Century, Cambridge: University Press.

Sedlák, Jan (1915), Jan Hus, Praha: V Praze Nákl. Ddictví sv. Prokopa.

Seeberg, Reinhold (1953), Lehrbuch der Dogmengeschichte, vol. 3: Die Dogmengeschichte des Mittelalters, 5th ed., Basel: Benno Schwabe.

Wernisch, Martin (2014), Luther and Medieval Reform Movements, Particularly the Hussites, in: R. Kolb/I. Dingel/Ľ. Batka, (ed.), The Oxford Handbook of Martin Luther's Theology, Oxford: Oxford University Press, 62–70.

Wernisch, Martin (2015), Luther und Hus, Communio viatorum, 57, 272–282.

Volker Leppin

Augustin zwischen Wittenberg, Zürich und Löwen

Die frühen Kontroversen der Reformationszeit

Das Bewusstsein, dass die Reformation sich besonders mit dem Erbe Augustins verbinde, ist im evangelischen Gedächtnis tief verankert. Das entspricht sicher, wie gleich noch darzustellen sein wird, dem Selbstverständnis insbesondere der Wittenberger Bewegung. Es steht aber in einer gewissen Spannung dazu, dass Augustin für die mittelalterliche Theologie die wichtigste Referenz nach der Bibel ist. Auch die Bedeutung, die Aristoteles insbesondere seit dem Aufkommen der Universitäten um 1200 gewann, hat Augustin aus dieser herausragenden Bedeutung keineswegs verdrängt, da allein schon der spirituelle Resonanzraum den Unterschied zwischen dem insbesondere für logische Analysen gut brauchbaren paganen Philosophen und dem auf zahlreichen Kanzeln sichtbaren Kirchenvater bewusst hielt. Diese Spannung in der Wahrnehmung der Bedeutung Augustins für Mittelalter und Reformation hat Walter von Loewenich treffend zum Ausdruck gebracht: "Augustin ist der Vater des mittelalterlichen Katholizismus und doch zugleich der Kirchenvater der Reformation."[1]

Nicht einmal der Zusatz, die Reformation habe eben besonderes Augenmerk auf den antipelagianischen Augustin gelegt, wird den Verhältnissen ganz gerecht. Denn natürlich war auch dieses spezielle Segment augustinischen Schrifttums in der Scholastik keineswegs vergessen. Das Schimpfwort "pelagianisch" konnte auch von solchen Denkern verwendet werden, die wie Wilhelm von Ockham später selbst in den Geruch des Pelagianismus gerieten[2] – von denen, die sich für eine scharfe Lektüre Augustins gegen jeden Pelagianismus einsetzten, wie Gregor von Rimini und Thomas Bradwardine, ganz zu schweigen.[3] Die Besonderheit des Wittenberger Ansatzes liegt also hier wie auch in anderen Zusammenhängen nicht einfach in einer bestimmten Einzelaussage, sondern in seiner gegen jede Form der Harmonisierung gerichteten Differenzhermeneutik[4], welche Augustin mit Stoßrichtung gegen eine Anthropologie las, die unter Verwendung des Aristoteles auch

---

1 Loewenich: 1959, 76.
2 Ockham: 1980, 588f.
3 S. zu der heute etwas ruhiger gewordenen Diskussion: Oberman (1958); (1981); (1991); und Leff: (1957); (1961). Für Bradwardine liegt mittlerweile eine bemerkenswerte zweisprachige Ausgabe vor: Bradwardine (2013).
4 S. hierzu Leppin: 2018b, 29.

Augustin so zu lesen vermochte, dass das Tun des Menschen eine eigene Würdigung erfuhr. Augustin wurde zwischen Mittelalter und Reformation offenkundig unterschiedlich wahrgenommen. Diesen verschiedenen Perzeptionen Augustins als unterschiedlichen Modi der Erfassung Augustins selbst nachzugehen, ist das Anliegen der folgenden Zeilen, die ausschnitthaft auf einige grundlegende Konflikte der frühen Reformationszeit unter dem Gesichtspunkt eingehen, inwiefern in ihnen sich dieses unterschiedlichen Augustinbilder spiegeln.

1. Universitätsreform im Namen Augustins: Wittenberg

Dass an einer Theologischen Fakultät, deren frühe Prägung durch den General der Augustinereremiten geschah, und die sich an einer Universität befand, deren Patron Augustin war,[5] der afrikanische Kirchenvater eine besondere Bedeutung besaß, wird kaum überraschen. Eine hohe Bedeutung hatte er auch für Luther persönlich, der bekanntlich in der Genesisvorlesung berichtete, dass er den Ordensnamen Augustinus erhalten habe.[6] Freilich liegen die Dinge auch hier nicht ganz einfach: Berndt Hamm hat darauf hingewiesen, dass Luther bereits 1516 gegenüber Spalatin bestritten hatte, dass er seiner Ordenszugehörigkeit wegen Augustin gegenüber Hieronymus vorziehe – erst durch die Lektüre der Bücher Augustins habe er ihn zu schätzen gelernt.[7] Allerdings hat Hamm selbst die Bedeutung dieser Bemerkung durch die Erinnerung daran eingeschränkt, dass Luther schon in seiner Erfurter Zeit intensiv Augustin gelesen und annotiert hat.[8] Auch wenn dieses frühe Augustininteresse sich eher auf die trinitätstheologischen Spekulationen richtete als auf die Rechtfertigungstheologie, weist es doch darauf hin, dass die Distanzierung

---

5 Lohse: 1990, 89.
6 WA 44,213,5f: "Ego in Baptismo nominatus sum Martinus, postea in Monasterio Augustinus". Eine ausführliche Betrachtung des systematischen Zusammenhangs zwischen Luthers Sündenverständnis und Augustin bietet Pereira (2013).
7 WA.B 1,70 [Nr. 27, 17–21]: "Ego sane in hoc dissentire ab Erasmo non dubito, quod Augustino in scripturis interpretandis tantum posthabeo Hieronymum, quantum ipse Augustinum in omnibus Hieronymo posthabet. Non quod professionis meae studio ad b. Augustinum probandum trahar, qui apud me, antequam in libros eius incidissem, ne tantillum quidem favoris habuit".
8 Hamm: 1982, 314; s. die Notizen in AWA 9,149–249. Das klassische Werk zum Thema, das aber leider nur bis 1518 reicht, ist Hamel (1934–1935). Die Sentenzenvorlesung untersucht Hamel vorwiegend unter dem Gesichtspunkt der Gnadenlehre und kommt hier zu dem Ergebnis, dass Luther Augustin inhaltlich im Wesentlichen durch die Augen der Via moderna gelesen habe (a. a. O. I,24). Nach wie vor eine unerschöpfliche Quelle für Luthers Augustingebrauch ist auch Delius (1984) – ein Buch, das allerdings zugleich wissenschaftsgeschichtlich daran erinnert, wie solche Fragen vor dem digitalen Zeitalter angegangen wurden.

gegenüber einer Ordensprägung eher der Rhetorik der Objektivierung in der Auseinandersetzung mit Erasmus im genannten Brief zu verdanken ist, als dass es echte Erinnerung widerspiegelte. Umgekehrt ist deutlich, dass sich die Faszination über Augustin auf den Ordenszusammenhang nicht reduzieren lässt beziehungsweise innerhalb dessen einen sehr konkreten Entdeckungszusammenhang hat: Johann von Staupitz hat den Kirchenvater nicht nur sehr explizit als "*Augustinus noster*" bezeichnet,[9] sondern mit der Prädestination auch in seinen Nürnberger Adventspredigten von 1516 und dem daraus hervorgegangenen "*Libellus de exsecutione aeternae praedestinationis*" eines der heikelsten Probleme augustinischer Theologie in den Vordergrund gehoben und dabei auch bereits unterschiedliche Lesarten Augustins thematisiert beziehungsweise in Stellung gegeneinander gebracht: Der Augustin zugeschriebene Satz: "Wenn Du nicht prädestiniert bist, mach, dass du prädestiniert wirst", sei sachlich falsch[10]. Seine augustinische Rechtfertigungstheologie spitzte sich darauf zu, dass die Rechtfertigung "aus reiner Gnade und den Werken Christi" fließe, "ohne dass unsere Werke etwas hierzu tun",[11] und dies "aus freier Wahl Gottes".[12] Dass diese Aussagen zwar eine gewisse Schärfe der Differenz zwischen Christus und unseren Werken ausdrückten, ihr Augustinismus aber nicht so umfassend differenzhermeneutisch gedacht war wie später der Luthers, bedarf hier nicht der ausführlichen Begründung[13] – es mag der Hinweis genügen, dass Staupitz diese Rechtfertigungslehre ausdrücklich mit einem Konzept der *fides caritate formata* verband, nach welcher alle Werke des Gerechtfertigten eigentlich Christus zum Subjekt haben, formal aber dem Menschen zuzuordnen sind.[14] Dem entspricht es, dass Staupitz die augustinische Vorstellung von einer durch die Prädestination umfassten Willensfreiheit des Menschen[15] so stark betonte, dass er sich gegen die Annahme wenden konnte, Prädestination hebe die Möglichkeit eines *arbitrium* auf.[16]

Dies ist offensichtlich der Punkt, an welchem sich Luther von den Auffassungen seines Lehrers und Beichtvaters löste, so sehr er diesem bekanntlich gerade zur

---

9 Staupitz: 1979, 92 (= *De exsecutione aeternae praedestinationis* IV,17). Zur Augustinrezeption in Staupitz' Tübinger Predigten s. Wetzel: 2018, 223–265 (Übers. v.: ders., Wetzel: 1991, 72–115).
10 Staupitz: 1979, 104 (= *De exsecutione aeternae praedestinationis* V,28): "Si non es praedestinatus, fac praedestineris".
11 Staupitz: 1979, 112 (= *De exsecutione aeternae praedestinationis* VI,33): "mera gratia est et ex Christi meritis – praevisis vel exhibitis – fluit, operibus nostris ad hoc nihil facientibus".
12 Staupitz: 1979, 114 (= *De exsecutione aeternae praedestinationis* VI,34): "ex libera dei electione".
13 Ausführlicher stellt die Unterschiede im Ansatz zwischen Staupitz und Luther (und auch Karlstadt) Lohse (1990) dar.
14 Staupitz: 1979, 122ff (= *De exsecutione aeternae praedestinationis* VII,40).
15 S. hierzu Drews: 2009, 178–185.
16 Staupitz: 1979, 234 (= *De exsecutione aeternae praedestinationis* XIX,170).

Prädestinationslehre entscheidende Hinweise verdankte.[17] Denn zu den markanten Gestaltungen von Luthers Augustinismus zählte eben die Bestreitung des freien Willens, die entsprechend auch in die Verurteilungen der Bannandrohungsbulle einging.[18] Die darin liegende Verschiebung in der Wahrnehmung Augustins hängt offenbar an jenem besonderen Komplex, in welchem Luther Augustin wahrnahm: Wohl durchaus unter dem Einfluss von Staupitz hatte er sich bekanntlich Tauler zugewandt und dessen Predigten zusammen mit der bald ihm zugespielten "Theologia deutsch" in einen gedanklichen Komplex hineingeformt, der eben aus dem Erbe der Mystik, Paulus und Augustin gebildet war.[19] Innerhalb dieses Komplexes kann man die "Theologia deutsch", obwohl sie den Namen Augustins nicht erwähnt, als eine Gestalt eines zugespitzten Augustinismus verstehen, welcher sich, wie Lydia Wegener gezeigt hat, auch in der Frage der Willensfreiheit niederschlägt: Die "Negation des Eigenwillens" in der "Theologia deutsch" nämlich, gehe, so Wegener, in einem gewissen "Jargon der Ausschließlichkeit" über die konventionelle mystische Kritik am Eigenwillen hinaus.[20] Er sei konsequent nur auf Negatives ausgerichtet.[21] Daher kann die "Theologia deutsch" über den Willen sagen:

> Aber wo man sich freiheit an nympt, (…) Da ist nicht eyne ware, gottlich freiheit auß eyme waren, gotlichen lichte, sonder das ist eyn naturlich, yngerecht, falsch, betrogen tufels freiheit auß eim naturlichen, falschen, betrogenen lichte.[22]

---

17 S. Luthers Erinnerung an den "Prädestinationsratschlag": "Disputatio de praedestinatione omnino fugienda est. Et Staupitius dicebat: Si vis disputare de praedestinatione, incipe a vulneribus Christi, et cessabit; sin pergis disceptare pro illa, perdes Christum, verbum, sacramenta et omnia etc. Ich vergiß alles, das Christus vnd Gott ist, wen ich in dieße gedancken kome, vnd kom wol dohin, das Gott ein boßwichtg sey. In verbo manendum est nobis, in quo Deus nobis revelatur et offertus salus, si illi credimus. In cogiatione autem praedestinationis obliviscimur Dei, vnd das laudate hort auff, vnd das blasphemate gehet an. In Christo autem omnes thesauri sunt absconditi; extra ipsum omnes clausi. Ideo hoc argumentum praedestinationis simpliciter negandum est." (WA.TR 2, S. 582,15–24 [Nr. 2654a]); zu den quellenkritischen Problemen s. Leppin: 2013, 55ff.

18 DH 1486. Den späteren Streit um diese Frage kann man nur recht nachvollziehen, wenn man bedenkt, dass Erasmus sich in seinem Votum für den freien Willen explizit gegen Luthers Verteidigung dieser These in der *Assertio omium articulorum M. Lutheri per bullam Leonis X. novissimam damnatorum* wandte (s. hierzu Leppin: 2019, 13f).

19 S. hierzu Leppin: 2018a, 130–153.

20 Wegener: 2016, 304.

21 Wegener: 2016, 308.

22 Franckforter: 1982, 147, 107–112 (= *Theologia deutsch* 51): "Aber wo man sich Freiheit anmaßt (…), da ist nicht eine wahre, göttliche Freiheit aus einem wahren, göttlichen Licht, sondern da ist eine natürliche, ungerechte, falsche, betrogene Teufelsfreiheit aus einem natürlichen, falschen, betrogenen Licht."; cf. hierzu Wegener: 2016, 309.

Dass Martin Luther, der 1518 in der Vorrede zu der nun vollständigen Ausgabe der "Theologia deutsch", die auch erstmals diese Passage aus Kapitel 51 enthielt,[23] erklärte, dieses Buch sei ihm "nehst der Biblien und S. Augustino" zur besonderen Quelle seines Lernens geworden,[24] in eben demselben Jahr auf der Heidelberger Disputation erklärte: "Der freie Wille nach der Sünde ist eine Sache bloß dem Namen nach, und solange er tut, was in ihm ist, begeht er Todsünde",[25] lässt jedenfalls einen dichten gedanklichen Zusammenhang mit der "Theologia deutsch" erkennen und macht die Annahme plausibel, dass Luthers Augustinismus seine Charakteristik unter dem Einfluss der "Theologia deutsch" gewonnen hat.

Dies gilt um so mehr, als die Heidelberger Disputation in dieser 13. These ebenso wie auch in den Thesen zur *theologia crucis* weniger als eine Fortsetzung der 95 Thesen gegen den Ablass erscheint denn als eine weitere Ausführung zur Weise des Theologietreibens, also als eine Fortführung eigentlich eher der sekundär so benannten *Disputatio contra scholasticam theologiam* vom 4. September 1517, die auch bereits die Abweisung des freien Willens – hier mit dem Begriff *"liber appetitus"* – enthielt.[26] Eben damit aber sind wir bei dem für den Wittenberger Augustinismus entscheidenden Text, denn die Disputation gegen die scholastische Theologie legt den Grund genau für die eingangs angesprochene im Protestantismus kulturprägende Diastase zwischen Augustin und Aristoteles. Das machte schon die erste These deutlich: "Zu sagen, dass Augustin gegen die Häretiker übertrieben formuliert habe, heißt zu sagen, dass Augustin beinahe überall gelogen habe".[27] Die "*contra dictum commune*" gerichtete Spitze lässt sich tatsächlich mit einer Aussage bei Gabriel Biel verbinden, die dieser wiederum aus Bonaventura übernommen hatte.[28] Die Verallgemeinerung, bekanntlich eine durchgängige Strategie Luthers in dieser Disputation, resultierte nicht nur daraus, dass Luther in Erfurt ja Theologie tatsächlich vornehmlich durch die Brille Biels gelernt hatte, sondern auch darum, dass die Klimax der Thesen auf eine Abweisung der gewohnten Zuordnung von Aristoteles und theologischer Arbeit zulief: Nicht dass man ohne Aristoteles nicht Theologie werden könne, sei wahr, sondern im Gegenteil gelte: "Theologe wird niemand, wenn das nicht ohne Aristoteles erfolgt".[29] Verteidigung Augustins und

---

23 Zum Umfang der ersten Ausgabe von 1516 s. Zecherle: 2019, 71.
24 Luther, Vorrede zur vollständigen Ausgabe der "deutschen Theologie" (WA 1,378,20–22).
25 Luther, *Disputatio Heidelberga habita*. These 13 (WA 1,354,5f): "Liberum arbitrium post peccatum res est de solo titulo, et dum facit quod in se est, peccat mortaliter."
26 Luther, *Contra scholasticam theologiam 5f* (WA 1,224,15–18).
27 Luther, *Contra scholasticam theologiam* 1 (WA 1,224,7f): "Dicere, quod Augustinus contra haereticos excessive loquatur, Est dicere, Augustinum fere ubique mentitum esse."
28 Biel: 1984, 594,25f (= *Sentenzen II d. 23 q. un. A. 3 dub. 2*).
29 Luther, *Contra scholasticam theologiam* 44 (WA 1,226,16): "immo theologus non fit nisi id fiat sine Aristotele."

gänzliche Verbannung des Aristoteles aus der Theologie, das war – wenn auch Letzteres eine rhetorische Übertreibung darstellen dürfte – das Programm, das Luther sich und der Wittenberger Bewegung auf die Fahnen geschrieben hatte: Schon einige Monate zuvor, am 18. Mai 1517 hatte er in einer berühmten Bemerkung an seinen Ordensbruder Johannes Lang geschrieben:

> Unter Gottes Beistand machen unsere Theologie und Sankt Augustin gute Fortschritte und herrschen an unserer Universität. Aristoteles steigt nach und nach herab und neigt sich zum nahe gerückten ewigen Untergang. Auf erstaunliche Weise werden die Vorlesungen über die Sentenzen verschmäht, so dass niemand auf Hörer hoffen kann, der nicht über diese Theologie, d. h. über die Bibel, über Sankt Augustin oder über einen anderen Lehrer von kirchlicher Autorität lesen will. Gehab dich wohl und bete für mich.[30]

Augustin gegen Aristoteles: Das war das Wittenberger Reformprogramm, dem sich auch mehr und mehr die Kollegen anschlossen.

Dass es hierbei tatsächlich nicht um die Neueinführung der Autorität Augustins ging, sondern um die Durchsetzung jener spezifischen, gnadentheologischen und antivoluntativen Zuspitzung der Augustindeutung, die Luther der "Theologia deutsch" entnommen hatte, macht niemand mehr deutlich als Andreas Karlstadt in seinem berühmten Bericht über seine Bekehrung zur spezifischen Wittenberger Theologie: In dem Widmungsbrief an Staupitz, den er der Veröffentlichung seiner Vorlesung über "De spiritu et littera", die ab 1517 in Wittenberg erschien, voranstellte, schilderte er, wie er die Bibelauslegung Luthers, vor allem dessen Berufung auf Augustin, für unglaubwürdig gehalten habe[31] – ausdrücklich berief er sich hierfür auf sein "Verständnis" (*intelligentia*). Den Anstoß bildete für ihn wohl die Doktorpromotion des Bartholäus Bernhardi aus Feldkirch aus dem September 1516,[32] die das augustinische Programm, das Luthers Römervorlesung durchzog, wirksam präsentierte und dabei den Gedanken in die Debatte einführte, der bald darauf Furore machen sollte: dass der menschliche Wille ohne die Gnade nicht frei sei.[33] Jedenfalls berichtete Luther seinem Freund Lang, er habe in diesem

---

30 Luther an Johannes Lang, 17. Mai 1517 (WA.B 1, 99 [Nr. 41,8–13]): "Theologia nostra et S. Augustinus prospere procedunt et regnant in nostra universitate Deo operante. Aristoteles descendit paulatim inclinatus ad ruinam prope futuram sempiternam. Mire fastidiuntur lectiones sententiaeriae, nec est, ut quis sibi auditores sperare possit, nisi theologiam hanc,id est bibliam aut S. Augustinum aliumve ecclesiasticae auctoritatis doctorem velit profiteri. Vale et ora pro me".
31 Karlstadt: 2017, 561,20–30 (= *De spiritu et littera. Widmungsschreiben*).
32 Matthias: 2001, 90; Zur Disputation s. Leppin: 2015b, 43–57; zur Datierung s. Baral: 2014, 57–68.
33 Luther, *Quaestio de viribus et voluntate hominis sine gratia disputata concl. 2 cor. 2* (WA 1,147,38f.). Im selben Jahr 1516 hat Luther die erste Ausgabe der Theologia deutsch, freilich, wie eben erwähnt, noch unvollständig herausgebracht.

Zusammenhang viele, insbesondere aber Karlstadt, durch seine Bestreitung der Autorschaft Augustins am "*Liber de vera et falsa poenitentia*" gegen sich aufgebracht.[34]

In Auseinandersetzung mit Luthers Augustindeutung, habe Karlstadt, so berichtete er, im Januar 1517 in Leipzig eine Ausgabe der Werke Augustins von Amerbach aus dem Jahre 1505/1506[35] – erworben,[36] um den Kollegen zu widerlegen. Jens-Martin Kruse verweist zu Recht darauf, dass sich in diesem Vorgehen die humanistische Haltung, *ad fontes* zu gehen, um Sachfragen zu klären, niederschlägt.[37] Doch es kam zu einem Geschehen, das man mit Markus Matthias als veritables Bekehrungserlebnis bezeichnen kann.[38] Karlstadt fasst es in die Worte: "Ich stutzte, ich verstummte, ich erzürnte"[39] – und er erkannte, dass er aufgrund der Befangenheit in scholastische Auffassung einem Irrtum aufgesessen war.[40] Im Weiteren kam ihm dann noch ein vermutlich verschollenes Brieflein von Staupitz zu Hilfe.[41] Am Ende jedenfalls war er von der Auffassung des Kollegen überzeugt und stand nun auf seiner Seite – dass dabei seine eigene Beschäftigung mit Mystik[42] den Wandlungsprozess unterstützt hat, kann man nur vermuten. Er war jedenfalls bereit, rasch in die Offensive zu gehen: Schon am 26. April 1517 veröffentlichte er eine Thesenreihe, die in mancher Hinsicht Luthers Disputation gegen die scholastische Theologie präludierte. Das galt zum einen für die Form der scharfen knappen Abweisung von Gegenpositionen,[43] aber auch für die schroffe Gegenüberstellung der Kirchenväter zu Aristoteles. Letzterer sei für das Durcheinander in der Theologie verantwortlich,[44] während nicht nur für Augustin, sondern für die

---

34 Luther an Johannes Lang, Mitte Oktober 1516 (WA.B 1, 65f [Nr. 26,29f]).
35 Karlstadt, Kritische Gesamtausgabe 550, Anm. 102f, in Korrektur von Karlstadt und Augustin. Der Kommentar des Andreas Bodenstein von Karlstadt zu Augustins Schrift De spiritu et littera, ed. v. Ernst Kähler, Halle [Saale] 1952, 54*.
36 Karlstadt: 2017, 562,15–21 (= *De spiritu et littera. Widmungsschreiben*).
37 Kruse: 2002, 87.
38 Matthias: 2001, 92.
39 Karlstadt: 2017, 562,21f (= *De spiritu et littera. Widmungsschreiben*): "obstupui: obmutui: succensui".
40 Karlstadt: 2017, 562,25f (= *De spiritu et littera. Widmungsschreiben*).
41 Karlstadt: 2017, 562,28–30 (= *De spiritu et littera. Widmungsschreiben*); Matthias (2001, 95) erklärt zu Recht, dass es nicht genügend Anhaltspunkte gibt, um dieses "*epistolium*", wie es Kähler, in: Karlstadt und Augustin 5, tut, mit "*De exsecutione aeternae praedestinationis*" zu identifizieren. Karlstadt (2017) folgt auf Seite auf Seite 562 Anm. 23, Kählers Identifikation, Seite 552 Anm. 115, hingegen – wohl zu Recht – der Problematisierung von Matthias.
42 S. Hasse (1993).
43 S. dazu Leppin: 2015a, 141f, dort auch mit Hinweis auf die textkritische Problematik: Die knappen *contra*-Positionierungen finden sich nicht in der handschriftlichen Fassung, könnten also sekundär in den erst nach 1517 entstandenen Druckfassungen zugefügt worden sein (s. Kolde: 1890, 450 Anm. 1).
44 Karlstadt: 2017, 499, 5f 11 (= *Centum Quinquagintaunum Conclusiones de natura, lege et gratia* 3. 7) u. ö.

Kirchenväter insgesamt gelte: "Die Aussprüche der heiligen Väter dürfen nicht bestritten werden".[45] Und das bezog sich ausdrücklich auch auf die heiklen Aussagen Augustins zur Willensfreiheit: "Der Wille erlangt die Gnade nicht aufgrund von Freiheit, sondern ganz im Gegenteil."[46] Karlstadt war somit Teil jener Wittenberger Augustindeutung, die in den Vordergrund ihres Verständnisses die Anthropologie mit der Bestreitung des freien Willens und die ihr korrespondierende Ausschließlichkeit der Gnade Gottes hob. Gerade die Weise, wie Karlstadt und Luther[47] diesen Augustinismus vielleicht nicht in einem "Jargon", sondern eher in einer "Rhetorik der Ausschließlichkeit" antiaristotelisch und antischolastisch zuspitzen und so ihre Differenzhermeneutik mittelalterlicher Harmoniehermeneutik entgegensetzten, bedeutete eine Inszenierung des Wittenberger Augustinismus ungeachtet aller auch vorhandenen Anknüpfung an Vorgegebenes – nicht zuletzt die "Theologia Deutsch" – als Neuheit. Das provozierte und polarisierte.

2. Mit Augustin für das Schriftprinzip: Zwingli

Dass die Verhältnisse bei Zwingli anders liegen als bei den Wittenbergern, hat Alfred Schindler, dem wir die gründlichste Untersuchung zum Thema verdanken, sehr klar auf den Punkt gebracht:

> Es scheint mir deshalb schlechterdings unmöglich, die Formung der reformatorischen Theologie Zwinglis, die wir Anfang 1523 als abgeschlossen ansehen dürfen, auf einen irgendwie besonders gearteten Einfluss Augustins zurückzuführen.[48]

Dieses ernüchternde Ergebnis steht im Zusammenhang des Bemühens, die Erforschung von Zwinglis reformatorischer Entwicklung positiv wie negativ aus dem Schatten Luthers zu holen.[49] Bezeichnenderweise stammt das einzige Zeugnis, in

---

45 Karlstadt 2017, 499,3 (= *Centum Quinquagintaunum Conclusiones de natura, lege et gratia 1*): "Dicta sanctorum patrum non sunt neganda". In These 2 schränkte Karlstadt allerdings ein, dies gelte nur, wenn sie nicht korrigiert oder zurückgenommen worden seien (ebd. 499,4).

46 Karlstadt 2017, 12f (= *Centum Quinquagintaunum Conclusiones de natura, lege et gratia 21*): "Voluntas non libertate consequitur gratiam. sed econtra"; zur Bedeutung der antipelagianischen Schriften Augustins in diesen Thesen s. Kruse: 2002, 90.

47 Zu Luthers Wertschätzung von Karlstadts Thesen s. Kruse: 2002, 93.

48 Schindler: 1984, 38; für einen breiteren Blick auf Zwinglis Gebrauch der Kirchenväter insgesamt s. Backus: 1997, 627–660. Die folgenden Ausführungen beziehen sich konzentriert auf die Anstöße Augustins für die Entwicklung Zwinglis – dass er insbesondere im Zusammenhang der Entwicklung seiner Abendmahlslehre reichlich Gebrauch von einschlägigen Augustinstellen machte, zeigt in diesem Band eindrucksvoll der Beitrag von Amy Nelson Burnett.

49 Schindler: 1984, 40; cf. die bahnbrechende Studie von Bolliger (2003).

welchem Zwingli seine reformatorische Entwicklung mit dem Namen Augustins verbindet, dem Streit mit Luther, nämlich der *Amica Exegesis* von 1527.[50] Das hat nicht nur offensichtlich apologetischen Charakter, sondern ist in seiner Struktur auch so formuliert, dass Zwingli sehr deutlich macht, dass er Augustin hauptsächlich als Hilfe zur Erkenntnis des Sinns der Heiligen Schrift wahrgenommen hat, ihm aber keine eigene Bedeutung zumisst.

Auch der Blick in die frühen Schriften lässt keine intensivere Auseinandersetzung mit Augustin erkennen: In der Werkausgabe, die er von dem am Verlegerkonsortium beteiligten Johannes Froben selbst erhalten hat, hat Zwingli bis etwa 1519 vorwiegend grammatische Randbemerkungen hinterlassen – unter ihnen ist zwar, wie Walter Köhler vermerkte, eine "köstlich",[51] der Stoßseufzer zu *De civitate Dei* 13 c. 11 nämlich: "ach got das Adam nit biren aasz".[52] Theologisch trägt dies aber wenig aus – und in Zwinglis Randbemerkungen zu anderen Texten fällt auf, dass Origenes und Hieronymus eine weit größere Bedeutung haben als Augustin.[53] Zwar wird dieser gelegentlich auch rechtfertigungstheologisch angeführt,[54] aber dass diejenigen Züge seiner Lehre, die Luther beeindruckt haben, eine besondere Bedeutung für Zwingli gehabt hätten, wird man kaum behaupten können.

Vielmehr wird Augustin herangezogen, wenn und soweit er dem Anliegen Zwinglis entgegenkommt, und das heißt für ihn, in Transformation der scotistischen Unterscheidung zwischen Endlichem und Unendlichem,[55] vor allem wo er das Schriftprinzip unterstützt, das, um noch einmal Schindler zu zitieren, "als solches freilich (…) überhaupt kein spezifisches Anliegen altkirchlicher Autoren" war.[56] Entsprechend ambivalent ist der Befund bei ihnen, und das war im Blick auf Augustin auch Zwingli bewusst: Im *Apologeticus Archeteles*, seiner Antwort an den Bischof

---

50 Zwingli, *Amica exegesis* (CR 92 / Z 5, 713,2–714,2): "Nam de me ipso coram deo testor, euangelii vim atque summam cum Joannis Augustinique tractatuum lectione didici, tum diligenti Gręcanicarum Pauli epistolarum, quas hisce manibus ante undecim annos exscripsi, quum tu annis iam octo regnes.".
51 CR 99 / Z 12, 136.
52 CR 99 / Z,12, 156.
53 CR 92 / Z 5, 713 Anm. 3.
54 Zwingli, *Auslegung der Artikel* 20 (CR 89/ ZII, 186,26–29): "Und obschon got mit sinem wort lon verheißt, belonet er nüt anderst dann sin eigen werck, das er gewürckt hat, als ouch Augustinus spricht und der herr selbs bedüt". Die Herausgeber verweisen in Anm. 7 auf "In Ioannis evangelium tractatus CXXIV 82. Richtiger dürfte aber der Verweis auf Augustin, *Epistola* 194 sein: "Quod est ergo meritum hominis ante gratiam, quo merito percipiat gratiam, cum omne bonum meritum nostrum non in nobis faciat nisi gratia et, cum deus coronat merita nostra, nihil aliud coronet quam munera sua?" (CSEL 57, 190,12–15), das von Petrus Lombardus überliefert wurde als: "cum coronat merita nostra, nihil aliud coronat quam munera sua", Lombardus: 1971, 484, 14f.
55 S. hierzu in weiterführender Anknüpfung an Bolliger, *Infiniti contemplatio*, Leppin: 2017, 51–64.
56 Schindler: 1984, 37.

von Konstanz aus dem August 1522, setzte Zwingli sich zunächst mit dem berühmten Diktum auseinander: "Ich aber würde dem Evangelium nicht glauben, wenn mich nicht die Autorität der katholischen Kirche dazu bewegte".[57] Hier wandte er sich kritisch nicht nur gegen dessen Gebrauch, sondern wohl auch gegen seinen Urheber, der allzu kühn und unklug gesprochen habe[58] – wobei er sich freilich, wie Irena Backus gezeigt hat, auf eine nicht nur vom Original, sondern auch von Zwinglis eigener Augustinausgabe abweichende Textfassung bezog, in welcher das Verb "*approbare*" vorkam und die somit einen kirchlichen Rechtsakt auszudrücken schien.[59] Der Sache nach war Zwinglis Argument im Kern: Das Evangelium sei ja älter und sachlich unabhängig von Augustin als Botschaft von der Gnade Gottes gegeben gewesen.[60] Gegenüber diesem explizit kritischen Umgang mit Augustin gab es aber auch eine positive Aufnahme. Zwingli konnte sich darauf beziehen, dass Augustin in einem Schreiben an Hieronymus erklärt hatte: "Ich habe gelernt, allein jenen Büchern, die man kanonisch nennt, diese Ehre zukommen zu lassen, mit Gewissheit zu glauben, dass keiner ihrer Schreiber in Irrtum gefallen ist".[61] Allerdings führte Zwingli dieses Zitat zunächst aufgrund seiner Aufnahme in *Decretum Gratiani* D. 9 c. 5 an,[62] erst sekundär aufgrund des Ursprungs bei Augustin. Von einer spezifischen Augustinrezeption wird man auch hier nicht sprechen können. Eher macht Zwingli den Eindruck sich Augustins dort zu bedienen, wo es ihm nützlich erscheint, die Autorität des Kirchenvaters also zugunsten des von ihm jeweils präferierten Arguments auszuspielen.

---

57 Augustin, *Contra epistolam fundamenti* (CSEL 25,197,22f): "Ego vero euangelio non crederem, nisi me catholicae ecclesiae commoveret auctoritas"; cf. Zwingli, *Apologeticus Archeteles* (CR 88 / Z 1, 293,6f): "Euangelio non crederem, nisi ecclesia adprobasset euangelium." Um diese Deutung ist offenbar noch ein Streit mit Chorherr Hofmann entstanden; s. Zwingli an Konrad Hofmann, 11. April 1524 (CR 95 / Z 8, 168,7–169,4 [Nr. 332]); cf. Schindler: 1996, 82 Anm. 88.
58 Zwingli, *Apologeticus Archeteles* (CR 88 / Z 1, 293,8f).
59 Backus: 1997, 641; zu Zwinglis Textfassung s. o. Anm. 57.
60 Zwingli, *Apologeticus Archeteles* (CR 88 / Z 1, 293,9–15).
61 Augustin, Epistola 82 (CSEL 6,354,4–8): "ego enim fateor caritati tuae solis eis scripturarum libris, qui iam canonici eppellantur didici hunc timorem honoremque deferre, ut nullum eorum auctorem scribendo errasse aliquid firmissime credam"; bei Zwingli aufgenommen in Zwingli, *Apologeticus Archeteles* (CR 88 / Z 1, 306,26–30).
62 Zwingli, *Apologeticus Archeteles* (CR 88 / Z 1, 303,9f); cf. Corpus: 1879, 17. Auch an der Stelle, an welcher Zwingli auf die Autorschaft Augustins an dem Zitat im *Decretum* rekurriert, verweist er zunächst auf "*vestros sacrosanctos canones*" (CR 88 / Z 1, 306,26f).

3. Latomus: Pochen auf das rechte Augustinverständnis

Die Vielfalt der Reaktionen auf die Reformation kann in einer schmalen Pilotstudie wie dieser nicht aufgeführt werden, sondern es ist nur ein exemplarischer Einblick möglich. Soll dieser inhaltlich zugespitzt erfolgen, so muss er sich nach dem bislang Dargelegten auf die altgläubige Reaktion auf den Wittenberger Augustinismus richten. Ungeachtet dessen, dass Augustin – auch etwa im Blick auf die Frage der Geltung der kanonischen Schriften – in der Leipziger Disputation eine große Rolle spielte[63] soll daher im Folgenden nicht diese detailliert aufgearbeitet werden. Vielmehr kommt derjenige in den Blick, der sich sehr früh und intensiv mit den Folgen der reformatorischen Rechtfertigungslehre für die Anthropologie auseinandergesetzt hat: Jacobus Latomus, der in seiner gegen Luther gerichteten *Ratio* zugleich auch den Anspruch erhob, nicht allein für seine individuelle Lehre zu sprechen, sondern auch die durch seine Löwener Fakultät ausgesprochene Verurteilung Luthers[64] zu begründen. Besonders ausführlich erfolgt dabei die Beschäftigung mit Augustin, wie Hannegreth Grundmann in ihrer Latomus-Studie gezeigt hat, im Zusammenhang der Auseinandersetzung von Latomus mit Luthers achtem Argument zur ersten *Conclusio* seiner *Resolutiones* der Leipziger Disputation.[65] Luthers *cunclusio prima* besagte, dass der Mensch beständig sündige und beständig Buße tue.[66] Im achten Argument führte er unter Berufung auf Ps 143:2 aus, dass kein Mensch ohne Sünde sein könne[67] und so deutlich werde, dass nach der Taufe Sünde bleibe und in jedem guten Werk Todsünde enthalten sei.[68] In dieser Argumentation spielen drei Augustinzitate eine Rolle,[69] deren Beweiskraft entsprechend von Latomus widerlegt wird – folglich kann man die unterschiedlichen Ansprüche auf Augustin hier besonders deutlich nachvollziehen:

- Mit Augustin, *Confessiones* 9, 13,34 ("Wehe selbst einem löblichen Menschenleben, wenn ich es ohne Mitleid prüfe")[70] begründete Luther, dass es keine in der Sünde selbst liegende Unterscheidung von Todsünde und lässlicher Sünde geben könne:

---

63 *Leipziger Disputation* (WA 59,473,1262–1266; 480, 1469–1475); cf. auch den Streit um seine Deutung von Matt 16:18: WA 59, 459,830–840; 464,998–465,1017; 470,1170–1185; 476,1356–1369.
64 S. *Facultatis Lovaniensis condemnatio doctrinae Martini Lutheri* (WA 6,175–178) – darin wird Augustin nicht explizit erwähnt.
65 Grundmann: 2012, 162.
66 Luther, *Resolutiones super propositionibus Lipsiae disputatis* concl. 1 (WA 2,403,6–9).
67 Luther, *Resolutiones super propositionibus Lipsiae disputatis* concl. 1 (WA 2,415,18–27).
68 Luther, *Resolutiones super propositionibus Lipsiae disputatis* concl. 1 (WA 2,421,1–3).
69 S. Grundmann: 2012, 128–133.
70 Augustin, *Confessiones* 9,13,34 (CSEL 33,223,23f): "uae etiam laudabili uitae hominum, si remota misericordia discutiam eam".

allein aufgrund der Barmherzigkeit Gottes könne eine Sünde, die ihrem Kern nach Widerstand gegen den göttlichen Willen sei, als lässliche Sünde angesehen werden.[71] Dem hielt Latomus entgegen, dass Augustin, der an der von Luther herangezogenen Stelle über seine Mutter sprach,[72] dieser in anderem Zusammenhang durchaus auch gute Werke zuspreche, die Stelle also nicht, wie Luther sie deutete, besage, jedes menschliche Werk sei "Sünde oder mit Sünde vermischt" ("peccatum, aut mixtum cum peccato"). Vielmehr sei sie so zu verstehen, dass auch ein löblich lebender Mensch keineswegs nur gute Werke tue, sondern gelegentlich sündige und für diese Werke dann der Barmherzigkeit Gottes bedürfe:[73] Das Argument Luthers, das auf eine Unfähigkeit des Menschen zu Sündenfreiheit zielte, wandte Latomus also zu einer Möglichkeit des Sündigens auch durch Gerechte.[74] Will man den Gegensatz im Sinne der eingespielten Formeln deuten, so argumentierte Luther mit dieser *Confessiones*-Stelle für ein *non posse non peccare*, Latomus hingegen mit derselben Stelle für ein *posse (non) peccare* des Getauften, etwas tiefergehend gesagt: Luther sah in dem Zitat ein Indiz für die umfassende Erbsünde, angesichts deren die Qualifizierung auch guter Werke ganz unter das Vorzeichen der Sünde tritt, während Latomus Aktualsünden von aktuellen guten Taten unterschied. Ebenso differenziert Latomus auch die Aussagen über die Barmherzigkeit Gottes. Sie führten nicht zu einer Aufhebung des Gegensatzes zwischen Todsünde und lässlicher Sünde, sondern verwiesen lediglich darauf, dass Gott jederzeit barmherzig sei und handle.[75]

– Ein weiteres Augustinzitat, das Luther anführt, entstammt *Retractationes* l. 1 c. 18: "Alle Gebote Gottes also können als erfüllt betrachtet werden, wenn was nicht geschieht, vergeben wird."[76] Hieraus folgerte der Reformator, dass die Erfüllung der Gebote eben nicht in der menschlichen Handlung liege, sondern allein im Verzeihen Gottes – und dieses Verzeihen wiederum könne sich allein auf die in den Werken implizierte Sünde richten, woraus sich ergibt, dass es keine Werke und vor allem kein Verdienst ohne Sünde gebe.[77] In ganz ähnlicher Weise wie bei dem *Confessiones*-Zitat deutet Latomus diese Aussage aus den *Retractationes* im Horizont eines an Aktualsünden orientierten Denkens nicht auf eine Qualifizierung jeglicher Tat als auch der Vergebung bedürftig,

---

71 Luther, *Resolutiones super propositionibus Lipsiae disputatis* concl. 1 (WA 2,416,10–20).
72 Hierauf verweist auch Grundmann (2012, 128), erweckt aber den Eindruck, der kontextuelle Bezug auf die Mutter sei das entscheidende Argument von Latomus. Er nutzt dies lediglich, um anhand des Bezuges deutlich zu machen, wie die Aussage zu verstehen ist, relativiert die Aussage also nicht durch den biographischen Kontext.
73 Zu dieser durchgängigen Argumentationsstrategie von Latomus und dem damit verbundenen Augustinverständnis s. Vind: 2019, 127.
74 Articvlorvm: 1521, h 3^r.
75 Articvlorvm: 1521, h 3^r.
76 Augustin, *Retractationes* L.1 c. 18,5 (CSEL 36, 90, 10f): "Omnia ergo mandata facta deputantur, quando quidquid non fit ignoscitur."
77 Luther, *Resolutinoes super propositionibus Lipisiae disputatis* concl. 1 (WA 2,417,1–6).

sondern in dem Sinne, dass einzelne Taten gut und richtig sein könnten, anderer hingegen sündig.[78] Hierfür führte er dann noch weitere Aussagen Augustins an, insbesondere aus *De peccatorum meritis* 16.23, wo Augustin die Unfähigkeit des Menschen sündenfrei zu sein, damit erklärte, dass kein Mensch so weit gelange, dass er keine Sünde beginge[79] – für Latomus ein klarer Beleg, dass seine Augustindeutung der Aufteilung von Sünde und Sündenfreiheit auf einzelne Akte und nicht auf eine Qualifizierung jeglicher Tat als sündig, dem Kirchenvater entspreche.[80] Er kam zu dem scharfen Ergebnis: "Hier siehst du ganz deutlich, wie Martin diesen Ausspruch Augustins gewaltsam verdreht, wenn er aus ihm ableiten will, dass die Gebote nicht durch das Tun der Menschen erfüllt würden, sondern durch Gottes Vergebung, und dass in eben dem Werk, durch welches das Gebot erfüllt wird, Sünde innewohne".[81]

– Schließlich verweist Luther auf *Ep. 167 an Hieronymus*, wo Augustin über die *caritas* schreibt, die in manchen mehr, in anderen weniger in einigen gar nicht gegeben sei. In Luthers Lektüre gipfelte dies in dem Zentralsatz: "Aufgrund dieses Fehlers gibt es auf Erden keinen Gerechten, der Gutes täte und nicht sündigt. Aufgrund dieses Fehlers wird kein Lebender vor Gottes Angesicht gerechtfertigt",[82] in dem Augustin seine Überlegungen mit Zitaten aus Koh 7:20 und Ps 143:2 verband. Luther folgerte hieraus, dass die im Menschen verbliebene *concupiscentia* in jeglichem menschlichen Werk

---

78 Articvlorvm: 1521, h 3ᵛ; zu Latomus' Argumentationsgang s. Grundmann: 2012, 129f.
79 Augustin, *De peccatorum meritis* l. 2,16,23 (CSEL 60,95,16–96,8) "Neque negandum est hoc Deum iubere ita nos in facienda iustitia esse debere perfectos, ut nullum habeamus omnino peccatum. nam neque peccatum erit, si quid erit, si non divinitus iubetur ut non sit. cur ergo iubet, inquiunt, quod scit nullum hominum esse facturum? hoc modo etiam dici potest, cur primis illis hominibus iusserit, qui duo soli erant, quod sciebat eos non esse facturos. neque enim dicendum est ideo iussisse, ut nostrum aliquis id faceret, si illi non facerent; hoc enim, ne de illa scilicet arbore cibum sumerent, non nisi illis solis Deus iussit, quia, sicut sciebat quid iustitiae facturi non erant, ita etiam sciebat quid iustitiae de illis erat ipse facturus. eo modo ergo iubet omnibus hominibus ut non faciant ullum peccatum, quamvis sit praescius neminem hoc impleturum, ut, quicumque impie ac damnabiliter eius praecepta contempserint, ipse faciat eorum damnatione quod iustum est, quicumque autem in eius praeceptis oboedienter et pie proficientes nec tamen omnia quae praecepit implentes, sicut sibi dimitti volunt, sic aliis peccata dimiserint, ipse faciat in eorum mundatione quod bonum est. quomodo enim dimittenti dimittitur per dei misericordiam, si peccatum non est? aut quomodo non vetatur per dei iustitiam, si peccatum est?".
80 Articvlorvm: 1521, h 3ᵛ–4ʳ.
81 Articvlorvm: 1521, h 4ʳ: "Hic clare vides quod hanc. Aug. sententiam M. violenter torquet, cum ex ea vult inferre quod mandata non impleantur operantibus hominibus, sed ignoscente deo, et quod in ipso opere quo mandatum impletur sit pecccatum".
82 Augustin, *Ep. 167*, 15 (CSEL 44,602,16–18): "Ex quo vitio non est iustus in terra, qui faciat bonum, et non peccabit: ex quo vitio non iustificabitur in conspectu Dei omnis vivens"; Cf. Luther, *Resolutiones super propositionibus suis Lipisiae disputatis* (WA 2,417,20–22).

Sünde verursache.[83] Die Differenz zu Latomus zeigt sich gerade am Umgang hiermit, denn für diesen war das, was nach der Taufe über blieb allein der *fomes peccati*, so dass sich die Aussage Augustins lediglich auf ein Sündigen "*ex vitio fomitis*" beziehen könne.[84] Wiederum aber bedeute dies lediglich, dass auch Getaufte *frequenter* sündigen,[85] nicht aber, dass, wie Luther folgerte, jegliches Tun des Menschen von Sünde belastet sei.[86]

Anna Vind hat darauf hingewiesen, dass insbesondere die letztgenannte Differenz zwischen Latomus und Luther damit zu tun hatte, dass Augustins Verständnis von *concupiscentia* zwischen einer Deutung als Sünde selbst oder als Anreiz zum Sündigen geschwankt hat.[87] Das unterstreicht, dass es bei den durchgehenden Differenzen in der Augustindeutung zwischen Luther und Latomus letztlich um unterschiedliche Gesamtsichten des Kirchenvaters geht. Sie verweisen auf das, was Christoph Markschies ähnlich wie Vind als das Phänomen von "zwei 'Reihen' von Beschreibungen des Sachverhaltes (…) oder zwei 'Sprechweisen'" in Augustin charakterisiert hat.[88] Die Auseinandersetzung um Augustin hat ihren Grund auch in der mangelnden Geschlossenheit des Werkes Augustins selbst. Das hat im 16. Jahrhundert heftige Streitigkeiten provoziert. Im 21. Jahrhundert kann man diese Streitigkeiten als Beitrag zur Entdeckung der Vielfalt Augustins verstehen.

Quellen und Literatur

Quellen

Größere Reihen wie die Weimarer Aussage u. ä. werden hier nicht eigens aufgeführt, sondern in den Fußnoten mit den Abkürzungen aus IATG³ (Siegfried Schwertner, Internationales Abkürzungsverzeichnis für Theologie und Grenzgebiete, 3. Auflage Berlin 2012) zitiert.

ARTICVLORVM (1521), Articv-| lorvm Doctrinae Die|tris Martini Lutheri per theologos | Louanienses damnatorum Ratio | ex sacris literis, & veteribus | tractationibus, per Iacobum | Latomum sacrae theologiae | professorem, Antwerpen: Hillenius.

---

83 Luther, *Resolutiones super propositionibus suis Lipisiae disputatis* (WA 2,417,26–28): "Haec clarissimi patris clarissima sententia, nonne predicta omnia confirmat, quod defectu charitatis reliquam nimirum concupiscentiam causam facit peccati in quolibet opere bono?"
84 Articvlorvm: 1521, i 1ʳ.
85 Articvlorvm: 1521, i 1ʳ.
86 Articvlorvm: 1521, i 1ᵛ.
87 Vind: 2019, 120.
88 Markschies: 2001, 103f.

GABRIELIS BIEL (1984) Collectorium circa quattuor libros Sententiarum. Liber secundus, Wilfried Werbeck/Udo Hofmann (ed.), Tübingen: Mohr Siebeck.

ANDREAS BODENSTEINS VON KARLSTADT (1952), Kähler, Ernst, ed., Karlstadt und Augustin. Der Kommentar des Andreas Bodenstein von Karlstadt zu Augustins Schrift De Spiritu et litera. Einführung und Text, Halle a.d. Saale.

ANDREAS BODENSTEINS VON KARLSTADT (2017), Kritische Gesamtausgabe der Schriften und Briefe, Thomas Kaufmann (ed.), vol. I/2, Göttingen: Hubert & Co.

THOMAS BRADWARDINE (2013), De causa Dei contra Pelagium et de virtute causarum. Auszüge Lateinisch – Deutsch, ausgew., übers. u. annotiert v. E. Anna Lukács, Göttingen: V & R Unipress.

CORPUS (1879), Corpus Iuris Canonici, Emil Friedberg (ed.), vol. 1., Leipzig: Bernhard Tauchnitz.

FRANCKFORTER (1982), "Der Franckforter" ["Theologia deutsch"]. Kritische Textausgabe, Wolfgang von Hinten (ed.), München/Zürich: Artemis Verlag.

PETRI LOMBARDI (1971), Sententiae in IV libros distinctae, Vol. 1, Grottaferrata: Quaracchi.

GUILLELMI DE OCKHAM (1980) Opera Theologica, Joseph C. Wey (ed.), vol. 9, New York: New York: Franciscan Institute, University of St Bonaventure.

JOHANN VON STAUPITZ (1979) Sämtliche Schriften, Lothar Graf zu Dohna/Richard Wetzel (ed.), vol. 2: Lateinische Schriften II, Berlin/New York: De Gruyter.

Literatur

BACKUS, IRENA (1997), Ulrich Zwingli, Martin Bucer and the Chruch Fathers, in Irena Backus (ed.), The Reception of the Church Fathers in the West. From the Carolingians to the Maurists, 2 vol., Leiden: Brill, 627–660.

BARAL, MATTHIAS (2014), "Theologia nostra". Die Disputation des Bartholomäus Bernhardi von 1516 und Luthers Römerbriefvorlesung. Eigenständige Fortentwicklung oder unkritische Reproduktion?, in ZKG 125, 57–68.

BOLLIGER, DANIEL (2003), Infiniti Contemplatio. Grundzüge der Scotus- und Scotismusrezeption im Werk Huldrych Zwinglis. Mit ausführlicher Edition bisher unpublizierter Annotationen Zwinglis, Leiden/Boston: Brill.

DELIUS, HANS-ULRICH (1984), Augustin als Quelle Luthers. Eine Materialsammlung, Berlin: Evangelische Verlagsanstalt.

DREWS, FRIEDEMANN (2009), Menschliche Willensfreiheit und göttliche Vorsehung bei Augustinus, Proklos, Apuleius und John Milton. Vol. 1: Augustinus und Proklos, Frankfurt: De Gruyter.

GRUNDMANN, HANNEGRETH (2012), Gratia Christi. Die theologische Begründung des Ablasses durch Jacobus Latomus in der Kontroverse mit Martin Luther, Arbeiten zur Historischen und Systematischen Theologie 17, Berlin: Lit Verlag.

Hamel, Adolf (1934–1935), Der junge Luther und Augustin. Ihre Beziehungen in der Rechtfertigungslehre nach Luthers ersten Vorlesungen 1509–1518 untersucht, 2 vol., Gütersloh: C. Bertelsmann.

Hamm, Berndt (1982), Frömmigkeitstheologie am Anfang des 16. Jahrhunderts. Studien zu Johannes von Paltz und seinem Umkreis, BHTh 65, Tübingen: Mohr Siebeck.

Hasse, Hans-Peter (1993), Karlstadt und Tauler, Untersuchungen zur Kreuzestheologie, Gütersloh: G. Mohn.

Kolde, Theodor (1890), Wittenberger Disputationsthesen aus den Jahren 1516–1522, in ZKG 11, 448–471.

Kruse, Jens-Martin (2002), Universitätstheologie und Kirchenreform. Die Anfänge der Reformation in Wittenberg 1516–1522, VIEG 187, Mainz: Zabern.

Leff, Gordon (1957), Bradwardine and the Pelagians. A Study of his "De causa Dei" and its Opponents, London: Cambridge University Press.

Leff, Gordon (1961), Gregory of Rimini. Tradition and Innovation in Fourteenth Century Thought, New York: Barnes and Noble.

Leppin, Volker (2013), Erinnerungssplitter. Zur Problematik der Tischreden als Quelle von Luthers Biographie, in Katharina Bärenfänger/Volker Leppin/Stefan Michel (ed.), Martin Luthers Tischreden. Neuansätze der Forschung, Spätmittelalter, Humanismus, Reformation 71, Tübingen: Mohr Siebeck, 47–61.

Leppin, Volker (2015a), Der Einfluss Johannes Ecks auf den jungen Luther, in Luther 86, 135–147.

Leppin, Volker (2015b), Zuspitzung und Wahrheitsanspruch. Disputationen in den Anfängen der Wittenberger reformatorischen Bewegung, in Herman J. Selderhuis/Ernst-Joachim Waschke (ed.), Reformation und Rationalität, Refo500 Academic Studies 17, Göttingen: Vandenhoeck & Ruprecht, 43–57.

Leppin, Volker (2017), Zwinglis Transformation des Scotismus, in Schweizerische Zeitschrift für Religions- und Kirchengeschichte 111, 51–64.

Leppin, Volker (2018a), Die Verbindung von Augustinismus und Mystik im späten Mittelalter und in der frühen reformatorischen Bewegung, in LuJ 85, 130–153.

Leppin, Volker (2018b), Transformationen. Studien zu den Wandlungsprozessen in Theologie und Frömmigkeit zwischen Spätmittelalter und Reformation, Spätmittelalter, Humanismus, Reformation 86, Tübingen: Mohr Siebeck.

Leppin, Volker (2019), Luther und der Humanismus, Jacob Burckhardt-Gespräche auf Castelen 35, Basel: Schwabe Verlag.

Loewenich, Walter von (1959), Von Augustin zu Luther. Beiträge zur Kirchengeschichte, Witten: Lutherverlag.

Lohse, Bernhard (1990), Zum Wittenberger Augustinismus. Augustins Schrift De Spiritu et Littera in der Auslegung bei Staupitz, Luther und Karlstadt, in Kenneth Hagen (ed.), Augustine, the Harvest, and Theology (1300–1650), Essays Dedicated to Heiko Augustinus Oberman, Leiden: Brill, 89–109.

Markschies, Christoph (2001), Taufe und Concupiscentia bei Augustinus, in Theodor Schneider/Gunther Wenz (ed.), Gerecht und Sünder zugleich?, Ökumenische Klärungen, DialKir 11, Freiburg/Göttingen: Vandenhoeck & Ruprecht, 92–108.

Matthias, Markus (2001), Die Anfänge der reformatorischen Theologie des Andreas Bodenstein von Karlstadt, in Ulrich Bubenheimer/Stefan Oehmig (ed.), Querdenker der Reformation. Andreas Bodenstein von Karlstadt und seine frühe Wirkung, Würzburg: Religion & Kultur Verlag, 87–109.

Oberman, Heiko (1958), Augustinus, Archbishop Thomas Bradwardine. A Fourteenth-Century Augustinian. A Study of his Theology and its Historical Context, Utrecht: Kemink & Zoon.

Oberman, Heiko (ed.) (1981), Gregor von Rimini. Werk und Wirkung bis zur Reformation. Berlin/New York: De Gruyter (Neuausgabe 2017).

Oberman, Heiko/James, Frank A. (ed.) (1991), Via Augustini. Augustine in the Later Middle Ages, Renaissance and Reformation, FS Damasus Trapp, Leiden/New York: Brill.

Pereira, Jairzinho Lopes (2013), Augustine of Hippo and Martin Luther on Original Sin and Justification of the Sinner, Göttingen: Vandenhoeck & Ruprecht.

Schindler, Alfred (1984), Zwingli und die Kirchenväter, 147. Neujahrsblatt zum Besten des Waisenhauses Zürich, Zürich: Beer.

Schindler, Alfred (1996), Das Anliegen des Chorherrn Hofmann, in Zwingliana 23, 63–88.

Vind, Anna (2019), Latomus and Luther. The Debate: Is every Good Dead a Sin?, Refo500. Academic Series 26, Göttingen: Vandenhoeck & Ruprecht.

Wegener, Lydia (2016), Der "Frankfurter"/"Theologia Deutsch". Spielräume und Grenzen des Sagbaren, Berlin/Boston: De Gruyter.

Wetzel, Richard (1991), Staupitz Augustinianus: An account of the reception of Augustine in his Tübingen sermons, in Heiko Augustinus Oberman/Frank A. James, III (ed.), Via Augustini. Augustine in the later Middle Ages, Renaiccanse and Reformation, SMRT 48, Leiden: Brill, 72–115.

Wetzel, Richard (2018), Staupitz Augustinianus. Eine Bestandsaufnahme der Rezeption Augustins in seinen Tübinger Predigten, in Lothar Graf zu Dohna/Richard Wetzel, Staupitz, theologischer Lehrer Luthers, Spätmittelalter, Humanismus, Reformation 105, Tübingen: Mohr Siebeck, 223–265.

Zecherle, Andreas (2019), Die Rezeption der "Theologia Deutsch" bis 1523. Stationen der Wirkungsgeschichte im Spätmittelalter und in der frühen Reformationszeit, Spätmittelalter, Humanismus, Reformation 112, Tübingen: Mohr Siebeck.

Stefania Salvadori

The Reception of Augustine in Karlstadt's Writings from 1517 to 1521

Scholars have repeatedly explored the reception of Augustine and the Wittenberg Reformation as interrelated topics. This also applies to authors who have sometimes fallen into the historiographical background, such as Andreas Bodenstein von Karlstadt.[1] Indeed, among his best-known early works the long commentary on the anti-Pelagian treatise *De spiritu et litera* has been the focus of important studies, since Karlstadt accomplished his final transition to the Augustinian doctrine of grace and thus to the Reformation while working on it.[2] And yet, if the rediscovery of Augustinian theology through *De spiritu et litera* was fundamental to Karlstadt's theological career, as the literature has often pointed out, it is also true that his relationship to the writings of the Bishop of Hippo was much more multifaceted and lasting than those set down in that famous commentary. This contribution tries to reconstruct in their essential features the different and in part still unexplored phases of Karlstadt's reception of Augustine from 1517 to 1520, at the same time setting out their specific biographical and theological conditions.[3] How did the Wittenberg Professor discover and read Augustine in order to develop his doctrine of grace? For which polemical – as well as theological, methodological and juridical – purposes did he use Augustinian works in the decisive years 1519–1520? How did Augustine underpin Karlstadt's radical understanding of the principle of *sola scriptura*?

To answer these questions, this essay is divided into four parts: After a brief overview on Karlstadt's Augustine before 1517–1518, the commentary on *De spiritu et litera* (and the contemporary *151 Conclusiones*) will be briefly discussed. Subsequently the famous Leipzig debate and the use of Augustinian writings in the two disputations between Karlstadt and Eck has to be outlined. Finally, this essay analyzes the beginning of a new theological phase in Karlstadt's thought and a new

---

1 See the classic and always valuable studies: Barge (1968); Bubenheimer (1977); (2001); Burnett (2011).
2 Cf. e. g. Kähler (1952); Lohse (1990); Leppin (2005). See also note 25. A new comprehensive study on Karlstadt's commentary on Augustine is to be expected by Alyssa Lehr Evans, who recently submitted her PhD Thesis on this subject in Princeton.
3 The critical edition of Karlstadt's letters and writings currently in the works and edited by Thomas Kaufmann provides new insight into the intellectual development of the Wittenberg theologian. The present contribution refers in particular to the first three volumes, KGK I–III, which cover the here discussed timespan 1507–1520.

conception of the notion of *auctoritas*, once again by recalling Augustine in his *De canonicis scripturis*, published in Wittenberg in late summer 1520. Besides the setting-up and development of the doctrine of grace, which Karlstadt derived from the anti-Pelagian writings, the homogeneity of polemical and juridical intentions against the scholastically oriented tradition is the background for his reception of Augustine, which is a dynamic process, constantly reshaped in order to respond to concrete historical urgencies.

1. Augustine, Scholasticism, and Luther.

Karlstadt was in some way acquainted with Augustine and his writings even before his "conversion" to the doctrine of grace, marked in 1517/1518 by his commentary on *De spiritu et litera*. Indeed, the theologian pointed to Augustine as an important *auctoritas* already in his early works, even if it was an indirect reading mediated by the scholastic tradition, as was standard at that time.[4] In *De intentionibus* and *Distinctiones Thomistarum*, both published in 1507, Karlstadt always refers to the Church Father – mostly *De Trinitate* and *De diversis quaestionibus* – indirectly, i. e. quoting intermediary sources, especially Thomas Aquinas.[5] Similarly indirect is the reference in his *Conclusiones* to the theses of Giovanni Pico della Mirandola (1516), where he refers once again to *De Trinitate* using a collection – *Quodlibeta* – of the medieval theologian Henrich of Ghent.[6] However the sources mentioned in the writings of this period show how Karlstadt, who received his doctorate *utriusque iuris* in Rome in 1516,[7] approached Augustine through the mediation of not only scholastically oriented literature, including the *Sententiae* of Petrus Lombardus, but also and especially of the *Decretum Gratiani*.[8] This epoch-making legal textbook is in large part a collection of quotations from the Church Fathers and especially from Augustine, who was one of the main authorities in canon law itself. Karlstadt mentioned and exploited repeatedly the *Decretum Gratianum* in his writings, more or less directly, but always intensively until 1520. Augustine probably aroused Karlstadt's open sympathy also for reasons internal to the university agenda: As

---

[4] See here the contributions by Leppin and Strohm. For a broader analysis of the impact of the thought and works of Augustine in the late Middle Ages, see Saak (2012); (2013a).

[5] See KGK I.1, 57 note 188, 61 note 205, 178 note 63. The influence of Thomas Aquinas on Karlstadt is analyzed in Bollbuck (2016). See also Bollbuck's introductions to *De Intentionibus* and *Distinctiones Thomistarum* in KGK I.1, 1–10 and 161–168.

[6] KGK I.1, 365–371 and especially 371.

[7] Bubenheimer: 1977, 61f, 71–77.

[8] For an overview see Saak (2013b).

dean of the theological faculty, Karlstadt repeatedly praised the Church Father, patron of the *Leucorea* since 1508.[9]

To sum up, Karlstadt did not systematically read Augustine and subsequently his writings were not perceived as a coherent theological system. Individual quotations from the Church Father simply belonged to the traditional collections, to the *florilegia*, from which it was possible to draw norms or authoritative validations of an argument. The reception of Augustine is thus mainly functional in the first years of Karlstadt's activity as Professor in Wittenberg. In this respect, Karlstadt certainly represents no exception but, on the contrary, fully corresponds to the theological discourse of the time. With this background, however, what Karlstadt meant when he described his rediscovery of Augustine in 1517 in terms of a real conversion becomes clear.

The historical circumstances that led to this "conversion" are well known.[10] During his doctoral disputation *De viribus et voluntate hominis sine gratia* on September 25, 1516, Bartholomäus Bernhardi von Feldkirch discussed the theological views of his teacher Luther with reference, among other things, to Augustinian anti-Pelagian writings.[11] The disputation had dazed not only the Erfurt but also the Wittenberg theologians, and namely the scholastic oriented professors among them. Karlstadt belonged to this group. They all were particularly upset that Luther would not attribute *De vera et falsa poenitentia* to the Church Father, although both Gratian and Peter Lombard had used this treatise as a genuine Augustinian authority.[12] The clash between the two Wittenberg theologians also entailed the central question concerning the essence of a theological evidence and escalated to such an extent that Luther urged Karlstadt to examine for himself whether the scholastics he held in such high esteem could still appear trustworthy at all in comparison with the Church Fathers.[13] Karlstadt accepted this request and bought editions of the patristic texts. On January 13, 1517, he acquired in Leipzig the complete edition of Augustine's works in eleven volumes published by Amerbach in 1505–1506.[14]

---

9 Friedensburg: 1926, 20 Nr. 22.
10 See the introduction to the new critical edition of this treatise in KGK I.2, 537–559 and Bubenheimer: 1980, 16. See also for bibliographic references, Matthias (2001); Salvadori (2018).
11 The theses to this disputation – *Quaestio de viribus et voluntate hominis sine gratia disputata* – are edited in WA 1, 142–151 und LuStA 1, 153–162. For bibliographic references on Bernhardi see KGK I.2, 548 note 90.
12 So Luther reported in his letter to Johannes Lang dated middle October 1516, in WA.B 1, 65,18–66,30.
13 So Karlstadt in his dedicatory epistle to Johannes von Staupitz in his Commentary on Augustine, edited in KGK I.2, 562,10ff.
14 As in the previous note, here KGK I.2, 562,15ff. The Amerbach Edition is the following: Aurelius Augustinus, Prima (– Undecima) pars librorum, Basel: Johann Petri/Johann Amerbach/Johann Froben, 1505–1506, corresponding to the identification Nr. VD 16 A 4147.

The reading of patristic texts, and especially of Augustine, marked a radical shift in Karlstadt's intellectual career, as his *151 Conclusiones* affixed in Wittenberg on April 26 and 27, 1517 clearly show.[15] These theses not only lay out the basic principles that inaugurate Karlstadt's new theological method, but also clarify his first attempt to position himself publicly in the growing controversy surrounding the at that time emerging Reformation movement. Karlstadt had definitively adopted Augustine's theology of grace, to which Luther had urged him, no later than spring 1517. The reception of the Bishop of Hippo became emancipated from all intermediary sources, such as the late medieval authors or the *Decretum Gratiani*. On the contrary, Augustine slowly turned into the fundamental *auctoritas* Karlstadt's argumentation relied upon. Indeed the *Conclusiones* consist largely of quotations from Augustine and reveal Karlstadt's intensive and direct work on Augustine at that time. Augustine's Anti-Pelagian writings are the most often quoted, such as *De peccatorum meritis et remissione*, *De baptismo parvulorum*, *De correptione et gratia*, *De gratia et libero arbitrio*, and of course especially *De spiritu et litera*.

The theological program outlined in the *151 Conclusiones* was completely in line with these anti-Pelagian Augustinian sources. The first seven theses arrange the classical *auctoritates* into a hierarchy, acknowledging the priority of the Holy Scripture over all human texts and over all Church Fathers. Among them, Augustine was considered nevertheless the most credible in moral questions.[16] The following theses (Th. 8–20) describe the ontological corruption of postlapsarian man.[17] Karlstadt's radical change of perspective and his consequent teaching of the doctrine of grace become evident on the theological level in the remaining theses. Both the relationship between justifying grace and free will (Th. 21–64) and between law and gospel (Th. 65–110), as well as the question of predestination (Th. 111–151) are discussed and underpinned by Augustinian quotations.[18] How profound and structural – but also evidently programmatic – the reception of the Bishop of Hippo was to Karlstadt's theological positioning in 1517–1519 appears even more clearly in the commentary on *De spiritu et litera* shortly thereafter.

---

15 See the introduction to the critical edition of these theses in KGK I.1. See also Bubenheimer (2018).
16 In These Nr. 6, KGK I.1, 499,11.
17 KGK I.1, 499f.
18 Also in his *151 Conclusiones* Karlstadts refers largely to Augustine's anti-Pelagian works, thus revealing the substantial homogeneity of sources and themes between these theses and the contemporary commentary on Augustine.

2. The Commentary on Augustine.

During the summer semester of 1517, Karlstadt explained the first nine chapters of Augustine's *De spiritu et litera* in his lectures.[19] Thus, the long process of the composition of his renowned commentary began. At the request of his students, after a brief recapitulation of the first eight chapters, he continued his lectures in the following winter semester 1517/1518. Probably in order to provide his students with the corresponding texts discussed in the lecture, he had the first part of his commentary printed in single sheets in the first half of January 1518. They included the interpretation of the first chapter to the middle of the fourth chapter. In the following weeks, the sheets with the interpretation from the fifth to the tenth chapter, which Karlstadt was at that time explaining in his lectures, appeared in two steps in Wittenberg.[20] After this publishing phase at the beginning of the year 1518, the printing of the commentary on Augustine was suspended. While Karlstadt continued to read on *De spiritu et litera* also during the summer semester 1518, the last six sheets with the explanation up to the twelfth chapter were not published until the fall and printed only in January 1519.[21] The intent announced at the end of his commentary to explain and publish the remaining two parts – namely 24 chapters – of *De Spiritu et litera*[22] remains at present not supported by historical sources. Karlstadt's commentary on the first twelve chapters of the Augustinian treatise definitely marked a new phase in his theological career and a clear cut with the scholastic tradition that shaped his first treatises.

Karlstadt described the process channeled by the reading of Augustine and laid down in the commentary on *De spiritu et litera* with clear rhetorical features similar to a conversion. In his dedicatory letter to Staupitz,[23] he expressed in detail the transition he experienced from his old error of mixing scholastic theology and metaphysics – thus ignoring the true saving message of the Scriptures – to the doctrine of grace. The Bishop of Hippo and especially his book *De spiritu et litera* made possible this "conversion".[24] It is therefore not surprising that Augustine became the primary source in Karlstadt's process of recognizing divine truth. This does not regard alone the partially rhetorical narrative of the conversion in the dedication letter, but also and especially the theological program of the commentary,

---

19 See Kähler: 1952, 6 and for the complete publication process KGK I.2, 553ff.
20 The publication took place in single sheets. By March 1517 (*terminus ante quem* is provided by Luther's letter to Johannes Lang dated 21 March, WA.B 1, 154,4–9) there were nine available with signature A,B,C,Cc,Ccc,Di,D,E,F.
21 See Karlstadt's letter to Spalatin from the beginning of 1519 in KGK II, 86.
22 KGK I.2, 722.
23 KGK I.2, 560–564.
24 See in particular KGK I.2, 562ff.

which clearly shows how much Karlstadt had internalized Augustine's doctrine of grace. The anti-Pelagian treatises of the Church Father are – here as in the *151 Conclusiones* – the most quoted and constantly underpin the argumentation of the Wittenberg Professor. To answer the central question of whether man can justify himself before God by his own works and natural powers, Karlstadt endorsed the anti-Pelagian thesis of *De spiritu et litera* and demonstrated how sin – and especially its source, *concupiscentia* – cannot be destroyed by natural human efforts. Only under the guidance of God, who saves believers by accrediting them the righteousness of his Son, can human beings obtain the forgiveness of their sins and the subsequent redemption. The relationship between postlapsarian human nature and justifying grace is then described using the Pauline dynamic of law (pedagogically intended as killing *baculus*) and gospel (i. e., mercy proclaimed in Christ, which realizes *sola fide* the *imago Dei* in true believers).[25]

Besides these rhetorical and theological facets, two others characterize Karlstadt's reception of Augustine in the years 1517/1518 in a more concrete way. The commentary on *De spiritu et litera* was part of a broader program of academic reform at the University of Wittenberg at that time.[26] Immediately after the dedication letter to Staupitz, Karlstadt addressed a brief preface to the – real and potential – students of the Leucorea.[27] This preface is also a collective manifesto of the theological faculty as a whole: The University of Wittenberg offered a series of lectures in which the Holy Scriptures and the Church Fathers were rediscovered and interpreted. The goal of this academic program is to dismantle the inconsistency of all sophisms and collections of the scholastic tradition and recognize the Bible as the only source for the revelation of the saving truth. To frame the program in an even more concrete way, Karlstadt announced to the students the lecture schedule for the year 1518: Petrus Lupinus was reading on Ambrose, Luther on the Epistle to the Hebrews, Johannes Rhagus on Jerome, and Karlstadt precisely on Augustine and his *De spiritu et litera*.[28] Even if the reception of the writings of the Bishop of Hippo had a decisive influence on Karlstadt's theological reorientation and on the entire theological faculty, it was still part of a broader rediscovery of patristic texts and of a direct reading of the Scriptures, as the Commentary on Augustine itself demonstrates.

In addition to *De spiritu et litera*, Karlstadt's commentary openly refers to a wide variety of patristic sources. For many of them, the exact accuracy of the quotations made it possible to identify the edition used, thus reconstructing part of the library

---

25 A detailed analysis of this commentary is expected by Alyssa Evans. See for a first overview again Matthias (2001) and Salvadori: 2018, 251–257.
26 See for an overview Kruse (2002) especially 139–144.
27 KGK I.2, 568f.
28 KGK I.2, 569.

of the Wittenberg theologian. Karlstadt cited a total of 25 single writings, all of them from the Augustine edition published by Amerbach in 1505/1506,[29] as well as the *Epistolae*, *Sermones* and *Enarrationes* from other editions.[30] Such a broad reception of Augustine interlaced the rediscovery of other Church Fathers: Ambrose from his *Opera* published in Basel in 1516[31] as well as Jerome quoted from the 1516 Basel edition edited by Erasmus;[32] to a lesser extent, Karlstadt refers also to single works by Bernhard, Cyprian, and Gregory the Great.[33] All these patristic sources are constantly combined to underpin not only Karlstadt's explanation of *De spiritu et litera*, but primarily the interpretation of those biblical passages that announce the doctrine of grace, which is ultimately the core thesis of the Commentary itself. In this sense, the patristic quotations are functional to the interpretation of the Scripture – quotes from the *Vulgata* as well as from Erasmus' *Novum Instrumentum*[34] –, to which Karlstadt constantly points as the definitive source of divine truth.

This hermeneutical method of referring to Augustine and the Church Fathers for the purpose of a genuine scriptural interpretation was not only more and more practiced by Karlstadt in his personal theological development from January 1517 till fall 1518, but it also represented an essential part of his pedagogical task. In other words, students as well were trained in this hermeneutical method. As the extensive handwritten notes in the nine surviving print copies of the commentary on Augustine attest,[35] Karlstadt dictated in the classroom terminological clarifications

---

29 See note 14.
30 Respectively from the following editions: Aurelius Augustinus, Liber Epistolarum, Paris: Jean Petit/Berthold Rembolt, 1515 (Moreau II, 1014); Aurelius Augustinus, Opera Sermonum, Paris: Berthold Rembolt, 1516 (Moreau II, 1259) and Aurelius Augustinus: Prima (– Tertia) Quinquagena [Enarrationes in psalmos], Basel: Johann Amerbach, 1497 (GW 2911).
31 Ambrosius Mediolanensis, Omnia opera accuratissime revisa: atque in tres partes nitidissime excusa, Basel: Adam Petri, 1516 (VD 16 A 2178).
32 Sophronius Eusebius Hieronymus, Omnium Operum [...], Tomus primus (– nonus), Basel: Johann Froben u.a, 1516 (VD 16 H 3482).
33 Among the different works by these three Chruch Fathers mentioned in the commentary, Karlstadt quoted part of them from the following editions: Bernardus Claraevallensis, Opus preclarissimum Epistolarum [...], Basel: Nikolaus Kessler, 1494 (GW 3926); Thascius Caecilius Cyprianus, Opera hinc inde excerpta, Paris: Berthold Rembolt/Jean Waterloose, 1512 (Moreau II, 289); Gregorius Magnus, Liber Moralium in beatum Job, Basel/Köln: Adam Petri/Ludwig Hornken, 1514 (VD 16 G 3133).
34 Desiderius Erasmus Roterodamus, Novum Instrumentum, Basel: Johannes Froben, 1516. References to Erasmus – especially in the handwritten notes he dictated to his students (see the following paragraph) – are not only formal, but also reveal Karlstadt's active interest in the humanistic philological method. Erasmus will remain a key source and a pivotal authority on the issue of translation and interpretation of the sacred text even in Karlstadt's writings of the years 1519–20, see for instance *Verba Dei* (KGK III, 9–102) and *De canonicis scripturis* (KGK III, 257–362).
35 A detailed description of the 9 surviving copies by Ulrich Bubenheimer in KGK I.2, 539–546.

or longer theological digressions to his hearers, in order to delve into and point out specific themes that the printed text had not extensively taken into account. These notes testify not only to Karlstadt's progressive fine-tuning and revision of his own doctrine of grace, but also his effort to introduce students into their own independent research on Scripture. Thus, Karlstadt's hearers were able to observe directly their teacher's work in refining his own interpretations drawing on new sources during the lecture. Moreover, Karlstadt quoted the patristic and biblical passages – both in the printed text and in his oral digressions – with extreme accuracy, referring to the *folia*, *columnae* and even lines of the editions he had employed, so that students could get back to the mentioned sources and so check for themselves whether the suggested interpretation was plausible.[36]

To sum up, Karlstadt's reception of Augustine in the years 1517–1518 was profound and dynamic and represented a pivotal part of a broader rediscovery of patristic sources. Furthermore, it has a concrete character since Karlstadt experienced and shared his theological and methodological innovation actively with his students. However, as soon as the Wittenberg theologian had to project "his" Augustine from the private writing desk and the university lecture hall into the arena of academic disputation, he was dramatically forced to reformulate his position.

3. Challenging Augustine in the Leipzig Disputation.

The wide range of quotations that Karlstadt collected from his extensive reading of Augustinian sources, especially during the work on his commentary on *De spiritu et litera* between 1517 and 1519, became a reservoir that he could easily draw on in the following months. Nevertheless, his interpretations of the Bishop of Hippo progressively changed through the course of 1519. A significant transformation both in content and in method appeared already in the last paragraphs of the Commentary on Augustine. While the first ten chapters explain in detail Augustine's teaching and discuss theologically the new doctrine of grace, the last two sections – which refer to the eleventh and twelfth chapters of *De spiritu et litera* – contain a sharp polemic against the cult of saints of late medieval devotion, citing several references and sources, including even scholastic texts.[37] The genuine commentary on the anti-Pelagian text and the philological and Bible-centered hermeneutic remains on the contrary in the background. The historical context in which these concluding chapters were written largely explains such a shift.

---

36 See again Salvadori: 2018, 257–263.
37 See KGK I.2, 681–724.

As Karlstadt wrote the last part of his commentary, he became involved in a sharp controversy. The polemical scenario progressed during the summer/winter 1518. His *Apologeticae Conclusiones*, written in June 1518 in defense of the Scriptures and of the Wittenberg University, declared in a public academic debate the new doctrine of grace he had previously developed in the commentary on Augustine.[38] The methodological, juridical, and theological fundamentals set forth in those theses are in total coherence with Karlstadt's earlier works. Similarly, they resort to a massive use of anti-Pelagian writings by Augustine. The criticism and even the rejection of the scholastic-oriented tradition and adversaries – above all Eck, whose Obelisks were the polemical target of the theses 102–213[39] – is however clearly radicalized. Eck reacted to the *Apologeticae Conclusiones* in the following August with a *Defensio*,[40] which Karlstadt in turn countered in the fall with his own *Defensio*.[41] Both theologians declared themselves in their defensive texts ready to debate with the opponent in a public debate.[42] After many negotiations between December 1518 and May 1519 they finally agreed to carry out their plan in Leipzig, and published theses in which each one concisely stated the central issues of the doctrine they wanted to defend. Luther too became involved in the controversy and took part in the Leipzig Dispute, where he arrived with Karlstadt on June 24, two days after Eck.[43]

Karlstadt and the Ingolstadt theologian began their first disputation on the 27th of June. Then Luther and Eck followed from the 4th to the morning of the 14th of July. That same afternoon, Karlstadt began his second disputation, which ended the next day.[44] Referring to his *17 Conclusiones* – published in May[45] – Karlstadt reaffirmed

---

38 The theses are edited with a detailed introduction in KGK I.2, 789–862.
39 Eck wrote some polemical remarks on Luther's ninety-five thesis in spring 1518. Luther reacted renaming Eck's comments as Obelisks and responding with his own Asterisks in May. Karlstadt entered the dispute and joined Luther and the Wittenberg theological faculty shortly after with the *Apologeticae Conclusiones*. For a more detailed review of the historical context, see Evans (2019); Bubenheimer (2018). Karlstadt's thesis 102–213 against Eck were published also as a separate print and are now edited both in KGK I.2, 813–834 and in KGK I.2, 871–898. Thesis 214–324 of the *Apologeticae Conclusiones* discuss Eck's doctrine of grace; see KGK I.2, 834–848.
40 See Eck's defensive work (which corresponds to VD 16 E 307) in modern edition by Joseph Greving in Eck: 1919.
41 Edited in KGK I.2, 903–994.
42 See Eck: 1919, 81f. and KGK I.2, 785ff, 907.
43 For the historical background of the Leipzig disputation, Karlstadt's role in it and the publication of the acts may here be referred to Salvadori (2019); see also Bühmann (2019) and again Evans Lehr (2019).
44 See the critical edition of the acts of the Leipzig disputation with introduction in KGK II, respectively 315–414 and 285–314. See also the preparatory documents and agreements to the disputation – also for bibliographic references – in KGK II, 269–284.
45 Critical edition of these theses in KGK II, 155–174.

his doctrine of grace, borrowed from the Church Father. However, his use of Augustine during the two Leipzig disputations with Eck diverges significantly from the theological argumentation of the previous year. Compared to the Commentary on Augustine, Karlstadt did not introduce substantially new theological theses in Leipzig. However, the reasoning became more punctilious and radical, in part also because of the back and forth of the disputation which left no room for a nuanced position. The focus of the disputation revolved in particular around the question of a possible cooperation between divine grace and human free will. Karlstadt confirmed once again his thesis: human freedom is just to sin, while with regard to good works nothing is accomplished without divine action and government.[46] In this regard, he repeatedly quoted anti-Pelagian writings by Augustine, but gradually combined them with other patristic and biblical *auctoritates*, so that the voice of the Bishop of Hippo resounded in a broader chorus.[47]

However due to the fluidity, if not the discrepancy of emphases and formulations that occur within the Church authors, the disputation between Eck and Karlstadt quickly degenerated into a rhetorical battle. They accused each other of ineptitude in argumentation, ignorance of the Holy Scriptures, or incoherency, and they provocatively drew conclusions from the opponent's argument by claiming that the latter, without realizing it, ended up supporting his own thesis. They pushed all doubts or blurry definitions to such extremes that the arguments often became contradictory or untenable, so that they were forced to constantly refine their thesis with new and more intricate arguments, thus increasing the criticism of the opponent, who could easily find new details to raise further objections. More concerned with defending their own opinion than with finding a common ground, the theologians quickly turned their disputation into the vicious circle of a rhetorical whirlwind.

Augustine became the main object of this rhetorical battle. Both Eck and Karlstadt claimed to quote the Church Father more sincerely than their opponent, without being able to agree on the interpretation of a single passage. Even referring to the same Augustinian quote, Eck and Karlstadt rather advocated opposing theses. For instance, the pseudo-Augustinian metaphor from the third book of the *Hypognosticon*, where free will is compared to a horse and grace to its rider, was interpreted in differing ways: Eck saw in it an evidence of cooperation between the two forces. Karlstadt, on the other hand, confirmed the passivity of free will in relation to the leading role of grace. The two theologians disputed days over the interpretation of

---

[46] The argument was introduced at the beginning of the disputation, KGK II, 317–322. The discussion on free will spans completely the first disputation, KGK II, 317–376.
[47] In addition to Augustine, Karlstadt and Eck repeatedly refer to Bernhard, Ambrose, und Jerome.

this passage, each arguing that their opponent used it inappropriately or interpreted it incorrectly.[48]

Such a confrontation with Eck may have urged Karlstadt to reconsider the limits of theological reasoning based on non-scriptural *auctoritates*, including Church Fathers and Augustine itself. Indeed, the Wittenberg Professor dramatically experienced during the Leipzig disputation how an improper use of Church authors could even corrupt the comprehension of the Bible. To explain an obscure scriptural passage – e. g., during the first disputation, Sirach 15:14 – Karlstadt drew on several verses from the New or Old Testament and combined them with several patristic sources, such as Augustine's *De gratia et libero arbitrio*. However, his argumentation failed repeatedly, since Eck quoted further biblical passages and Augustinian writings to temper Karlstadt's doctrine of grace and adapt it to his own doctrine of cooperation between grace and free will.[49] Which Augustine should one ultimately lean on? How many different Augustines could be evoked in interpreting Scripture?

After all, the public disputation in Leipzig with its rhetorical and polemical structure – as well as the literary controversy between Eck and the Wittenberg theologians in the following fall/winter 1519/1520 – made it clear to Karlstadt how a tendentious interpretation of the divine truth could find proof even in – for this purpose accurately selected – patristic quotations.[50] On July 14–15, during their second Leipzig disputation, for instance, Karlstadt rebutted a passage of Chrysostom, that Eck had cited to confirm the free agreement of human will and grace,[51] by referring to Augustine, who – according to the Wittenberg theologian – was to be preferred to the Greek Church Father.[52] Eck, in turn, tempered the teaching of the Bishop of Hippo through Jerome, whose anti-Pelagian writings attributed at least the beginning of good works to human beings, their accomplishment however only to God.[53] This opposition of patristic authorities, decontextualized and selected according to purely rhetorical argumentative criteria, represented to Karlstadt an

---

48 KGK II, 332–346, with reference to Ps. Aug. hypomn. 3,11,20.
49 KGK II, 318–322; 325–328; 332f.
50 See the conflicting accounts of the Leipzig disputation sent to Frederick the Wise by Eck and the Wittenberg theologians in KGK II, 415–428 and 431–460. Karlstadt further radicalizes his conflict with Eck and his critique of his opponent's theological approach between the fall of 1519 and the spring of 1520. See in particular the new critical edition of Karlstadt's *Epistola adversus ineptam et ridiculam inventionem Ioannis Eckii* (October/November 1519), *Verba Dei* (Februar 1520) and *Confutatio adversus defensivam epistolam Ioannis Eckii* (March 1520) and their introduction – for bibliographical references and historical overview of the literary controversy with Eck of that time – respectively in KGK II, 515–578 and KGK III, 9–102 and 111–180.
51 Eck's quotation from Chrys. hom. 84 in Mt. in KGK II, 379.
52 KGK II, 385f.
53 KGK II, 388, with reference to Hier. adv. Pelag. 1,14ff.

intolerable peril, especially to uneducated Christians.[54] Eck's sophistic rhetoric could persuade them to the doctrine of an active cooperation of the human will and grace, since he presented in a credible manner even sin as an (apparent) virtue by quoting Augustine or the Scripture. In other words, Karlstadt became aware, how a theological principle based on non-scriptural arguments and – even patristic, not to speak of scholastic and philosophical – *auctoritates* resulted in the inextricable chaos of human opinions. Not even Augustine was safe from ending in this chaos. Indeed, as long as arguments were based on *ius humanum*, human fallible ideas, divine truth could be constantly misrepresented and adapted to personal interests. The inference Karlstadt comes to is that true theologians must ground their argument on a more solid basis, namely the *ius divinum*, to which all, including Augustine, must submit.

4. Ius divinum and Augustine in De canonicis scripturis

Karlstadt's rediscovery of the Augustinian theology of grace is linked from the very beginning to the rediscovery of the Bible, whose authority his *Apologeticae Conclusiones* had placed above council, pope, and Church authors.[55] Yet, the Wittenberg theologian tested during and immediately after the Leipzig disputation[56] how difficult it was to assert this principle without denying a certain coherence of the patristic tradition with the Scripture. In Karlstadt's eyes, Eck used – or rather manipulated – the Church Fathers and even Augustine to support his insane thesis of free human will. In winter 1519, Karlstadt first mentioned his intention to systematically address the problem of the biblical canon and thus of divine law, in order to identify a firm criterion to distinguish the true from the false in theological discussions.[57] However, his proposal only assumed a definitive structure in the spring/summer of the following year with the publication of *De canonicis scripturis*.[58]

This treatise is divided into two parts: the first pursues programmatic and polemical goals; the second one offers a three-level division of the biblical canon and its varying interpretation in Augustine and Jerome. Suffice here to recall that in this latter part Karlstadt preferred Jerome's interpretation to that of the Bishop

---

54 This is a central issue also in Karlstadt's *Verba Dei*, edited in KGK III, 9–102.
55 In the 12th thesis, see KGK I.2, 797,3–798,2.
56 Cf. note 50.
57 See KGK II, 577; 585.
58 A first appraisal of this treatise in Barge: 1968, vol. 1, 186–200; see for the hermeneutical and historical framework of this treatise Bubenheimer: 1977, 165–167 and Keßler (2016). It may be referred here also to the new edition with critical introduction in KGK III, 257–362.

of Hippo with respect to several questions concerning the division of the biblical texts. In view of the reception of Augustine, however, the first section – with its methodological premises, which was intended to enable all Christians to interpret the Bible – clearly shows the radical shift that occurred in *De canonicis scripturis*: from a reception centered on content such as the doctrine of grace, Karlstadts turn now to a methodological and juristic use of Augustine.

The central issue that Karlstadt wished to settle in the opening paragraphs concerns the secure basis through which all Christians could discern divine truth from human opinions. After the Leipzig Disputation, the Wittenberg theologian considered the recourse to the Church Fathers as authoritative sources for the interpretation of a biblical passage to be unsatisfactory. He turned therefore to the *sola scriptura* principle more decidedly and regarded the sacred texts as the rule of their self-interpretation.[59] Consequently, obscure biblical passages had their explanation in other biblical passages. For Karlstadt, it was not enough to state this principle. Rather, *De canonicis scripturis* aimed to deconstruct the entire scholastic system with its traditional theological methodology largely based on the recourse to collections of non-scriptural authoritative sources. For this purpose, Augustine provided the Wittenberg theologian with the decisive arguments to both reject papal primacy and subject all traditions as well as church authors to Scripture. Augustine, in short, helped Karlstadt to overcome Augustine himself and to establish the principle of *sola scriptura*.

Inspired by the Bishop of Hippo, the Wittenberg theologian defined the divine nature of Scripture as a God-given oracle, whose intentional distortion represents sacrilege.[60] In addition, the divine nature of Scripture manifests itself in its indisputable authority and supremacy: Scripture is "reginam et dominam, et iudicem" of everything and everyone, it cannot be contradicted, and yet it is accessible even to the unlearned. Referring to this eternal, divine norm – transmitted and preserved by and in the biblical Canon – anyone can judge even the papal decrees, which Karlstadt regarded as human, that is, transitory and fallible opinion.[61]

Once he elaborated this general principle of the superiority of the Bible, Karlstadt dealt directly with its consequences in the church. First, human habits and traditions should be swept away and burned like straw mixed into the wheat.[62] Karlstadt reaffirmed the perfection and clarity of Scripture against the *theologistae* who defended human decrees and doctrines by asserting that the Scriptures are not sufficient to regulate every aspect of Christian life and to remove all doubts. In this context, he resorted to the metaphor of the bee and the spider, which each extract

---

59 See the introduction to the critical edition of this treatise, KGK III, 263–269.
60 KGK 272f. with reference to Aug. civ 10.
61 KGK III, 273–276 with reference to Aug. Gn. Litt. 2; nat. et gr. 61 and pecc. mer. 1.
62 KGK III, 276 with reference to Jer 23,28f.

honey and poison from the same flower.[63] The spider represents educated people and theologians who (mis)interpret the Scripture, subjecting it to their human postlapsarian reason and *prudentia*. The bee represents instead the simple believers who trust in God alone and understand the Scriptures with a pure heart.[64]

Karlstadt radicalized the contrast between true faith and human *sapientia* even further in the following sections: canonical scriptures alone define divine truth, not human interpretations, no matter how holy and learned their authors may be. Human exegesis was to be considered true only when confirmed by the canonical scriptures, and not vice versa. This conclusion allows Karlstadt to criticize not only theologians like Eck, but also the mendicant orders, who were more concerned with human *auctoritates*, i. e. with their patron saints or with papal decrees, than with the Scriptures. To dismantle their perversion Karlstadt reminded his opponents how even Augustine, the prince of theologians, subordinated his own works to the canonical writings and was therefore still condemning for this reason the superstition of the "fraterculi".[65]

Karlstadt, however, did not want to primarily criticize the mendicant orders, but rather the doctrine based on canon law that distinguished between the truth in Scripture and the authority to interpret it. The Wittenberg theologian claimed instead that an interpretation is inseparable from the interpreted text. And this because, in Karlstadt's opinion, Christ himself inhabited the Scriptures, speaking through it to all believers, so that everyone could understand and interpret the Bible without mediation. Moreover, God enabled in this way all Christians – lay and clerical, secular and ecclesiastical – to perform the function of prophets, that is, to develop a scriptural explanation whose authority matched with that of Christ and thus surpassed that of bishop, pope and church council.[66]

Karlstadt drew further practical implications from these premises and underpinned his reasoning once again with Augustinian quotations, mentioned both in the *Decretum Gratiani* and in his previous *Apologeticae conclusions*.[67] If Scripture alone was always true and had therefore primacy over all human interpretations and decrees, these latter were sometimes erroneous and had to be improved according to the hierarchy of authorities within the church. With Augustine, the Wittenberg theologian distinguished three ways to evaluate and ameliorate episcopal and papal decrees or sentences, i. e., in comparing them with better-founded and more expert

---

63 The metaphor revises a proverb already known in the Middle Ages (cf. Werner (1912)) and also used by Erasmus in his *Enchiridion* (ASD V-8, 248,375ff).
64 KGK III, 277f.
65 KGK III, 279–281 with reference to Aug. trin. 3,1,2 (CCSL 50, 128,38– 41). This passage is also quoted in the 3rd *canon* of the 9th distinction of the *Decretum Gratiani* (cf. CICan 1,17).
66 KGK III, 275 and 281f.
67 Cf. KGK I.2, 797,3–7 und here note 69. See also Bubenheimer: 1977, 67ff.

opinions, or in submitting them to the judgement of a bishop with more authority and wisdom, or, lastly, to the judgment of church councils. Councils in turn were so arranged: general councils could improve local ones, older the recent ones.[68]

In the concluding paragraphs of the first part of *De canonicis scripturis*, Karlstadt further supported this hierarchy of authority within the church and the resulting improvement mechanism almost exclusively with quotations by the Bishop of Hippo, which were also the basis for crucial passages of the *Decretum Gratiani*.[69] Theological teachings and juridical arguments were thus so closely intertwined that these central paragraphs of *De canonicis scripturis* represent a kind of commentary, especially on Distinctions 8 and 9 of the first part of the *Decretum Gratiani*, even if Karlstadt quoted in 1520 directly from Augustinian sources. And yet for sure, these latter sounded familiar to all canonists, i. e., to the polemical target group of the first part of his treatise. Such a theological-legal argumentative approach is not surprising considering the structural and ecclesiastical change Karlstadt was suggesting by recognizing Holy Scripture as the exclusive normative authority in theological debates and by opening the scriptural interpretation to all Christians. That same Augustine who in 1517/1518 had freed him from the obstacles of scholasticism and had provided him with the key to accessing "true theology" of the doctrine of grace; that same Augustine through whom, during the Leipzig disputation, he had tried in vain to definitively refute his adversaries and their doctrine of free will; that Augustine who, between 1519 and 1520, had finally proved insufficient to convert hearts, had also made it possible for Karlstadt to take the last step: to turn away from Augustine himself in order to submit him as a human author definitively to the *ius divinum*, i. e. to the sacred scripture, the only and certain source of divine truth.

Bibliography

BARGE, HERMANN (1968), Andreas Bodenstein von Karlstadt, 2 Vol., Leipzig: Brandstetter 1905, ND Nieuwkoop: B. De Graaf.

BUBENHEIMER, ULRICH (1977), Consonantia Theologiae et Iurisprudentiae. Andreas Bodenstein von Karlstadt als Theologe und Jurist zwischen Scholastik und Reformation, Tübingen: Mohr Siebeck.

BUBENHEIMER, ULRICH (1980), Andreas Rudolff Bodenstein von Karlstadt. Sein Leben, seine Herkunft und seine innere Entwicklung, in: Wolfgang Merklein (ed.), Andreas

---

68 KGK III, 283–287, with reference primarily to Aug. bapt. 2,3,4, also quoted in the 8th chapter of the 9th distinction of the *Decretum Gratiani* (cf. CICan 1,17). See also in the *Apologeticae conclusiones*, KGK I.2, 797.
69 See the previous note and KGK III, 292ff.

Bodenstein von Karlstadt 1480–1541. Festschrift der Stadt Karlstadt zum Jubiläumsjahr 1980, Karlstadt: Arbeitsgruppe Bodenstein, 5–58.

Bubenheimer, Ulrich/Oehmig, Stefan (ed.) (2001), Querdenker der Reformation. Andreas Bodenstein von Karlstadt und seine frühe Wirkung, Würzburg: Religion u. Kultur Verl.

Bubenheimer, Ulrich (2018), Andreas Karlstadts und Martin Luthers frühe Reformationsdiplomatie. Thesenanschläge des Jahres 1517, Luthers Asterisci gegen Johannes Eck und Wittenberger antirömische Polemik während des Augsburger Reichtages 1518, in: Wolfgang Breul (ed.), Andreas Bodenstein von Karlstadt und die frühe Wittenberger Reformation (Ebernburg-Hefte 52), Speyer: Verlagshaus Speyer, 31–68.

Bollbuck, Harald (2016), St. Thomas in Wittenberg. Thomism before and in the Early Reformation. The Case of Karlstadt, Angelicum 93, 281–295.

Bühmann, Henning (2019), Wittenberg's Disputation Culture and the Leipzig Debate Between Luther and Eck, in: Mickey L. Mattox/Richard J. Serrina, Jr./Jonathan Mumme (ed.), Luther at Leipzig: Martin Luther, the Leipzig Debate and the Sixteenth-Century Reformations, Leiden/Boston: Brill, 61–92.

Burnett, Amy Nelson (2011), Karlstadt and the origins of the Eucharistic controversy, A study in the circulation of ideas, Oxford: Oxford University Press.

Eck, Johannes (1919), Defensio contra amarulentas D. Andreae Bodenstein Carolstatini invectiones, Corpus Catholicorum 1, Münster in Westfalen: Aschendorff.

Evans Lehr, Alyssa (2019), Defending Wittenberg: Andreas Bodenstein von Karlstadt and the Pre-history of the Leipzig Debate, in: Mickey Mattox/Richard J. Serina Jr./Jonathan Mumme (ed.), Luther at Leipzig. Martin Luther, the Leipzig Debate, and the Sixteenth-Century Reformations, Boston/Leiden: Brill, 31–60.

Friedensburg, Walter (ed.) (1926), Urkundenbuch der Universität Wittenberg, vol. 1 (1502–1611), Magdeburg: Selbstverl. der Historischen Kommission.

Kähler, Ernst (1952), Karlstadt und Augustin, Der Kommentar des Andreas Bodenstein von Karlstadt zu Augustins Schrift De Spiritu et Litera, Halle: Max Niemeyer Verlag.

Kessler, Martin (2016), Andreas Bodenstein von Karlstadt, De canonicis scripturis libellus (1520), in: Oda Wischmeyer (ed.), Handbuch der Bibelhermeneutiken, Berlin/New York: De Gruyter, 297–312.

KGK (2017–), Kritische Gesamtausgabe der Schriften und Briefe Andreas Bodensteins von Karlstadt, Thomas Kaufmann (ed.), Vol. I.1 and 2: 2017, Vol. II: 2019; Vol. III: 2020; IV: 2022, Gütersloh: Gütersloher Verlagshaus.

Kruse, Jens-Martin (2002), Universitätstheologie und Kirchenreform, Die Anfänge der Reformation in Wittenberg 1516–1522, Mainz: von Zabern.

Leppin, Volker (2005), Die wittenbergische Bulle: Andreas Karlstadts Kritik an Luther, in: Mariano Delgado/Gotthard Fuchs (ed.), Die Kirchenkritik der Mystiker, Vol. 2, Fribourg: Acad. Press, 117–129.

Lohse, Bernhard (1990), Zum Wittenberger Augustinismus: Augustins Schrift De Spiritu et Littera in der Auslegung bei Staupitz, Luther und Karlstadt, in: Kenneth Hagen (ed.),

Augustine, the Harvest, and Theology (1300–1650): Essays Dedicated to Heiko Augustinus Oberman in Honor of his Sixtieth Birthday, Leiden/New York: Brill.

MATTHIAS, MARKUS (2001), Die Anfänge der reformatorischen Theologie des Andreas Bodenstein von Karlstadt, in: Ulrich Bubenheimer/Stefan Oemig (ed.), Querdenker der Reformation, Andreas Bodenstein von Karlstadt und seine frühe Wirkung, Würzburg: Religion u. Kultur Verl., 87–109.

SAAK, ERIC L. (2012), Creating Augustine: Interpreting Augustine and Augustinianism in the Later Middle Age, New York: Oxford University Press.

SAAK, ERIC L. (2013a), Augustine and his Late Medieval Appropriations (1200–1500), in: Katia Pollmann (ed.), The Oxford Guide to the Historical Reception of Augustine, 3 vol., New York: Oxford University Press, vol. 1, 39–50.

SAAK, ERIC L. (2013b), The Augustinian Renaissance: Textual Scholarship and Religious Identity in the Later Middle Ages (1200–1500), in: Katia Pollmann (ed.), The Oxford Guide to the Historical Reception of Augustine, 3 vol., New York: Oxford University Press, vol. 1, 58–67.

SALVADORI, STEFANIA (2018), Der Augustinkommentar des Andreas Bodenstein von Karlstadt zwischen der Stilisierung einer Bekehrungsgeschichte und der (Wieder-)Entdeckung der biblisch- patristischen Quellen, in: Wolfgang Breul (ed.), Andreas Bodenstein von Karlstadt und die frühe Wittenberger Reformation (Ebernburg-Hefte 52), Speyer: Verlagshaus Speyer, 7–30.

SALVADORI, STEFANIA (2019), Andreas Bodenstein von Karlstadt und die Leipziger Disputation, in: Markus Hein/Armin Kohnle (ed.), Die Leipziger Disputation von 1519. Ein theologisches Streitgespräch und seine Bedeutung für die frühe Reformation, Leipzig: Evangelische Verlagsanstalt, 135–158.

WERNER, JAKOB (1912), Lateinische Sprichwörter und Sinnsprüche des Mittelalters, aus Handschriften gesammelt, Heidelberg: Winter.

Mark W. Elliott

Melanchthon und Augustinus

Brüche in der Soteriologie mit besonderem Bezug zu den Römerbriefen.

1. Einleitung

Dieser Vortrag zielt auf die folgende Frage ab: welche Art von heilender/(er)rettender Gnade fand Melanchthon im Argument von Paulus im Römerbrief? Nach dem Reformator veränderte sich der "Augustin als Spitzenausleger mit hermeneutischem Einfluss" vom 1540 Kommentar in einen Exegeten, der in der 1556 Auflage manchmal hilfreich war, jedoch ab und an auch einen Anlass zur Peinlichkeit bot. War sich Melanchthon darüber im Klaren, dass Augustin bereits zu den tridentischen Katholiken gehörte? Als in seiner letzten Auflage Melanchthon Osiander erwähnte, was war die angebliche oder implizite Beziehung Osianders auf Augustin und dessen Logik um Römer 5:5?[1]

Zum Erscheinen des Kolosserbriefkommentars Melanchthons sodann wurde der Spruch von Martin Luther überliefert: "Lebte Augustinus noch, würde er sich freuen, dieses Buch zu lesen, auch wenn er darin oft kritisiert werde."[2] Dies spiegelt die Meinung Luthers wider, dass man von einem Vorgänger am meisten profitiert, wenn der eigene Ansatz aus einer Mischung von Ehre und Kritik bestehe. (Man denkt an Calvin und Wyclif.) Ganz anders als man versuchte, die biblische Texte und deren Verfassern zu erklären, welche einer Haltung von Huldigung und Aufgesschlossenheit bedürfen; so beklagte Luther die Auslegung von Origenes, Hieronymus und Thomas von Aquin, worin gab es mehr von ihnen selbst als von den biblischen Schriftstellern.[3] Bereits 1519 schrieb der künftige *Praeceptor Germaniae*

---

[1] Claus Bachmann versucht eine Erklärung von Osianders Beziehung auf Luther: Das Kreuz mit der Alleinwirksamkeit Gottes: Die Theologie des Nürnberger Reformators und protestantischen Erzketzers Andreas Osiander im Horizont der Theosis-Diskussion', in (2003, 252): "Blickt man vor hier aus auf Luthers 'fröhlichen Wechsel' – am eindrucksvollsten im Sermon Von der Freiheit eines Christenmenschen'(1520) entfaltet – so ergibt sich ein ganz anderes Bild: Die fröhliche 'Wirtschaft' zwischen dem Bräutigam Christus und dem 'armen Hürlein' von menschlicher Seele scheint gar kein gestern und heute zu kennen. Christus nimmt das 'arm voracht böse hürlein' zur Frau, entkleidet sie im Nu aller Übel und ziert sie mit seinen Gütern. So hatt Christus alle gütter und Seligkeit, die seyn der Seelen eygen. So hatt die seel alle untugent und sund auff yhr, die werden Christi eygen."
[2] Luthers Vorwort zu 1529 2. Aufl. von Melanchthons Kolosserbrief; cf. Matsuura: 2004, 13.
[3] WA 10,2., 309.

in einer Antwort an Johannes Eck: "Divus Augustinus contra Donatistas ait, Scriptura Canonicam veteris ac novi testamenti omnibus posterioribus Episcoporum literis ita praeponi".[4] Mit anderen Worten: Augustin ist Autorität, und so sollte der Prinz der Kirchenväter hoch geschatzt werden, auch wenn alle die Kirchenväter niedriger als die Heilige Schrift gelten. Gleichfalls fast am Ende seines Lebens hat Melanchthons es so ausgedrückt: wir trinken von den Flüssen Augustins, oder eher von ihm werden wir nach den Quellen geleitet, die sind reiniger als irgendwelche Schrift von Menschen.[5]

2. Römerbrief 1540

Erstens, wie war es mit dem Kommentar von 1540, dier im selben Jahr wie derjenige von Johannes Calvin erschien?[6] Augustin sagte es richtig: Liebe verdient das Wachstum der Liebe. Er spricht dann nicht von Zuschreibung (*imputatio*) sondern von Gaben und Zugebung. Die Gaben nehmen mit Gebrauch zu und verdienen sogar einen Anstieg. Sie laden auch die Größe von der göttlichen Barmherzigkeit ein, die dieses arme, bettlerische und vielfältig infizierte Gehorchen auf noch für gut zu halten fordert, und verurteilt sich selbst von ihr in seiner Ehre getroffen zu sein. Sie laden auch ein anderer notwendiger Lohn ein vom Leben und Kirche und in seinem Ort zu suchen, welche zu den Übungen des Glauben vorgestellt werden, damit Friede gewinnt von guten Erfolg in Berufungen, in Untersuchungen, in der Regierung von Kirche und Republik, die Frömmigkeit der freien Menschen, Tugend und Freude.[7] Soweit, so Augustinisch und oekumenisch.

Aber die Stimmung wechselt sich bald. Laut Melanchthon:

> Zu Röm 2:14–16, schwitze Augustin sehr, als er darzustellen versuchte, was Paulus damit sagen wollte, dass die Völker das Gesetz erfüllt haben; redet Paulus hier nur über ein paar Heilige wie etwa Hiob und seinesgleichen? Nein, er hielt nicht um Besonderheiten, aber um die gemeinsame Natur, weil das Gesetz nicht wirklich machbar ohne den heiligen

---

4 CR 1 143, in Fraenkel: 1961, 17.
5 MBW (*Melanchthons Briefwechsel*) 5890 (CR 7: 65if.): "Bibimus enim rivulos Augustini, vel potius ab ipso ad fontes deducimur, qui sunt puriores, quam ulla hominum scripta." Cf. MBW 7929–7932 (CR 8: 827–31); 28 August [1556].
6 *Corpus Reformatorum* (CR) XV, ed. von C.G. Bretschneider, Halle, 1848.
7 CR XV, 515: "Recte illud Augustinus: Dilectio mèretur augmentum dilectionis non enim loquitur de imputatione, sed de donis. Dona crescunt usu, et merentur in crementa. Invitent et magnitudo misericordiae Dei, quod hanc miseram, mendicam, et tam varie contaminatam obedientiam, tamen approbat, et per eam se honore affici iudicat. Invitent et alia praemia necessaria vitae et Ecclesiae, et suo loco expetenda, quae fidei exercitiis proposita sunt, ut victus pax, boni successus in vocationibus, in studiis, in gubernatione Ecclesiae et Reipublicae, liberorum pietas, virtus, et felicitas."

Geist ist, indem Paulus sagt, die Völker aus ihrer Natur zumindest gelegentlich machen. Augustin wirft diese Probleme auf Paulus. Denn der Satz selbst ist nicht bisher dunkel. Denn erstens bezeichnet Natur vor allem natürliche Kenntnis. Paulus reflektiert hier mit seiner eigenen Vernunft über Wissen und Gericht.[8]

Melanchthon geht einen Schritt weiter, als ein melanchthonisches Merkmal in seiner Auslegung von Kapitel 5 hervortritt: die Herrlichkeit findet sich in Bedrängnissen, ja in der Tat unsere gegenwärtige Heiligkeit besteht aus unseren Leiden und Gehorsam bedeutet Geduld. Auch zu Römer 8:24 klingt dieses Lied: die Leiden sind die Erstlinge von dem Geist und der künftigen Herrlichkeit. "Es müsse, so sagt Melanchthon, an dem Leiden der Heiligen deutlich werden, daß sie Gott prinzipiellen Gehorsam leisteten und nicht im Hinblick auf Belohnungen und Nützlichkeitserwägungen".[9] Hier kommt die Kreuzexistenz der Kirche vor: ein gemeinsames Leben, geführt von *non humanis consiliis*.

Nun ist das was der Geist beiträgt keine Liebesgnade sondern die Versicherung und der Glaube daran, dass Gott uns liebe. Obwohl es keine Erwähnung von Augustin hier gibt, ist dieses dennoch eine Auslegung, "als ob Augustin nicht existiert hat". In der Meinung Melanchthons sind die Noten von "Liebe in unsere Herzen gegossen" stillschweigend. Auch die Lehre der Ursünde wurde Anselm, nicht Augustin zugeschrieben. Stattdessen liegt die Möglichkeit von Errettung in unserem Bewusstsein bzw. *conscientia*, wenn wir auf Christus blicken (re. Röm 6:14).

Es handelt sich seltsamerweise um Augustin vor allem in der Mitte der Betrachtung des 14. Kapitels des Römerbriefs. In Kapitel 14 gibt es einen Excursus (*De Ecclesiasticis Scriptoribus*), worin Augustin sich unter verschiedenen frühen Christlichen Schriftstellern, Origenes und (Pseudo-)Dionysius eingeschlossen, findet. Es gibt einiges, wofür wir dem Bischof von Hippo dankbar sein sollten. Nach alldem hatte er die Lehre von der Gnade kämpferisch verteidigt, auch wenn wir auf die Ursünde pochen, nur weil die heiligen Schrift uns so anweist. Eines seiner Hauptwerke, *De spiritu et littera*, war und ist noch für die heutigen Theologen ein sehr hilfreiches Werk. Jedenfalls gab Melanchthon *De spiritu et littera* von Augustin

---

8 CR XV, 578: "Quare noticiae illae sunt verae, et sunt- lex divina, ut supra dictum est. In hoc loco valde sudat Augustinus, cum nihil habeat obscuri. Primum disputat, quid velit Paulus, cum ait, Gentes legem fecisse, an loquatur de aliquibus sanctis, ut de Iob et similibus. Secundo disputat de particula, natura, cum lex non possit vere fieri sine Spiritu sancto, quare Paulus dicat, Gentes natura fecisse. Has difficultates affert ad Paulum Augustinus. Nam ipse textus non usque adeo obscurus est. Primum enim natura significat principaliter noticiam naturalem. Paulus enim ratiocinatur, de noticia et de iudicio."
9 Cf. Jung: 2000, 276.

(1545) mit einem Vorwort heraus.[10] Laut diesem Exkurs um Römerbrief 14 meinte Melanchthon wie dankbar alle Christen für Augustin waren, und zwar nicht nur für die Erbsündenlehre, sondern auch für den Unterschied zwischen Gesetz und Evangelium, und dazu den Gegensatz von *littera* und *spiritus* wie er in den biblischen Texten angewendet wird. Augustin reiht sich somit in das Glied der Ausleger ein, die auf Grund ihrer exegetischen Anwendbarkeit eine Erwähnung wert waren.

Die *Loci Communes* von 1521 beweist darauf, dass der junge Melanchthon eine ziemlich 'necessitarian' Verständnis von Vorherbestimmung verwendet.[11] Aber die Auflage von 1535 machte klar: die Ausnahme ist Sünde, die belegt dass unsere Wahl kontingent ist, was man als "im Gegensatz zu 1521" beschreiben darf. Wenn *necessitas* existiert, existiert ein *necessitas consequentiae*,[12] notwendig auf Grund etwas anderem.[13]

Im Römerbriefkommentar von 1540 Melanchthon legt er Römer 8:29 aus: Warum ist dieses (Heil) von Erwählung beherrscht? "Welche er aber verordnet hat, die hat er auch berufen." Meine Antwort: Paulus wollte die ganze Reihenfolge vom Anfang der Heilsgeschichte bis zum Ende ergriffen zu werden, wodurch die Kirche von Gott gegründet wird. Erstens erinnert er uns daran, dass die Erwählung die Ursache von Berufung, und keineswegs menschliches Verdienst oder gesetzliche Gerechtigkeit ist. Dieses Wissen ist nützlich, damit wir Trost bekommen, gegen die Meinung von 'Verdienst', ebenso gegen die Leute, die zu sich selbst auf Grund der gesetzlichen Gerechtigkeit die Bezeichnung 'Kirche' zuschreiben. Dann müssen wir bestätigen, dass die Kirche 'erwählte' ist ohne menschliche Ehre und Verdienst, ohne gesetzliche Gerechtigkeit, ohne Vorrecht von Erbfolge. Paulus fügt hier hinsichtlich der Berufung das Wort hinzu und noch dazu eine Ermahnung: die Berufung ist nicht wirkungslos (*irritus*). Gott ist tatsächlich in seiner Berufung anwesend, um die zu rechtfertigen und endlich zu verherrlichen. Dem Wunsch des Paulus nach müssen wir unseren Beruf behalten und dürfen dabei nicht seine göttliche

---

10 In dieser Erklärung von 1539 hat Melanchthon auf ein Reden von Luther verwiesen, 22 Jahre früher gehalten (1517) in seiner *Oratio de vita divi Augustini* ist Augustin als ein humanistisches Vorbild dargestellt. Man kann seine Hermeneutik von littera et spiritus, die gleich wie Gezetz-Evangelium war, und sein Kampf um die Ursünde, auch wenn seine Soteriologie unvollständig war. Melanchthons Hauptsache war der Mangel Augustins von rhetorischem *genus demonstrativum*. In 1545 hat Joseph Klug eine Auflage von Augustinus' *De spiritu et littera* veröffentlicht; Cf. Maurer: 1964, 196: "In ähnlicher Weise deutet er die Rechtfertigung des Frommen im Neuen Testament als ein nie ganz abgeschlossenes, sukzessives Geschehen, da der Mensch zwar immer noch unter der Sünde leidet und den- noch in der Hoffnung der Vollendung steht."
11 CR 21,89.
12 Vos: 2016, 54; bezüglich *Loci communes 1535*, 50.
13 CR 13.

Herstellung vergessen, damit wir daran ausharren, den Gott anwesend bei seiner Berufung und seinem Wort. [14]

Und noch einmal zu Römer 9:22: Meine Antwort: Ich gebe zu, dass niemand sich bekehrt es sei denn durch die Notwendgkeit der Konsequenz. Weiter ist es wahr, dass die verworfene Menge nicht bekehrt werden kann, aber verworfen wegen ihrer eigenen Gottlosigkeit sein muss. Die gute Nachricht: wenn man zum anrufenden Gott sich anpassen kann, dann ist man nicht unter den Verworfenen gerechnet. Also antwortet er mit Zugeständnis und fügt die folgende Worte hinzu:

> warum Gott hat es so bestimmt, namentlich dass jeder Zorn und Barmherzigkeit offensichtlich widerspiegeln kann? Wenn ich Paulus so zusammenfassen darf: wieso streitet ihr mit Gott? Wenn ihr den wunderbare Rat von Gott anseht, der die Minderheit erwählt und die Mehrheit verworfen hat, solltet ihr Gott hören und habt ihr Angst vor seinem Urteil, damit ihr das Vorbild von vielen Menschen verfolgt, Seid bewusst, dass Gott seine Barmherzigkeit unter uns um uns zu schützen und Zorn unter diejenigen, die gestraft werden müssen offenbart.[15]

3. Römerbrief, 1556[16]

In seinem Versuch von 1556 (bzw. 1553, das Jahr von der Haltung der Vorträge) einen reiferen und gründlicheren Kommentar zu verfassen, wird Augustin ziemlich selten erwähnt auch wenn noch häufiger als andere Namen mit der Ausnahme von Osiander.

In Bezug auf die '1556' Auflage, bleibt die Rechtfertigungslehre offensichtlich Schlüssel-Dogma. Paulus kämpfte mit den Pharisäern. Fünf Sachen sind unverzichtbar, wenn man Theologie treiben will. Außer der Erwähnung in einer Liste von anti-origenistischen Kirchenvätern in der Einleitung, kommt Augustin zuerst anlässlich von Röm 2 vor. Gerade vorab im Kapitel 1 macht Melanchthon viel aus den griechischen Philosophen und die Vorbilder der im Römischen Reich verbreiteten Lästern. Als Kontrast ist der Kain ein Vorbild von brüderlichen Liebe, *storge*, oder im Gegenteil: ein Mangel von *storge*. Zu Adam kam die Verheißung nach seinem Fall (Gen 3:15), aber mit David sieht man den Vorgang: Gottesfurcht und dann Trost. Die Verheißungen sind uralt, und gehören zum Zeitalter der Patriarchen. Die Propheten haben diese erklärt und der Sohn Gottes und seine Apostel

---

14 CR XV, 675.
15 CR XV, 684.
16 Zuerst muss ich erklären: sehr hilfreich war das Buch Defending Faith von Timothy Wengert, obwohl sein Interesse mehr mit Osianders Beziehung auf und Auseinandersetzung mit Melanchthon zu tun hat. Wengert (2012); Siehe dazu: Frank (1995).

haben diese noch weiter, tiefer und mit glänzenden Klarheit enthüllt. Noch einmal wird das Thema von Rechtfertigung aus Glauben allein als Hauptsache bestätigt: ("[...]Et fides est illaipsa res, quae est initium novitatis, et qua vivificamur ad vitam aeternam, iuxta illud: Iustus fide sua vivet.") Das bedeutet die geistige Wahrheit: jeder Gläubiger sucht vom Anfang der christlichen Leben an nach ewigem Leben mit Gott.

Er setzt sich mit fünf Argumenten seiner Gegnern auseinander, die alle mit der protestantischen Entkoppelung von Glauben und Liebe durch Hoffnung zu tun haben. Es ist überhaupt nicht der Fall, dass Vergebung der Sünden und Akzeptanz einer Person eine Veränderung in jedem (*mutatione in nobis*) überhaupt bedarf. Der Glaube besteht *propter mediatorem*, und nicht von unseren eigenen Tugenden.[17] Die Reise und unsere Bewegung ist äusserlich, nicht innerlich.

Problematisch und schuldig ist das Virus von Pelagiani, dessen Nachfolger in jüngerer Zeit sind diejenige wie Thomas, Scotus und weitere, die glauben, dass man durch Bussdisziplin das Gesetz Gottes erfüllen kann. Zum zweiten Kapitel vom Römerbrief hatte Augustin angeblich eine zu pessimistische Anthropologie;[18] er hat nie sein Festhalten zur Ursünde-Erbsünde Lehre mit der Wahrheit, dass das natürliche Gesetz auf jedes Herz geschrieben worden ist, ausgeglichen. Sicherlich hat der berühmte augustinische Skeptizismus gegen die Moralität der romanischen Helden Melanchthon beeinflusst, eine allzu positive Meinung zurückzuweisen, aber dennoch wollte dazu, dass wir an das Benehmen und eheliche Treue von Scipio schauen. Es gab und gibt in jedem Menschen teilweise etwas Gutes. Das göttliche Gesetz für Menschen verändert sich nie.

> Er selbst verdeutliche dies an den Gepflogenheiten der Skythen, die ihre Gäste als Menschenopfer darbrachten, wie der Geschichtsschreiber Herodot zu berichten wusste. Wer Besucher jedoch nicht schütze, sondern opfere und ihnen die Haut abziehe, handle wider das Naturrecht.[19]

Weiter hatten Pompeius, Brutus und Cato alle einen Sinn von Verantwortungsbewußtsein aufgrund ihres Glaubens an Recht und Vorsehung. Das Verständnis, dass Naturrecht als Wissen in unseren Seelen niedergeschrieben worden ist, hat bei Melanchthon zunehmende Bedeutung gewonnen.

Leider gab es auch verschiedene und vielfältige Arten von Lästern binnen der Kirche, in der jüngeren Zeit nicht zuletzt. Deshalb kann zum Beispiel Thomas Monetarius, ein verdorbener Mönch der sein Kloster als Reich Gottes auf Erden

---

17 CR XV, 811.
18 CR XV, 829.
19 Kuropka: 2010, 76.

schätzte, mit Catalina, der Erzfeindin von römischen Tugenden leicht verglichen werden. Jeder falsche Christ ist wohl schlechter als die schlechtesten der heidnischen Übeltäter. Das ist insofern bedeutsam, was das Thema vom Kapitel 2 angeht, wie gerade beobachtet, dass Augustin eine angeblich zu negative Anthropologie hatte. Es gibt in allen Menschen gutes und schlechtes. Es geht um die Möglichkeit, moralisches Recht und Falsch zu nennen, aber gar nicht um die Fähigkeit bzw. 'posse' alles zu tun was sie für Recht hielten, wie die Pelagianer vorgaben/lügen. [20]

Die Liste der menschlichen Typen, die ohne *storgé* (brüderliche Liebe) lebten, schliesst Kain, Medea, Atreus und Thyestes ein. Kain zuerst, weil er der erste war, der seine freie Wahl leider missbraucht hat, als er entschieden hat seinem bösen Trieb zu folgen. Jeder ist für sich selbst verantwortlich und Gott ist nicht voreingenommen: sein Urteil ist weit von Willkür entfernt. "Nec sunt in Deo contradictoria voluntates, quia Deus est verax": da Gott wahr ist, gibt es bei ihm keine entgegensetze Willen. "Gott will, daß alle Menschen errettet werden und zur Erkenntnis der Wahrheit kommen" (1. Timotheus 2:4).

Osiander glaubte, dass im wiedergeborenen Menschen Gott selbst wohnte (*ipsum Deum habitantem in renato*). Deswegen ist Gerechtigkeit etwas, das zu Gottes Wesen gehört.[21] Gott bewegt den Gläubigen, damit dieser das Gute tue. Aber was hier bemerkenswert ist: er (Osiander) war überzeugt davon, dass seine Person durch Neuigkeit (*novitate*) und Werke gerecht ist, genau wie die Papisten meinten. Das Urteil Claus Bachmanns um Osiander ist hier treffend: Der rechtfertigende 'Infekt' mit dem Sinn von Jesu Christi ist seine Einwohnung *secundum divinitatem*— die wiederum einen menschlichen Sinn für den Nächsten entwickelt.[22] Gottes *amor sui*, Heiliger Geist und Nächstenliebe - sie sind nur Momente des Zirkels, den Gott um sich schlägt.[23] Obwohl diese Art von Neoplatonismus ganz anders ist als derjenige, der von Augustin stammen könnte, destoweniger ist das Merkmal von bonum diffusivum sui für Osiander und Augustin (und dazu Bonaventura *et alii*) beide gemeinsam. Bachmann schritt vor mit seinem Hauptargument, dass bei Osiander das Gewicht woanders liegt als auf dere gemeinsame angenommen Menschheit, wie bei Augustin.

---

20 CR XV, 846: "Postea disputant Augustinus, An Gentes legem fecerint, et an natura fecerint? Paulus tantum hoc ratiocinari vult, in Gentibus esse noticiam legis quod inde ratiocinator, quia multi tantum fecerint iudicio naturali, quantum Iudaei lege scripta: Et diiudicari in conscientiis honesta et turpia. Hoc sequitur, si tantum disciplina et externa facta considerentur. Scipio non attigit sponsam alterius, quia sciebat adulterium turpe esse, et a Deo puniri. Fecit igitur opus legis et Paulus non dicit, Gentes legem fecisse, sed ea quae sunt legis, id est, aliqua legis opera."
21 CR XV, 855.
22 Bachmann: 2003, 254.
23 Bachmann: 2003, 258.

Osiander geht damit weit über die augustinische Vorstellung einer *conditio humana* hinaus, mit der Gott dem gefallenen (!) Menschen gewissermaßen kommunikationstechnisch entgegenkommt. Bei Augustin verliert Adam durch den Fall seine unmittelbare Geistesgegenwart, so dass er jetzt nur auf dem Umweg über die Sinnlichkeit und über die Distanz zwischen Zeichen und Bedeutung hinweg zur intelligiblen Wahrheit in den Genuss der ewigen Güter gelangt... Bei Osiander braucht die Gnade allerdings nicht auf den *homo* zugeschnitten zu werden, weil die Sinnlichkeit des Wortes Gottes keineswegs eine Konzession an die (postlapsarische) Beschränktheit der menschliehen Natur darstellt![24]

Nein, wir sollen Gott suchen durch Schmerzen und Angst vor dem Zorn Gottes. Das hat mit 'Neuigkeit' nichts zu tun, zeugt aber von einem tiefen Sinn und Bewusstsein von unserer Unreinheit und dem Gewicht von Sünde, wie es die Heilige Schrift belegt. Der Grund der Versöhnung ist kaum unsere Würde, sondern diejenige unseres Erlösers. Wir Sünder vertrauen Gott, uns zu retten, ohne dass Gott in uns einwohnen und eine solche Reinigung dafür notwendig ist. Wir schauen an die Barmherzigkeit, die durch Christus verfügbar ist. [25]

Melanchthon kämpfte an zwei Fronten, sowohl gegen Osiander als auch gegen die Römischen Theologen von Trient. Aber was die beiden Feinde verbindet ist die 'samosatische' Idee (die auf den Erzhäretiker Paul von Samosata um Jahr 250 zurückgeht), nämlich: das 'Logos' bedeute nur 'decretum' in Gott zur Errettung von Menchen (*decretum in deo de salvandis hominibus*), und was eigentlich galt war der Verdienst des Menschen Christi.[26] Stattdessen brauchen wir laut Melanchthon eine 'hohe' Christologie, nachdem Gott der Sohn mit großer Liebe herabstiegen und bis zum schmerzhaften Tod gegangen ist. Der Messias ist Sohn (*filius*) als auch Opfer um die Kirche zu sammeln, durch die Ausgabe vom ewigen und fruchtbaren Leben (: "et quod Messias non tantum sit victima sed quid filius [...] sit ab initio, ut Ecclesiam colligax et in ea sit efficax, sicut inquit Ego vitam aeternam do eis.") Was am wichtigsten für unser Verständnis ist, ist die Meinung von Melanchthon über seine Gegner, nicht der Unterschied und Abstand zwischen seiner Vorstellung und dem was Osiander und Trient hielten.

Von Beginn an in seiner Lehrtätigkeit hat Melanchthon den frühchristlichen Schriftsteller Origenes heft kritisiert, und zwar dahingehend, dass der Alexandriner den paulinischen Geist/Buchstabe mit dem oberflächlichen Unterschied zwischen 'buchstäblich' und 'geistig' bzw. allegorischen Sinn von einem biblischen Text verwechselt. Zusätzlich war Origenes anzulasten, dass er eine bösartige Veränderung

---

24 Bachmann: 2003, 247, Anm. 48: Cf. etwa *De doctrina christiana* 1, 11, 11 (CChr.SL 32, 12, 1–10); *Epistula* 55, 11, 21 (CSEL 34/2,191,20–192,13); 'De agone Christiano' 11,12 (CSEL 41,114,16 f.).
25 CR XV, 856.
26 CR XV, 862.

des Evangelium Pauli hervorgebracht hat, als er meinte, dass Paulus nur gegen das zeremonisches Gesetz war, und deshalb hat Christus das moralische Gesetz nie aufgehoben.[27] Laut Origenes sind Güte Werke grundlegend für unsere Heil. Nein: Was am wichtigsten ist: gerechtfertigt zu werden braucht die Annahme vom Erlass der Sünden und Versöhnung und Anrechnung der Gerechtigkeit.[28] Mit anderen Worten: jeder muss Gottes Annahme akzeptieren.

Zu Röm 3:31 ("Heben wir denn das Gesetz auf durch den Glauben? Das sei ferne! Sondern wir bestätigen das Gesetz") teilt uns Melanchthon mit: Augustin mochte diesen Vers sehr und hat ihn oft benutzt. Seiner Meinung nach wird das Gesetz stabiler durch Glauben, weil es die Hilfe beschafft, die man braucht um das Gesetz zu gehorchen. Aber diese Erklärung ist sehr dünn und fehlerhaft. In der Tat bot Osiander eine treffendere Auslegung an: die innerliche, tiefe und durchgehende Sünde bleibt, und was der heilige Geist uns gebe wäre Trost, und in diesem Glauben ruhen wir in unserem Mittler, während der Geist in uns bestimmte Bewegungen verursacht, welche Er dann mit seiner eigenen Charakter entzünden oder inspirieren lässt. Dennoch ist dieses unfertige Gehorchen in uns noch weit weg von der Vollständigkeit des Gesetzes. Sogar Osiander hat ja richtig gesagt: Gott wohnt in den Gläubigen, aber gleichzeitig ist leider die Menge von Sünden die in uns noch bleibt ganz groß. Hier hat Melanchthon seinen Feind Osiander benützt als Gegengift zu Augustin.[29] Es gab kein Platz für geschöpfte Gnade (*gratia creata*) oder etwas unschuldige geschaffene Menschheit am Besten (gewohnt, verdaut, 'ein Teil von uns' werdende Gnade) in jedem von uns.

Erbsünde bedeutet einen Mangel an ursprünglicher Gerechtigkeit, wie Anselm die Lehre von Augustin entwickelt hat.[30] Aber dieser Stand ist keineswegs forensisch zu verstehen, wie die mönchischen Theologen irren, da der Mensch tatsächlich Finsternis und Zweifeln in seinem Geist hat, und eine Aversion des Willens gegen den Willen Gottes, wütend und mit Hartnäckigkeit im Herzen.[31] Wenn Rechtfertigung forensisch gemeint ist, im Fall der Sünde ist der Sinn gegensätzlich. Nochmal klingt die Meinung von Augustinus ausgesprochen kritisch.

Augustin band sich in Knoten hinsichtlich der Frage: wie kann ewiges Leben ist beides Gabe und Lohn gleichzeitig sein? Eigentlich ist es eine Gabe, weil die einzige Ursache nachdem das ewige Leben gegeben wird, ist Christus und deswegen kostenlos in seiner Bekehrung zum Gläubiger gegeben ist, laut das Recht vom Gelübde: Wie ich lebe, sagt

---

27 CR XV, 861.
28 CR XV, 878.
29 CR XV, 888.
30 CR XV, 917.
31 CR XV, 942: "Röm 7, Sed ipsa, depravationes, id est, tenebres et dubitationes in intellectu, et aversionem voluntatis a Deo, contentum et fomentum adversus Deum et cordis contumaciam."

der Herr, ich habe kein Gefallen am Tode des Sünders. Also wird Gerechtigkeit wegen etwas anderes (*aliud*) gegeben, das kommt zu dem Mensch her, als ob es Entschädigung oder Vergeltung für Werke wäre – genauso wie ein Erbe gegeben ist, in dem er Sohn ist, aber nachdem später er das Erbe bekommt, wie eine Vergeltung für Aufgaben, wenn man darin beharrt. Diese ist die wahre und einfache Erklärung.[32]

Was fällt uns vor allem auffällt in seiner Behandlung von Röm 8:29–30 ist seine Entscheidung nichts darüber zu sagen! Es geht um sein Verbot, Prädestination zu erwähnen. Wie Gregory Graybill richtig bemerkt hat (auch wenn seine weitere These über den 'evangelischen freien Willen' nicht ganz überzeugend war):

> He [Melanchthon] was even capable of expressing disapproval of the word ['predestination'] itself, as used in a specific context. In relation to Romans 1:4, he took issue with the Vulgate translation, which called Jesus "the predestined Son of God with power according to the Spirit of holiness by resurrection from the dead, Jesus Christ our Lord." Melanchthon argued that 'declared' was a better word than 'predestined' because 'this word [i. e. predestination] gives birth to multiple inept disputations. Even when Melanchthon did use a word like 'elect', he did not define it, and indeed, 'elect' seemed to mean for Melanchthon those who have faith in Christ, and not necessarily a finite number of individuals preordained for salvation. Additionally, when he came to Romans 8:29 (which explicitly mentioned predestination) and 9:22 (the text most conducive to an argument for reprobation), Melanchthon had not a single word of commentary. This silence stood in stark contrast to the *Annotations on Romans* of 1522, where at this point Melanchthon offered a lengthy and detailed passage on election, reprobation and divine determinism.[33]

Also hat die Probleme mit 'Christus Praedestinatus' (Röm 1:4), einen Einwand hervorgebracht und Melanchthons vorgeschlagenen Lösung: Jesus wird 'der Sohn Gottes' erklärt. 'Die Erwählten' heißen einfach diejenigen, die an Jesus Christus glauben, und nicht eine vorherbestimmte Nummer von Einzelnen und in Bezug auf Römerbrief 8:29 (und 9:22) – sie fehlen vollkommen im Kommentar. Martin Jung hat gegen Theodor Mahlmann reagiert und gesagt: ja, Melanchthon hat seine Meinung über Predestination geändert. 'Die Erwählungslehre' ist zweitrangig und gehöre zur Ekklesiologie. In diesem Aspekt hat Melanchthon wohl die mittlere

---

32 CR XV, 955: "Augustinus torquet se, quomodo vita aeterna et donum sit ac merces, sed vera explicatio est, Proprie donum est, quia sola causa, propter quam datur vita aeterna, est Christus, et propter hunc gratis datur credenti in conversione, iuxta ius iurandum: Vivo ego, dicit Dominus, nolo mortem peccatoris etc. Deinde cum propter aliud data sit, accidit ei, ut sit etiam compensatio seu merces laborum, sicut datur haereditas, quia filius est, et tamen postea accidit haereditatem ut sit compensatio officiorum, si qua praestiteris. Haec est vera et simplex explicatio."
33 Graybill: 2010, 206.

Jahre-Augustins (anti-donatistische) vorgezogen gegenüber den späteren Anti-Pelagianischen.

Wir überspringen die Kommentare zum Kapitel 9 bis 11, in denen Melanchthon ein ekklesiozentrische Auslegung entwickelt. Man könnte sagen, dass ein Geruch vom augustinischen 'Die Stadt Gottes' (*De civitate Dei*) – Begriff answesend und einflussreich ist. Wenn dem so ist, war dieser 'Einfluss' ziemlich versteckt, ohne explizite Zitate auf den Bischof von Hippo. Also erreichen wir an der berühmten Text im Kapitel 13, die entscheidend für die Bekehrung Augustins im Garten war: "Lasset uns ehrbar wandeln als am Tage, nicht in Fressen und Saufen, nicht in Kammern und Unzucht, nicht in Hader und Neid; sondern ziehet an den HERRN Jesus Christus." (Rom 13:14 b: ἀλλὰ ἐνδύσασθε τὸν κύριον Ἰησοῦν Χριστὸν καὶ τῆς σαρκὸς πρόνοιαν μὴ ποιεῖσθε εἰς ἐπιθυμίας.) Melanchthon kommentiert:

Bei jüngeren Übersetzungen finden wir hier 'Macht mal Sorge für den Fleisch' (*Providentiam carnis facite*). Augustin hat diese fremde Übersetzung in Frage gestellt: Damit sie den fleischlichen Rat *nicht* folgen, zum Beispiel Geiz, damit man nach fleischlichem Rat viel Reichtum durch die Wucherzinsen nicht suchen, oder damit man einen Reichtum mit widerrechtlichen Methoden nicht erobern soll. Aber der Satz bedeutet etwas anderes. Paulus befiehlt ein Pflegen des Körpers obwohl auch mit Vernunft des Fleisches bzw. Körpers, mit anderen Worten: Erwägt was die Gesundheit des Körpers fordert aber mit gerechter Methode und ordentlich.[34]

Es geht um die Weisheit des weltlichen Lebens, positiv verstanden. Man denkt an die Anweisungen Salomos, die alttestamentlichen Sprüche, ein beliebtes Buch von unserem Phillip.

Man denkt hier auch an die Exegese von Erasmus in 1517: "Dennoch kann ich nicht erraten was hat bei Augustin Anstoss erregt [...] Da Paulus uns nicht verbiet, dem Fleisch zu pflegen und deswegen ἐπιφονεῖ fügt, sozusagen 'in Begierden' hinzu."[35] Erasmus war einer von der 'jüngeren Übersetzen', die hier Melanchthon angreifen würde.

Oder in Melancthons eigener Kommentar zum Ersten Korintherbrief (posthum. 1564) bekommt Augustin eine letzte und treffende Ehrung: "Propheten hier (im NT) sind Ausleger, die mit einer besonderen Begabung ausgerüstet wurden zur

---

34 CR XV, 1022: "Iuniores considerent phrasin: Providentiam carnis facite. Hic enim peregrinam interpretationem quaerit Augustinus, Ne sequantur carnali consilio, ut dici posset avaro, ne carnali consilio quaerat opes per usuras: et cupido dominationis dici posset. Ne invadas regnum illicitis modis. Sed phrasis aliud significat. Iubet Paulus curare corpus, sed habere rationem carnis seu corporis, id est, considerare quid corporis incolumitas postulet, sed iusto modo et ordine. Sic Demomsthenes inquit: ποιεῖσθαι πρόνοιαν ἐορτῆσ, id est, habere rationem festi."

35 D. Erasmus, *Annotationes ad Romanos* [1517] ad loc; LB VI638C–E.

Erbauung von der christlichen Lehre, wie Augustin in seiner Zeit und Luther in unserer Zeit."[36]

4. Schluss

Wilhelm Maurer hat uns gelehrt:

> Als Humanist hätte er [Melanchthon] die Kirchenväter als die maßgeblichen, weil zeitlich und sprachlich am nächsten stehenden Interpreten der Schrift ansehen müssen. Melanchthon hat die Schrift den Vätern übergeordnet, noch ehe er den sittlicher Sinn der anti-pelagianischen Schriften Augustins erkannt hatte.

Und was wohl noch wichtiger ist: "Melanchthons Weg zum Verständnis des reformatorischen Evangeliums hat nicht über Augustin geführt."[37] Aber hinsichtlich der überschnittenen gesamtkirchliche Erfahrung von Sünde dann Heil ist ein Spur von Augustinus zu entdecken. Nochmal Maurer:

> Sein Verständnis jenes Nebeneinanders grenzt vielmehr nahe an das heilsgeschichtliche von ein an der, das sich sowohl im Leben des Einzelnen wie in der Geschichte des Volkes Gottes, in der Ablösung des Gesetzes durch das Evangelium abspielt… Für diese sukzessive Lösung der Spannung von Sünde und Gerechtigkeit kann sich Melanchthon mit Recht auf Augustin berufen.

Oder, mit Timothy Wengert:

> Finally, the witness of Augustine rested on two central principles of Melanchthon's own theology: the distinction between law and gospel (which included both definition and effect) and the distinction between philosophical righteousness and the divine righteousness given by God.[38]

Fraenkel hat seinen eigenen Schluss gezogen: "Even more striking is his claim to St Augustine's support for the definition of 'fiducia' as sure trust in God's promise, by

---

36 "Prophetae hic sunt interpretes, qui ad instaurationem doctrinae singulari dono instructi sunt, ut Augustinus suo tempore, Lutherus nostro tempore."; Ad 1Cor 13; CR XV, 1134.
37 Maurer (1964).
38 Wengert: 2008, 263; Vor allem (2012).

which we chase away all doubt and seize the declaration of divine forgiveness."[39] D.h. sie teilen eine Vorstellung von 'Glaube als Vertrauen', die in unserem Herz alle Zweifel austreiben kann und die Erklärung von Vergebung ergreift. Und ähnlich wie Augustin hat Melanchthon darauf bestanden, dass wir Christen mit der Hilfe des Geistes das Gesetz erfüllen können. Aber, Melanchthon ohne Recht gebe es vor, dass nach der Lehre Augustins wir Christen keine Gerechtigkeit besitzen. Falsch, schrieb Fraenkel: "Augustins Meinung nach sollen wir mit unserer Gerechtigkeit uns nicht rühmen, was nicht das gleiche ist."[40] Am Ende steht Melanchthon fest, die Rechtfertigung geht in christliches Leben weiter vor, weil man jeden Tag einen erneuerten Blick auf Christus braucht, damit ist der Glaube mehr als nur Zugang zum christlichen Leben. Forensisch aber täglich und 'relational', im Unterschied zu Osianders Gewicht auf eine 'Einwohnungsmetapher'. Osianders Lehre ist zu nah in Wirkung zu der 'innere Gerechtigkeit' von Augustin, auch wenn die Kraft aus göttlichen statt übernatürlichen Energien bestehe. Ohne dieses melanchthonische Korrektiv bleibt der Glaube an einem allmählichen Aufwärtssteigen zu optimistisch. Eine Mannschaft muss sowohl wissen, wie man verteidigt, als auch wie man die Tore schießt.

5. Fazit: Theologische Ergebnisse (oder, Antworten Melanchthons zu modischen Themen)

Wenn Sünde als etwas metaphysisch und einheitlich behalten wird, dann lauert die Gefahr, dass die verschiedenen Sünden (alle möglicherweise tödliche) ausgeblendet werden dürfen. Laut Melanchthon aber ist Sünde typisch voluntarisch und deshalb Situations-bedingt, eher als metaphysisch und unbewusst, wie bei Augustinus.

Wenn Bussen ein alltäglicher Lebensstil wäre, dann ist unsere Feinsinnigkeit für Gut und Böse, sogar für das Gestalt von unserer Verantwortlichkeit entschärft. Wenn alles heilig ist, denn ist fast nichts heilig. Das ist nicht der Weg Melanchthons. Stattdessen: wenn Reue hat mit unserer Haltung zu Christus zu tun, dann ist der Mensch von Angesicht zu Angesicht Gottes in Beziehung gesetzt.

Wenn alles politisch ist, den ist Ethik zurückgetreten. Biblische Ethik bleibt wichtig, weil es eine äußerliche Prüfung von unserem Benehmen anbieten kann.

---

39 Fraenkel: 1961, 303: "testator se fidem intelligere non tantum historiae notitiam sed fiduciam, qua confidimus nobis remitti peccata propter Christum" (De Ecclesia et Autoritate Verbi Dei CR 23/624.) Cf. Latomus, *Ep to L .Crucius*, 32: "Quod autem adiungit Augustinum dicere homines legi non satisfacere, intelligens de iustificatis et sanctificatis, falsum est et contra Augustinum et Paulum."

40 Prefatio, CR 5,806: "Renati faciunt legem per gratiam, id est placent Deo imputata iusticia propter mediatorem, et simul Spiritus sanctus in eis inchoatam fidem et novam obedientiam, quae tamen non satisfacit legi Dei, sed placet propter mediatorem fide."

Dem melanchthonischen Meinung nach liegt der *secundus usus* des Gesetz – persönlich/verurteilend und vergebend – im Kern und wie Voraussetzung des *tertius* (moralisch) und des *primus* (staatlich-gesetzlich) *usus*/Gebrauch.

Quellen und Literatur

BACHMANN, CLAUS (2003), Das Kreuz mit der Alleinwirksamkeit Gottes: Die Theologie des Nurnberger Reformators und protestantischen Erzketzers Andreas Osiander im Horizont der Theosis-Diskussion, in Kerygma u. Dogma 49, 247–275.

BACHMANN, CLAUS (2006), Die Selbstherrlichkeit Gottes: Studien zur Theologie des Nürnberger Reformators Andreas Osiander, Neukirchen-Vluyn: Neukirchener theologische Dissertationen und Habilitationen.

FLOGAUS, RAINER (2000), Luther versus Melanchthon? Zur Frage der Einheit der Wittenberger Reformation in der Rechtfertigungslehre, Archiv für Reformationsgeschichte 91, 6–46.

FRAENKEL, PETER (1961), Testimonia Patrum: The Function of the Patristic Argument in the Theology of Phillip Melanchthon, Geneve: Droz.

FRANK, GÜNTER (1995), Die theologische Philosophie Philipp Melanchthons (1497–1560), Leipzig: Benno.

GRAYBILL, KENNETH (2010), Evangelical Free Will Phillipp Melanchthon's Doctrinal Journey on the Origins of Faith, New York-Oxford: OUP.

JUNG, MARTIN H. (1998), *Frömmigkeit und Theologie bei Philipp Melanchthon: Das Gebet im Leben und in der Lehre des Reformators*, Tübingen, Germany: Mohr Siebeck.

JUNG, MARTIN H. (2000), Leidensefahrungen und Leidenstheologie in Melanchthons Loci, in: G Frank (ed.), Der Theologe Melanchthon, Stuttgart Thorbecke (MSSB 5), 259-290.

KEEN, RALPH (1998), Melanchthon and His Roman Catholic Opponents, Lutheran Quarterly 12: 419–429.

KOLB, ROBERT (2005), Bound Choice, Election, and Wittenberg Theological Method from Martin Luther to the Formula of Concord, Grand Rapids, MI: Eerdmans.

KRAMER, HOWARD (trans.) (2010), *Commentary on Romans*, 2nd ed. by Philip Melanchthon. Saint Louis: Concordia.

KUROPKA, NICOLE (2010), Melanchthon, Tübingen: Mohr Siebeck.

MATSUURA, JAN (2014), Martin Luther: Annotationen zu Melanchthons Pauluskommentaren (um 1536), Luther Jahrbuch 81: 11–53.

MAURER, WILHELM (1964), Der Einfluß Augustins auf Melanchthons theologische Entwicklung, in: Wilhelm Maurer, Melanchthon-Studien, Gütersloh: Gütersloher, 67–102.

PHILLIP MELANCHTHON (1540), Commentarius in Epistularum Pauli ad Romanos, in: Carolus Gottlieb Bretschneider/Henricus Ernestus Bindseil (ed.), Corpus Reformatorum XV, Halis Saxonum: C. A. Schwetschke und Sohn.

PHILLIP MELANCHTHON (1556), Enarratio Epistularum Pauli ad Romanos, in: Carolus Gottlieb Bretschneider/Henricus Ernestus Bindseil (ed.), Corpus Reformatorum XV, Halis Saxonum: C. A. Schwetschke und Sohn.

SCHEIBLE, HEINZ (2016), Melanchthon: Vermittler der Reformation: eine Biographie, München: C.H. Beck.

VOS, ANTON (2016), Philip Melanchthon on Freedom and Will, in: Andreas Beck (ed.), Melanchthon und die Reformierte Tradition, Refo500 Academic Studies 6, Göttingen: Vandenhoeck & Ruprecht, 47–62.

WENGERT, TIMOTHY J. (1999), "Qui vigilantissimis oculis veterum omnium commentarios excusserit": Philip Melanchthon's Patristic Exegesis, in: David C. Steinmetz (ed.), Die Patristik in der Bibelexegese des 16. Jahrhunderts, Wiesbaden: Harrassowitz, 1999.

WENGERT, TIMOTHY J. (2008), Philip Melanchthon and Augustine of Hippo, LuJ 22, 249–267.

WENGERT, TIMOTHY J. (2012), Defending Faith: Lutheran Responses to Andreas Osiander's Doctrine of Justification 1551–1559, Tübingen: Mohr Siebeck.

Amy Nelson Burnett

Reading Augustine in the Early Eucharistic Controversy

Augustine was without question the church father most frequently cited in the early Eucharistic controversy. Both sides used the bishop of Hippo to support their own understanding of the sacrament (Burnett: 2012). It might therefore be expected that a chapter exploring the role of Augustine in that controversy would focus on how his ideas were accepted, modified, or rejected by participants in the debate. Underlying this expectation are two implicit assumptions: that the reformers had ready access to Augustine's writings, and that they studied them dispassionately. Neither of these assumptions holds true for the early years of the eucharistic controversy.

To look at the second assumption first: scholars do not live in ivory towers with unlimited time available for study and writing. This was no less true in the early sixteenth century than it is today. The reformers were pastors, professors, and church organizers, and the eucharistic controversy was only one of many challenges they faced in the later 1520s. In the heat of debate, they had little free time to study Augustine's writings intensively, and when they did, they read him instrumentally – that is, they looked for statements that supported their own views. They did not regard Augustine as an authority who was to be accepted simply because he was a witness to the teachings of the early church. Instead, each interpreter began with the assumption that he had found the proper understanding of the Lord's Supper in Scripture, and Augustine was a witness to the same – correct – position. In other words, the interpreter did not agree with Augustine; instead, Augustine agreed with the interpreter, because they both held to the true teaching of Scripture.

This observation suggests that the reformers had little interest in understanding Augustine's sacramental theology on its own terms, and it may give the impression that it is therefore not worth studying Augustine's role in the early eucharistic controversy. There are other questions that can be answered by such an examination, however, and this leads to the first assumption: that the reformers had full access to Augustine's writings. In fact, into the third decade of the sixteenth century access to the full range of Augustine's works was still fairly limited. The second half of the 1520s was a key period in the transition from the older medieval use of Augustine based on excerpts from his writings to the newer humanist study of Augustine's works as a whole. The early debate over the Lord's Supper provides a particularly illuminating example of how one's reading and use of Augustine was conditioned by the sources used to access the African father's thought.

In order to demonstrate the connection between access and use, this essay will describe the ways that the Protestant reformers had access to Augustine's discussions of the Eucharist in the second half of the 1520s. It will then examine their use of Augustine, which can be divided into three phases. The Swiss reformers Huldrych Zwingli and Johannes Oecolampadius laid the foundation for later debate with their citations of Augustine in their publications of 1525. Between 1526 and 1528, both sides used Augustine to support their understanding of the Eucharist, with the most important exchange taking place between Oecolampadius and the Nuremberg humanist Willibald Pirckheimer. A final phase began with the Marburg Colloquy in 1529, where the interpretation of Augustine became part of the debate. The exchange of pamphlets between Philipp Melanchthon and Oecolampadius concerning the patristic understanding of the sacrament in the wake of Marburg was the last major discussion of the topic until the renewed outbreak of polemics in the mid-sixteenth century.

1. Access to Augustine's Works

There were two contrasting ways of approaching Augustine's understanding of the Eucharist in the mid-1520s. The first came through study of Augustine's *Opera Omnia,* printed in Basel by Johann Amerbach in 1505–1506. Although individual works by Augustine were available in print and in manuscript before this time, the Amerbach edition made available the entire range of the church father's thought. Arnoud Visser (2011, 13–27) has characterized that edition as deeply traditional in its presentation of the Augustinian texts but at the same time radical because it presented readers with the full text of all of Augustine's works. Printed in eleven folio volumes, the Amerbach edition was organized according to the order in Augustine's *Retractiones,* and the major works were provided with scholastic commentaries. Those works not mentioned in the *Retractiones* – including a number of pseudo-Augustinian texts – were printed in the last three of the eleven volumes.

Although the Amerbach edition was a landmark in the history of patristic scholarship, it was not ideal for those seeking to understand Augustine's sacramental theology. To begin with, potential users had to have access to that edition, whether they had purchased the volumes when they were published or could consult the set in a nearby library. The fact that already in 1517 a new edition of Augustine was considered economically viable suggests that the Amerbach edition was difficult to find (Visser: 2011, 31f). Beyond that, although Augustine discussed the Eucharist in many of his works, he did not write anything exclusively on that topic. It was a daunting task to read through all eleven folio volumes to find his discussions of the sacraments. For that reason, busy reformers might prefer to approach the church father's understanding of the Eucharist through reading excerpts from his writings contained in textbooks and *florilegia*. The most important of these collections was Gratian's *Decretum*. The second distinction of Book III (entitled *De consecratione*) contained 97 canons devoted to the Eucharist, and about one-third of these were attributed to Augustine (Friedberg: 1879–1881, 1:1326–1351).[1] The discussion of the sacrament of the altar in the fourth book of Peter Lombard's *Sentences* also cited extensively from Augustine, especially Distinction 9, concerning the relationship of spiritual and sacramental eating, and Distinction 10, which condemned as heresy the position that the consecrated bread and wine were only signs.

These two twelfth-century compilations offered significant advantages for anyone wanting to know what Augustine said about the Eucharist. They were readily available and already familiar to those with a formal theological education, and they brought together a number of relevant passages from Augustine's diverse body of writings. These advantages were countered, however, by the fact that the two collections drew from pseudo-Augustinian works as well as from genuine ones. Even where the work quoted was genuinely Augustinian, citations were divorced from their original context and sometimes garbled in transmission. Most of the canons in the *Decretum* were only two or three sentences long, and so they worked better as proof-texts than as keys to understanding Augustine's thought.

A third source became available in the fall of 1529 with the publication of a new complete edition of Augustine's work by the Froben press. Erasmus spent much of the 1520s working on this edition, which was printed in ten folio volumes. In contrast to the earlier Amerbach edition, which framed Augustine's work with scholastic paratextual material, the Froben edition provided a humanist framework for reading Augustine. The edition did not include extensive scholia, but Erasmus provided marginal notes and brief evaluations focusing on the text itself. He also clearly labeled dubious or spurious works, an important step in view of the incorporation of pseudo-Augustinian writings into both the *Sentences* and the *Decretum* (Visser: 2011, 29–45). By the time this edition was published, the most intense discussion of the Lord's Supper, and of Augustine's understanding of the sacrament, had already occurred, but as we shall see, work on the Froben Augustine edition would influence the debate in a rather unexpected way.

How one accessed Augustine's statements proved to be an important factor in the early eucharistic controversy. Those who defended the presence of Christ's body in the elements relied chiefly on the medieval compilations for their use of Augustine, and even Huldrych Zwingli had only a limited knowledge of Augustine's works. The only contributor to the controversy who drew directly and extensively from Augustine's writings was the Basel reformer Johannes Oecolampadius.

---

1 The canons attributed to Augustine were c. 36f, 41, 44–48, 50ff, 54, 57–68, 70, 72, 75, 81, 90ff. Fourteen of these would be cited in the early years of the eucharistic controversy.

2. Foundations: The Swiss Reformers

Augustine's influence on the Swiss theologians was apparent from the very beginning of the public debate, but there was a significant difference in the way the bishop of Hippo was used by the reformers of Zurich and Basel. Huldrych Zwingli's few references to Augustine in the spring of 1525 suggest that the Zurich reformer's knowledge of Augustine's sacramental theology was based almost entirely on Augustine's homilies on the Gospel of John. Zwingli preached on that gospel in the spring and summer of 1524, which probably prompted his careful study of both those homilies and Augustine's Gospels harmony. Citing the Gospels harmony, he asserted that John said nothing about Christ's body and blood in his description of the Last Supper because he had written more fully about it earlier in his Gospel. Zwingli also cited Augustine's homily on John 15:13 to defend his understanding of the Lord's Supper as a remembrance of Christ's death (Z 3: 814f; cf. *De consensus evangelistarum* III.1.2, MPL 34: 1158; *In Ioan. evang.* 84.1, MPL 35: 1846f).

The homilies on John 6 would be particularly important for the Zurich reformer. Zwingli began his discussion of the Lord's Supper in both his published letter to Matthaeus Alber and *De vera et falsa religione commentarius* with a paraphrase of John 6 that betrayed Augustine's influence (Z 3: 335–39, 776–85).[2] Zwingli asserted that the church father's homily on John 6:41–49 made clear how Augustine distinguished between sacramental and spiritual manducation, and he illustrated this point by citing Augustine's statement, at the end of that homily, that eating and drinking Christ's body and blood was simply abiding in Christ (Z 3: 351f, 814f, cf. *In Ioan. evang.* 26.18, MPL 35: 1614). Two passages from the homily on John 6:60–72 were used to support his view that eating Christ's flesh was of no use (Z 3: 810; cf. *In Ioan. evang.* 27.1–2, 5, MPL 35: 1616). More generally, from the summer of 1524 Zwingli no longer spoke of Christ's body and blood in the sacrament but instead referred to "the sacrament of Christ's body and blood," using the word *sacramentum* as a synonym for sign. This phrasing suggests that his reading of the homilies had given him a new appreciation of the sacraments as signs (Burnett: 2019, 75f, 98–102).

Zwingli's only other reference to Augustine's writings in these two publications was a quotation from Augustine's exposition of Psalm 3 that Christ "commended a figure of his body and blood to the disciples" (Z 3: 346, 809, Z 4: 918; cf. *Enarr. in Ps. 3:1*, MPL 36: 73). He interpreted this wording as support for Tertullian's statement that Christ gave his disciples "a figure of his body." Tertullian's statement would be

---

[2] The influence of Erasmus's paraphrase of this chapter is equally strong, but Erasmus too was influenced by Augustine. Zwingli differed from both Augustine and Erasmus, however, in positing a much sharper division between flesh and spirit.

discussed extensively over the next few years, but Zwingli's citation of Augustine's discussion of Ps. 3 was ignored.

As the debate over the Lord's Supper grew, Zwingli sought out other statements from Augustine that supported his position, but he did not expand his reading of the church father's works to any significant extent. In the *Klare Unterrichtung*, published in February 1526, he mentioned two further passages from Augustine's homilies on John (Z 4: 826, cf. *In Ioan. evang.* 45.9, MPL 35: 1723; Z 4: 852, cf. *In Ioan. evang.* 62.1, MPL 35: 1802). More important was his use of several statements attributed to Augustine in the *Decretum*, which Zwingli used to support his claim that the "papists'" own law taught a symbolic understanding of the sacrament (Z 4: 809, 820f, 855, 861; cf. *Decretum* III, Dist. II, c. 36, 44, 47, 51, 59; Friedberg 1: 1327, 1330–3, 1336f). Two of these canons repeated a statement, attributed to Augustine, that "Christ commended his body and blood in this sacrament," while a third contained Augustine's well-known assertion, "why do you prepare your teeth and stomach? Believe, and you have eaten."[3] The most important of the citations was c. 44. This was a lengthy quotation attributed to Augustine that ended with the proclamation that, "Until the end of the age, the Lord is above, but nevertheless the truth, the Lord, is also here with us. For the body in which he arose must be in one place, but his truth is everywhere diffused" (Z 4: 820f; cf. Friedberg 1: 1330).[4]

Zwingli was not the first to cite c. 44, for Johannes Oecolampadius had discussed the passage in *De Genvina Verborum domini (…) iuxta uetutissimos authores expositione*, published the previous summer. There it played a central role in supporting the Basel reformer's argument that Christ's body was in heaven and so could not be contained in the bread and wine of the Eucharist. Oecolampadius did not rely on canon law alone, however, for he also cited Augustine's letters to Evodius and to Dardanus to support this claim (Oecolampadius: 1525, B8v, K7v).

In fact, Oecolampadius had a much deeper knowledge of Augustine's works than did Zwingli, and throughout *De Genvina Expositione* he cited from or referred to a dozen works by the bishop of Hippo, whether letters, sermons, treatises or commentaries. *De Genvina Expositione* opened with a discussion of Augustine's description of signs and miracles in Book III of *De trinitate*. Oecolampadius ([1525],

---

3 The first statement, which is not found in Augustine, probably came from Bede the Venerable and was cited in *Decretum* III, Dist. II, c. 36 and c. 62. *Decretum* III, Dist. II, c. 47 attributed Augustine's statement, *Crede, et manducasti*, to *De remedio penitenciae*, but as Zwingli well knew, it came from *In Ioan evang.* 25.12 (MPL 35: 1602).

4 *Decretum* III, Dist. II c. 44 wrongly attributed most of this passage to Augustine's exposition of Psalm 54 and the final sentences to *In Ioan evang.* 30, but the passage also drew from his exposition of Ps. 98 and *In Ioan evang.* 27. The last two sentences were also found in *Sent.* IV.10.1 (MPL 192: 860) where they were wrongly identified as coming from Augustine's exposition of Psalm 34 and his letter *ad Dardanum*.

A7r–A8r) interpreted this passage as arguing that corporeal things used by men could be regarded as holy, but there was no miraculous change to their substance. Augustine's goal was to teach what was signified by the bread, which did not require any miracle. The Basel reformer endorsed Augustine's neoplatonic subordination of flesh to spirit, and he followed the bishop of Hippo in seeing deeper spiritual truths taught through a typological understanding of Scripture and the use of figurative language. He therefore cited with approval Augustine's three-fold interpretation of "daily bread" in the Lord's Prayer as physical bread, Christ's teaching, and the sacrament of the Lord's body (F8r, G2r–v). This approach to exegesis underlay Oecolampadius's discussion of the relationship between sacramental and spiritual eating, particularly as illustrated by the parallels Augustine drew in his sermon *De utilitate agenda poenitentiae* between manna and the Eucharist, based on 1 Cor 10:1–4 and John 6 (C2r, D1v–D2r). Oecolampadius argued against a "crass" interpretation of Augustine's letter *ad Bonifacium* that made no distinction between Christ's body and the sacrament as sign of Christ's body (K2v–K3v), and he rejected Prosper of Aquitaine's attempt, cited in *Sentences* IV.10.2, to explain away Augustine's statement that "the flesh of Christ is the sacrament of Christ's flesh" (K2v). Last but not least, he used Augustine's discussion, in his exposition of Psalm 73, of the differences between the sacraments of the Old and New Testaments to argue that the latter made God's promises clearer but did not effect that which they signified (D2v).[5]

Unlike Zwingli, Oecolampadius did not cite directly from Augustine's homilies on the Gospel of John, but he did refer to several canons in Book III, Dist. II of the *Decretum* that included excerpts from Tractates 25–27 on John 6. In addition to his discussion of c. 44 just mentioned, the most important of these was c. 47, "Believe, and you have eaten" (Oecolampadius: [1525], F5r). The Basel reformer was as likely to challenge the interpretation of Augustine in canon law as he was to endorse it, however. The *Decretum*'s use of Augustine to uphold transubstantiation was problematic, and so Oecolampadius emphasized that the church father's statements had to be understood in their original setting. For instance, he cited c. 92's citation from Augustine's interpretation of Ps. 33:1 as a foretelling of Christ's bearing his body in his own hands when he said, "this is my body." The Basler then discredited this interpretation by describing the context of the passage within Augustine's homily on the psalm and by pointing out that Augustine used qualifying words so that his statement could not mean that Christ actually held his own body (A6r–A7r).[6]

---

5 Oecolampadius was using Augustine's statement to argue against the understanding of sacraments as efficacious signs in *Sent.* IV.1.2, MPL 192: 839.

6 Another example was his criticism of c. 45, a citation from Augustine's exposition of Ps 98:5 (Oecolampadius: [1525], K4r–v; cf. Friedberg, 1330f).

3. The Development of the Debate

In contrast to Oecolampadius, those who defended the Wittenberg position drew almost entirely from the citations attributed to Augustine in the *Decretum*, which interpreted the church father as teaching the true presence of Christ's body and blood in the elements. Although he emphasized that his party relied on Scripture rather than the teachings of the church fathers, Johannes Brenz argued in the *Syngramma* that Augustine did not support the Swiss. Brenz pointed out that when Augustine described the various types of miracles in *De trinitate*, he never explicitly denied that the bread could be the body of Christ (Brenz: 1970, 239). Similarly, although the bishop of Hippo sometimes referred to the bread as a symbol, in his letter to Januarius he stated simply that the disciples received Christ's body and blood, without referring to that body and blood as a sacrament. While Brenz's discussion suggests some familiarity with Augustine's writings, the passage he cited from *ad Januarium* was included in the *Decretum*, which is probably how Brenz became aware of it (Brenz: 1970, 245; cf. *Ep. 54 ad Januarium* VI.8, MPL 33: 203; *Decr*. III, Dist. II, c. 54, Friedberg 1:1333f).

The one work that Brenz may have read directly was Augustine's homilies on the Gospel of John. Like Zwingli, Brenz cited Tractate 27 on John 6:63, but he chose a section from that homily that lay between the two excerpts used by the Zurich reformer. In this section, Augustine stated that the flesh alone was of no use, but when the spirit was added it was of much benefit (Brenz: 1970, 271f; cf. MPL 35: 1617). Brenz also linked Augustine's interpretation of John 6:63 in Homily 27 with the bishop of Hippo's explanation of John 15:1–3 in Homily 80.3. In the latter sermon, Augustine described the efficacy of baptism with the famous statement, "the word approaches the element, and it becomes a sacrament/a sacrament is made."[7] Brenz applied this concept to the element of bread to argue that the bread became Christ's body when the words, "this is my body, which is given for you" were added to it (Brenz: 1970, 239; cf. MPL 35: 1840).

Far more important for opposing Oecolampadius's interpretation of Augustine was the response to his treatise by the Nuremberg humanist Willibald Pirckheimer. Although he was known chiefly as a Greek scholar, Pirckheimer did not hesitate to challenge Oecolampadius's interpretation of Augustine. Like Brenz, he rejected Oecolampadius's use of Augustine's *De trinitate* to argue against any miraculous change in the bread and wine. Pirckheimer interpreted the passage not as teaching that there was no miracle, but rather as demonstrating that humans could not know how the miracle occurred, and he argued that Augustine's discussion proved that he believed there was some miraculous change. To defend this position, he

---

7 Irène Rosier-Catach (2004, 86f) discusses the ambiguity of the phrase *et fit sacramentum*.

(like Brenz) alluded to Augustine's definition of a sacrament in his homily on John 15:1–3: No one believed that a person could convert the bread and wine into Christ's true body and blood, but when the word "this is my body" was added, the bread became Christ's body (WPBW 6: 442–5). Pirckheimer also accused Oecolampadius of twisting Augustine's statement, in his exposition of Ps. 33, that Christ bore his body in his own hands, and he cited an earlier passage from the same Psalm to prove that Augustine meant his words to be taken literally and not explained away as a figure of speech (WPBW 6: 441–2, cf. MPL 36: 303). He pointed out that Augustine's emphasis on the spiritual eating of Christ's body could not be used to disprove the presence of Christ's corporeal body. Although he believed that one ate Christ's body truly and not simply as a figure of that body, that flesh had to be received spiritually, a point Augustine had also emphasized (WPBW 6: 476, 487). Last but not least, Pirckheimer took aim at Zwingli by citing the section of Augustine's sermon on John 6:63 that the Zurich reformer had skipped over in his discussion (WPBW 6: 495f, cf. *In Ioan. Evang.* 27.5, MPL 35: 1617).

Pirckheimer's extensive discussion of these works suggests that he had Augustine's texts in front of him as he wrote, but that does not mean that he had an extensive knowledge of Augustine himself.[8] The Swiss reformers had already identified the sources for these quotations, and so it was fairly easy for Pirckheimer to locate them. Most of his other citations from Augustine were taken from the *Sentences* and the *Decretum*. So, for example, he pointed out that Augustine's statement, "believe, and you have eaten," which was quoted in both collections, simply distinguished between spiritual and sacramental eating (WPBW 6: 439). He also cited passages attributed to Augustine in the *Sentences* that distinguished between Christ's visible body and the invisible body that was eaten, and between the bread before and the body after consecration (WPBW 6: 440; cf. *Sent.* IV.10.2, MPL 192: 860, *Decr.* III. dist. II, c. 45, Friedberg 1: 1330f; WPBW 6: 447; cf. *Sent* IV.10.4, MPL 192: 861). Significantly, his only other references to Augustine were to the pseudo-Augustinian sermon *De vigilia nativitatis Christi* (WPBW 6: 447; cf. MPL 40: 1266) and to Augustine's *Epistola ad Vincentium*, which concerned the use of allegory in interpreting Scripture (WPBW 6: 472f; cf. MPL 33: 334).

One is left with the impression that despite his scholarly reputation, and in sharp contrast to Oecolampadius, Pirckheimer had little unmediated knowledge of Augustine. The difference between the two writers is only more apparent in their continued public debate. Pirckheimer had attacked Oecolampadius for seeing a

---

8 Pirckheimer's citation of Augustine's homily on John 6:63 may be the exception, but Brenz's *Syngramma* circulated in manuscript since the late autumn of 1525 and was printed at the beginning of 1526. Pirckheimer wrote his response to Oecolampadius before the *Syngramma* was published, but his own treatise was not published until March of 1526. The criticism of Zwingli occurs in the last pages of the book, and it is possible that Pirckheimer added it after reading the *Syngramma*.

trope in the words, "this is my body." In his response to Pirckheimer, Oecolampadius defended his interpretation of the passages from the exposition of Psalm 33 and from *De trinitate*, adding yet another citation from the latter work (Oecolampadius, 1526b: c14, d6r-v, d7v-e3r). He also introduced citations drawn from several other treatises by Augustine, most importantly from Book III of *De doctrina Christiana*, where the bishop of Hippo warned against taking figurative expressions literally (b5r, b6v, c2r, d5v, f4r, g2r, h1v).[9] He also questioned the reliability of the Augustine citations from the *Sentences* and the *Decretum* that Pirckheimer had cited. For instance, he pointed out that the statement allegedly taken from Augustine's letter *ad Ireneum* actually came from the African bishop's exposition of Psalm 98 (d2r).[10] Last but not least, he brought up again the lengthy citation contained in the *Sentences* and repeated in c. 44 of the *Decretum* that the Lord's body must be in one place. After accusing the Lombard of twisting Augustine's clear statement, he referred Pirckheimer to Augustine's letter *ad Bonifacium*, which made clear that when the church father spoke of Christ's body, he meant the sacrament of that body (b4v-b5r).

The debate would continue in two further publications, but it is not necessary to give a detailed description of the use of Augustine. It is sufficient to note that the two men continued to disagree about the proper interpretation of the citations already described. Pirckheimer introduced a few new passages into the debate, some of them from the *Decretum*, others suggested to him by the Nuremberg pastor Thomas Venatorius (WPBW 7: 500–1, no. 1059a). Oecolampadius countered each of these citations and for the first time addressed Augustine's statement, "the word approaches the element," pointing out that Augustine had emphasized that it was not the word that was spoken but instead faith in the word that gave power to the elements (Oecolampadius: 1527a, b5r).[11] Needless to say, neither man convinced the other, but the debate revealed a significant difference in the range and depth of knowledge that each had of Augustine's works. I have argued elsewhere that Pirckheimer emerged as the victor in his public debate with Oecolampadius (Burnett, 2019, 158–77), but it should be emphasized that this was largely due to his skillful use of rhetoric to undermine Oecolampadius's authority, and not to his superior knowledge of the church fathers. Oecolampadius's scholastic training and

---

9 In addition to *De doctrina Christiana*, Oecolampadius drew from *contra Epistolam Manichei quam vocant fundamenti*, *Contra Faustum*, and *Contra Julianum*. In his *Antisyngramma*, Oecolampadius cited from *Contra Faustum* and *De doctrina Christiana* as well.
10 Oecolampadius was arguing against *Sent.* IV.10.2/*Decretum* III.II. c. 45, a statement that is also included in c. 44, where it is identified as coming from the exposition of Ps 54, Friedberg 1:1330f. He also questioned (1526b: d1v) a citation allegedly from Prosper's compilation of statements from Augustine cited in *Sent.* IV.10.4 (MPL 192: 860) and *Decr.* III.II. c. 41 (Friedberg 1: 1328).
11 Oecolampadius's interpretation of the statement thus accorded with that of Luther in 1522, who had stressed the importance of faith for sacramental efficacy (Zur Mühlen, 1993).

his patristic scholarship gave him a huge advantage over the Nuremberger when it concerned familiarity with Augustine's writings. Pirckheimer simply could not compete with him, and as the debate progressed the problematic nature of the Augustine citations incorporated into the *Sentences* and the *Decretum* became ever more apparent.

Citations from Augustine would play only a minor role in the debate between Martin Luther and the Swiss reformers in treatises published over the course of 1527 and 1528. Luther devoted a short section of his 1527 *Das Diese Wort (…) Fest Stehen wider die Schwermgeister* to the bishop of Hippo. He was familiar with the previous debate, but his own use of Augustine differed from that of others. He cited only a few of Augustine's own writings, and he used them not so much to prove that Augustine was on his side (although he did argue this), but instead to demonstrate that his opponents had twisted the church father's words, which left them with no clear and certain understanding of the text. Although Augustine used words like "sacrament, sign, invisible, and intelligible," Oecolampadius could not prove from this that the elements were mere bread and wine and that Christ's body was not present. Luther cited Augustine's definition of a sacrament as a visible form of an invisible grace to argue that the bishop of Hippo understood a sacrament to be "the form of a present but invisible thing," not a sign of something future or absent. This definition shed light on Augustine's distinction, in his exposition of Ps. 98, between Christ's visible and his invisible body and his statement, "believe, and you have eaten." Luther also cited Augustine's letter to Januarius to demonstrate that the father called the elements body and blood, and not just a sacrament of Christ's body and blood, and he told his readers that Augustine's statement concerning Psalm 33 was clear: "Christ said, 'this is my body,' and he bore that same body in his hands" (WA 23: 209–17 [citation at 213], 243). Last but not least, he accused his opponents of "childish fleshly thoughts" for arguing that Christ's body could not be in the bread on the basis of Augustine's statement (in c. 44 of the *Decretum*) that "Christ must be bodily in one place, but his truth is everywhere" (WA 23: 131).

In most of these cases, Luther cited the original work where the statement occurred, and he was certainly familiar with Augustine's exposition of the Psalms.[12] It can be questioned, however, whether he had paid much attention to Augustine's statements concerning the sacrament in that work until Oecolampadius drew his attention to specific passages. All of the Augustine quotations used by Luther were cited in the *Decretum*, the *Sentences*, or both, and the interpretation of several of them had been hotly debated in earlier works. Luther's condemnation of Oecolampadius's "uncertainty" in his explanation of Augustine on Ps 33 dismissed out

---

12 Tarald Rasmussen (1989, 21) identified Augustine's exposition on the Psalms as the most important source used by Luther in preparing his own lectures on that book.

of hand Oecolampadius's efforts to interpret this particular proof text within its original context. In Luther's eyes, there was no need for subtlety or nuance; in fact, these only obscured what was to him the clear meaning of Augustine's words. Taken as a whole, however, Luther's statements reflect his relative disinterest in Augustine's position. If the church father agreed with the truth, then he could be cited, but Luther showed no inclination to defer to Augustine.

This attitude was in sharp contrast to Oecolampadius (1528: W^2 20: 1385), who referred to Augustine as his earthly teacher. The Basler continued to cite the now-familiar passages from Augustine in the two treatises he wrote against Luther in 1527 and 1528, and he added new quotations, both from works used earlier and from new sources. In *Das der miszuerstand (...) nit beston mag. Die ander billiche antwort*, he referred to the letters *ad Bonifacium* (1527b, k2v; cf. W^2 20: 1381), *ad Dardanum* (1527b, e1r, f2v) and *ad Januarium* (k2r); he drew from *De doctrina Christiana* (c1r, k1v) and *De trinitate* (1527b: b3r, f2v, i4v; cf. W^2 20: 1428); and he discussed the passages from the expositions of Ps 33 (k2v) and John 6 incorporated into the *Decretum* (h2v, i4v, m2v, o4r–v). For the first time he cited Augustine's *ad Donatum* (m1v), his exposition of Psalm 65 (i4r) and his *de peccatorum meritis et remissione* (m1v). In his contribution to *Über Martin Luthers Buch, Bekenntnis genannt, zwo Antworten*, Oecolampadius cited *De agone Christiano* (W^2 20: 1409, 1413), and in both works he continued the debate over Tract. 80.3 from the homilies on John (1527b: m2v; 1528: W^2 20: 1399). Zwingli largely left the discussion of the church fathers to his Basel colleague, although he too cited a few now-familiar passages from Augustine in his final contributions to the debate (Z 6/2: 85 [*Ep. 54 ad Januarium* 3.4, MPL 33:202], 86 [*in Ioan evang.* Tract 62.1, MPL 35: 1802], 95 [*De consensus evangelistarum*, MPL 34: 1158]).

With the publication in the fall of 1528 of the Swiss reformers' *Zwo Antworten*, the debate over the sacrament came to a temporary halt. It would, however, be revived at the Marburg Colloquy.

4. The Marburg Colloquy and After

The debate at Marburg centered on the three issues that had come to define the two parties: whether "this is my body" should be understood figuratively or literally; whether Christ's body was limited to one place and so could not be simultaneously in heaven and in the consecrated bread; and whether Christ's teaching in John 6 on spiritual communion had any relevance for the presence of his body in that bread. Underlying these issues was a deeper metaphysical difference between the neoplatonic realism of the Swiss reformers and the Aristotelian nominalism of the Wittenbergers. The only church fathers mentioned in the surviving accounts of the discussion at Marburg were Augustine and Fulgentius, both of whom were cited by the Swiss against Luther. The extant accounts of the colloquy do not provide detailed information, but it is clear that the debate concerned passages familiar from earlier exchanges: Augustine's letters to Januarius and Dardanus, his homilies on John 6, his treatises *De trinitate* and *De doctrina Christiana*, and especially his statement that "[the Lord's body] must be in one place" cited by both Gratian and Peter Lombard. Ultimately Luther admitted that his opponents had Augustine and Fulgentius on their side, but the other church fathers supported his position (May: 1970, 20, 27f, 38, 49).

The citations from these two fathers were apparently persuasive enough that the Wittenbergers felt compelled to assemble a list of quotations taken from several other church fathers for Landgraf Philipp of Hesse. They acknowledged that the Swiss had used Augustine to argue persuasively that Christ's true body was limited to one place and that the sacraments were only signs. They argued, however, that much of what had been quoted was not written about the Lord's Supper and so was not relevant to the question of whether the bread was Christ's true body (MBW.T 3: 583–9, no. 823). This was the argument that Melanchthon would repeat in his *Sentenciae veterum aliquot scriptorum de Coena Domini*, published in the spring of 1530. In view of the similarities between the contents of the letter to Landgraf Philipp written in Marburg and Melanchthon's *Sentenciae*, it would not be an exaggeration to see the latter as the official Wittenberg statement concerning the patristic understanding of the Lord's Supper.

Melanchthon's use of Augustine in the *Sentenciae* is striking for both what he said and what he did *not* say (Burnett, 2021). The bishop of Hippo was discussed not in the first section of the treatise, which might be seen as the *confirmatio* of an oration, but instead in the second part, the *confutatio*. Melanchthon began by pointing out that c. 44 of the *Decretum* was a mishmash taken from several places, and that Augustine's words were twisted to apply to the Lord's Supper (CR 23: 745f). He observed that the church father was discussing the fruit of the sacrament, or spiritual eating, but this did not impede the ceremonial eating of Christ's body, whose purpose was to strengthen hearts and to engender faith. It is important to note here that when Melanchthon spoke of ceremonial or sacramental eating, he understood the phrase in the traditional way that meant the eating of Christ's true body in the bread, and not simply eating the signs of bread and wine, as the Swiss would define it (Hoffmann: 2011, 207ff).

The Wittenberger then turned to the final section of the canon, which he identified as taken from Augustine's homily on John 7:19–24. He cited the entire passage from the homily to support his contention that the statement, "[the Lord's] body must be in one place" had nothing to do with the Eucharist and so could not be used to argue against the presence of Christ's true body in the elements. He then quoted from Augustine's sermon on John 6:63 to demonstrate that Augustine did not separate Christ's divine and human natures. These were the only citations from

Augustine addressed in the *Sentenciae*, and Melanchthon made the telling comment that if one insisted on using this one passage from the *Decretum*, it could not stand against the clear testimonies of Hilary and Cyril, who openly stated that Christ's body was present in the Supper (CR 23: 745–9; cf. *In Joann. evang.* 30.1, MPL 35:1632; *In Joann. evang.* 27.4, MPL 35: 1617). His refusal to engage further with the bishop of Hippo could perhaps be taken as implicit agreement with Luther's concession that Augustine was on the side of the Swiss.

Although Melanchthon mentioned no names explicitly and asserted that he was not attacking anyone or seeking further disputes (CR 23: 748), his treatise was obviously a challenge to Oecolampadius. The Basel reformer responded with *Quid de Eucharistiae veteres (…) senserint. Dialogus*, published in the summer of 1530. The treatise was much more than a discussion of Augustine, for it displayed the full range of Oecolampadius' patristic scholarship, with almost eighty citations drawn from two dozen sources. Augustine was, however, the most frequently cited author, and Oecolampadius added to the now lengthy list of quotations used to illuminate the bishop of Hippo's understanding of the Eucharist and of the sacraments more generally. These included both new passages from previously cited works, such as *Contra Julianum* (1530: m5v), and new works such as *De diversis Quaestionibus octaginta tribus* (m7r), *Contra Adimantum* (n8r), and sermons 229 *de sacramentis fidelium* and 272 *ad infantes* (o2v–o3v). Although some of the citations he used were from the *Decretum*, Oecolampadius referred his readers to the original citation rather than to the more familiar canon.[13] More significantly, the *Dialogus* demonstrates that Oecolampadius had a far greater knowledge and deeper understanding of Augustine's thought than all of his Lutheran opponents combined. He emphasized Augustine's distinction between sign and signified and his approach to the figurative language used in scripture, underlining Augustine's statement that it was sinful to take Christ's statement about eating his flesh literally (f4r, f8r–v, n8r). He highlighted the bishop of Hippo's words concerning the location of Christ's body in one place as well as his identification of the faithful as the body of Christ (b6r, m7r–v, o2v–o3r).

By drawing attention to Oecolampadius's knowledge of Augustine, I do not absolve the Basler from his opponents' accusations of twisting Augustine's words or taking them out of context. He was by no means an unbiased and objective reader of St. Augustine for, as he wrote in 1526, he believed that "Augustine more openly agrees with me." (1526a: c3r). But of all the contributors to the early eucharistic controversy, he was the one who came closest to a genuine understanding of the

---

13 So, for instance, a reference to Sermon 229, cited in *Decretum* III, Dist. II c. 36 (1530: o3r–v), as well as the original sources of the much-discussed passage in *Decretum* III, Dist. II c. 44 (m6v–n1r); cf. his earlier discussions of the exposition of Ps 33 rather than c. 92.

bishop of Hippo's sacramental theology. He had clearly studied Augustine's works more deeply than they had and adopted Augustine's flesh/spirit dualism and his approach to figurative language in scripture. Oecolampadius's understanding of Augustine is the topic of a different paper, however, and so instead, and by way of conclusion, I will summarize the most important lessons to be drawn from this examination of how Augustine was used in the early eucharistic controversy.

Perhaps most unexpected is the continued importance of medieval collections of authoritative texts, despite the reformers' general commitment to humanism. One major factor contributing to this conservatism was the difficulty of obtaining the text of Augustine's works. Even a confirmed humanist like Pirckheimer could not approach Augustine as a humanist scholar unless he had a copy of the *Opera Omnia* to work with and the scholarly aids – even something as basic as an index – that would help him locate Augustine's statements on a particular topic. It is particularly striking that the *Decretum* remained an important source for Augustine's thought for the Wittenbergers through the later 1520s. Both it and the *Sentences* were compiled in the wake of the eleventh-century Berengarian controversy concerning the Eucharist, and both works interpreted Augustine's words in a way that supported the doctrine of transubstantiation. This was a distinct advantage for the Wittenberg party, and one senses their reluctance to admit that the "medieval" Augustine of the *Decretum* might not accord with the "humanist" Augustine revealed in the *Opera Omnia*. But Zwingli too used the *Decretum*, and the only work of Augustine that he seemed familiar with was the *Homilies on the Gospel of John*. Virtually all other references to the works of Augustine were introduced into the debate by Oecolampadius.

The second lesson concerns Oecolampadius's significance as a scholar of Augustine. The breadth and depth of his knowledge of Augustine was impressive already in 1525, and it only increased over the next few years. The Basel reformer may be the one exception to the general rule that the reformers did not have much time to sit at their desks and devote long hours of study to Augustine, although much of Oecolampadius's familiarity with Augustine may have predated the outbreak of the eucharistic controversy. In his 1526 response to Theobald Billikan, Oecolampadius described how he had tried to allay his doubts about a literal understanding of "this is my body" by reading the church fathers. He had discovered that although they often spoke of the body and blood of the Lord, they rarely explained "what kind of body and what kind of blood" (1526a: c3r). His words paint a picture of a humanist scholar who had begun to question the doctrine of transubstantiation and who discovered that the church fathers did indeed speak differently about the Eucharist than the scholastic theologians did. Although Oecolampadius was not here referring specifically to Augustine, it is easy to surmise that studying the African father's works opened his eyes to a new way of understanding the Eucharist and the sacraments more generally.

One of the factors that allowed Oecolampadius to run rings around his opponents was his long association with the Erasmian circle in Basel, and this leads to the final lesson: the importance of Basel as a center of humanist scholarship and patristic publications. The patristic scholarship initiated by Amerbach with his edition of Augustine was continued by the partnership between Erasmus and Johann Froben through the third decade of the sixteenth century. Not only were copies of the Amerbach edition readily available in Basel, but the knowledge and expertise of the scholars associated with preparation of the Froben edition could function as a sort of "living critical apparatus" to be consulted by others. Oecolampadius continued to have close ties with these men even after his relations with Erasmus had soured. Although he was not directly involved in Erasmus' new edition of Augustine, Oecolampadius certainly benefited from the preparatory work being done on it in the second half of the 1520s. This gave him a significant advantage over both Pirckheimer and Melanchthon, his two most important opponents.

This situation would change after the publication and frequent reprinting of Erasmus's edition made Augustine's works much more widely available and a younger generation had the opportunity to study them. This study of the use of Augustine in the early eucharistic controversy therefore functions as a snapshot, illustrating a brief but crucial stage in the transition from medieval to humanist patristic scholarship.

Appendix: Oecolampadius's Citations of Augustine's Works

The table below expands that of Northway (2008, 183–184), which is limited to citations in *De Gevnina Expositione* and *Dialogus*. In a few cases Oecolampadius only mentioned a work by Augustine, or he paraphrased or translated the passage in such a way that it cannot be identified more closely. I have marked with an asterisk those works that, as far as I can determine, were introduced into the debate by Oecolampadius.

ABA JOHANNES OECOLAMPADIUS (1527b), Das der miszuerstand D. Martin Luthers/ vff die wenig-bstendige wort/ Das ist mein leib/ nit beston mag. Die ander billiche antwort, Basel: Cratander, VD16: O 303.

APR JOHANNES OECOLAMPADIUS (1526b), Ad Billibaldum Pyrkaimerum de re Eucharistiae responsio. Zurich: Froschauer, VD16: O 281.

AS JOHANNES OECOLAMPADIUS, (1526a) Apologetica De Dignitate Evcharistiae Sermones duo. Ad Theobaldvm Billicanvm quinam in uerbis Caenae alienum sensum inferant. Ad Ecclesiastas Svevos Antisyngramma. Zurich: Froschauer, VD16: O 305/O283/O 288.

BA Johannes Oecolampadius (1526c), Billiche antwortt/ auff D. Martin Luthers bericht des sacraments halb/ sampt einem kurtzen begryff auff etlicher Prediger in Schwaben gschrifft die wort des Herren nachtmals antreffendt. Basel: Wolff, VD16: O 295–296; In W² 20: 582–633.

GVE Johannes Oecolampadius (1525), De Genvina Verborum domini, Hoc est corpus meum, iuxta uetutissimos authores expositione, liber. Strasbourg: Knoblauch, VD16: O 331.

QED Johannes Oecolampadius (1530), Quid de Eucharistia veteres tum Graeci, tum Latini senserint, Dialogus in quo Epistolae Philippi Melanchthonis et Joannis Oecolampadij insertae. Basel: Froben, VD16: O 381.

RP Johannes Oecolampadius (1527a), Ad Billibaldvm Pyrkaimervm, de Eucharistia, Ioannis Husschin, cui ab aeqalibus a prima adolescentia Oecolampadio nomen obuenit, Responsio posterior. Basel: Cratander, VD16: O 282.

ZA Johannes Oecolampadius (1528), Über Martin Luthers Buch, Bekenntnis genannt, zwo Antworten. Zurich: Froschauer, VD16: O 404; in W² 20: 1375–1438.

Source	Cited in	Edition
Confessiones IX.13	AS: Q1v	MPL 32: 778
*Contra Adimantum XII.3.5	QED: n84r	MPL 42: 144, 146
*Contra Epist. Manichaei	APR: b6v	
*Contra Faustum 19.13; 20.13, 21	AS: R2r; APR: g2r, h1v; RP: c2, c4v, e4r–v	MPL 42: 355f, 379, 385f
*Contra Iulianum	APR: d5v; QED: m5v (mention only)	
*De agone Christiano 24–25	ZA: W² 20: 1409, 1413	MPL 40: 304
*De civitate Dei	GVE: F8r (mention only)	
*De diversis Quaestionibus 83 (Q 20)	QED: m7r	MPL 40: 46
*De doctrina Christiana I (mention); III.5, 9, 16	AS: d6v–d7v, H5r, K7r; APR: b5r, c2r, f4r, RP: B8v, ABA: c1r, k1v; QED: f8r–v	MPL 34: 68–71
*De Genesi ad litteram 7.12	GVE: E6v	MPL 34: 362
*De peccatorum meritis et remissione I.24.34	ABA: m1v	MPL 44: 128
*De sermone domini in monte II.10.37	GVE: f8r, G2r–v	MPL 34: 1279–81, 1585
*De Trinitate III.4, 10	GVE: A7r–A8r, G2r–v; AS: H8v, I2v, APR: c1r, d7v–e3v; RP: d5v, ABA: b3r, f2v, ZA: W² 20: 1428	MPL 42: 876, 879f
*Decr. III d. II c. 36 Sent. IV.10.2	GVE: F4v; QED: o3r	Friedberg 1: 1326f MPL 192: 861
Decr. III d. II c. 41 Sent. IV.10.4 (Prosper)	RP: d1v	Friedberg 1: 1328 MPL 192: 861

Source	Cited in	Edition
*Decr. III d. II c. 44 Sent. IV.10.1	GVE: C6v; APR: b4v–b5r; PR: c3r–c4v, d3r; ABA: o4r–v; QED: m6v–n1r	Friedberg 1: 1330 MPL 192: 859f
Decr. III d. II c. 45 Sent. IV.10.2 (Enarr. In Ps. 98)	GVE: K4r; APR: b5r, d2r–v; RP: d2r	Friedberg 1: 1330f MPL 192: 860 MPL 37: 1263
*Decr. III d. II c. 47 Sent. IV.9.1 (In Ioan. Evang. 25.23)	GVE: F5r; APR: d5v; ABA: h2v, m2v	Friedberg 1: 1331 MPL 192: 858 MPL 35: 1602
Decr. III d. II c. 54 (Ep. 54 ad Januarium)	AS: K4r; ABA: k2r	Friedberg 1: 1333f MPL 33: 203
Decr. III d. II c. 72 (Paschasius)	RP: e4v	Friedberg 1: 1342
*Decr. III d. II c. 92 (Enarr. in Ps. 33:1)	GVE: A6r–v; AS: K4r; APR: d6r–v; RP: d4v; BA: W^2 23:213; ABA: f1v, k2v	Friedberg 1: 1351 MPL 36: 306, 308
*Ep. 98.9 ad Bonifacium	GVE: K2v–K3v; AS: L5r; RP: b8v, c6r, d2r; ABA: k2v; ZA: W^2 20: 20:1381	MPL 33 353f
*Ep 138 ad Marcellinum 1.7–8	GVE: d1v, k1r	MPL 33: 528
*Ep. 147 de videndo Deo	RP: c5r–v	MPL 33: 603
*Ep. 169 ad Evodium II.9	GVE: B8v; AS: K8v–L4r	MPL 33: 746
*Ep. 187 ad Dardanum (cf. Decr. III d. II c. 44)	GVE: k7v; APR: f7r; ABA: e1r, f2v; QED: b6r; m7r–v	MPL 33: 835f, 838f, 847
*Ep. ad Donatum	ABA: m1v	
In Ioan evang. 26.13	ABA: i4v; QED: o3r–v	MPL 35: 1614
In Ioan evang. 27.4–5	AS: S2r–v, QED: n4r	MPL 35: 1617
*In Ioan evang. 50	QED: n1r (mention only)	
In Ioan evang. 80.3	RP: b5r; ABA: M2v; ZA: W^2 20:1399; QED: h7v	MPL 35: 1840
*Enarr. in Ps. 65.17	ABA: i4r	MPL 36: 797f
*Enarr. in Ps. 73.2	GVE: D2v; QED: i6r	MPL 36: 931
*Retractiones	RP: d3r; QED: m5v (mention only)	
*Sermo 229 de sacramentis fidelium	QED: o3r–v	MPL 38: 1103f
*Sermo 272 ad infantes	QED: o2v–o3r	MPL 38: 1246
*Sermo 352 de utilitate agendae poenitentiae	GVE: C2r, D1v–D2r	MPL 39: 1551–3
*Sent. IV.10.2 (apud Prosper ad Irenaeum)	GVE: K2v	MPL 192: 860
*ad Petrum Diaconum 18 (Fulgentius)	GVE: D4r–v; RP: c7r	CChr 91A: 750

Abbreviations

CChr	Corpus Christianorum. Turnhout: Brepols.
Friedberg	FRIEDBERG, EMIL (ed.) (1879–1881), Corpus Iuris Canonici, 2 vol. 2nd ed., Leipzig: Tauchnitz.
MPL	MIGNE, J.P. (ed.) (1844–1864), Patrologiae cursus completes, Series Latina, Paris: Migne.
WPBW	REICKE, EMIL (ed.) (1940–2009), Willibald Pirckheimers Briefwechsel, München: C.H.Beck.
W^2	WALCH, JOHANN GEORG (ed.) (1881–1910), Dr. Martin Luthers Sämmtliche Schriften, 2nd edn, St. Louis: Concordia Publishing House.
Z	(1905–2013), Huldreich Zwinglis sämtliche Werke. Leipzig/Zürich.

Bibliography

BRENZ, JOHANNES (1970), Werke. Eine Studienausgabe. vol. 1: Frühschriften. Tübingen: Mohr Siebeck.

BURNETT, AMY NELSON (2012), "According to the Oldest Authorities": The Use of the Church Fathers in the Early Eucharistic Controversy, in: Anna Marie Johnson/John A. Maxfield (ed.), The Reformation as Christianization. Essays on Scott Hendrix's Christianization Thesis, Tübingen: Mohr Siebeck, 373–95.

BURNETT, AMY NELSON (2019), Debating the Sacraments: Print and Authority in the Early Reformation, New York: Oxford University Press.

BURNETT, AMY NELSON (2021), "What the Fathers Thought": Melanchthon and Oecolampadius on the Eucharist, in: Luka Ilic/Martin J. Lohrmann (ed.), Teaching Reformation: Essays in Honor of Timothy J. Wengert, Minneapolis: Fortress, 40–56.

HOFFMANN, GOTTFRIED (2011), Kirchenväterzitate in der Abendmahlskontroverse zwischen Oekolampad, Zwingli, Luther und Melanchthon: Legitimationsstrategien in der innerreformatorischen Auseinandersetzung um das Herrenmahl, Göttingen: Edition Ruprecht.

JOHANNES OECOLAMPADIUS ([1525]), Ioannis Oecolampadii De Genvina Verborum Domini, Hoc est corpus meum, iuxta uetustissimos authores, expositione liber [Strasbourg]: Knobloch.

JOHANNES OECOLAMPADIUS (1526a), Apologetica De Dignitate Evcharistiae Sermones duo. Ad Theobaldvm Billicanvm quinam in uerbis Caenae alienum sensum inferant. Ad Ecclesiastas Svevos Antisyngramma. Zurich: Froschauer.

JOHANNES OECOLAMPADIUS (1526b), Ioannis Oecolampadii Ad Billibaldum Pyrkaimerum de re Eucharistiae responsio. Zurich: Froschauer.

JOHANNES OECOLAMPADIUS (1527a), Ad Billibaldvm Pyrkaimervm, de Eucharistia, Ioannis Husschin, cui ab aeqalibus a prima adolescentia Oecolampadio nomen obuenit, Responsio posterior. Basel: Cratander.

Johannes Oecolampadius (1527b), Das der miszuerstand D. Martin Luthers/ vff die wenig-bstendige wort/ Das ist mein leib/ nit beston mag. Die ander billiche antwort. Basel: Cratander.

Johannes Oecolampadius (1528), Über Martin Luthers Buch, Bekenntnis genannt, zwo Antworten. Zurich: Froschauer. In W^2 20: 1375-1438.

Johannes Oecolampadius (1530), Quid de Eucharistia veteres tum Graeci, tum Latini senserint, Dialogus in quo Epistolae Philippi Melanchthonis et Joannis Oecolampadij insertae. Basel: Froben.

May, Gerhard (ed.) (1970), Das Marburger Religionsgespräch 1529, Gütersloh: Gütersloher Verlagshaus G. Mohn.

Northway, Eric W. (2008), The Reception of the Fathers & Eucharistic Theology in Johannes Oecolampadius (1482-1531), with Special Reference to the adversus haereses of Irenaeus of Lyons, Ph.D, Durham University.

Rasmussen, Tarald (1989), Inimici Ecclesiae: Das Ekklesiologische Feindbild in Luthers "Dictata Super Psalterium" (1513-1515) im Horizont der theologischen Tradition, SMRT 44, Leiden: Brill.

Rosier-Carach, Irene (2004), La parole efficace. Signe, rituel, sacré, Paris: Seuil.

Visser, Arnoud S.Q. (2011), Reading Augustine in the Reformation: The Flexibility of Intellectual Authority in Europe, 1500-1620, Oxford Studies in Historical Theology, New York: Oxford University Press.

Zur Mühlen, Karl-Heinz (1973), Zur Rezeption der Augustinischen Sakramentsformel, "Accedit verbum ad elementum, et fit Sacramentum," in der Theologie Luthers, Zeitschrift für Theologie und Kirche, 50-70.

Christoph Strohm

Augustin als Autorität bei Martin Bucer und in den Auseinandersetzungen um die Kölner Reformation[1]

In den Jahren 1598 bis 1613 erschienen insgesamt vier Bände einer *Medulla theologiae patrum*, zusammengestellt von dem kurpfälzischen Theologen und Hofprediger Abraham Scultetus.[2] Es handelt sich bei dem Werk um die erste umfassende Darstellung der Lehren der Kirchenväter im Bereich des reformierten Protestantismus. Tobias Dienst hat 2019 in einer Heidelberger Dissertation gezeigt, dass sich dieses Werk unmittelbar einer intensiven und kontroversen Debatte der kurpfälzischen calvinistisch-reformierten Theologen mit den nahen Mainzer Jesuiten verdankte.[3] Diese zwangen durch ihre Streitschriften die Kurpfälzer dazu, sich mit den Argumentationen der Kirchenväter vertraut zu machen und diese zur Begründung ihrer Auffassungen zu nutzen. Auf der anderen Seite zwangen die kurpfälzer Reformierten wiederum die Mainzer Theologen dazu, sich eingehend mit philologischen Fragen der Bibelauslegung zu befassen und zum Beispiel besser Griechisch zu lernen.[4] Die vermehrte Beschäftigung mit den Kirchenvätern und der verstärkte Rückgriff auf ihre Schriften ist somit ein unmittelbarer Ertrag der produktiven Kraft konfessioneller Konkurrenz in Folge der Reformation und der Spaltung der Christenheit in unterschiedliche Konfessionen.[5]

Was sich im Blick auf Scultetus' Darstellung der Theologie der Kirchenväter feststellen lässt, trifft in vergleichbarer Weise für Martin Bucers Umgang mit den Kirchenvätern im Allgemeinen und Augustin im Besonderen zu. Exemplarisch sichtbar wird das an Bucers Rückgriff auf die Kirchenväter in dem Streit um die Einführung der Reformation im Erzstift Köln seit dem Jahr 1542.[6] In dem mithilfe der Druckerpresse geführten Kampf um die Kölner Reformation sind in den Jahren 1542 bis 1547 mehr als 250 Werke zum Druck gelangt.[7] Bucers Hauptgegner Johannes Gropper berief sich wie andere Gegner auf die Kirchenväter und zwang

---

1 Verwendete Abkürzungen: BDS=Martin Bucers Deutsche Schriften, ed. von R. Stupperich/W.H. Neuser/G. Seebaß/Ch. Strohm, 19 vol., 1960–2016; BOL=Martin Bucer, Opera latina, ed. v. F. Wendel u.a., 1955ff.
2 Scultetus (1598–1613).
3 Cf. Dienst: 2019, 108–130.
4 Cf. Dienst: 2019, 80–108.
5 Cf. dazu grundlegend Strohm (2017).
6 Cf. Burnett (2001).
7 Theodor C. Schlüter hat insgesamt 266 relevante Drucke aufgelistet (cf. Schlüter: 2005, 159–355).

Bucer dazu, selbst wiederum die Kirchenväter für seinen Standpunkt heranzuziehen. Was über den verstärkten Rückgriff auf die Kirchenväter infolge der kontroverstheologischen Auseinandersetzungen insgesamt festzustellen ist, gilt mit einigen Besonderheiten auch für den Rückgriff auf Augustin.

1. Augustin beim frühen Bucer

Stephen Buckwalter hat im Jahr 2013 zusammenfassend festgehalten, dass Augustin der Kirchenvater ist, auf den Bucer mit Abstand am meisten verweist.[8] Während er (in den bis dahin in BDS und BOL publizierten Schriften) immerhin 670mal Augustin zitiert bzw. auf ihn verwiesen habe, erfolge das im Fall des am zweithäufigsten erwähnten altkirchlichen Autors Cyprian sowie der *Historia tripartita* nur ungefähr 240mal. Dann folge Chrysostomus mit ungefähr 200 Zitaten bzw. Verweisen. Interessanterweise finden sich in den ersten Texten Bucers nach der Hinwendung zur Reformation keine oder nur sehr spärliche Verweise auf Augustin. In der ersten zusammenfassenden Darstellung seines reformatorischen Programms aus dem Jahr 1523, einer unter dem Titel *Das ym selbs niemant, sonder anderen leben soll* gedruckten Predigt,[9] findet sich kein Verweis auf Augustin. In der bald darauf entstandenen zusammenfassenden Darstellung seiner Predigt für den Rat der Stadt Weißenburg grenzt er sich gegen den Papst und die Bischöfe ab, "die stocknarren, [die] in irem eygen Decret etlich sprüch Augustini eingeführt haben".[10] In den angeführten Canones wird Augustin mit der Mahnung zitiert, seine eigenen Werke nicht zu kanonischen Schriften zu machen.

Schon Bucers Rede von den "stocknarren, [die] in irem eygen Decret etlich sprüch Augustini eingeführt haben", macht deutlich, dass die Beschäftigung mit Augustin bzw. der Rückgriff auf ihn Bucer durch die Argumentation der Gegner aufgenötigt wird. Zudem zeigt sich, dass die autoritativen Augustin-Worte nicht zuletzt durch ihre Aufnahme in das *Decretum Gratiani* überkommen sind.[11] Es war bekanntlich in der Mitte des 12. Jahrhundert aus einer Fülle rechtlich relevanter Texte der Alten

---

8 Cf. Buckwalter: 2013, 715. Das Urteil bezieht sich auf die Werke, die bis dahin in *Martin Bucers Deutschen Schriften* und den *Opera Latina* veröffentlicht worden sind.
9 Bucer: BDS 1,(29)44–67; cf. Koch: 1962, 20–26; Greschat: 1990, 68ff.
10 Bucer: BDS 1,(69)79–147, hier: 87,31f; mit Bezug auf: Decretum Gratiani I, dist. 9, c. 3–11, Friedberg I,17f; cf. auch BDS 1,313,13.
11 Zu Bucers Rückgriff auf das kanonische Recht in den Auseinandersetzungen um den Kölner Reformationsversuch cf. Strohm: 2002, 123–145, bes. 128–134; Wright: 2002, 102–121. Bucer gibt mitunter ausdrücklich an, dass er sich auf die im *Decretum Gratiani* gesammelten "spruch Augustini" bezieht (cf. z. B. Bucer: BDS 3,224,17f). Bucer hat aber wohl auch die von Johannes Amerbach, Johannes Petri und Johannes Froben auf den Weg gebrachte elfbändige Augustin-Ausgabe, die 1506 in Basel erschien, benutzt: Augustini (1506) (cf. BDS 3,303 Anm. 529).

Kirche zusammengestellt worden. Wie bei der zeitgleich entstandenen Sammlung von Väter-Sentenzen durch Petrus Lombardus in den *Sententiarum libri quatuor* ist Augustin der mit großem Abstand am häufigsten herangezogene Autor.

Weiterhin ist charakteristisch für Bucers frühe Bezugnahmen auf Augustin, dass sie sich gehäuft da finden, wo er Luthers reformatorische Lehren wiedergibt[12] oder als Übersetzer tätig ist.[13] Dieser Befund eines vergleichsweise zurückhaltenden Rückgriffs auf Augustin entspricht dem Sachverhalt, dass Bucer als Dominikanermönch – anders als zum Beispiel der Augustiner-Eremit Luther – primär in der Theologie Thomas von Aquins geschult worden ist.[14] Zwar kam bald ein starker Einfluss Erasmus von Rotterdams hinzu,[15] aber ein frühes Verzeichnis der Bücher Bucers aus dem Jahr 1518 enthält bezeichnenderweise kein Werk Augustins.[16] Die ersten umfangreicheren Bezugnahmen auf Augustin beim frühen Bucer finden sich dann auch in der Auseinandersetzung mit dem Augustiner-Eremiten Konrad Treger, seit 1517 Prior des Klosters in Straßburg und seit 1518 Provinzial der rheinisch-schwäbischen Ordensprovinz der Augustiner-Eremiten.[17]

In der Auseinandersetzung mit Treger beruft sich Bucer auf Augustins Kampf gegen die Pelagianer als Vorbild für den gegenwärtigen Kampf gegen menschliche Lügen und Irrtümer,[18] ebenso auf dessen Auffassung von der ewigen unsichtbaren Kirche[19] und der Sakramentslehre[20]. Wenn es Kennzeichen des Ketzertums sei,

---

12 So beim Hinweis auf Luthers Auslegung von 1 Kor 2:15 ("der geistliche Mensch richtet alle Ding"), cf. Bucer: BDS 1,313,12f: "Des stond feine, herliche spruch uss dem Augustino ouch im decret dist. ix." Hier erwähnt Bucer ausdrücklich, dass er die Augustin-Stelle aus dem *Decretum Gratiani* kennt (cf. Decretum Gratiani I, dist. 9, c. 3–11, Friedberg I,17f). In ähnlichem Sinn hatte sich schon Erasmus von Rotterdam, mit dem sich Bucer eingehend beschäftigt hat, in seiner Vorrede zum Novum Instrumentum Graece von 1516 auf Augustin berufen, cf. Allen: 1910, 166,14ff); cf. auch BDS 1,314,12ff: "Mer wirfft man disem grundt engegen [sic!] den spruch Augustini: Ich glaubt dem Euangelio nit, ich glaubet dan der kirchen, daruss sy wöllen einfüren, der kirchen sy mer zu glauben dan der schrifft, [...]" (mit Zitat von: Augustin, Contra epistulam Manichaei quam vocant "fundamenti" V,6, PL 42,176). Cf. schon Luther: WA 2,430,12–23.
13 Cf. Bucer: BDS 1,413,3–6 (Augustin über das Paulus-Wort: "Wir predigen nit uns selbs, sunder unsern herren Jesum christum" [2 Kor 4:5]); BDS 1,420,16–19 (Augustin gegen die Selbstsucht von Bischöfen und Hirten); BDS 1,422, 31–33 (Augustin in der Auslegung des Johannesevangeliums über die wahren Hirten, die anders als Papst und Pfaffen die Wölfe meiden).
14 Cf. Greschat (1976).
15 Cf. Krüger (1970).
16 Cf. Greschat (1975).
17 Zu Treger cf. Vermeulen (1954); Zumkeller (1988); Zschoch (1997).
18 Cf. Bucer: BDS 2,57,38.
19 Cf. Bucer: BDS 2,123f (Bucer beruft sich für die Lehre von der ewigen unsichtbaren Kirche auf Augustin und andere Kirchenväter); cf. auch BDS 2,135,25.
20 Cf. Bucer: BDS 2,121 (Bucer verweist auf das Fehlen der gegenwärtigen Sakraments- und Messopferlehre bei Augustin und anderen Kirchenvätern).

Irrtümer mit der Heiligen Schrift zu überwinden, müsse man Augustin und andere Kirchenväter als Ketzer bezeichnen.[21] In der Auseinandersetzung mit Treger grenzt sich Bucer aber auch von Augustin ab, wenn dieser – wie von Treger angeführt – die Autorität der Kirche überschätze.[22] In Anspielung an Formulierungen des Paulus im 1. Korintherbrief betont Bucer, dass es darum gehe, Christus-gläubig zu sein, nicht Augustin-gläubig. Es sei viel besser, sich von Augustin als von Christus zu scheiden. Augustin selbst sei es ja auch um Übereinstimmung mit der Heiligen Schrift gegangen.[23] Gegenüber Augustins Satz "Ich glaub dem Evangelio nit, mich ermant dann darzu das ansehen der gemeynen Kirchen, [...]" äußert er deutliche Vorbehalte.[24] Bucer versäumt es auch nicht, darauf hinzuweisen, dass der späte Augustin ja selbst früher getätigte Aussagen korrigiert habe, und zwar gerade im Blick auf die rechte Schriftauslegung und ihr Verhältnis zur kirchlichen Autorität.[25]

2. Augustin als Autorität im Streit um das Abendmahl

Der Themenbereich, in dem Bucer im Lauf der 1520er Jahre am häufigsten auf Augustin zurückgreift, ist spätestens seit dem Jahr 1528 die Abendmahlslehre. Zuerst einmal ist das natürlich dem Sachverhalt geschuldet, dass spätmittelalterliche Frömmigkeit wesentlich Sakramentsfrömmigkeit war und darum der Streit um das rechte Abendmahl sowohl die Auseinandersetzungen mit den Altgläubigen als auch unter den Reformatoren beherrschte. Entsprechend breiten Raum nimmt das Thema in Bucers Schrifttum ein. Die zahlreichen Bezüge auf Augustin in der Abendmahlslehre sind aber auch dadurch zu erklären, dass der als Erasmus-Anhänger zur Reformation gekommene Bucer[26] sein eigenes Abendmahlsverständnis hier treffend zum Ausdruck gebracht fand. Er sah bei dem Kirchenvater

---

21 Cf. Bucer: BDS 2,130,29 (Bucer betont, dass Ketzer allein mit der Heiligen Schrift zu überwinden seien. Wenn die Berufung auf die Heilige Schrift Kennzeichen von Ketzern sei, dann müssten Augustin und andere Kirchenväter Ketzer sein).
22 Cf. Bucer: BDS 2,94,20ff (zur Frage der Autorität der Kirche).
23 Cf. Bucer: BDS 2,100,9–19; cf. auch BDS 2,100,27–101,2.
24 Cf. Bucer: BDS 2,100,12–19. Das Augustin-Zitat ist hier falsch nachgewiesen (richtig: Augustin, Contra epistulam fundamenti V, CSEL 25/1,197,22f); cf. auch BDS 2,94,20ff (mit demselben – von Treger angeführten – Augustin-Zitat); zur Interpretation des Augustin-Zitats in dem 1540/41 gemeinsam mit J. Gropper verfassten Wormser Buch cf. BDS 9/1,417f.
25 Cf. Bucer: BDS 2,142,14 (rechte Schriftauslegung ist entscheidend für die Kirche; bei Augustin und Hieronymus Widerruf früherer Aussagen); cf. auch BDS 2,138,22.
26 Zur folgenreichen Begegnung mit Luther bei der Heidelberger Disputation vom April 1518 und seinem begeisterten Bericht an Beatus Rhenanus, der die erasmianische Wahrnehmung Luthers zeigt, cf. Greschat: 1990, 39–43.

wesentliche Ansatzpunkte für einen Konsens in der Abendmahlslehre. Das betraf sowohl die Auseinandersetzungen zwischen Luther und Zwingli als auch die Differenzen zu den Altgläubigen.[27]

Bucer versucht, die Realpräsenz Christi im Abendmahl, die Luther auf dem Höhepunkt des Streits mit Zwingli in der Schrift *Vom Abendmahl Christi. Bekenntnis* 1528 profiliert herausgestellt hatte, nicht zuletzt mit Hilfe Augustins zu erläutern und damit konsensfähiger zu machen. In der *Vergleichung D. Luthers und seins gegentheyls*[28] wird der Ertrag seines Studiums von Augustins wirkungsreicher Auslegung des Johannesevangeliums – im Zuge der Vorbereitung eines eigenen Kommentars zum Johannesevangelium – sichtbar.[29] Das Wort Jesu "Wer mein fleysch isset und mein blut trincket, hat das ewig leben" (Joh 6,54) habe Augustin besser als Luther verstanden,

> dann er drüber schreibt, das wol das Sacrament dieser speisen ettliche zum verderben nehmen, die speiß aber selb diene yederman nur zum leben und niemandt zum verderben, dann niemandt mag solcher teylhafft werden, der nit in Christo sey und bleibe.[30]

Im Sinne eines tropischen Verständnisses bedeute das Essen des Fleisches bei Augustin "des leidens Christi teylhafftig werden und eindenck sein".[31] Augustin habe darauf beharrt, dass der Leib "leiblich am himmlischen Ort" sei[32] und "das Gott dem fleysch Christi unsterblichkeyt geben und aber die natur nit entnommen habe".[33] Schließlich ruft Bucer Augustins Verständnis des Sakraments als "eyns heyligen dings zeychen" in Erinnerung, da diese Formulierung den Anliegen Zwinglis entgegen kommt, zugleich aber Luther der Autorität Augustins hier kaum widersprechen kann.[34]

Auch in anderen Texten der 1530er Jahre greift Bucer in der Abendmahlslehre ausführlich auf Augustin zurück, um zwinglianisch-oberdeutschen Anliegen bei

---

27 Zur konsensstiftenden Funktion der Augustin-Verweise im Wormser Buch siehe unten S. 104.
28 Abgedr. in: Bucer: BDS 2,(295)305–383.
29 Cf. Bucer: 1528, Straßburg; wiederabgedr. in: BOL 2; cf. auch die Verweise auf Augustins Auslegung des Johannesevangeliums in der 1530 entstandenen Confessio Tetrapolitana, Bucer: BDS 3,130, 132.
30 Bucer: BDS 2,360,31–360,2, mit Bezug auf: Augustin, In Ioannis Evangelium Tractatus XXVI,15, CChr.SL 36,267f.
31 Bucer: BDS 2,318,2–6, mit Verweis auf: Augustin, De doctrina Christiana III,16 (tropisches Verständnis des Essens des Fleisches: "so vil gelte, als des leidens Christi teylhafftig werden und eindenck sein"); cf. auch Bucer: BDS 2,362,18ff.
32 Bucer: BDS 2,322,8–10, mit Verweis auf: Augustin, Ep. 187,41, PL 33,848 (Ermahnung, fest zu glauben, dass der Leib leiblich am himmlischen Ort sei).
33 Bucer: BDS 2,344,8–10, mit Verweis auf: Augustin, Ep. 187,10, PL 33,835 (Betonung, "das Gott dem fleysch Christi unsterblichkeyt geben und aber die natur nit entnommen habe").
34 Cf. Bucer: BDS 2,313,4f, mit Verweis auf: Augustin, De civitate Dei X,5, CChr.SL 47,277,16.

den Anhängern Luthers mehr Anerkennung zu verschaffen. Denn Augustins Betonung des Zeichencharakters des Abendmahls und seine spiritualisierenden Tendenzen entsprachen eher Zwinglis als Luthers Deutungen, konnten aber von letzterem nicht so einfach abgewiesen werden. Dafür sprechen die Augustin-Bezüge in der *Confessio Tetrapolitana* von 1530,[35] ihrer Apologie von 1531[36] oder auch in dem *Bericht, was zu Frankfurt am Main geleret* von 1533, in dem Bucer sich gegen Vorwürfe Luthers verteidigt.[37] Bezeichnenderweise lobt Bucer Augustins Deutung der Himmelsbrotrede Joh 6 im Kommentar zum Johannesevangelium als "herrlich[e]" Auslegung.[38]

3. Augustin und die Verantwortung der weltlichen Obrigkeit in Religionsangelegenheiten

Mitte der 1530er Jahre greift Bucer in einem weiteren Themenbereich, der Frage obrigkeitlicher Kompetenz in Religionsangelegenheiten, umfassend auf Augustin zurück. Bucers unermüdliches Bemühen um die Ausbreitung und Etablierung der Reformation im Südwesten des Reiches hatte große Erfolge gezeigt. Zugleich stand man allerorten vor dem Problem gefährlicher Parteiungen. Nicht nur die Auseinandersetzungen zwischen den Anhängern Luthers und Zwinglis, die schon aufgrund der Nähe Zürichs unausweichlich waren, sondern auch die Anwesenheit von Täufern und Spiritualisten im Südwesten bedeutete eine bedrohliche Schwächung der aufkeimenden Reformation.

Besonders dramatisch stellte sich die Situation in Augsburg dar. Hier wurden die Auseinandersetzungen nicht nur mit besonderer Heftigkeit geführt, sondern aufgrund der Präsenz des Bischofs und der Nähe des katholischen Herzogtums Bayern schien die Reformation hier besonders gefährdet. In dieser Situation sah Bucer keine andere Möglichkeit, als die weltliche Obrigkeit für die Durchführung der Reformation der Kirche in die Verantwortung zu nehmen.[39] Kräftigen Anhalt dafür fand er in den Bemühungen Augustins, das Donatisten-Problem mithilfe der weltlichen Obrigkeit zu "lösen". So erörterte er Mitte der dreißiger Jahre in mehreren Schriften die Kompetenz obrigkeitlichen Handelns in Religionsangelegenheiten

---

35 Cf. bes. Bucer: BDS 3,120f; 128ff; 132.
36 Cf. Bucer: BDS 3,208; 212; 215; 223ff; 228–232; 240ff; 252; 265; 270; 273f; 276ff; 285; 289; 295; 301ff.
37 Cf. Bucer: BDS 4,486,1f; 488,32f; 490f; 495,26; 497,10–16.
38 Cf. Bucer: BDS 3,229,30f, mit Verweis auf: Augustin, In Ioannis Evangelium Tractatus XXVI, CChr.SL 36,260ff; cf. auch Bucer: BDS 3,240,30–35, mit Verweis auf: Augustin, In Ioannis Evangelium Tractatus XXVII, CChr.SL 36,271ff; Bucer: BDS 3,231,3–18, mit Verweis auf: Augustin, In Ioannis Evangelium Tractatus XXVI, CChr.SL 36,263.
39 Cf. dazu eingehend Strohm: 2016, 42–47; cf. auch Greschat: 1990, 122–125.

bzw. das Verhältnis von Kirche und Staat. Dies erfolgte unter breitestem Rückgriff auf Augustin.

Bucer veranlasste den von ihm nach Augsburg entsandten Prediger Wolfgang Musculus dazu, Augustins Brief an den weströmischen Feldherrn Bonifatius zu übersetzen, in dem es eben um die Verantwortung der weltlichen Obrigkeit für die Sorge um die rechte Gottesverehrung ging.[40] Er selbst verfasste zu dieser Schrift ein Vor- und Nachwort mit dem programmatischen Titel "Vom Ampt der Oberkait".[41] In dem auf den 10. März 1535 datierten Vorwort vertrat Bucer unter anderem die Unterscheidung von niederen ("undren") und übergeordneten Obrigkeiten ("obren"), um die Verantwortung der städtischen Obrigkeiten in Religionsangelegenheiten auch im Gegensatz zum katholischen Kaiser zu begründen.[42] Auch eine weitere Schrift zum Thema, die *Dialogi oder Gesprech Von der gemainsame vnnd den Kirchen übungen der Christen Vnd was yeder Oberkait von ampts wegen auß Göttlichem befelch an den selbigen zuuersehen vnd zu besseren gebüre*,[43] ist zur unmittelbaren Wirkungsgeschichte Augustins zu zählen. In der während eines Aufenthalts in Augsburg im Mai 1535 verfassten Schrift erläuterte er ausführlich seine Auffassungen über die Kompetenz der weltlichen Obrigkeit in Religionsangelegenheiten. Bucers Rückgriff auf Augustin in dieser Sache hat im reformierten Protestantismus und weit darüber hinaus unter dem Stichwort des Erastianismus außerordentlich weitreichende Folgen gezeitigt.[44]

4. Augustin als Autorität im Streit um den Kölner Reformationsversuch

Zur unmittelbaren Vorgeschichte der Kölner Reformation gehört Bucers Engagement in den Reichsreligionsgesprächen der Jahre 1540/41.[45] Denn hier kam es zur Begegnung mit dem Kölner Juristen und Theologen Johannes Gropper, der

---

40 Cf. Greschat: 1990, 124f; zu vergleichbaren Auseinandersetzungen in Straßburg und Bucers Voten darin cf. W. Delius, Einleitung, zu: Vom Ampt der Oberkait, Bucer: BDS 6/2,20f.
41 Abgedr. in: Bucer: BDS 6/2,17–38.
42 "Dabey will ich auch auß beystand unsers Herren Jesu auß göttlicher geschrifft und auch der Christlichen Kayser gesetzen gnugsam anzaigen, wes die undren oberkaiten on verletzung der waren gehorsame, auch on ainig zerrüttung guter Pollicey gegen den obren oberkaitten in sachen der Religion und besserung der Kirchen zu handlen haben und mit der hilff Gottes wol auch gantz schleünig und fridlich vermögen" (Bucer: BDS 6/2,29,27–30,5).
43 Abgedr. in: Bucer: BDS 6/2,39–188.
44 Zur weitreichenden Wirkungsgeschichte in Gestalt des sog. Erastianismus cf. bereits Heckel: 1962, 62–74; cf. ferner Kingdon (1980); Maissen (2015).
45 Zu Bucers Aktivitäten und Voten bei den Religionsgesprächen des Jahres 1540/41 cf. Ortmann (2001).

Bucers wichtigster Partner bei den Konsensbemühungen wurde.[46] Gerade der Rückgriff auf Augustin ermöglichte Gropper und Bucer die Abfassung eines Konsensdokuments, das als Wormser und dann Regensburger Buch eine beträchtliche Wirkungsgeschichte entfaltet hat, auch wenn es schließlich doch nicht zu einer Konkordie oder gar Wiedervereinigung der getrennten Konfessionen gekommen ist.[47]

Man bezog sich auf die Sünden- und Gnadenlehre des späten Augustin, um in der umstrittenen Rechtfertigungslehre zu einem Konsens zu gelangen. Augustins antipelagianische Schriften wie *De spiritu et littera* boten hierzu das Vorbild.[48] Der Konsens unter Rückgriff auf Augustin gelang aber nur um den Preis eines Kompromisses, der mit seinem Ansatz einer doppelten Rechtfertigungslehre[49] von Luther bald harsch abgelehnt wurde.[50]

Erzbischof Hermann von Wied hatte Bucer auf den Reichsreligionsgesprächen 1540/41 als kompromissorientierten Theologen kennengelernt. So berief er ihn 1542 in sein Kölner Erzbistum, um eine Reformation durchzuführen. Wider Erwarten stellte sich schnell heraus, dass sein vertrauter Berater Gropper mit der Berufung Bucers keineswegs einverstanden war. Es kam zu heftigen Angriffen von Seiten Groppers und anderer Kölner Theologen aus dem Bereich der Universität, des Domkapitels und der Orden.[51]

Die Vertreter des Domkapitels im Landtag sprachen Bucer im Februar 1543 in einer später gedruckten *Sententia delectorum* grundsätzlich die Berechtigung zum Predigtdienst im Erzbistum Köln ab.[52] Abgesehen davon, dass er die verurteilte Lehre Luthers vertrete,[53] sei er weder ordnungsgemäß unter Zustimmung der

---

46 Zu Gropper cf. Lipgens (1951); Lipgens (1966); Meier (1977).
47 Die Lehre von der doppelten Rechtfertigung bestimmte dann auch den auf dem nachfolgenden Regensburger Reichstag (vom 5. April bis 29. Juli 1541) verglichenen Artikel über die Rechtfertigung, der im Rahmen des sog. Regensburger Buches veröffentlicht wurde (cf. Hergang: 1858, 98–107). Zu den verschiedenen, auf den Religionsgesprächen des Jahres 1540/41 vertretenen Modellen der Rechtfertigungslehre cf. Lexutt (1996).
48 Cf. bes. Bucer: BDS 9/1,359f; 376f; 378f; 399.
49 Der Kompromiss bestand darin, dass man von zweierlei "Gerechtmachung" sprach. Neben der allein aus Gnade und durch den Glauben empfangenen gebe es eine Gerechtmachung, die "ist von wercken, so auß der wurtzel des glaubens vnd der liebe endtspringen vnd den glauben [...] vollfueren" (Bucer: BDS 9/1,354,19–21).
50 Cf. Luther: WA.B 9,356,17–25; cf. auch Luther und Bugenhagen an Kurfürst Johann Friedrich, 10. od. 11.5.1541, WA.B 9,407,15–39; Luther an Justus Jonas, 16.7.1541, WA.B 9,474,24–27; Luther an Justus Menius, 10.1.1542, WA.B 9,590,9f; WA.TR 5, Nr. 5461.
51 Zu Bucers Mitwirkung am Kölner Reformationsversuch cf. Köhn (1966).
52 Sententia delectorum per venerabile capitulum ecclesiae Coloniensis, de uocatione Martini Buceri, in: Gropper: 1544, Bl. Bb6b–Cciijb; jetzt abgedr. in: Bucer: BDS 11/1,433–446.
53 Cf. Bucer: BDS 11/1,439.

Kirche berufen worden noch erfülle er die notwendige Voraussetzung eines untadeligen Lebenswandels. Der Bruch der Mönchsgelübde, mangelnde Enthaltsamkeit und die Heirat einer Witwe würden klar gegen die alten Canones verstoßen.[54] Hier verweisen die Kritiker Bucers ausdrücklich auf eine entsprechende, in das *Decretum Gratiani* aufgenommene Aussage Augustins[55] und unterstreichen dies noch durch einen weiteren expliziten Verweis auf ein Kapitel in dessen *Liber de bono conjugali*.[56]

Bucer antwortete auf die Vorwürfe sogleich im März 1543 mit einer ersten umfangreichen Verteidigungsschrift *Was im namen des Heiligen Euangeli vnsers Herren Jesu Christi / jetzund zu Bonn im Stifft Coellen / gelehret vnnd gepredigt würdt*.[57] Den ersten Teil widmet Bucer der Darstellung seiner Lehre.[58] Durch zahlreiche Verweise sucht Bucer die Übereinstimmung mit der Heiligen Schrift, aber auch der Alten Kirche zu erweisen. Dabei greift er mehrfach ausdrücklich auf Augustin zurück, zum Beispiel um zu betonen, dass die "Heiligen vätter sich alweg allein der lehr vnnd ordnung göttlicher schrifft on alles ferners beweren vnnd nochfragen gentzlich vnderworffen [...]" hätten.[59] Auch für eine Praxis der Heiligenverehrung, die sich auf "vereerung der liebe vnd gemeinschafft" beschränkt und Opfer und Anrufung ausschließt, wird Augustin in Anspruch genommen.[60] Besonders ausführlich kommt Augustin zu Wort, wenn Bucer die Messopferlehre, die dem priesterlichen Amt eine konstitutive Rolle zuspricht, zurückweist.[61] Bei der Widerlegung der Kritik an der Legitimität seiner Berufung und seinem Lebenswandel oder auch der Legitimität der Wiederverheiratung einer Witwe spielt Augustin neben Chrysostomus, Hieronymus und anderen Kirchenvätern ebenfalls eine wichtige Rolle.

---

54 Cf. Bucer: BDS 11/1, 438f.
55 Cf. Bucer: BDS 11/1, 438,23ff, mit Verweis auf: Decretum Gratiani II, Causa 27, qu. 1, c. 41, Friedberg I,1060.
56 Cf. Bucer: BDS 10/1,439,2f, mit Verweis auf: Augustin, De bono conjugali XVIII,21, PL 40,387f.
57 [Bonn] 1543; Bonn ²1544; abgedr. in: Bucer: BDS 11/1,19–131.
58 Cf. Bucer: BDS 11/1,29–70.
59 Bucer: BDS 11/1,38, mit Verweis (in der Marginalie) auf: Augustin, De baptismo II,3, PL 43,128f.
60 Cf. Bucer: BDS 11/1,42,21–25, mit Verweis auf: Augustin, De civitate Dei VIII,27, CChr.SL 47,248f; XXII,10, CChr.SL 48,828; Augustin, Contra Faustum XX,21, CSEL 25/1,561–565.
61 "Wie wir dann dem Herren alda entpfahen sollen, daß wir in im vnd er in vns lebe, so sagen sie auch, daß die gemeinde Christi alda sich selb vffopfere zu einem solchen angenemen opfer, wie Paulus rhümet [Röm 15,16], das er die Heyden Gott zum opfer geheyliget vnnd vffgeopfret habe. Dauon der H. Augustinus sagt: 'Dis ist das opfer der Christen, sacrificium, wir viel sindt ein leyb in Christo, welches die kirchen auch im Sacrament, das den glaubigen bekandt ist, haltet, da je angezeyget wirdt, das in dem opfer, das sie opfret, in ea oblatione, sie selb vffgeopfert wirdt.' Hec ille. Vnd mercke hie, das der Heilig Lehrer sagt, Die gemein opfer, dan das der Priester thut, das thut er von wegen der gantzen versamlung Christi, Ja die versamlung durch jn" (Bucer: BDS 11/1,52,19–29, mit Zitat von: Augustin, De civitate Dei X,6, CChr.SL 47,279,52–55).

Der gleiche Befund wie in der ersten Verteidigungsschrift ergibt sich bei der Analyse der Augustin-Bezüge in der von Bucer zusammen mit Melanchthon 1543 erarbeiteten Kölner Reformationsordnung, dem *Einfältigen Bedenken* Erzbischof Hermann von Wieds.[62] Auch hier dient der ausdrückliche Verweis auf die Kirchenväter und insbesondere Augustin zum Beleg der rechten Lehre.[63] Das zeigt sich gerade bei den umstrittenen Lehrinhalten. Gleich zu Beginn des *Einfältigen Bedenkens* wird Augustin als Zeuge dafür zitiert, dass auch die herausragenden Lehrer der Alten Kirche sich ganz und gar der Heiligen Schrift untergeordnet und um ihre Unvollkommenheit gewusst hätten.[64] Wieder wird Augustin ausdrücklich gegen die Messopferlehre in Stellung gebracht:

> Vnd als die alten Vätter die handlung dieses H. Sacraments offt Sacrificium vnnd Oblationem nennen vnnd etwan [=manchmal] schreiben, das der Priester, der das H. Abendtmal haltet, Christum da opffere, Sollen die Prediger wissen, auch andere des berichten, das die alten Vätter des Priesters opfferen in diesem handel nit von dieser Application verstanden, die hernach erdichtet vnd mit anderen mißbreuchen eingerissen ist, Sonder wie Augustinus spricht, Es heisse Sacrificium i.[=id est] memoria sacrificij, das man da das opffer Christi mit predigen, brauch des H. Sacraments vnd glauben betrachten vnd die frucht des selbigen in warem glauben niessen solle.[65]

Grundsätzlich unterscheidet sich Bucers Rückgriff auf Augustin nicht von den Verweisen auf andere Kirchenväter. Sie werden herangezogen, um dem eigenen Standpunkt mehr Durchschlagskraft zu verleihen. Augustin eignet sich hier aus drei Gründen noch besser als andere Kirchenväter. *Erstens* ist er als der wirkmächtigste Kirchenvater der westlichen Christenheit eine auf allen Seiten unangefochtene Autorität. *Zweitens* legt schon die schiere Menge seines Schrifttums einen besonders zahlreichen Rückgriff nahe. Und *drittens* eignet sich der spezifische Charakter vieler seiner Briefe und Schriften zur Begründung des eigenen Standpunkts im Streit um den Kölner Reformationsversuch. Augustin stand sein Leben lang in der

---

62 Von Gottes genaden, vnser Hermans Ertzbischoffs zu Coelln, vnnd Churfürsten etc. […], Bonn 1543; Bonn ²1544; [Bonn] ³1545; abgedr. in: Bucer: BDS 11/1,(147)163–432.

63 Cf. z. B. Bucer: BDS 11/1,182,3f (Zweinaturenlehre); BDS 11/1,193,6 (Erbsündenlehre); BDS 11/1,203,35 (bleibendes Miteinander von Altem und Neuem Testament); BDS 11/1,254,8 (gegen die Leidenssucht der Donatisten); BDS 11/1,421,19 (Vergeblichkeit der Wiederherstellung des Mönchtums der Alten Kirche).

64 Cf. Bucer: BDS 11/1,171,28–35, mit Zitat (in der Marginalie) von: Augustin, Ep. 82, c. 1, PL 33,277; CSEL 60,380,10ff.

65 Bucer: BDS 11/1,332,15–23, mit Zitat von: Augustin, De fide ad Petrum, c. 62 (XIX), CChr.SL 91A,750f. Das früher Augustin zugeschriebene Werk stammt von Fulgentius von Ruspe (462/7–526/31).

Auseinandersetzung mit Gegnern, welche die katholische Christenheit zu bedrohen schienen, zuerst mit den Manichäern, dann mit den Donatisten und schließlich mit Pelagius und seinen Anhängern. Augustin wird als Verteidiger der rechten katholischen Lehre gegen alle möglichen Arten von Irrlehre rezipiert. Nicht wenige Worte und Schriften, die in den verschiedenen Auseinandersetzungen formuliert worden waren, wurden von verschiedenen Synoden aufgenommen. Das wiederum führte – wie gesagt – zu einem außerordentlich umfassenden Rückgriff auf Aussagen Augustins in der ersten Sammlung des (späteren) kanonischen Rechts, dem *Decretum Gratiani*. Schon die Natur der gegen Bucer erhobenen Vorwürfe, die ihm ganz grundsätzlich die Legitimität seines reformatorischen Wirkens absprachen, bewirkte eine vermehrte Rezeption gerade solcher die Legitimität des Amts und die kirchliche Autorität betreffender, oft im *Decretum Gratiani* überlieferter Worte Augustins.

Im weiteren Verlauf der Auseinandersetzungen um den Kölner Reformationsversuch bleibt es bei vielfachen Bezugnahmen auf die Kirchenväter. Auf die andauernde massive Kritik des Kölner Karmelitenprovinzials Eberhard Billick[66] antwortete Bucer noch im Sommer 1543 mit einer zweiten Verteidigungsschrift.[67] Wieder führt er zahlreiche Bibelstellen an und wieder werden die Kirchenväter Cyprian, Ambrosius, Hieronymus, Chrysostomus und mehr als alle anderen Augustin als Autoritäten angeführt.

Bucers dritte, außerordentlich umfangreiche Verteidigungsschrift, die 1545 gedruckte *Beständige Verantwortung*,[68] antwortet einer Schrift Johannes Groppers. Dieser hatte in der Schrift mit dem Titel *Christliche vnd Catholische gegenberichtung eyhns Erwirdigen Dhomcapittels zu Cöllen* der Kölner Reformationsordnung zahlreiche Irrlehren nachzuweisen versucht.[69] Dazu führte er eine Fülle von Aussagen der Kirchenväter und allen voran Augustins an.

Gleichsam programmatisch stellte Gropper seinem Werk eine Auflistung der Kirchenväter im Osten wie Westen sowie der altkirchlichen Konzilien voran.[70] Unter mehrfachem Verweis auf Augustin erläutert er die Auffassung, dass die katholische Lehre nicht allein auf der Heiligen Schrift beruhe, sondern auch auf den apostolischen Traditionen. Diese seien zuerst nicht schriftlich überliefert und erst

---

66 Cf. Billick (1543); cf. dazu Varrentrapp: 1878, 165ff; Schlüter: 2005, 179.
67 Abgedr. in: Bucer: BDS 11/2,(21)31–247; cf. dazu Schlüter: 2005, 193; Varrentrapp: 1878, 171–176.
68 Abgedr. in: Bucer: BDS 11/3,(11)23–672; cf. dazu Schlüter: 2005, 239–243.
69 Cf. Gropper (1544). Bereits im März 1544 erschien bei dem Kölner Drucker Jaspar von Gennep eine von Eberhard Billick erstellte lateinische Übersetzung: Antididagma.
70 "Der Cathalogus oder die namen der heiligen Vätter / so von zeit der Apostell Christi / beide in Occidentalischer vnd Orientalischer Kirchen geleucht haben. Wölche neben der götlicher geschrift in disem Gegenbericht angezogen seynd / vnd dem zeugnis geben" (Gropper: 1544, f. [b6]ᵛ).

später von den Kirchenvätern festgehalten worden.[71] Unter den hier angeführten Kirchenvätern wird Augustin besonders hervorgehoben: "Aber der andern alle von wegen der kurtze vmbgangen / Gibt der vnuergleichlich mann / der heiliger Augustinus / hier über eynen fast schönen bericht."[72] Danach gebe es *zum einen* Gewohnheiten/Traditionen, die schnell ("stracks") als im Widerspruch zur Heiligen Schrift erwiesen worden seien. *Zum anderen* aber gebe es "eyn herkommens das dem glauben nicht zu entgegen" sei, und hier seien wiederum drei Formen zu unterscheiden.[73] Es gebe *erstens* Traditionen, die in der gesamten Kirche einhellig gehandhabt und durch die Schrift geboten würden.[74] *Zweitens* gebe es besondere Gebräuche und Ordnungen, die nicht überall gleichmäßig gehalten würden, aber der Erbauung dienten.[75] Und *drittens* gebe es auch Dinge, die weder in der Heiligen Schrift noch durch die allgemeinen Konzilien geboten seien. Wenn sie nicht zu begründen und nutzlos seien oder gar zur knechtischen Beschwerung des christlichen Volks führen, seien sie abzutun. "Dan dauon alleyn Christus geredt hab / Vergeblich ehren sie mich mit menschen gesätzen etc. Doch sagt er das die abtuhung nit ohn grosse bescheidenheit beschehen sol."[76] Gropper unterstreicht die Bedeutung und quasi-rechtlich begründete Geltung der Einteilung Augustins durch einen Verweis auf deren Aufnahme in das *Decretum Gratiani*.[77]

Dagegen führt Bucer in der *Beständigen Verantwortung* selbst wiederum Äußerungen Augustins und anderer Kirchenväter an. Augustin habe beklagt, dass "schon zu seinen zeyten alles voll war mit menschlichen vermessenheiten."[78] Auch habe er (wie andere Väter) ausdrücklich betont, dass seinen Lehren nicht Geltung zukomme, weil sie von "alten, heyligen vnd gelehrten Vättern gelehrt und geschrieben seindt", sondern allein darum, "das diese Lehren vnd fürgebungen mit göttlicher Schrifft oder sonst bewegenden vrsachen bewäret werden".[79] Augustin und andere Väter hätten auch ein Bewusstsein dafür gehabt, dass sich in ihren Schriften Fehler fänden und diese von der Heiligen Schrift her zu korrigieren seien.[80]

Bucers Verweise auf Augustin in der *Beständigen Verantwortung* sind im Wesentlichen durch Groppers Augustin-Rückgriffe vorgegeben. Sie finden sich über

---

71 Gropper: 1544, f. i^r–iiii^r.
72 Gropper: 1544, f. ij^v.
73 Cf. Ebd.
74 Gropper: 1544, f. ij^v–iij^r.
75 Cf. Gropper: 1544, f. iij^r.
76 Gropper: 1544, f. iij^v.
77 Cf. Gropper: 1544, f. iij^v–iiij^r, mit Verweis auf: Decretum Gratiani I, Dist. 11, c. 8, Friedberg I,25.
78 Bucer: BDS 11/3,88,13ff, mit Verweis auf: Augustin, Epistola 55,19,35, PL 33,221; CSEL 34/2,209f.
79 Bucer: BDS 11/3,89,26ff.
80 Cf. Bucer: BDS 11/3,89,29–90,5, mit Verweis auf: Augustin, Epistola 148,4,15, PL 33,628f; CSEL 44,344f; Augustin, De baptismo contra Donatistas I,3,4, CSEL 51,148–150; cf. auch Bucer: BDS 11/3,75,26–29.

dessen gesamte *Christliche vnd Catholische gegenberichtung* verteilt. Schwerpunkte der Augustin-Rezeption Groppers sind neben der skizzierten Verhältnisbestimmung von Schrift und Tradition die Sündenlehre, die Lehre von der Anrufung der Heiligen, die Tauflehre und die Abendmahlslehre.

In der Sündenlehre geht es Gropper darum aufzuzeigen, dass das *Einfältige Bedenken* Augustins Auffassung von der sündentilgenden Wirkung der Taufe und den Überresten, die von der Sünde blieben, widerspreche.[81] Sowohl die frühen gegen den manichäischen Dualismus verfassten Schriften Augustins als auch die späten antipelagianischen wie *De spiritu et littera* werden herangezogen.[82] Gropper sieht im *Einfältigen Bedenken* die radikale Sündenlehre wiederkehren, die Augustin den Manichäern vorgeworfen habe.[83] Bucer wiederum meint, dass die "Gegengelehrten dem H. Augustino seine wort" verkehren.[84]

Für die Anrufung der Heiligen und die verschiedensten Aspekte der in der Alten Kirche geübten Praxis findet Gropper zahlreiche Belege bei Augustin.[85] Bucers ausführliche Auseinandersetzung damit greift hingegen zuvorderst auf die Heilige Schrift zurück.[86] Aussagen Augustins werden in diesem Abschnitt der *Beständigen Verantwortung* nur vereinzelt angeführt bzw. erläutert.[87] Groppers zahlreiche Verweise auf Augustin im Abschnitt "Von administration der heiliger Tauff" beziehen sich weniger auf grundlegende Lehrfragen als auf verschiedenste Gebräuche.[88] Bucer ist in seiner Gegenschrift kaum auf diese Rückgriffe eingegangen.[89]

Die Darstellung der umstrittenen Abendmahlslehre nimmt in Groppers *Gegenberichtung* naturgemäß breiten Raum ein.[90] Neben Augustin wird insbesondere auch Ambrosius mehrfach zitiert.[91] Bucers Auseinandersetzung damit in der *Beständigen Verantwortung* umfasst nicht weniger als 200 Druckseiten in der modernen

---

81 "Von dem vberpleib der Erbsunde / Unn was nach der Tauff eygentlich vor sunde zu halten sey" (Gropper: 1544, f. vi^v–x^r).
82 Cf. z. B. Gropper: 1544, f. vij^v, mit Verweis auf: Augustin, De Genesi ad litteram X,12,20, CSEL 28/1,309,8–X,12,21; CSEL 28/1,311,10; De spiritu et littera 66, CSEL 60,228,3–23.
83 Cf. Gropper: 1544, f. x^r.
84 Bucer: BDS 11/3,123,9–28 (Zitat in: Marginalie), mit Verweis auf: Augustin, De spiritu et littera 36, CSEL 60,223–229.
85 Cf. Gropper: 1544, f. xxix^v; xxx^{r-v}; xxxi^r; xxxij^{r-v}; xxxiij^v; xxxv^v.
86 Cf. Bucer: BDS 11/3,221–243.
87 Cf. Bucer: BDS 11/3, 224,7ff; 236,18–24; 236,27–237,8; 239,17f; 240,28.
88 Cf. Gropper: 1544, f. xiviij^v; xlix^{r-v}; l^v; li^v; lij^r–liij^v; liiij^v–lv^r; lvi^r.
89 Cf. Bucer: BDS 11/3,271–295.
90 "Von dem heiligen Sacrament des leibs vnd bluts Christi / vnd desselben administration" (Gropper: 1544, f. lix^r–cxiiij^r).
91 Zu Augustin cf. Gropper: 1544, f. lx^r; lxij^{r-v}; lxiiij^{r-v}; lxiiij^v–lxv^r; lxvij^{r-v}; lxx^r (mit anderen Kirchenvätern); lxxi^{r-v}; lxxij^v–lxxiiij^r; lxxxi^r; lxxxviij^v–lxxxix^r; xci^v; xciiij^v; xcv^v–xcvi^v; xcviij^v–xcix^v; c^{r-v}; ci^v; cij^v; ciiij^{r-v}; cv^v; cxij^v; zu Ambrosius cf. Gropper: 1544, f. lxi^r; lx^v–lxi^r; lxx^r; lxxij^r; lxxiij^r; xc^v; xcv^r; xcviij^r; xcviij^r; cxiij^v.

Ausgabe.⁹² Primäre Argumentationsquelle sind Bibeltexte. Augustin wird nur vereinzelt herangezogen, wo es die von den "Gegengelehrten" angeführten "Sprüch Augustini" notwendig erscheinen lassen.⁹³ Allein bei der Abwehr der Messopferlehre kommt es zu einer durch mehrere Verweise unterstrichenen Präsentation der Deutung Augustins, der den Gedächtnischarakter des Opfers betont hatte.⁹⁴ Bucer verteidigt damit die in der Reformationsordnung vertretene Auffassung, dass das "wort Oblationem vnd Sacrificium bey den H. Vättern [be]deute, das es mehr nit sey, dan die gedechtnüß halten deß Opffers Christi".⁹⁵

Anders als in der Messopferlehre hält sich der Streit um die rechte Deutung Augustins in der Rechtfertigungslehre in Grenzen. Zwar moniert Gropper hier, dass das *Einfältige Bedenken* von den drei Arten der Rechtfertigung, die Augustin in der Schrift *Contra Julianum* erläutert habe, nur eine kenne.⁹⁶ Weitere Differenzen finden aber nicht Niederschlag in unterschiedlichen Augustin-Deutungen. Das dürfte dem Sachverhalt geschuldet sein, dass Gropper zu den reformorientierten katholischen Theologen gehörte und sich entschieden auf die Sünden- und Rechtfertigungslehre des späten, antipelagianischen Augustin berief.⁹⁷ So scheint der Kompromiss, der drei Jahre zuvor im Wormser Buch in der Sünden- und Rechtfertigungslehre zwischen Gropper und Bucer gefunden worden war,⁹⁸ trotz des persönlichen Zerwürfnisses nicht vollständig verloren gegangen zu sein.

5. Résumé

Im Unterschied zu Thomas von Aquin und Erasmus von Rotterdam scheint Augustin den jungen Dominikanermönch Martin Bucer nicht besonders beeinflusst oder geprägt zu haben. Die bald festzustellenden Bezugnahmen auf Augustin sind durch die Argumentationen der Gegner vorgegeben. Auch führt der Anschluss an

---

92 Cf. Bucer: BDS 11/3,299–502.
93 Cf. Bucer, Bestendige Verantwortung, 335,17–23. Wie in früheren Texten zur Abendmahlslehre verweist Bucer vermehrt auf Augustins Kommentar zum Johannesevangelium: cf. z. B. Bucer, Bestendige Verantwortung, 336f, mit Verweis auf: Augustin, In Ioannis Evangelium Tractatus LXXX,3, CChr.SL 36,529,5f; Augustin, In Ioannis Evangelium Tractatus LXXX,3, CChr.SL 36,529,4f; Bucer, Bestendige Verantwortung, 365, mit Verweis auf: Augustin, In Ioannis Evangelium Tractatus XXV,12, CChr.SL 36,254,8f; Bucer, Bestendige Verantwortung, 370, mit Verweis auf: Augustin, In Ioannis Evangelium Tractatus XXVI,11, CChr.SL 36,265.
94 Cf. Bucer, Bestendige Verantwortung, 406–408; 451f; 469.
95 Bucer, Bestendige Verantwortung, 494,14ff.
96 Cf. Gropper: 1544, f. xix^r.
97 Zu Groppers Sünden-, Gnaden- und Rechtfertigungslehre cf. Braunisch (1974); cf. auch Meier (2018).
98 Siehe oben S. 104 mit Anm. 49.

Luthers Reformation zu einem verstärkten Rückgriff auf Augustin. Ein Schwerpunkt ist die Abendmahlslehre, in der Bucer Augustins Zurückhaltung gegenüber einer leiblichen Realpräsenzvorstellung, die Erläuterung des Zeichencharakters und die Betonung des Gedächtnisses des Opfers gegen die spätmittelalterliche Messopferlehre herausstellt. In der Sünden- und Gnaden- bzw. Rechtfertigungslehre bringt er in verschiedenen Kontexten Aussagen des späten Augustin zur Geltung. Nicht unterschätzt werden darf der Einfluss Augustins auf Bucers Lehre von der Verantwortung der weltlichen Obrigkeit in Religionsangelegenheiten. Die für große Teile des reformierten Protestantismus charakteristische Betonung der Verantwortung der weltlichen Obrigkeit für die wahre Gottesverehrung kann man, wie die Mitte der 1530er Jahre im Blick auf die schwierige Situation in Augsburg entstandenen Texte zeigen, im weiteren Sinn der Wirkungsgeschichte Augustins zurechnen. Das gilt auch für die Geschichte des Widerstandsrechts, da Bucer seine wichtige Unterscheidung von über- und untergeordneten Obrigkeiten und das mögliche Widerstandsrecht der inferiores magistratus in Religionssachen ebenfalls in diesem Kontext entfaltet hat.

Die Auseinandersetzungen um die Kölner Reformation zeigen: Bucers Rückgriff auf Augustin und andere Kirchenväter ist in erheblichem Maß durch die kontroversen Debatten mit altgläubigen Theologen hervorgerufen. Gleichwohl zeigt die Auseinandersetzung mit Johannes Gropper in den Jahren 1544/45 und der Vergleich ihrer Schriften bleibende Unterschiede. Trotz der Vielzahl der Verweise auf Kirchenväter – und hier vor allem Augustin – in Groppers *Gegenberichtung* bleibt Bucer seiner Überzeugung treu, dass im Streit um die rechte Lehre und Praxis zuerst und zuvörderst mit der Heiligen Schrift zu argumentieren sei. Trotz aller kontroverstheologischer Herausforderungen bleibt Bucers reformatorische Theologie zuallererst Schriftauslegung.

Quellen und Literatur

Quellen

Percy Stafford Allen (ed.) (1910), Opus epistolarum Des. Erasmi Roterodami, denuo recognitum et auctum, vol. 2: 1514–1517, Oxford: Oxford University Press.

Aurelius Augustinus (1506), Prima [-undecima] pars librorum divi Aurelii Augustini, [Basel: Johannes Amerbach, Johannes Petri, Johannes Froben].

Eberhard Billick (1543), Ivdicivm cleri et vniversitatis Coloniensis de doctrina et uocatione Martini Buceri ad Bonnam, Köln: Novesianus.

Martin Bucer (1528), Enarratio in evangelion Iohanni, Straßburg [wiederabgedr. in: Martin Bucer (1987), Enarratio in evangelion Iohanni, Irena Backus (ed.), Leiden : Brill, Opera latina, vol. 2].

MARTIN BUCER (1955), Opera latina, François Wendel (ed.), Paris/Gütersloh: Presses Universitaires de France/C. Bertelsmann Verlag.

MARTIN BUCER (1960–2016), Deutsche Schriften, Robert Stupperich/Wilhelm H. Neuser/ Gottfried Seebaß/Christoph Strohm (ed.), 19 vol., Gütersloh: Gerd Mohn.

[MARTIN BUCER / PHILIPP MELANCHTHON (1543; 1544^2; 1545^3),] Von Gottes genaden / vnser Hermans Ertzbischoffs zu Cölln / vnnd Churfürsten einfaltigs bedencken, warauff ein Christliche, in dem wort Gottes gegrünte Reformation an Lehr, brauch der Heyligen Sacramenten vnd Ceremonien, Seelsorge vnd anderem Kirchendienst, biß vff eines freyen, Christlichen, Gemeinen, oder NationalsConcilij oder des Reichs Teutscher Nation Stende, im Heyligen Geyst versamlet, verbesserung, bey denen so vnserer Seelsorge befolhen, anzurichten seye, Bonn: Laurentius Mullen.

EMIL FRIEDBERG (ed.) (1879; 1995), Corpus Iuris Canonici, 2 vol., Leipzig: B. Tauchnitz; Graz: Akademische Druck- u. Verlagsanstalt.

JOHANNES GROPPER (1544; 2006), Christliche vnd Catholische gegenberichtung eyhns Erwirdigen Dhomcapittels zu Cöllen, wider das Buch der gnanter Reformation, so den Stenden Ertzstiffts Cöllen vff junxtem Landtage zu Bonn vorgehalten, Köln; photomechanischer Nachdruck, Gütersloh; latein. Übersetzung v. Eberhard Billick: Antididagma, seu christianae et catholicae religionis […] propugnatio, Köln/Gütersloh: Jaspar von Gennep/ Gütersloher Verlagshaus.

MARTIN LUTHER, (1883ff; 1912ff; 1930ff), Werke. Kritische Gesamtausgabe, vol. 1ff, Tischreden, 1ff; Briefwechsel, 1ff, Weimar: Hermann Böhlau.

ABRAHAM SCULTETUS (1598–1613), Medulla theologiae patrum, qui a temporibus apostolorum ad concilium usque Nicenum floruerunt, 4 vol., Amberg/Heidelberg/Frankfurt a. M.: Forsterus.

Forschungsliteratur

BRAUNISCH, REINHARD (1974), Die Theologie der Rechtfertigung im "Enchiridion" (1538) des Johannes Gropper, Münster: Aschendorff.

BUCKWALTER, STEPHEN E. (2013), Bucer, Martin (1491–1551), in: Karla Pollmann/Willemien Otten (ed.), The Oxford Guide to the Historical Reception of Augustine, vol. 2, Oxford: Oxford University Press, 715–718.

BURNETT, AMY (2001), Martin Bucer and the Church Fathers in the Cologne Reformation, Reformation & Renaissance Review 3:1, 108–124.

DIENST, TOBIAS (2019), Konfessionelle Konkurrenz. Gelehrte Kontroversen an den Universitäten Heidelberg und Mainz (1583–1622), Diss. theol., Heidelberg: Mohr Siebeck, 108–130.

GRESCHAT, MARTIN (1975), Martin Bucers Bücherverzeichnis von 1518, Archiv für Kulturgeschichte 57, 162–185.

GRESCHAT, MARTIN (1976), Martin Bucer als Dominikanermönch, in: Marijn de Kroon/ Friedhelm Krüger (ed.), Bucer und seine Zeit, Wiesbaden: Franz Steiner Verlag, 30–53.

GRESCHAT, MARTIN (1990), Martin Bucer. Ein Reformator und seine Zeit, München: C. H. Beck.

HECKEL, JOHANNES (1962), Cura religionis, ius in sacra, ius circa sacra [1938]. Sonderausgabe, Libelli 49, Darmstadt: Wissenschaftliche Buchgesellschaft, 62–74.

HERGANG, KARL THEODOR (1858), Das Religions-Gespräch zu Regensburg i.J. 1541 und das Regensburger Buch, nebst andren darauf bezüglichen Schriften jener Zeit, Kassel: Kessinger Publishing.

KINGDON, ROBERT M. (1980), The political thought of Peter Martyr Vermigli. Selected Texts and Commentary, THR 178, Genf: Librairie Droz.

KOCH, KARL (1962), Studium Pietatis. Martin Bucer als Ethiker, BGLRK 14, Neukirchen-Vluyn: Neukirchener, 20–26.

KÖHN, MECHTILD (1966), Martin Bucers Entwurf einer Reformation des Erzstiftes Köln. Untersuchung der Entstehungsgeschichte und der Theologie des "Einfaltigen Bedenckens" von 1543, UKG 2, Witten: Luther-Verlag.

KRÜGER, FRIEDHELM (1970), Bucer und Erasmus. Eine Untersuchung zum Einfluß des Erasmus auf die Theologie Martin Bucers (bis zum Evangelien-Kommentar von 1530), VIEG 57, Wiesbaden: Franz Steiner Verlag.

LEXUTT, ATHINA (1996), Rechtfertigung im Gespräch. Das Rechtfertigungsverständnis in den Religionsgesprächen von Hagenau, Worms und Regensburg 1540/41, FKDG 64, Göttingen: Vandenhoeck & Ruprecht.

LIPGENS, WALTER (1951), Kardinal Johannes Gropper, 1503–1559, und die Anfänge der katholischen Reform in Deutschland, Münster: Aschendorff.

LIPGENS, WALTER (1966), Gropper, Johannes, NDB 7, Berlin, 133–136.

MAISSEN, THOMAS (2015), Thomas Erastus und der Erastianismus. Der innerreformierte Streit um die Kirchendisziplin in der Kurpfalz, in: Christoph Strohm/Jan Stievermann (ed.), Profil und Wirkung des Heidelberger Katechismus. Neue Forschungsbeiträge anlässlich des 450jährigen Jubiläums. The Heidelberg Catechism: Origins, Characteristics, and Influences. Essays in Reappraisal on the Occasion of its 450th Anniversary, SVRG 215, Gütersloh: Gütersloher Verlagshaus, 189–206.

MEIER, JOHANNES (1977), Der priesterliche Dienst nach Johannes Gropper (1503–1559). Der Beitrag eines deutschen Theologen zur Erneuerung des Priesterbildes im Rahmen eines vortridentinischen Reformkonzeptes für die kirchliche Praxis, RST 113, Münster: Aschendorff.

MEIER, JOHANNES (2018), Johannes Gropper (1503–1559) – Theologie für eine Erneuerung der Praxis der Kirche, Archiv für mittelrheinische Kirchengeschichte 70, 127–146.

ORTMANN, VOLKMAR (2001), Reformation und Einheit der Kirche. Martin Bucers Einigungsbemühungen bei den Religionsgesprächen in Leipzig, Hagenau, Worms und Regensburg 1539–1541, VIEG 185, Mainz: Von Zabern.

SCHLÜTER, THEODOR C. (2005), Flug- und Streitschriften zur "Kölner Reformation". Die Publizistik um den Reformationsversuch des Kölner Erzbischofs und Kurfürsten Hermann von Wied (1515–1547), Buchwissenschaftliche Beiträge aus dem Deutschen Bucharchiv München, 73, Wiesbaden: Harrassowitz.

STROHM, CHRISTOPH (2002), Die Berufung auf kanonisches Recht, römisches Recht und Reichsrecht in der Auseinandersetzung um die Kölner Reformation 1543–1546, in: Christoph Strohm/Henning P. Jürgens (ed.), Martin Bucer und das Recht. Beiträge zum internationalen Symposium in der Johannes a Lasco Bibliothek Emden vom 1. bis 3. März 2001, THR 361, Genf: Librairie Droz, 123–145.

STROHM, CHRISTOPH (2016), Martin Bucer und die südwestdeutsche Reformationsgeschichte, in: Christoph Strohm/Thomas Wilhelmi (ed.), Martin Bucer, der dritte deutsche Reformator. Zum Ertrag der Edition der Deutschen Schriften Martin Bucers, Akademiekonferenzen, 26, Heidelberg: Winter, 29–51.

STROHM, CHRISTOPH (2017), Die produktive Kraft konfessioneller Konkurrenz für die Rechtsentwicklung, in: Christoph Strohm (ed.), Reformation und Recht. Zur Kontroverse um die Kulturwirkungen der Reformation, Tübingen: Mohr Siebeck, 131–171.

VARRENTRAPP, CONRAD (1878), Hermann von Wied und sein Reformationsversuch in Köln. Ein Beitrag zur deutschen Reformationsgeschichte, Leipzig: Duncker & Humblot.

VERMEULEN, ADEODATUS (1954), Der Augustiner Konrad Treger. Die Jahre seines Provinzialates, 1518–1542, Nijmegen: Institutum Historicum OESA.

WRIGHT, DAVID F. (2002), Martin Bucer and the Decretum Gratiani, in: Christoph Strohm/ Henning P. Jürgens (ed.), Martin Bucer und das Recht. Beiträge zum internationalen Symposium in der Johannes a Lasco Bibliothek Emden vom 1. bis 3. März 2001, THR 361, Genf: Librairie Droz, 102–121.

ZSCHOCH, HELLMUT (1997), Treger, Konrad, BBKL 12, Herzberg, 438–442.

ZUMKELLER, ADOLAR (1988), Konrad Treger OESA (ca. 1480–1542), in: Erwin Iserloh (ed.), Katholische Theologen der Reformationszeit, vol. 5, Münster: Aschendorff, 74–87.

Willem van Vlastuin

Calvin's un-Augustinian concept of Catholicity

Introduction

In the ecclesiastical debate of the Reformation, the appeal to Augustine was an important issue as the representatives of the medieval church used this appeal to legitimise the continuity and historical unity of the church. But it was also important for the representatives of the Reformation to be able to appeal to Augustine to prove that the Reformation did not want to establish a new church, but to assert that the church of the Middle Ages had deviated from its old track.[1] It is telling that Calvin quoted Augustine more than two thousand times.

In this contribution I focus on the concept of Catholicity and strive to answer the research question: how did Calvin's concept of Catholicity relate to that of Augustine? In answer, I outline the contours of Augustine's concept of Catholicity and describe Calvin's concept of Catholicity[2] in order to make a comparison between both theologians and draw a conclusion.

1. Augustine's concept of Catholicity

1.1 Universal Catholicity

When Augustine returned from Milan to Africa, he came across a small Catholic Church opposite a large church of Donatists.[3] Yet, he did not choose the church of the Donatists, because unity was too dear to him. God "create(d) two separate beings, male and female, but one man; and from this one man He made woman. Why did He do this? Why did He begin the human race from one man, if not to commend unity to mankind?"[4]

---

1 For previous research about Augustine in the Reformation, cf. Burger (2005) and Visser (2011).
2 Both descriptions refer to the chapters on Augustine and Calvin in Vlastuin: 2020, 45–58, 85–100.
3 P. Brown wrote: "So his writings against the Donatists will mark a final stage in the evolution of Early Christian ideas on the church, and its relation with society as a whole" (1967, 217). Cf. about Augustine's ecclesiology Mara (2007) and Noordmans (1981). Anti-Donatist writings by Augustine are found in Migne, *Patrologia Latina* 43.
4 Sermo 268.3. For the references to Augustine I used http://www.augustinus.it/latino/index.htm (accessed on September 28, 2020).

It should be noted that Augustine's participation in the international church of Christ convinced him that the issue of Donatism was a regional problem. A scrupulous zeal to preserve one's own identity was not congruent with his understanding of Catholicity, "The clouds roll with thunder that the House of the Lord shall be built throughout the earth; and these frogs sit in their marsh and croak, 'We are the only Christians!'"[5]

Augustine wrote these words in his treatise about Psalm 96. In this Psalm, God's dominion over the whole of creation and all nations is praised prophetically. So, the universal character of the church was clearly a given in the Scripture.

We also find telling sayings in his explanation of Psalm 22:27–28 which speaks of "all the ends of the earth" which will repent, and God's kingdom among all nations.[6] Augustine says that the Donatists limit these texts. All the ends of the earth, all the generations and all the kingdoms were bought by Christ, rather than just the province of Africa or Mauritania. Whereas Christ calls to the ends of the earth, Donatus limits his call to only a part of Christianity.

According to Augustine, the Donatists say, "Keep what you have: you have your sheep, I have mine. Leave my sheep in peace as I leave yours." Here we learn that the Donatists handle the church as if it was their own possession. They think in terms of allotment and groups, so that one part belongs to one group, and the other part to another group, as if the church is the possession of people and groups.

That is why Augustine writes the meaningful words:

> You split up the unity, you seek for possessions of your own. And why have they the name of Christ attached to them? Because to guarantee your own property you have affixed to it the title of Christ […] Similarly with those who possess the baptism of Christ; if they return to unity, we do not change or destroy their title, but we acknowledge the title of our King, the title of our Commander. What are we to say? O wretched patrimony, let Him whose title you bear own you; you bear the title of Christ, do not be the property of Donatus.[7]

1.2 Holy Catholicity

But didn't the church father have to recognise the holiness claim of the Donatists? Didn't the Donatists have a point when they criticised the yielding of the *tradi-*

---

5 Augustine: *Enarrationes in Psalmos* 95.11.
6 Augustine: *Enarrationes in Psalmos* 21.27–28.
7 Augustine: *Enarrationes in Psalmos* 21.31.

tors? Augustine did indeed consider the *traditor* to be a criminal, but he saw the schismatic as a worse criminal.[8]

Just like the Donatists, Augustine drew a sharp distinction between God's church and the world. However, Augustine had seen the destructive consequences that occurred when people drew a dividing line. That is why the mystery of invisible predestination is just as important in the conflict with the Donatists as it was in the debate with Pelagius.

For Augustine the starting point of the holiness of the church was not in the holy members, but in the holiness of the Word and in the effect of the sacraments. That is why holiness in the church preceded the holiness of the members, and why he accepted sinners in the church.

Moreover, believers continually receive remission of sins in the community of the church. When Augustine, in his sermon about confession, says that baptism is like the Red Sea, in which all the enemies were drowned, he continues:

> But since we are destined to live in this world where no one lives without sin, on that account the remission of sin depends not solely on the washing in holy baptism but also on the Lord's Prayer that you will receive after eight days. In that prayer you will receive, as it were, your daily baptism, so that you may give thanks to God who has given to his church this gift that we acknowledge in the creed. Thus, when we have said, 'I believe in the holy church', let us add, 'and in the remission of sins'.[9]

So, for Augustine it is essential that, in the creed, the church precedes the remission of sins, because the remission of sins continually takes place in the community of the church.

In making this point, an important decision is also made about the nature of the church. In contrast to the Donatists, this means that the world is not only outside the church, but also inside it. Where the Donatists, in fact, deny there is chaff amongst the wheat, for Augustine, this point is fundamental and vital to his understanding of the church.

This approach makes his attitude towards the church a very realistic one. When Augustine tells beginners in the Christian faith to persevere on the narrow way to eternal life and to be on the alert for temptations, he says that they should be most on their guard for temptations in the church, where they would encounter drunkards, misers, fraudsters, gamblers, adulterers and superstitious people.[10]

---

8 'Si traditio Codicum scelerata est […], quanto sceleratius est sacrilegium schismatis', Augustine: Epistola 76.4.
9 Augustine: Sermo 213.9.
10 Augustine: *De catechizandis rudibus* 25.48.

Apparently, the Bishop of Hippo cared deeply for the multitude and wanted to share the Gospel with them. He did not consider sinners in their position as sinners, but considered how the Gospel could renew them. Augustine reasons more from the potential of Word and Spirit, than he does from the church as a closed institution where the Spirit resides. For Augustine, Catholicity arises from the authority of the Gospel, because the Word of God is the source and the mark of real Catholicity.

1.3 Christological Catholicity

This 'people's church' approach raises the question: how did Augustine deal with the high title of the church as the body of Christ? Can the church still be seen as an ark of salvation? Is baptism a seal of the forgiveness of sins, or does the church degrade into an institution for evangelisation?

We begin to understand his thoughts if we look again at the quotation from the preceding section about the Creed in which faith in the church is mentioned.[11] There he states that we believe *in* the church. This is an intriguing expression because this approach can be used to place belief *in* the church on the same level as believing *in* the Father, the Son and the Holy Spirit (cf. Beek: 2012, 186–191, 392, 420).

Augustine's speaking about faith *in* the church becomes even deeper when we are made aware of the fact that, with respect to the relationship between Christ and His body, he spoke of *totus Christus* (cf. Bavel (2011)). With this in mind, he can say that the whole Christ is made from the church which is added to His flesh.[12] So, speaking about the church is speaking about Christ, and vice versa.[13] This approach reveals that the church is God's work, but is also the body of Christ. It shows us that we should speak about the church in a sacramental manner, because Christ Himself is present.

Do his words about faith *in* the church imply that we believe in the church just as we believe in the Father, the Son and the Holy Spirit? When we look at the church father's explanation, it becomes clear that he characterises the church as the wife of the great heavenly Bridegroom. This is how the church, according to Augustine, is the mother of all believers. Whilst this does confirm the importance of the church, it does not imply that the church must be put on the same level as the Trinity.

This is confirmed when we look at a different sermon about the creed by the Bishop of Hippo where it becomes clear that he does not attach much value to the

---

11 Augustine: Sermo 213.8–9.

12 The church father wrote above his explanation of John 5:20–23, "Gratulemur et agamus gratias, non solum nos christianos factos esse, sed Christum," Augustine: In Evangelium Ioannis, tractatus 21. In the first sermon about the epistle to John he wrote, "Illi carni adiungitur Ecclesia, et fit Christus totus, caput et corpus," *In Epistolam Joannis ad Parthos*, tractatus 1.2.

13 Augustine: *Enarrationes in Psalmos* 30.2, 4. Compare also *Enarrationes in Psalmos* 140.3.

expression "believing *in* the church". He does not use the words *in ecclesiam*, but *per ecclesiam*.[14] Although the way to salvation is the way of the church, there is a clear distinction drawn between the Trinity and the church. Speaking about the church as only having an instrumental function obviously isn't adequate, but there remains a clear distinction between the Son and the Holy Spirit on the one hand, and the church on the other.

1.4 Pneumatological Catholicity

Besides this, Augustine's broad 'people's church' approach did not detract at all from this view of the church as the temple of the Holy Spirit. Just like earlier church fathers, Augustine was very much aware of the indwelling of the Spirit in God's church. So, those who are outside the church, do not have the Holy Spirit.[15] In this context, Augustine uses the metaphor of body and soul. The whole of the body is indwelled by one spirit,

> What our spirit, that is our soul, is to the parts or members of our body, that the Holy Spirit is to the members of Christ, to the Body of Christ, the Church. […] Is this Body alive? It's alive. What with? With one Spirit. […] So consider, brothers and sisters, the case of our own bodies, and grieve for those who cut themselves off from the church. […] But now, if a member is cut off from the body, the spirit doesn't follow, does it? And yet the member can be recognised for what it is; it's a finger, a hand, an arm, an ear. Apart from the body it retains its shape, it doesn't retain life.

For the church father, the presence of the Spirit in the church is connected with love, which he explains in an Ascension Day sermon.[16] It is very clear to him that the indwelling of the Spirit is inseparably connected with love and that one cannot have love outside the church, because one does not have the Spirit outside the church. Those who cut themselves off from the church are natural people without the Spirit. With this in mind, we can understand his zeal for unity, because he believed the Donatists outside the church to be without the Spirit and without salvation.

In the controversy with the Donatists, it becomes clear how seriously Calvin took love. After years of tensions and complications between Donatists and Catholics, a public conference was held in 411, at which 286 Catholic bishops were present and 279 Donatist bishops. The Catholics won the debate. One might have expected Augustine to say that the Donatists must give up their offices. But the very opposite

---

14 Augustine: Sermo 215.9.
15 Augustine: Sermo 268.2.
16 Augustine: Sermo 265.

was true. If there were two bishops in a certain town or city, the Catholic bishop would withdraw in favour of the Donatist bishop.

In this way, Augustine shows us that we must not simply assume that God connects His blessing to our holiness, but that He gives His blessing where brethren dwell in unity (Ps 133). In this approach we can also see that Augustine does not treat the schismatic Donatists as heretics, because they have the same faith, the same Scriptures and the same sacraments. Nevertheless they do lack Catholicity and love.

Augustine does not make it a theological principle, but here an opening is given to a broader pneumatology. He says that there are many wolves inside the church and many sheep outside it.[17] Firstly, this means that the Spirit is not bound to the church in an absolute sense. Secondly, we can see that a lot of attention is given to individual persons.[18] Thirdly, it means that the actual characteristics of the *ecclesia catholica* are of a spiritual nature. This underscores his belief that the church is a temple of the Holy Spirit.

To summarise: in this approach the church father emphasises that the Spirit focuses on unity. Whomever is in the Christian church and is not focused on this unity, does not have the Holy Spirit, and therefore sins against the Holy Spirit. Augustine even describes this as unforgiveable blasphemy against the Spirit, the greatest sin.[19]

1.5 Assessment

What should we conclude about Augustine's idea of Catholicity? Firstly, it is striking that the principle of universality is essential. Secondly, the indwelling of the Holy Spirit in the Catholic Church is very important to Augustine. He emphasises that this is what makes the church a living spiritual reality, especially in the exercise of love. This also influences his understanding of the validity of baptism. Augustine stresses that Christ lives together with sinners in His church, so that, on the one hand, the remaining remission of sin also functions within the church, and on the other hand, we cannot say that the church is without sin. Another aspect is that Augustine connects the hidden election with his understanding of the church – without the Catholic Church evaporating into an invisible reality.

---

17 Augustine: *In Iohannis evangelium*, tractatus 45.12. In *De baptismo* V.27.38 Augustine also writes that many who seem to be without are in reality within, and many who seem to be within yet really are without.
18 Augustine: *Soliloquia* 1.2.7.
19 Augustine: Sermo 71.33–38.

2. John Calvin's concept of Catholicity

2.1 Personal Catholicity

As Calvin gave his own description of Catholicity, we will choose this as our starting point:

> For unless we are united with all the other members under Christ our head, no hope of the future inheritance awaits us. Hence the Church is called Catholic or Universal [Aug. Ep. 48], for two or three [churches, WvV] cannot be invented without dividing Christ; and this is impossible. All the elect of God are so joined together in Christ, that as they depend on one head, so they are as it were compacted into one body, being knit together like its different members; made truly one by living together under the same Spirit of God in one faith, hope, and charity, called not only to the same inheritance of eternal life, but to participation in one God and Christ [*Institutes* 4.1.2].

This interpretation of Catholicity leads one to make a number of observations. Firstly, Calvin chooses spiritual communion with Christ as the starting point of his understanding of Catholicity. This enables him to interpret the church from its invisible dimension; a dimension which is based on the hidden election.[20] This is also clear from the beginning of the section in which the quotation about Catholicity was taken from. With respect to the confession of the church, "reference is made not only to the visible Church of which we are now treating, but also to all the elect of God, including in the number even those who have departed this life". In this expression we hear that most of the words about the church actually relate to the invisible church.

This information reveals that Calvin, in the end, chooses the starting point for developing his view of the church in the invisible church and the personal relationship with Christ (cf. Plasger: 2009, 323).[21] That this is his starting point is further confirmed by the structure of the *Institutes*. It is striking that Calvin deals with the doctrine of the church in the fourth volume, in the context of "the external means or helps by which God invites us to fellowship with Christ, and keeps us in it". According to G. Plasger (2009, 323), this indicates that Calvin divided the Apostles' Creed over the four volumes of the *Institutes*. He discusses the work of

---

[20] It is telling that Calvin, also in the *Catechism of Geneva* primarily defines the church from God's election, cf. Q. 93. In Question 100 he emphasises, once again, that the article about the church is actually about the church of election.

[21] D.G. Butner (2016, 238) emphasises that Calvin speaks of the election in Christ, and thus of the election of the one Person in Christ. These notions in *Institutes* 3.22.1–2 do not detract from the character of personal election.

the Holy Spirit as a unity in the third volume, and does not define the church from only the perspective of the Holy Spirit. This definition certainly has substantive consequences.

Firstly, it must be pointed out that the church, when defined in this way, is treated as an instrument. So, for Calvin, it is not a question about whether we can speak of faith *in* the church (*Institutes* 4.1.2). He explicitly rejects this interpretation. Where Calvin's structural order gives the church a position as serving the body of Christ, Augustine called the body of Christ the church and vice versa.

Secondly, this change in structure has consequences for the relationship between church and remission. According to Calvin, in the Apostles' Creed, the forgiveness of sins is placed in the context of the church, so we can speak about forgiveness without mentioning the church. The forgiveness of sins becomes something between God and the individual person.[22] Although external means such as the church, sacraments and preaching are necessary, there is much more emphasis placed on the individual's relationship with God, at the expense of the corporative aspect of the church.

Undoubtedly, this approach reveals a criticism of the absolutising of the power of the church of the Middle Ages (cf. Oberman: 2009b, 998; Spijker: 2009). While all the emphasis was placed on the external and visible church in the Middle Ages, this Reformed theologian emphasised its invisibility.

Moreover, the approach from the invisible church enabled an attacked church to be recognised as the church. Although Calvin, personally, served in the great city church of Geneva, he was aware that many Protestants were 'divided and dispersed' (*Institutes* 4.1.9). In Calvin's days there were many refugees who fled to Geneva and other places (Neuser: 1990, 7). Oberman (2009a, 177–194) speaks of the "Reformation of the Refugees". In this context, the comfort of God's election shone forth (Oberman: 2003, 111–115).

This also indicates that Calvin's considerations emanate from his belief in the universality of the church, namely the totality of often insignificant and vulnerable local churches (cf. De Boer: 2016, 12ff). As an ecumenical theologian, Calvin made a "heroic effort to unite the Protestants in the dispersion" under one church roof (Noordmans: 1986a, 403).

At the same time, when we consider Calvin's understanding of Catholicity, we must take into account the cultural context. The Reformation was part of a culture in transition, where a turn was taking place to the subject (Taylor: 2007, 146); in this respect, Calvin was a child of his time. Bavinck also notices this development in a religious sense, "The Reformation – deliberately and freely – took its position

---

22 According to B. Gordon (2016, 145), in this way Calvin facilitated individualism in the protestant tradition.

in the religious subject, in the faith of the Christian, in the testimony of the Holy Spirit" (Bavinck: 2003, 1:583, cf. Kooi: 2008).

Calvin also considered the corporate aspect of Christ's body. For example, in Calvin's exegesis of Ephesians 1:23 we find him speaking of *totus Christus* when he says that Christ, in a sense, is not complete without believers. The fourth volume of the *Institutes* places the external aids within the framework of the communion with Christ. On the other hand, the personal focus of salvation was clearly present in the Early Church, so this was not new in the Reformation.

2.2 Catholic unity

This perspective – of the individual toward the visible church could be seen as a source of the fragmentation of the church. But, for Calvin, it did not function like that at all. From the perspective of hidden election and Christ's hidden body, the meaning of the visible local church is highlighted (Wendel: 1997, 296). It is the believers' precious calling to give form to this unity; visible form too. There is a striking sentence in the *Institutes,* which connects the invisible church to the visible church: "Moreover, this article of the Creed relates in some measure to the external church" (*Institutes* 4.1.3). Again, it is clear that Calvin actually applies the article from the Creed to the invisible church, but that, from the invisible church, something can be said of the visible church.

There is a distinction between the visible and invisible church, but this distinction cannot be made too great. In any case, there cannot be an opposition between the visible and the visible church, although some tension remains. The direction of thinking is clear: from the invisible to the visible church; from the spiritual reality of the church to the visible revelation of the church. This also implies that the visible church, "in some measure" has the same importance as the invisible church, so the importance of the visible church is clearly emphasised. In other words: it is certainly not true that the visible church is less important than the invisible church.

This connection between the invisible and visible church places an enormous claim on the unity of the church. Calvin, in his exegesis of Ephesians 4:4 is decisive in his emphasis that there is no eternal life if we do not live in unity in this world. God regards an individual who alienates themselves from any Christian society as a "deserter of religion" (*Institutes* 4.1.10). Calvin can be so decisive because he is not speaking of a high human ideal, but of Christ Himself, of His body.[23] If one loses sight of the unity in Christ, one is also vulnerable to heresy and schism (*Institutes* 4.2.6).

---

23 In this context, Hesselink (2010, 70) says decisively, "His commitment to the unity of the church was not despite his high view of the church, but precisely because of it!"

It is clear that Calvin was sincere. When he was banished from Geneva (Niesel: 1957, 196), the people who had supported him and his policy, planned to stop participating in the Lord's Supper. Calvin, however, admonished them to do so, despite the broken situation in Geneva.

Another effect of this way of thinking, is Calvin's effort to reach agreement in theology. He took part in the colloquies of Hagenau, Worms and Regensburg (Stolk: 2004) where, for the sake of the unity of the mediaeval church, he was willing to speak of a justification of our works.[24] Unfortunately, this Catholic attitude did not have the desired result as demonstrated at the Council of Trent, where the reformatory approach was rejected. In any case, Calvin had done his utmost to reach agreement. He had shown his willingness to compromise.

This was also how he conversed with all Protestants. He was friends with Melanchthon, even though they did not agree about free will and divine predestination and, despite some reservations, he also supported Melanchthon's *Confessio Augustana*. He also came to an agreement with Bullinger concerning the Lord's Supper (*Consensus Tigurinus*) – even though they held very different views concerning election and reprobation.

We should also mention Calvin's boundless efforts on behalf of the Waldensians, when terrible massacres took place among them. He wrote to Archbishop Cranmer that he looked forward to organising an ecumenical-Protestant council to devise a confession that would be acceptable to all Protestants, saying, among other things:

> It is to be reckoned among the worst evils of our day that the churches are so ripped apart that the holy communion of Christ's members, which all profess with the mouth, is sincerely practised only by a few. [...] Thus it comes to pass that, the members being divided, the body of the Church lies down as if it has been ripped apart. Respecting myself, if it should appear that I could be of any use, it would not be hard for me even to cross ten oceans if necessary. [...] With respect to such an important matter, namely the agreement of learned men, according to the rule of Scripture rightly assembled, by which the Churches, which are now so far away from each other, would grow together and be united, I think it would be unlawful for me to spare any labour or trouble to effect it.[25]

Calvin did not write this in the context of divided Reformed denominations, of course, but in regard to the lack of unity between the different local, regional or national churches (Wendel: 1997, 310). In summation, we can conclude that Calvin acted like a 'bridge builder'.

---

24 In a letter to Farel, 11 May 1541. Cf. Lane: 2002, 46–60; 2004a; 2004b.
25 Calvin: *Calvini Opera* 14:314.

2.3 Catholic Reformed

This existential concern, and boundless striving, for the unity of the church as the expression of the one body of Christ, raises the question: how could Calvin account for the existence of the church besides the mediaeval church? A question which becomes even more urgent when we realise that Calvin was not averse to tradition in an Anabaptist sense. Moreover, one could not hurt him more deeply than by saying that he was responsible for schisms (cf. Nauta: 2009).

When we study this at greater depth, the *doctrina* (doctrine) turns out to be of vital importance.[26] Calvin accuses the church of the Middle Ages of having forsaken the Word by appealing to the Spirit (Calvin: 2002, 35).[27] So Calvin not only accuses the fanatics of having broken the bond of Word and Spirit, but he also says that Rome is to blame. An appeal to the Spirit without the Word leads to error and heresy, sect and schism.

This belief brings him to give the following description of the church, in his famous reply to Cardinal Sadolet,

> Now, if you can bear to receive a truer definition of the Church than your own, say, in future, that it is the society of all the saints, a society which, spread over the whole world, and existing in all ages, yet bound together by the one doctrine, and the one Spirit of Christ, cultivates and observes unity of faith and brotherly accord. (Calvin: 2002, 37)

This quotation shows that unity in Christ is defined by the doctrine of Christ. Calvin's well known exegesis of Acts 2:42 states that what the soul is to the body, doctrine is to the body of Christ.[28] It is not very easy to explain what Calvin means by doctrine. It is clear though that he certainly does not understand doctrine in an absolutely systematic or rational sense. We can say that he consciously considers the doctrine which is confessed to be of greatest importance (Hesselink: 2010, 75n23). In this way, he can also reject and reverse the accusation of schism. It

---

26 "But the most serious charge of all is, that we have attempted to dismember the Spouse of Christ" (Calvin: 2002, 66; Nijenhuis: 1959, 231, 272).

27 Compare other expressions in Calvin: 2002, 50: "In fine, ours the Church, whose supreme care it is humbly and religiously to venerate the word of God, and submit to its authority." See also (2002, 52) "Hence, I observe, Sadolet, that you have too indolent a theology, as is almost always the case with those who have never had experience in serious struggles of conscience." Calvin can also say, "For such is our consciousness of the truth of our doctrine, that it has no dread of the heavenly Judge, from whom, we doubt not, that is proceeded", (2002, 55). According to W. Nijenhuis (2009, 956), Calvin's letter to Sadolet provides his deepest view of the unity of the church. According to Calvin's analysis, the Romana is sectarian (1959, 273).

28 Cf. Calvin: 2002, 57f: "Always, both by word and deed, have I protested how eager I was for unity [...] I behoved to purchase it with the denial of thy truth."

was not the reformers who created the schism, but the mediaeval church when it separated itself from the Early Church in such an 'uncatholic' way (Nijenhuis: 1959, 231). He accuses Sadolet, as a representative of the mediaeval church, of elevating the traditions of men above Christ, as a result of which the church has become corrupted (Calvin: 2002, 41). This corruption is particularly in evidence in regard to the confession of justification by faith, in which the glory of Christ shines forth brightly (Calvin: 2002, 41).

Although Calvin could be mild with respect to differences in doctrine, the deviations in the church of the Middle Ages were nevertheless important to him, "Nay, even in the administration of word and sacraments defects may creep in which ought not to alienate us from its communion" (*Institutes* 4.1.12).[29] In the same breath, he adds: "for all the heads of true doctrine are not in the same position." For him it is essential to have agreement about faith in God, God's Son and the absoluteness of God's grace, but there may be differences of opinion about the place of souls after this life. In a reply to Joachim Westphal, Calvin also mentions the doctrine of depravity, the manner of justification, the offices of Christ, repentance and its exercises, and faith and prayer as unity-creating practices (Hesselink: 2010, 88). According to Calvin, the controversy with Rome, however, was about giving up the full Christ,[30] and making him choose between Rome and Christ (*Institutes* 4.2.6).

Calvin, however, maintained his ambivalent attitude towards the Church of Rome. He did not completely write it off, because he recognised traces and remnants of the church within it. He recognised that there are "churches" in the Roman-Catholic Church, where, locally, justice is done to the Word of God, but considering the "the whole body, as well as every single assembly, [...] the form of a legitimate Church" is wanting (*Institutes* 4.2.12; Hesselink: 2010, 78).[31]

Where the Church of Rome can be seen to be moving away from the Early Church, the reformation movement, on the contrary, intends only "to renew that ancient form of the Church" (Calvin: 2002, 37).[32] In fact this indicates that Catholicity implies historicity and apostolicity, and that reformation is mainly restoration (Nijenhuis: 1959, 231). Just like Luther, Calvin did not intend to form a new church, but to reform the Catholic Church. He did not place himself outside the Catholic

---

[29] In Calvin: *Institutes* 4.1.13–16 Calvin shows that even serious defects are not reason enough for leaving the church (Cf. Wendel: 1997, 310f).

[30] Cf. commentary to Gal. 1:5. See also Calvin: *Institutes* 4.2.2; 4.6–9.

[31] A restoration of the Romana is not impossible (Walker: 1984, 216).

[32] Calvin concludes (2002, 49): "Expostulate with us, if you can, for the injury which we inflicted on the Catholic Church, by daring to violate its sacred sanctions [...] in all these points, the ancient Church is clearly on our side, and opposes you." See also (2002, 37): "Our agreement with antiquity is far closer than yours."

Church, but he implicitly refuted the claim that the Church of Rome was Catholic. That is why Calvin called on people to distance themselves from the numerous mediaeval renewals and join the true Catholic Church of all times (Calvin: 2001).

2.4 Qualitative Catholicity

Calvin did not make much effort to encourage use of the term Catholicity (Lane: 2012, 225). This is striking since he was himself Catholic in his agreement with the Apostles' Creed, the Nicene Creed, and the Athanasian Creed, all three of which use the term 'Catholic'.

Perhaps Calvin does not use the term Catholicity because he is afraid of being identified with the mediaeval church. But this suspicion does not seem to be grounded. If it were true, the Reformer would have decided not to formally use the word 'Catholic', but would have paid a great deal of attention to its substance. But the opposite is true. When we investigate the extent to which Calvin used the theologians from the Early Church's considerations about Catholicity, we discover that Calvin does not quote the views of Ignatius, Cyprian or Cyril on Catholicity at all (Cf. Lane: 1999, 55–61).

This reinforces the idea that Calvin was not especially interested in Catholicity. But this is not the whole story. Although Calvin interpreted the term Catholicity mainly quantitatively and geographically, Calvin's qualitative perspective sheds a surprising light on the Catholic character of the whole of Calvin's theology.[33] In this sense, Calvin was more Catholic than he realised.

As the qualitative aspect of Catholicity relates to the fullness in Christ and His gracious dominion, it is not hard to discover Calvin's Catholicity.[34] Even though there may be some historical nuances when speaking of the solas of the Reformation, substantively nothing is wrong with characterising the theology of the Reformation using these terms. Calvin wanted to go back to the Catholic fullness in Christ and that is why *solus Christus* was a reality to him. Because of the *solus Christus*, the *sola scriptura, sola gratia* and *sola fide* also functioned in his beliefs.

From this perspective, the break with Rome was a lot more final than we might have concluded from the preceding section. Calvin was not only concerned with individual doctrinal points, but with the whole structure of the church. The reality

---

33 I use the word 'geographically' in a different sense than Noordmans, who uses it with respect to the church's connection to a certain city such as Rome, Jerusalem or Geneva (Kooi: 1992, 284f).
34 According to W. Balke (1990, 277) Calvin is "the greatest Catholic thinker from the history of the church". H. Berkhof (1962, 105) said, "Calvin was a Catholic thinker par excellence." Berkhof elaborates this mainly by referring to the dominion of Christ in the church and the world. In this sense, this view of Calvin is at odds with his analysis that, in Reformed circles, a qualitative understanding of Catholicity was never developed, 19.

of a living Christ, who reigns over His church Himself, is contrary to a structure which has a pope as a successor of Christ who is in control (Noordmans: 1986a, 399, 401, 406, cf. Noordmans: 1986b; Kooi: 1992, 287, 291).

This personal dominion of Christ also sheds light on the cohesion between Word and Spirit. It is Christ, Who personally uses the Word and Spirit to feed His body. This underlines Christ's liberty, in comparison to a *presentia realis* which is bound to matter or historical forms. This liberty also implies great dynamics for the church. We might speak of a 'coming to pass' of the church, because the gracious presence of God is not an automatism or possession.

From the perspective that Christ commands the Word to be preached, it also becomes clear why Calvin concentrated on the main points of the doctrine. By doing so, he expressed the Word-structure of the church which is made effective by the Spirit in the life of the congregation. Zillenberg (1993, 140–143, 150f) thinks that Calvin's focus on doctrine is new with respect to the Early Church. There is, indeed, a difference with Augustine. Whereas Augustine mentions the Spirit and love as the soul of Christ's body, Calvin mentions doctrine (*Institutes* 1.11.13; cf. Lane: 1999, 50; Noordmans: 1986c, 439). The explicit way in which Calvin expresses the Word-structure of the church is new. However, we cannot conclude from this that the focus on doctrine is completely new.

This is also clear from the substantive aspects that Calvin discusses. In the articles about God, the Trinity, the creation, providence, predestination and eschatology, hardly any changes are made. While the Early Church emphasised the doctrine of creation, the resurrection of Christ and of believers, these things are not spearheads for Calvin. As these concepts were not so contentious in the church of the Middle Ages, there was also great continuity with mediaeval theology (Muller: 2000; 2003a; 2003b; Steinmetz: 1999; Asselt: 2001). This continuity also existed in the scholastic way of reasoning. In Calvin's writings, numerous philosophical nuances and distinctions can be found (McGrath: 1993, 47). In the understanding of the Reformation, the doctrine of Christ *was* actually at stake in ecclesiology and soteriology, and with respect to the doctrine of the sacraments. All these doctrines concerned the glory of Christ which was why the Reformation focused on them.

Calvin speaks of justification and sanctification to do justice to the Catholic fullness in Christ. It is characteristic of him to speak often in word couples: Law and Gospel, Word and Spirit, election and responsibility, procuring and effecting, inward and outward, church and state. For him, this *complexion oppositorum* is an expression of a high unity in Christ.

This exploration of the Christocentric character of Calvin's theology shows that his Catholicity is primarily an anonymous Catholicity. Instead of consciously claiming Catholicity, he practices Catholicity by living and theologising from the fullness in Christ. In a Catholic way, he does not limit Christ's dominion to the soul but believes that all areas of life are under His dominion.

2.5 Assessment

At the end of this investigation, we weigh Calvin's attitude. Calvin bases Catholicity on the spiritual unity in Christ. At the same time, his awareness of the heavenly Christ is his main reason for interpreting the church from Him.

The individualisation of modern times handed Calvin a concept which was manageable in his context. Instead of starting from a visible Catholicity, by starting from the invisible unity with Christ, he could continue to speak of an invisible Catholicity. In this way, the reformation of the church could be accounted for, in contrast to a rigid visible Catholicity.

Catholicity was mainly used as an expression of universality, without any explicit attention being given to the qualitative concept of the fullness of the Christian faith. At the same time, this qualitative concept of Catholicity appears to be present in Calvin's writings. Calvin seeks unity and truth in Christ. His lifelong dedication to true doctrine and his striving for unity can be understood as a passion for Christ. In this sense, his formula would not have been that we seek unity in truth, but truth and unity in Christ. Just as sanctification is not a fruit of justification but, like justification, a reality in the communion with Christ, we cannot separate truth from Christ.

3. Comparison, Consideration and Conclusion

If we compare Calvin's concept of Catholicity to Augustine's concept, we see several similarities. Both theologians' reasoning is based on the universality of the church. Although it was an explicit theme in Augustine, it was implicitly present in Calvin's approach. Both theologians have a deep conviction that Christ is the head and the owner of the church. Augustine makes this explicit in his attack of the Donatists who understood themselves to be the owners of the church, while it was one of the deepest issues of contention between Calvin and the representatives of the Middle Age church. The church father and the reformer also agree on the relativisation of the office-bearers in the church, while stressing the authority of God's Word. Both theologians interpreted the church as the body of Christ and could use the concept of *totus Christus*. For both thinkers, accepting this concept did not mean that there was a massive sinless church. Their rejection of this ecclesiology cohered with their distinction between belief in God and belief in the church. Although neither of them absolutised the church as the temple of the Spirit, both church leaders understood the church as the Spirit's temple. Their emphasis on the Spirit, also gave both leaders a sensitivity to God's hidden election and the invisible dimension of the church; both leaders also had a zeal for the visible unity of the church.

Although there are contextual differences between Augustine's and Calvin's interpretation of the Catholicity of the church, these do not really separate them from each other. Augustine focuses a lot on the multitude, while Calvin ignores it. But Augustine's focus on the multitude is related to his particular historical context. Because of Donatist's claim that office-bearers and members of the church should be holy, Augustine emphasised the transformative power of Word and Spirit. Even Augustine's focus on love as an effect of the Spirit and Calvin's focus on the Christian doctrine do not exclude the other's position, because the indwelling of the Spirit in the church has different applications in different situations. For Augustine it was relevant to apply the indwelling of the Spirit to the love of the members for one another, while the Spirit was important for Calvin because he leads in all truth. This is also true for Calvin's implicit Catholicity, because it can be explained and justified in some way by its historical context.

Despite these comparable ecclesiological patrons, on a deeper level there is also a profound difference in ecclesiological structure, because Calvin structurally reverses the relationship of the church and forgiveness. Augustine put forgiveness in the context of the church, while the Augustinian theologian Calvin dealt with forgiveness independently of the church. Where Augustine thought about the individual from the position of the visible corporate unity, Calvin thinks about the visible church from the position of the invisible relationship between Christ and the individual. Augustine could reflect on the invisible election in the framework of the visible church, while Calvin treated the invisible election before he reflected on the church as a means of keeping believers in communion with Christ. So, Calvin treated the visible church ultimately in the context of the individual election.

Despite his appeal to the Early Church and his desire to furnish church life in continuity with the Early Church, Calvin changed the understanding of Catholicity. While Augustine understood Catholicity to be primarily concerned about the visible church, Calvin applied Catholicity primarily to the invisible church. We have to conclude, therefore, that Calvin had an un-Augustinian understanding of the concept of Catholicity.

Bibliography

Asselt, Willem J./Dekker, Eef (2001), Reformed Scholasticism, An Ecumenical Enterprise, Grand Rapids: Baker.
Augustine, Aurelius, De baptismo
Augustine, Aurelius, De catechizandis rudibus
Augustine, Aurelius, Enarrationes in Psalmos
Augustine, Aurelius, Epistolae
Augustine, Aurelius, In Epistolam Ioannis ad Parthos tractatus decem

AUGUSTINE, AURELIUS, In Evangelium Ioannis tractatus centum viginti quatuor
AUGUSTINE, AURELIUS, Sermones 71, 213, 215, 265, 268.
AUGUSTINE, AURELIUS, Soliloquia
BALKE, WILLEM (1990), De eigenschappen van de kerk, in: Willem van 't Spijker (ed.), De kerk. Wezen, weg en werk van de kerk naar reformatorische opvatting, Kampen: Kok, 259–282.
BAVEL, TARSICIUS. J. VAN (2011), De idee van Christus totus, in: Tarsicius J. van Bavel (ed.), Sint-Augustinus, Brussel: Mercatorfonds, 263–271.
BAVINCK, HERMAN (2003), Reformed Dogmatics, 4 vol., John Bolt (ed.), John Vriend (trans.), Grand Rapids: Baker (originally Kampen 1930).
BEEK, ABRAHAM VAN DE (2012), Lichaam en Geest van Christus. De theologie van de kerk en de Heilige Geest, Zoetermeer: Meinema.
BERKHOF, HENDRIK (1962), De katholiciteit der kerk, Nijkerk: G.F. Callenbach.
BOER, ERIK A. DE (2016), 'Verspreid en verstrooid'. Ecclesiologie van de diaspora van de reformatie van de Lage Landen (inaugural address 19 February, Theologische Universiteit Kampen).
BROWN, PETER (1967), oHoAugustine of Hippo, a biography, Berkeley: University of California Press.
BURGER, CHRISTOPH (2005), De receptie van Augustinus' genadeleer: Gregorius van Rimini, Hugolinus van Orvieto, Erasmus en Luther, in: Paul van Geest/Johannes van Oort (ed.), Augustiniana Neerlandica. Aspecten van Augustustinus' spiritualiteit en haar doorwerking, Leuven: Peeters, 413–425.
BUTNER, D. GLENN (2016), Reformed Theology and the Question of Protestant Individualism. A Dialogue with Henri de Lubac, Journal of Reformed Theology 10.3, 234–256.
CALVIN, JOHN, Institutes.
CALVIN, JOHN, Catechism of Geneva.
CALVIN, JOHN, letter to Farel, 11 May 1541, CO 11, 215–216.
CALVIN, JOHN, Calvini Opera.
CALVIN, JOHN (2002), Reply by John Calvin to a Letter by Cardinal Sadolet to the Senate and People of Geneva', in: John Calvin, Henry Beveridge (trans.), Calvin's Tracts relating to the Reformation, Eugene: Wipf and Stock, 1:25–68.
CALVIN, JOHN (2001), Come Out From Among Them. 'Anti-Nicodemite' Writings of John Calvin, Seth Skolnitsky (trans.), Dallas: Protestant Heritage Press.
GORDON, BRUCE (2016), John Calvin's Institutes of the Christian Religion: A Biography, Princeton: Princeton University Press.
HESSELINK, I. JOHN (2010), Calvinus Oecumenicus. Calvin's Vision of the Unity and Catholicity of the Church, in: Eduardus A.J.G. van der Borght (ed.), The Unity of the Church, A Theological State of the Art and Beyond, Leiden: Brill, 69–93.
KOOI, AKKE VAN DER (1992), Het heilige en de Heilige Geest bij Noordmans, Een schets van zijn pneumatologisch ontwerp, Kampen: Kok.

Kooi, Cornelis van der (2008), The appeal to the inner testimony of the Spirit, especially in H. Bavinck, Journal of Reformed Theology 2.2, 103–112.

Lane, Anthony N.S. (1999), John Calvin. Student of the Church Fathers, Edinburgh: T&T Clark.

Lane, Anthony N.S. (2002), Justification by Faith in Catholic-Protestant Dialogue. An Evangelical Assessment, London: T&T Clark.

Lane, Anthony N.S. (2004a), Twofold Righteousness. A Key to the Doctrine of Justification, in: Mark Husbands/Daniel J. Treier (ed.), Justification. What's at Stake in the Current Debates, Downers Grove: InterVarsity Press, 205–224.

Lane, Anthony N.S. (2004b), Calvin and the Article 5 of the Regensburg Colloquy, in: Herman J. Selderhuis (ed.), Calvinus Preacepter Ecclesiae, Genève: Droz, 231–261.

Lane, Anthony N.S. (2012), Calvin's Attitude towards Catholicity, in: Herman J. Selderhuis (ed.), Calvinus clarissimus theologus. Papers of the Tenth International Congress on Calvin Research, Göttingen: Vandenhoeck & Ruprecht, 206–227.

Mara, Maria G. (2007), De kerk bij Augustinus, in: Tarsicius J. van Bavel (ed.), Sint-Augustinus, Brussel: Mercatorfonds, 205–217.

McGrath, Alister E. (1993), A Life of John Calvin. A Study in the Shaping of Western Culture, Oxford: Wiley-Blackwell.

Muller, Richard A. (2000), Scholasticism in Calvin. A Question of Relation and Disjunction', in: Richard A. Muller, The Unaccommodated Calvin. Studies in the Foundation of a Theological Tradition, New York/Oxford: Oxford University Press, 39–61.

Muller, Richard A. (2003a), Post-Reformation Reformed Dogmatics. The Rise and Development of Reformed Orthodoxy, ca. 1520 to ca. 1725, 4 vol., Grand Rapids: Baker.

Muller, Richard A. 2003b), After Calvin. Studies in the Development of a Theological Tradition, Oxford/New: Oxford University Press.

Nauta, Doede (2009), Calvijns afkeer van een schisma, in: William de Boer/Herman J. Selderhuis (ed.), Opnieuw Calvijn. Verzameling Nederlandse Calvijnstudies, Apeldoorn: Instituut voor Reformatieonderzoek, 853–870.

Neuser, Wilhelm H. (1990), 'Calvin and the Refugees,' in: Adrianus D. Pont (ed.), Calvin – France – South Africa. Papers read at the third South African Congress on Calvin Research Stellenbosch, 26–27 July 1988, Pretoria: Kital, 1–10.

Niesel, Wilhelm (1957), Die Theologie Calvins, München: Chr. Kaiser Verlag.

Nijenhuis, Willem (1959), Calvinus oecumenicus. Calvijn en de eenheid der kerk in het licht van zijn briefwisseling, 's Gravenhage: Marinus Nijhof.

Nijenhuis, Willem (2009), De eenheid der kerk bij Luther en Calvijn, in: William den Boer/Herman J. Selderhuis (ed.), Opnieuw Calvijn. Verzameling Nederlandse Calvijnstudies, Apeldoorn: Instituut voor Reformatieonderzoek, 943–961.

Noordmans, Okke (1981), Verzamelde werken, Kampen: Kok, vol. 3:134–148.

Noordmans, Okke (1986a), 'Het calvinisme en de oecumene', Verzamelde Werken vol. 6, 397–409.

Noordmans, Okke (1986b), De Reformatie en Rome, Verzamelde Werken, Kampen: Kok, vol. 6, 415–427.

Noordmans, Okke (1986c), Natuur en genade bij Rome, Verzamelde Werken, Kampen: Kok, vol. 6, 428–451.

Oberman, Heiko, A. (2003), The Two Reformations. The Journey from the Last Days to the New World, New Haven: Yale University Press.

Oberman, Heiko, A. (2009a), John Calvin and the Reformation of the Refugees, Genève: Droz.

Oberman, Heiko, A. (2009b), De katholieke kerkvader. De hele waarheid voor de gehele wereld, in: William den Boer/Herman J. Selderhuis (ed.), Opnieuw Calvijn. Verzameling Nederlandse Calvijnstudies, Apeldoorn 2009, 988–998.

Plasger, G. (2009), Ecclesiology, in: Herman J. Selderhuis (ed.), The Calvin Handbook, Grand Rapids: Eerdmans, 312–332.

Spijker, Willem van 'T. (2009), De kerk bij Calvijn: theocratie', in: William den Boer/ Herman J. Selderhuis (ed.), Opnieuw Calvijn. Verzameling Nederlandse Calvijnstudies, 2 vol., Apeldoorn: Instituut voor Reformatieonderzoek, 1515–1531.

Steinmetz, David C. (1999), The Scholastic Calvin, in: Carl R. Trueman/Robert S. Clark (ed.), Protestant Scholasticism. Essays in Reassessment, Carlisle: Paternoster, 16–30.

Stolk, Johannes Maarten (2004), Johannes Calvijn en de godsdienstgesprekken, Kampen: Kok.

Taylor, Charles (2007), A Secular Age, Harvard: Harvard University Press.

Visser, Arnoud S.Q. (2011), Reading Augustine in the Reformation. The Flexibility of Intellectual Authority in Europe, 1500–1620, Oxford: Oxford University Press.

Vlastuin, Willem van (2020), Catholic Today. A Reformed Conversation about Catholicity, Göttingen: Vandenhoeck & Ruprecht.

Walker, George Stuart Murdoch (1984), 'Calvin and the Church', in: Donald K. McKim (ed.), Readings in Calvin's Theology, Grand Rapids: Baker, 212–230.

Wendel, Francois (1997), Calvin. Origins, and Developments of His Religious Thought, Grand Rapids: Baker.

Zillenbiller, Anette (1993), Die Einheit der katholischen Kirche. Calvins Cyprianrezeption in seinen ekklesiologische Schriften, Mainz: Philipp von Zabern.

Herman J. Selderhuis

Augustine in Reformed tradition: an impetus for further research

1. Introduction

When it comes to the reception of Augustine in the Reformed tradition, the impression can arise that it has been intensive, substantive and long lasting. This impression is mainly based on the way Calvin dealt with Augustine, a theme on which several thorough studies have been published.[1] In doing so, however, two essential questions have to be addressed. The first is the question as to what extent there really is an actual reception of Augustine in Calvin. The frequent references Calvin makes to Augustine do not mean that there is a substantive augustinian reception in the reformer's thinking. This thought should certainly be considered because Calvin – just like other reformers and just like Catholic controversial theologians – mainly used Augustine polemically.[2] Calvin expressed his relationship with the church father aptly by saying: "Augustine [...] totus noster est",[3] but that doesn't say too much since there was great unanimity between Protestants and Catholics regarding this appraisal of Augustine. Also defending one's own point of view with an appeal to Augustine says nothing about the reception of Augustine. In the past decades it has been established in Calvin's research that although Calvin liked Augustine dogmatically and saw himself as a supporter of resurgent Augustinianism, he preferred the exegesis of the Greek church father Chrysostom. The opposite, by the way, is also true because Augustine can have far-reaching influence on a theologian without this theologian naming Augustine by name. And even then it is questionable whether this influence is from Augustine or from the biblical ideas which can be found explicitly in Augustine or which have come further through him.

The second question that needs to be answered is actually the core of this contribution. This question is to what extent the tradition after Calvin can be seen as a disciple of Augustine. Calvin may mention and use Augustine a lot, but how is that

---

1 Lange van Ravenswaay (1990); Johannes van Oort: 1997, 661f; Smits (1957–1958); Visser (2011); Zahnd: 2017, 181–194. The most recent summary is Lane: 2013, 739–743. See also Seelbach: 2011, 75–98; and Han: 2008, 70–83.
2 Lane: 1999, 38f.
3 CO 8:266

true in the post-Calvin tradition as well? Only limited research has been done on this question and although the results are certainly worthwhile, there has been a wasteland here for a long time. Yet, it is a wasteland that does require some effort to exploit, especially when authors do not always mention their sources and thus Augustine can be theologically present without being mentioned.

Below, I take three periods from the history of theology after Calvin and question them about their use of Augustine. I speak with emphasis about 'the use' because it is not yet possible for me to say so much about Augustine's reception by means of these periods. The trio consists of the theological faculty of Heidelberg in the period 1583–1622, the period of Dutch Reformed Orthodoxy, and third, the socalled *Nadere Reformatie* – often rather awkwardly translated as 'Further Reformation' – as the Dutch version of the international Protestant piety movement from the seventeenth century in particular. This limited choice already indicates that for the Reformed tradition after Calvin, there are many other persons, movements and areas where the reception of Augustine could – and should – be examined.

2. Heidelberg

The years 1583–1622 in the history of Heidelberg University are those of the second Calvinist period and they belong to one of the most flourishing periods of this institution. A striking development at that time is the attention paid to the history of church and theology which resulted, among other things, in a major interest in patristics. Daniel Tossanus (1541–1602), French-born professor of theology, contributed to this interest with his posthumously published 'Synopsis de patribus' in which he gives an overview of the most important works of the church fathers, after first addressing questions about the authenticity and value of the patristic writings.[4] More extensive was the work of Abraham Scultetus (1566–1625), professor and court preacher, who between 1598 and 1613 published a manual for the reading of the church fathers in four volumes.[5] This is an elaborate publication in which an analysis is given of each work of all the Greek and Latin Fathers of the period before the Council of Nicea. In his preface he writes that he was asked by Bartholomew Pitiscus (1561–1613), theologian, mathematician and astronomer, to, in his spare time, focus more on the study of the early Church. The book written by Scultetus resulting from this exhortation is intended to help students find their way in the fathers by offering them, in this book, summaries of the most important

---

4 Tossanus (1603).
5 Scultetus (1603–1613); see about this: Benrath: 1963, 21–27. The work was published in one volume in 1634: Scultetus (1643).

patristic writings. Moreover, according to Scultetus, his book can also be of service to pastors. Scultetus begins his overview with the complaint that in his time there is an appalling lack of knowledge of the fathers,[6] and according to him this means that it is not recognized how many current discussions concerning them have already been played out before. As examples, Scultetus mentions the struggle over the trinity, christology and the doctrine of the Last Supper. If one knew the Fathers of the Church, a lot of the current discussion would be superfluous, because one could simply make use of what the fathers have already found and said. It would also be possible to expose new, and thus old, errors more quickly.

Scultetus is clear about the purpose of this publication. He wants to free the church fathers from papal decay and thus demonstrate that it is the church of the Reformation which has remained faithfully on the trail blazed by the early church. So the goal of this book is not so much the study of the Church Fathers in themselves so as to gain knowledge of their lives and works, but more so to prove that there is one line from the old church to the Reformation church. Scultetus mainly focuses on the work of Bellarminus, who wants to prove the opposite also from out of the church fathers, but from carefully taking notice of these sources it will become clear that the Protestants are rightly called the heirs of the fathers.[7] Students of theology can easily recognize, by means of Scultetus' Medullae, what is and what is not in accordance with the teachings of the old church.[8] Scultetus dates the patristic era from apostolic times up to the year 800.[9] The hallmark of the theologians of those centuries is that they used Scripture as a source for their comments. Those who come after 800 A.D. are the scholastics who are more concerned with commenting on the Sententiae of Peter Lombardus and, 'who have confused philosophy and theology'.[10] Nevertheless, Scultetus is of the opinion that the theologians before Nicaea are purer than those who came afterwards with the exception of Augustine.[11] It is only here that Scultetus speaks of Augustine, although, in view of the purpose of his patristic survey, it would have been obvious to present and recommend Augustine more fully. Apparently Scultetus considers the early church fathers more important than the later church fathers and Augustine is in this regard no exception.

---

6 "[…] nunquam tamen eos perinde misere atque hoc nostro seculo fuisse depravatos, detortos, & tantum non discerptos, ex eruditis dubitare credo neminem.", Scultetus: 1643, [4].

7 "[…] quod fraudum Bellarminicarum fontes tam pulchre nobis aperit: quanquam major, cedo, alter ille: quod doctrinae Patrum nucleum, & rationum quibus sua confirmarunt momenta singula, tanquam in tabella quadam descripta legentium oculis subjicit.", Scultetus: 1643, [7].

8 Scultetus: 1643, [8].

9 "Patres hodie vocantur Doctores Ecclesiae, qui a temporibus Apostolorum ad annum Christi octingentesimum vixerunt & interpretati sunt Scripturam", Scultetus: 1643, [23].

10 Scultetus: 1643, [23].

11 Scultetus: 1603–1613, [4].

This work by Scultetus is the first Reformed manual for reading the Church Fathers.[12] His approach is, on the one hand, confessional, which is mainly explained by the historical situation characterized by the polemic with Rome and with the Lutherans, and on the other hand, Scultetus deals with the material in a historically critical way, so that there is also attention paid to material that does not support the Reformed point of view. However, if a collision is imminent in the combination of both, Scultetus chooses the reformed-confessional approach.

Yet in spite of Scultetus' neglect of Augustinus, the church father is certainly in the picture in Heidelberg. The Heidelberg theologians actively participated in the discussions about the doctrine of predestination as it arose in the second half of the sixteenth century. The reason for this topic becoming the main issue of debate was the polemic that was used against the Calvinists from the Lutheran side to make it clear that the followers of Calvin did not actually belong to the Protestants and therefore did not fall under the protection of the religious peace of Augsburg (1555). In this polemic, the Lutheran theologians focused their arrows on the, as they said, 'Calvinistic' doctrine of predestiantion as being unbiblical and unreformed in the sense that it is not in line with the Reformation. They went so far as to say that when the Calvinists defended themselves by appealing to Luther's 'The servo arbitrio' they claimed that at the end of his life Luther had distanced himself from this work in a kind of *retractationes*, a view, however, for which they could not provide proof. For this reason the Calvinists' appeal to Augustine wouild be stronger than the appeal to Luther, and so the church father regularly appears in the works of the four theologians who participated in the aforementioned polemic: Georg Sohn (1551–1589), Herman Rennecherus (1550–?), Jacob Kimmedoncius (1554–1596) and the previously mentioned Daniel Tossanus (1541–1602).[13]

Georg Sohn invokes Augustine in his plea for treating the doctrine of predestination in the pulpit. The criticism against doing this was that the theme of predestination would be too difficult for the members of the congregation to deal with in sermons. Sohn reacts to this objection by giving four reasons why it can be preached: first of all predestination is a foundation of faith and people need to know that, second, everything in the Bible is useful and thus preaching predestination is also, third, the prophets, Christ and the apostles have passed on this doctrine and so we should do it too, and fourth, Augustine preached on predestination too and if he did it to give the people a more firm faith, we should do just the same.[14] Apart from this issue, Augustine is also prominently present in Sohn's work in general, for example when it comes to defending the doctrine of double predestination, that is

---

12 Backus: 2003, 222.
13 Lee (2009).
14 Lee: 2009, 66.

to say, the vision that God not only consciously elects sinners to rescue them from eternal death, but that as a result He also consciously rejects the unchosen. This doctrine was one of the targets of the Lutheran opposition, but Sohn defends these views with reference to Augustine who, in his De civitate Dei, speaks of two cities, one of which is destined by God for salvation and the other for judgment.[15]

In 1589 Herman Rennecherus published his 'Golden Chain of Salvation', which he dedicated to Queen Elisabeth of England.[16] In this work Rennecherus gives a detailed account of the causes and consequences of eternal election and of all the questions connected with it.[17] Although the reason is the discussion with Rome and the Lutherans, the book is hardly polemical. Rennecherus argues here only on the basis of biblical texts and only refers to Augustine as a post-Biblical theologian for his explanation of the Reformed vision of election.[18]

Heidelberg's most extensive contribution to this discussion is that of Jacob Kimedoncius. His book on redemption, to which a separate book on election has been added, contains more than 650 pages.[19] The work is an extensive dialogue mainly with Samuel Huber (1547–1624), the Lutheran theologian who had first been Reformed and who had already quarrelled with Beza and Musculus in Bern about predestination.[20] In the preface, Kimedoncius indicates that in this work he wants to oppose the Lutheran accusation that the Reformed deny that Christ died for all people. According to him, this is blatant slander, because, since it is according to Scripture, Reformed people certainly do confess this.[21] That does not mean, however, that every human being, without exception, with or without faith, is justified and saved. What he wants to say by this he indicates further on in this book, where he quotes with approval Thomas Aquinas, who said that the blood of Christ was enough for all men, but that not all men participate in the fruit of that blood.[22] It is striking not only that Kimedoncius juxtaposes Luther with Huber, but that

---

15 "Hinc sit ut Patres praedestinationem generatim intelligentes, non solum ad electos, sed etiam ad reprobos accommodent, ita ut utrique dicantur ab aeterno praedestinati: illi ad vitam, hi ad mortem aeternam. Sic Augustinus libro.15.cap.I. de civitate Dei. […]", Sohn: 1591, 1058.
16 This work appeared thus two years before William Perkins' famaous "A golden chaine", see Perkins (1591).
17 Rennecherus (1589).
18 Only once another theologian is cited, namely St. Bernardus and he is cited to support Rennecheru's statement, Rennecherus: 1589, 190.
19 Kimedoncius (1593). The 1592 edition has as numbering a total of 747 pages, but this is result of a misprint. After page 208 the printer numbered the following page 309. The 'De redemtione' covers pages 1–442, and 'De praedestinatione divina' pages 443–747.
20 Huber responds right away with also a massive publication: Huberus (1593). See on Hubers discussion with Tossanus, Cuno, Tossanus I 242–258.
21 "Impudens calumnia. Id enim secundum scripturas fatemur & nos.", De redemtione [7].
22 Kimedoncius: 1593, 63f.

he equates Luther with Augustine and Huber with the Pelagians.[23] Thus the two groups are opposite each other, on one side the Calvinists, Luther and Augustine, and on the other side the Lutherans, Huber and the Pelagians. Kimedoncius states that Augustine went through a development and initially was semi-pelagian in his thinking.[24] But while Augustine developed in his thought and came to realise that his original position was unbiblical, Huber remained so to speak where he stood. Considering this approach it is not surprising that Kimedoncius constantly quotes Augustine as a witness for the Calvinistic vision.[25]

As far as dealing with the Bible as Holy Scripture is concerned, Kimedoncius' book on the Bible is of great importance. In a work of more than nine hundred pages he presents materials for two books; the first dedicated to the city council and people of Middelburg, the other to those of Vlissingen, with all aspects of the written and unwritten Word.[26] In view of its contents, the book stands in the context of the polemic with Rome and in particular with Bellarminus. The second chapter of book one deals with the authority of Scripture. First Kimedoncius gives an overview of what the church fathers have said about this. Then he writes about the normativity of customs and traditions. The norm is always the 'lineal of Scripture', as Kimedoncius states it.[27] This also applies to the writings of the Church Fathers. No matter how much they may be of service with all that they have to offer in their explanations of Scripture, 'we cannot use them as the rule of truth'.[28] Striking in this chapter is the attention given to the question of the Pope's authority and position.[29] This brings Kimedoncius to the question of from whence the Bible derives its authority and there he cannot escape giving a detailed explanation of Augustine's statement that he would not believe the Gospel if it were not for the authority of the church. According to Kimedoncius, this statement doesn't mean that for Augustine it is the church that gives authority to the Scriptures, by which he wants to make clear that Augustine rejects the Roman Catholic viewpoint on this matter.

---

23 De redemtione, epistola dedicatoria.
24 "Et fuit Augustinus ipsemet in eadem sententia initio ante Episcopatum, ut apparet ex libro expositionum eius in Epist. ad Rom & ex Epist. Hilarij ad August.", Kimedoncius: 1593, 502.
25 Lee: 2009, 139–142.
26 Kimedoncius (1595).
27 "[…], sed eas quoque ad amussim scripturarum explorati oportere […]", Kimedoncius: 1595, 121.
28 Kimedoncius: 1595, 135.
29 Kimedoncius: 1595, 143–191.

3. Reformed Orthodoxy

As a second sampling in the history of reformed theology, a glance is worth taking at Augustine's presence in the Dutch authors belonging to so-called Reformed Orthodoxy. Since the theologions of this Reformed Orthodoxy were in general staunch supporters of the Canons of Dordt, it is not surprising that Augustine plays an important role in the descriptions of the doctrine of mercy and is invariably quoted as a witness for the Reformed doctrine. In the dogmatic handbook that was published in 1625 by four theologians of the Leiden faculty of theology and appeared under the name Synopsis Purioris Theologiae, no church father is referred to as much as Augustine.[30] The Utrecht theologian Gisbertus Voetius (1589–1676) generally had a rather ambivalent appreciation of the church fathers.[31] According to him, it was not really urgent for his students to study the fathers and it was better for them to focus on theologians of their own time. On the other hand, he quoted the Church Fathers frequently and felt that some of them had much to offer in a systematic or practical way. In this respect Augustine played the leading role with Voetius and was described by this Reformed theologian in the sermon which Voetius gave on Sunday 13 March 1636, immediately before the solemn consecration of Utrecht University, as "dien treffelycken Man Godts" (this outstanding man of God) .[32] Van Oort has already demonstrated the prominent presence of Augustine in the work of the young Voetius,[33] but a brief look at his later works shows that this church father had a lasting influence on the Utrecht theologian. Voetius' writings on the practice of godliness contain 46 references to Augustine, more than twice as many as to Ambrose, Cyprian and Hieronymus, each of which is mentioned around twenty times.[34] The nature of these references makes it clear that Voetius knew Augustine's work – he possessed at least eight volumes of the ten-volume edition published by Froben in Basel in 1556, according to the auction catalogue of his library[35] – and that he recommended to his readers his instructions for the practice of the faith. The fact that Voetius himself was also influenced by Augustine's spirituality is evident from reading one of his major works called the practice of godliness, but further investigation of the extent is certainly necessary. This research has been urgent for the whole of Voetius' work, since it is more than likely that

---

30 Velde (2015); Belt (2016).
31 Niet: 1997, 126–134; Goudriaan: 2007, 173–181; Asselt (2013); Oort: 1989a, 565–578; 1990, 997–1009.
32 Voetius (1636).
33 Oort: 1989b, 181–190.
34 Niet (1996). Here: Niet, I, lx.
35 See for more information Oort: 1989b, 188, note 80.

Augustine is also present in those places where Voetius does not mention him by name.

As in the Reformation, in Reformed orthodoxy Augustine is often summoned as a witness, mainly in the polemics with the Remonstrants and in those with Roman Catholic theology. In the discussion about the Synod of Dordrecht, for example, Augustine is repeatedly quoted as a defender of the vision of the Counter-Remonstrants.[36] Francis Gomarus, the man who in his vision of predestination went so far that the Synod even had to admonish him concerning his supralapsarism, was a great connoisseur of Augustine. In his student days he went to Oxford to hear Johannes Reinoldus (Raynolds) who, according to Gomarus's biographer, was known as "fierce anti-catholic, adorer of Augustine and his works, which he knew almost by heart".[37] The knowledge Gomarus had of Augustine came in handy for him in discussions with Arminius, who defended his point of view differing from that of Calvin and Beza by invoking Augustine and especially his view of sin.[38] Gomarus fought Arminius with quotes from other works of Augustine with the result that after this debate, Augustine's presence in Arminius' writings declined sharply. For Arminius this led to a relationship with Augustine which Aza Goudriaan refers to as 'ambivalent'.[39] On the one hand there is the appeal to Augustine to prove that Arminius is not unorthodox, on the other hand Arminius has difficulty with especially the later Augustine and his vision of predestination.

On the opposite side of this theological discussion, Jacobus Trigland could characterize Augustine in his counter-remonstrant historiographical overview 'Kerckelijcke geschiedenissen' (ecclesiastical histories) as 'that outstanding destroyer of Pelagian errors'.[40] Augustine and his writings have been so honourably received in the history of the church, because he, "pushed that issue of grace so broadly and seriously."[41] After Trigland, in reaction to Wtenbogaert, has quoted extensively from 'De dono perseverantia', he comes to the conclusion that "Augustine in his writings presents just the same grounds as the Reformed use in their debate with the remonstrants on the issue of the perseverance of the saints".[42] For George Abbott, Archbishop of Canterbury, it was quite clear. He had read the documents of the

---

36 See: Sinnema: 2018, 94, 132, 279, 385, 412, 515, 519, 603, 683, 738, 913, 922. For a concise overview: Bieber-Wallmann: 2007, 627–633. For the discussions in England on the Canons of Dordt in their relation to Augustine: Collier (2018).
37 Itterzon: 1979, 27.
38 See o. a. Stanglin (2010).
39 Goudriaan: 2009, 71f.
40 "[…] dien treffelijcken verpletteraer vande Pelagiaensche dwalingen", Trigland: 1650, 12.
41 "dat poinct vande ghenade soo breet ende ernstich dreef.", Trigland: 1650, 43.
42 "Augustinus leyt in schriften die selve gronden die de Gereformeerde leggen tegen den Remonstrantschen Afval der heyligen". Trigland: 1650, 25.

Arminians and his conclusion was that they would not have ended up 'in such Laberinth or errour' if they had read more Church Fathers and then 'especially St Augustine'.[43]

Knowledge of the works of the church fathers was important for the polemic with Rome in the question of who really followed in the footsteps of the early church. Johannes Coccejus (1603–1669), Voetius' theological opponent in the debate on the continuing validity of the Sabbath law and on the nature of forgiveness in the Old Testament, entered into discussions with Catholic theologians about how to interpret Augustine. An example of this is Voetius' polemic with the German Jesuit James Masenius (1606–1681), who asked the theologians of Leiden the question to what extent his view on the authority of the Bible differed from theirs as Reformed theologians.[44] After Coccejus reacted in 1656 with an exposition of the Reformed vision of Scripture, Masenius published a treatise on Augustine as the one who in their time had to be an arbitrator of disputes in which the authority of Scripture played a role.[45] Thus, the discussion shifted from being about the authority of Scripture, to the authority of Augustine in discussions about the interpretation of the Bible. Coccejus immediately wrote a reaction[46] in which he criticizes Masenius for applying a syllogism that is not correct according to the rules of scholasticism and accuses him of turning syllogism into sophistry. It is a syllogism in which the major thesis is that Augustine was orthodox in his doctrine, the minor thesis is that Augustine says the same as Roman Catholic theologians about present controversial matters, and the conclusion then is that Roman Catholic theologians are orthodox. Accordingly, according to Coccejus, Masenius wrongly introduced a fourth element, namely speaking about present controversial matters. According to Coccejus, who had fourteen works by and about Augustine in his library,[47] this church father cannot simply be put forward as a witness in current discussions as if nothing had happened between his time and the present one. Coccejus considers Augustine to have inhabited a time when church and theology were still on the right track, but after that so much has changed and especially changed negatively that what Augustine said and wrote is simply not applicable to what is going on today.

Melchior Leydecker (1642–1721) can be mentioned as a last example of the use of Augustine. Aza Goudriaan has referred to him as someone who has been involved with Augustine in terms of content, and has not used him just to defend his own

---

43 Sinnema: 2018, o.c., 913.
44 In detail on this polemic: Asselt: 1997, 135–154.
45 Masen (1656).
46 Coccejus (1657).
47 Asselt: 1997, 141.

position or that of Protestantism as a whole.[48] Leydecker enters into a discussion with Augustine on the persecution of Christians with a dissenting opinion. Probably it was also Leydecker who wrote the disputation that Bernardus Smytegelt, who would become one of the most influential representatives of the Dutch pietist movement, defended in 1686 at the conclusion of his studies at the university of Utrecht. The theses Smytegelt had to defend dealt with Augustine's De unitate ecclesiae.[49]

4. Reformed Pietism

Although no comprehensive research has yet been done on the reception of Augustine in the *Nadere Reformatie* (Further Reformation), the results of research that has been done seems to offer little hope for clarity.[50] John Exalto has researched how and to what extent Augustine was discussed in Reformed sermons after the Reformation.[51] His conclusion is that there is too little information to draw conclusions, but that it is clear that Augustine was mentioned in sermons, although to the hearers of those sermons he was not much more than a name from the past. Exalto does remark in his article that further research could yield more. W.J. op 't Hof has gone through the entire work of Willem Teellinck and arrives at a total of seventeen references to the work of Augustine.[52] Of those seventeen, fifteen appear in one work. For Op 't Hof this is reason to conclude that the church fathers in general were little used by this distinguished representative of the *Nadere Reformatie* and that he had less esteem for the fathers than for Protestant authors from the sixteenth and seventeenth centuries. "Among the church fathers there are more errors and less knowledge of the fundamental biblical languages".[53] According to Teellinck, the church fathers are just as much human beings as others and they are rather divided in their points of view. Moreover, by quoting church fathers there is a danger that not only will the Bible be pushed aside, but also that human institutions will be introduced. and where that can lead can be seen in Rome.[54]

---

48 Goudriaan: 2015, 25–36.
49 Post: 2006, 14.
50 As stated above, I am confining myself here to the Dutch branch of the Protestant piety movement of the late sixteenth and seventeenth centuries, but it would be worth making the same inventory of Augustine's reception by the Puritans.
51 Exalto: 2012, 195–214.
52 Hof: 2011, 244f.
53 Hof: 2011, 212.
54 Hof: 2008, 170.

Yet there are also theologians from this movement that do appreciate and use the church fathers. An example is Johannes Hoornbeeck (1617–1666), professor of theology in Leiden and particularly known for his homiletic work. Church Fathers are regularly quoted in his work, and his posthumous Miscellanea sacra (1677), for example, contains several treatises in which the importance of the Church Fathers is explicitly mentioned. This applies to the chapter "on the theology of the fathers", in which the lives and works of individual church fathers are discussed, but the views of church fathers are also discussed in the treatises on "the repentance of the ancients", "the baptism of the ancients", "the holy sacrament of the ancients", and "the synods of the ancients".[55] Nevertheless, Hoornbeeck chose to consult almost exclusively with theologians before 285 A.D., so that Augustine is only mentioned incidentally.

In his several times reprinted book 'De Wech des Levens'[56] Guiljelmus Saldenus (1627–1694), who in his works mainly dealt with the 'praxis pietatis', gives an overview of his sources and mentions 67 writers; among them classical authors like Seneca and Cicero.[57] This says something about the breadth of materials from which this representative of the *Nadere Reformatie* drew, but that his main source is Augustine is shown by the fact that he is mentioned more than forty times, while Bernard comes in second place with twenty mentions. Augustine is also present within the well-known author of edifying works Theodorus à Brakel (1608–1669). In his much read 'Trappen Des Geestelycken Levens'[58] the writer reacts hesitantly to the question of his son asking him to tell him something about his spiritual life. He wants to do it, but only just as holy men have done before him. He mentions then only two names of men from outside of the biblical tradition: Augustine and Luther.[59] The 'tolle, lege' moment in Augustine's life is mentioned as an example of the conversion that God works with power in a human life.[60]

Another bestseller of Reformed Pietism is 'Het Geestelyck Roer Van't Coopman's Ship' written by one of the founders of the Further Reformation, Godfrey Udemans (1581/82–1649).[61] Udemans was a preacher and was member of the Zeeland delegation to the Synod of Dordrecht. His 'Geestelyck Roer' is best known of all his works. In this book he describes in detail what the Bible says about subjects

---

55 Hoornbeek (1677). See about Hoornbeek: Itterzon: 1983, 259ff.
56 Saldenus (1657).
57 Spijker: 1989, 34f.
58 Brakel (1717).
59 "Soo heeft ook seer wijtloopigh gedaan de Oudtvader Augustinus in zijne belijdenisse […]", Brakel: 1717, 119.
60 "'t geene Augustinus van hem selven verhaelt in 't 8 Boek Cap.10. van sijne Confessie/ dat hij op de stemme die tot hem seyde *leest*, geleesen hebben[…]", Brakel: 1717, 124.
61 Udemans (1640).

like doing business with unbelievers, making profit, and slavery. In this economic handbook for the Christian businessman, Udemans frequently refers to what Augustine said about these themes, while reformers like Luther and Calvin, who also dealt with many of these subjects, remain almost unnamed. The same line can be found in Francis Ridderus (1620–1683), who refers to Augustine more often than to Calvin.[62] Ridderus quotes the church father in his exposition on the reliability of God's promises as expressed in the Bible.[63] He quotes Augustine with approval as a supporter of baptizing children of parents expelled from the church,[64] but also as a supporter of his warnings against showing off with clothes and jewellery as an expression of pride.[65] With his colleague Adriaan de Herder, preacher in Bleiswijk, Ridderus discussed how to interpret Augustine. Ridderus appealed to the church father to justify separation from a church in decline. On the other hand, Ridderus argues that Augustine remained faithful to the church in spite of its flaws and that he acted against schismatics.[66] Also in other – doctrinal as well as pastoral – subjects that Ridderus deals with in his works, Augustine is quoted repeatedly and it becomes evident that this representative of the *Nadere Reformatie* has thoroughly taken note of the work of the church father.

Dutch translations of Augustine are mainly Catholic publications in this period.[67] J. van der Haar mentions in his survey of Reformed publications only a translation of the Soliloquia which was translated and published by Caspar Staphorstius in 1632,[68] but he did not know at the time that this work is now attributed to Pseudo-Augustine. In 1621, a translation of De civitate Dei[69] by the Reformed preacher Johannes Lenaertsz Fenacolius (1577–1645) was published, who, however, does not belong to the movement of the *Nadere Reformatie*. Fenacolius used his translation of De civitate in his fight against government interference in ecclesiastical matters. This polemical use of Augustine is also the reason for a publication containing the translation of his writings on predestination and on perseverance in the faith.[70] This edition was published in 1621, two years after the closing of the Synod of Dordrecht. Dordt had spoken emphatically in favour of the perseverance of the saints and that in the presence of the remonstrants, who stated that a believer can lose their salvation. Dirck Vlack de Ionge, translator and publisher of this book,

---

62 Schaap (2008).
63 Schaap: 2008, 47.
64 Schaap: 2008, 115.
65 Schaap: 2008, 157.
66 Schaap: 2008, 246f.
67 For an overview see: Erven (2014).
68 Staphorstius: 1987, 279.
69 Lenaertsz Fenacolius (1621). A second edition appeared in 1646, a third in 1660–1661.
70 D. Vlack de Ionge (1621).

says in his preface that with this translation he wants to show that the doctrine as laid down by the Synod of Dordrecht in the canons of Dordt is not something new, as the remonstrants stated, but has always belonged to the doctrine of the Church of Christ and that the work of Augustine is proof of that. From the remonstrants' side it was stated that the perspective of Calvin and Beza, invoked by the Counter-Remonstrants, was an imported viewpoint, and foreign to the Dutch Reformed tradition. De Ionge states in his introductory letter ('Toe-eighen-Brief') to the magistrate of Gouda, that the work of Augustine proves that this doctrine was also known and confessed in the early church and that it was preached and proclaimed every time it came uner attack.[71] He therefore hopes that reading these two works of the Church Father will ensure that the proofs Augustine has given for this doctrine and which were based on the teachings of Christ, the Apostles, and the Prophets, will remain in the people's minds.[72]

From the above examples it is clear that there is indeed an 'Augustine reception' in the *Nadere Reformatie* and that it is thematically broader than just on discussions about predestination, sin and grace. Other themes are, for example, Augustine's vision of church and state as well as that of marriage and sexuality. Research on these topics will make clear that Augustine was more than just the church father who could fight against Roman Catholics, Remonstrants and other false teachers. When investigating Augustine's influence, it should be borne in mind that his influence can also be found through other authors, for example medieval theologians who were also used intensively by Reformed people such as Bernard van Clairvaux and Thomas Aquinas. In any case, this first analysis of the tradition after Calvin makes it sufficiently clear that there is still much to be done and most likely much to be achieved in the study of Augustine's reception in the Reformed tradition

5. Conclusion

This brief inventory of Augustine's use in so-called post-reformation theology is sufficient proof of the following:
1. Augustine was not only used polemically, but also as a witness to practical piety.
2. Augustine's conversion is used as a model for how God convinces people of sin and brings them to repentance.
3. Augustine's works have been used and read intensively by Reformed theologians.

---

71 "oock ten tijden van de *primitive* kercke bekent is gheweest/ick segghe niet alleen bekent/ maar dat de zelvde noodich gheacht heeft/ onderlingh wanneer de zelfde bevochten wierdt/ dese Leere den volcke te verkondighen." Toe-eighen-Brief, zp.
72 "dat de Bewijs-redenen Augustini/ gegrondet op de leere Christi/ der Apostelen/ ende Proppheten/ bij haer moghen beklijven." Toe-eighen-Brief, zp.

4. Research into the reception of Augustine in the Reformed tradition after Calvin is largely unexplored.
5. Protestant researchers would do well to consult their Catholic colleagues on this theme as these are generally more experienced in Augustine and his reception.

Bibliography

Sources

HENK VAN DEN BELT/ RIEMER FABER/ANDREAS BECK/WILLIAM DEN BOER, (2016), Synopsis Purioris Theologiae / Synopsis of a Purer Theology, vol. 2: Disputations 24–42, in: Studies in Medieval and Reformation Traditions: Texts and Sources, vol. 204, No. 8, Leiden: Brill.

THEODORUM À BRAKEL (1717), De Trappen Des Geestelycken Levens, Amsterdam: wed. van Gysbert de Groot en Antony van Dam.

JOHANNES COCCEJUS (1657), Admonitio de Principio Fidei Ecclesiae Reformatae XXV aphorismis comprehensa ad Jacobum Masenium, Lugd., Bat.

JOHANNES LENAERTSZ FENACOLIUS (1621), Van de stadt Godts: begrepen in 22 boecken ende verdeylt in vijf stucken / Den H. Outvader Aur. Augustinus; uyt den Latyne verduytscht door Johannes Fenacolius ... ende by hem verciert met de rijcke aenteeckekeninghen Lud. Vives, als oock syns eyghen selfs, Delff: Adriaen Gerritsz.

JOHANNES HOORNBEEK (1677), Miscellanea sacra: in quibus lectissimae, cujusvis argumenti, theologici, textualis, dogmatici, elenctici, ractici, historici et ritualis, Veteris et Novi Exercitationes, nec non orationes quaedam, continentur, Opus posthumum, Utrecht: Johannes Ribbius.

SAMUEL HUBERUS (1593), Contra Iacobum Kimedoncium Theologum Heidelbergensem, Qui Calviniano furore cum sociis accensus, Mahometismo fores aperit, & Evangelium Iesu Christi funditus extirpare conatur, Wittenberg.

VLACK DE JONGHE (1621), Twee tractaten, beschreven door den heylighen Oudt-Vader Augustinum. Het eene handelende van de Goddelijke Praedestinatie. Het ander van het goedt der Volhardinghe, wt het Latijn in Nederd. over geset door D. Vlack de Jonghe, Amst. 1621.

JACOBUS KIMEDONCIUS (1593), Synopsis de redemptione et praedestinatione, adversus Samuelem Huberum, Heidelberg.

JACOBUS KIMEDONCIUS (1595) De scripto Dei Verbo, libri octo, Ad senatum populumque Middelburgensem, Eiusdem De Verbo non scripto, libri duo, ad senatum populumque Flißinganum, Heidelberg: Abraham Smesmann.

JACOB MASEN (1656), D. Augustinus Controversiarum Fidei Huius Temporis Ex Sola S. Scriptura, Iuxta Orthoxae Apostolicaeque Ecclesiae mentem, arbiter ac decisor optimus: Serenissimis ac potentissimis Protestantium Principibus Rebusp. & Academiis ad spem pacis & approbationis universalis exhibitus; Cum Refutatione D. Joannis Cocceii

Batavo-Lugdunensis Theologi S. Scripturae interpretis, per oppositam D. Augustini interpretationem in praecipuis fidei articulis, & provocatione ad solidam Augustino adversanti responsionem, Coloniae Agrippinae: Busaeus.

WILLIAM PERKINS (1591), A golden chaine, or The description of theologie containing the order of the causes of saluation and damnation, according to Gods word. A view whereof is to be seene in the table annexed. Hereunto is adioyned the order which M. Theodore Beza vsed in comforting afflicted consciences, London: Edward White.

HERMAN RENNECHERUS (1589), Aurea salutis catena; continens et explicans omnes eius causas; ac singula Dei beneficia, ex aeterna electione ad nos per Christum descendentia, ordine enumerans & demonstrans: quae quidem beneficia universa scholiis perspicuis & orthodoxis illustrate sunt, Herborn: Christoph Rab.

GUILJELMUS SALDENUS (1657), De Wech des Levens, Ofte, Korte ende eenvoudige Onderwyzinge, Van de Natuer ende Eyghenschappen van de ware Kracht der Godsalicheyt, Den Schijn-heyligen tot beschaminge, ende alle oprechte Christenen tot noodighe Opweckinge ende Versterckinge voor-gestelt, Enkhuizen: Willem Evertsz.

ABRAHAM SCULTETUS (1603–1613), Medulla Theologiae Patrum, Qui A Temporibus Apostolorum ad Concilium usq[ue] Nicenum floruerunt: Methodo analytica & synthetica expressa, In gratiam eorum, qui vel ob Codicum temporisve defectum Patres ipsi legere non possunt, vel eosde[m] cum fructu evolvere volunt / Studio Abrahami Sculteti Grünbergensis Silesii, Cum praefatione Davidis Parei Theol. Doctoris, Ambergae: Ex typographeio Forsteriano.

ABRAHAM SCULTETUS (1634), Medullae Theologiae Patrum Syntagma: in quo theologia priscorum primitivae ecclesiae doctorum, qui ante et post concilium Nicaenum floruerunt, methodo analyticâ & syntheticâ expressa, atq[ue] à Roberto Bellarmini, Caesaris Baronii, Gregorii de Valentia, aliorumq[ue], pontificorium corruptelis ita vindicatur […] / authore D. Abrahamo Sculteto sacrarum litteratum in antiquissimâ Academiâ Heidelbergense olim professore, Francofurti: Jonae Rhodii.

DONALD SINNEMA/CHRISTIAN MOSER/HERMAN J. SELDERHUIS (ed.) (2018), Early Sessions of the Synod of Dordt, Acta et Documenta Synodi Nationalis Dordrechtanae (1618–1619), Vol. II/2, Göttingen: Vandenhoeck & Ruprecht.

GEORG SOHN (1591), Operum Georgii Sohnii Sacrae Theologiae Doctoris, vol. 2, Herborn: Christoph Rab.

CASPAR STAPHORSTIUS (1987), Een gulden tractaet, genaemt De alleenspraeck der siele tot Godt. / In voortyden beschreven door […] Aurelium Augustinum […], ende nu uyt het Latijn in de Nederlandtsche tale overgheset door Casparvm Staphorstivm, in: J. van der Haar (ed.), Schatkamer van de Gereformeerde Theologie in Nederland (c.1600–c.1800), Veenendaal: Antiquariaat Kool.

DANIEL TOSSANUS (1603), Synopsis De Patribvs, Sive Praecipvis Et Vetvstioribvs Ecclesiae Doctoribvs, Nec Non De Scholasticis, Heidelberg: Paul Tossanus.

JACOBUS TRIGLAND (1650), Kerckelycke Geschiedenissen, begrypende De swaere en Bekommerlijcke Geschillen, in de Vereenigde Nederlanden voor-gevallen, met derselver

Beslissinge, ende Aenmerckingen op de Kerckelycke Historie van Johannes Uutenbogaert. Uyt Autentycke stucken getrouwelijck vergadert, ende op begeerte der Zuyd en Noort-Hollantsche Synoden uytgegeven, tot nodige onderrichtinge, Leyden: Adriaen Wyngaerden.

GODEFRIDUM UDEMANS (1640), 't Geestelyck roer van't coopmans schip, dat is: trouwbericht, hoe dat een coopman, en coopvaerder, hem selven dragen moet in syne handelinge, in pays, ende in oorloge, voor God, ende de menschen, te water ende te lande, insonderheydt onder de heydenen in Oost ende West-Indien: ter eeren Gods, stichtinge syner gemeynten, ende saligheyt syner zielen: mitsgaders tot het tijtlick welvaren van het vaderlandt, ende syne familie, Dordrecht: Françoys Boels.

DOLF TE VELDE (ed.) (2015), Synopsis Purioris Theologiae / Synopsis of a Purer Theology; vol.1: Disputations 1–23, in: Studies in Medieval and Reformation Traditions 187, Texts and Sources 5, Leiden: Brill.

DIRCK VLACK DE IONGE (1621), Twee tractaten. Beschreven door den heylighen oudt-vader Avgvstinvm. Het eene handelende van de Goddelijcke praedestinatie. Het ander van het goedt der volhardinghe. / Wt het Latijn in Nederduytsch over geset door D. Vlack de Ionghe t'Amstelredam: Jan Evertsz Kloppenburgh.

GISBERTUS VOETIUS (1636), Sermoen van de nutticheyt der Academiën ende Scholen mitsgaders der Wetenschappen ende Consten die in de selve gheleert werden: gedaen in de Dom-kercke tot Vtrecht den 13. Martij Ouden stijls, des Sondaechs voor de Inleydinghe der nieuwer Academie aldaer, Utrecht: Aegidius/Petrus Roman.

Secondary Literature

ASSELT, WILLEM J. VAN (1997), Johannes Coccejus en de kerkvaders, Een fragment uit het zeventiende-eeuwse debat tussen protestanten en rooms-katholieken over het juiste gebruik van de kerkvaders in theologische geschillen, in: Johannes van Oort (ed.), De Kerkvaders in Reformatie en Nadere reformatie. Zoetermeer: Boekencentrum, 135–154.

ASSELT, WILLEM J. VAN (2013), Voetius, Gisbertus (1589–1676), Karla Pollmann/Willemien Otten (ed.) in: Te Oxford Guide to the Historical Reception of Augustine, vol. 3, 1879–1881, Oxford: Oxford University Press.

BACKUS, IRENA (2003), Historical method and confessional identity in the era of the reformation (1378–1615), Leiden/Boston: Brill.

BENRATH, GUSTAV ADOLF (1963), Reformierte Kirchengeschichtsschreibung an der Universität Heidelberg im 16. und 17. Jahrhundert, Speyer am Rhein: Zechnersche Buchdruckerei.

BIEBER-WALLMANN, ANNELIESE (2007). Remonstrantenstreit, in: Volker H. Drecoll (ed.) Augustin Handbuch, Tübingen: Mohr Siebeck, 627–633.

COLLIER, JAY T. (2018), Debating Perseverance: The Augustinian Heritage in Post-Reformation England, Oxford Studies in Historical Theology, Oxford/New York: Oxford University Press.

Cuno, Friedrich W. (1898), Daniel Tossanus der Ältere, Professor der Theologie und Pastor 1541–1602, 2 vol., Amsterdam

Erven, Willem (2014), Augustinus vertaald in het Nederlands, Selectief bibliografisch overzicht, Bibliotheek Augustijns Instituut Eindhoven, consultable at: https://www.augustinus.nl/pathtoimg.php?id=875 (accessed 4 February 2022).

Exalto, John (2012), Orating from the Pulpit: The Dutch Augustine and the Reformed Godly until 1700, in: Karla Pollmann/Meredith Gill (ed.), Augustine beyond the Book: Intermediality, Transmediality and Reception, Brill's Series in Church History/Religious History and Culture Series, no. 58/6, Leiden: Brill, 195–214.

Goudriaan, Aza (2007), De betekenis van de kerkvaders volgens Gisbertus Voetius, DNR 31, 173–181.

Goudriaan, Aza (2009), 'Augustine Asleep' or 'Augustine Awake'? Jacobus Arminius's Reception of Augustine, in: Theodoor M. van Leeuwen/Keith D. Stanglin/Marijke Tolsma (ed.), Arminius, Arminianism, and Europe, Jacobus Arminius (1559/60–1609), Leiden: Brill, 51–72.

Goudriaan, Aza (2015), Genade heeft geen wapens nodig: Melchior Leydeckers commentaar op Augustinus' geschrift Ad catholicos fatres, in: Jan van de Kamp/Aza Goudriaan/Wim van Vlastuin (ed.), Pietas Reformata: Religieuze vernieuwing onder gereformeerden in de vroegmoderne tijd, Zoetermeer: Boekencentrum, 25–36.

Han, Sung-jin (2008), An Investigation into Calvin's Use of Augustine, in: Dolf R.M. Britz/Victor E. d'Assonville (ed.), Prompte et sincere: John Calvin and the Exposition of the Word of God, Acta theologica, Supplementum 10, Bloemfontein, 70–83.

Hof, Willem J. op 't (2008), Willem Teellinck, Leven, geschriften en invloed, Kampen: De Groot Goudriaan.

Hof, Willem J. op 't (2011), De theologische opvattingen van Willem Teellinck, Kampen: De Groot Goudriaan.

Itterzon, Gerrit P. van (1979), Franciscus Gomarus, Groningen/Castricum: Bouma's Boekhuis.

Itterzon, Gerrit P. van (1983), Hoornbeek (Hoornbeeck, Horenbeek), Johannes, in: Doede Nauta (ed.), Biografsch Lexicon voor de Geschiedenis van het Nederlandse Protestantisme, 2, Kampen, 259–261.

Lane, Anthony N.S. (1999), John Calvin, Student of the Churchfathers, Edinburgh: T&T Clark.

Lane, Anthony N.S. (2013), 'John Calvin', in: Karla Pollmann/Willemien Otten (ed.), The Oxford Guide to the Historical Reception of Augustine, vol. 2, Oxford: Oxford University Press, 739–743.

Lange van Ravenswaay, Marius J. (1990), Augustínus totus noster, Das Augustinverständnis bei Johannes Calvin, Forschungen zur Kirchen und Dogmengeschichte, Band 45, Göttingen: Vandenhoeck & Ruprecht.

Lee, Nam Kyu (2009), Die Prädestinationslehre der Heidelberger Theologen 1583–1622, Reformed Historical Theology, volume 10, Göttingen: Vandenhoeck & Ruprecht.

Niet, Cornelis A. de (1996), Gisbertus Voetius, De praktijk der godzaligheid, TA AEKHTIKA sive Exercitia pietatis (1664), Monografieën gereformeerd piëtisme I/II; Utrecht: De Banier.

Niet, Cornelis A. de (1997), De kerkvaders in Voetius TA ASKHTIKA sive Exercitia pietatis (1664), in: Johannes van Oort (ed.), De kerkvaders in Reformatie en Nadere Reformatie, Zoetermeer: Boekencentrum, 126–134.

Oort, Johannes van (1989a), Augustinus, Voetius und die Anfänge der Utrechter Universität, in: Adolar Zumkeller (ed.), Signum pietatis. Festgabe für Cornelius Peter Mayer OSA zum 60. Geburtstag, Würzburg, 565–578.

Oort, Johannes van (1989b), De jonge Voetius en Augustinus. Een verkenning, in: Johannes van Oort/Cornelis Graafland/Aart de Groot/ Otto J. de Jong (ed.), De onbekende Voetius, Voordrachten wetenschappelijk symposium, Utrecht/Kampen: Kok, 181–190.

Oort, Johannes van (1990), Augustine's Infuence on the Preaching of Gisbertus Voetius, in: Bernard Bruning/Mathijs Lamberigts/Jozef van Houtem (ed.), Collectanea Augustiniana. Mélanges T.J. van Bavel, Leuven: University Press/Peeters, 997–1009.

Oort, Johannes van (1997), John Calvin and the Church Fathers, in: Irena Backus (ed.), The Reception of the Church Fathers in the West, From the Carolingians to the Maurists, Leiden: Brill, 661–700.

Post, Steef D. (2006), Bernardus Smytegelt, leven en werken, Kampen: De Groot Goudriaan.

Schaap, Gijsbert (2008), Franciscus Ridderus (1620–1683), Een onderzoek naar zijn theologie, bronnen en plaats in de Nadere Reformatie, Gouda: Vereniging voor Nederlandse Kerkgeschiedenis.

Seelbach, Larissa (2011), Augustin und Calvin, in: Michael Basse (ed.), Calvin und seine Wirkungsgeschichte, Berlin: LIT Verlag, 75–98.

Smits, Luchesius (1957–1958), Saint Augustin dans l'œuvre de Jean Calvin, vol. 2, Assen: van Grocum.

Spijker, W. van 't (1989), De bronnen van de Nadere Reformatie, in: De Nadere Reformatie en het Gereformeerd Piëtisme, 's Gravenhage: Boekencentrum, 34–35.

Stanglin, Keith D. (2010), The Missing Public Disputations of Jacobus Arminius. Introduction, Tekst and Notes, Brill's Series in Church History, vol. 47, Leiden: Brill.

Visser, Arnoud S.Q. (2011), Reading Augustine in the Reformation. The Flexibility of Intellectual Authority in Europe, 1500–1620, Oxford: Oxford University Press.

Zahnd, Ueli (2017), The Early John Calvin and Augustine: Some Reconsiderations, in: Papers presented at the Seventeenth International Conference on Patristic Studies held in Oxford 2015, Vol. 13: Augustine in Late Medieval Philosophy and Theology, Leuven, 181–194.

Mathijs Lamberigts

Augustine and/in Trent's Decree on Justification

1. Introduction

In this presentation I will focus on Trent's decree on justification, focusing on the presence of Augustine in the different drafts of this document.[1] As is known, it was Trent's ambition to increase and advance in esteem faith and Christian religion. It aimed at peace and unity in the Church, willing to reform the clergy and the Christian people, but had put on its program also the uprooting of heresies (*exstirpatio haeresum*), the dispelling of their darkness, and the crushing and extinction of the enemies of the Christian name.[2] However, in the officially approved texts of the Council, no reformer is explicitly mentioned by name.[3] The same was the case for the great hero of Trent, Augustine, who will only be mentioned in the footnotes of the decree under discussion. Augustine was for many Catholics and Protestants the authority *par excellence*. But people appealed to Augustine in the context of their own time, thus making use of Augustine in order to clarify, strengthen and underpin their own positions, which is not the same as presenting an historical study on Augustine. In a sense, one can say that Augustine was 'used' more to support positions than that he was studied *sine ira et studio*.

2. Augustine: A Problem

When the Council of Trent aimed at being faithful to what it considered as the Augustinian tradition,[4] the question could be asked, faithful but to which Augustine? How did they read Augustine?[5] If one reads Augustine in a chronological

---

[1] I discussed this issue briefly in Lamberigts: 2016, 156–159.
[2] *Concilium Tridentinum*, Sessio I (13 dec. 1545), *Decretum de inchoando concilio* (ed. Tanner, p. 660); Sessio II (7 jan. 1546), *Decretum de modo vivendi et aliis in concilio servandis* (ed. Tanner, p. 661). All references to the final text are taken from this edition.
[3] Luther, Lutherani, and Melanchton are regularly mentioned in the debates; see *Concilium Tridentinum* V, *ad indicem*.
[4] On the problem of the different "Augustinianisms", see the pertinent remarks of Janz: 1980, 117–127; on the different views on Augustinianism, see (1983); see also McGrath: 1981, 247–267; Fiorentino: 2008, 135–151.
[5] A very interesting example of different readings of Augustine is offered by Burger: 2020, 421–432.

way, one will see developments in the thought of Augustine. For the concept of justification, absent in the works of Augustine composed prior to his ordination to the priesthood, one has to wait until *Ad Simplicianum* (396/7). Here Augustine is adding some personal content to the Pauline texts, thus offering more than just paraphrases. But even then, one has to admit that Augustine is still rather vague, in comparison to later writings.[6] Augustine is thus developing his ideas. To give some examples, in the ecclesiological debate with the Donatists, the African hero Cyprian is regularly criticized by Augustine because the Donatists appeal to him. However, in the Pelagian controversy, the same Cyprian becomes the second most important source invoked to show the harmony between Augustine and his (African) predecessors.[7] In the dispute with the Pelagians, predestination does not play an important role,[8] while it becomes a key issue in the dialogue of Augustine with the monks of Hadrumetum and Marseille, which he considers as partners in a discussion, not as opponents in a debate.[9] Furthermore, Augustine's doctrine of predestination is not a static doctrine, but a doctrine that underwent a development.[10] Needless to say, that even for specific topics, appealing to Augustine, justified as it may be, must be carefully treated if one wants to avoid generalizations.

Augustine himself did speak of two forms of grace: the grace of creation, and the grace of salvation. The justification issue is to be situated on the second level. After the fall of Adam, the relation between human beings and God is one between sinful people and God revealing Himself to them so that they can know and love Him. The saving grace, as a result of Christ's suffering and death, is based on remission of sins and participation in the divine life. God operates in us, sinners, so that we may will (the good); He cooperates with us when we will and will in such a way that we may act according to his will. The operative grace happens without us, the cooperative grace results in regeneration and sanctification and in performing good works. In any case, no good works of piety can be done without God.[11] Grace, renewing the will, is primarily the direct work of God, but once renewed, this will can perform

---

6 See Schindler: 2004–2010, 861–863.
7 See Gaumer (2016) with a rich bibliography.
8 See Lamberigts: 2004, 282–288; see also Drecoll: 2012–2018b, 828. This study offers an impressive bibliography on the theme in Augustine.
9 Drecoll, 2012–2018b, 828f. One should keep in mind that the polemical term semi-Pelagian, used in the post-Tridentine controversies, was connecting groups which de facto had not that much in common. When speaking about Pelagians, some authors even speak of a myth; see Bonner (2018); for a critical review, see Lamberigts: 2020, 1–5.
10 See Lössl: 2002, 241–272.
11 *De gratia et libero arbitrio* 17,33, PL 44, 901: "Ut ergo uelimus, sine nobis operatur; cum autem uolumus, et sic uolumus ut faciamus, nobiscum cooperatur: tamen sine illo uel operante ut uelimus, uel cooperante cum uolumus, ad bona pietatis opera nihil ualemus."

good works and thus gain merits.[12] In his earlier works, Augustine clearly stated that God gave to everybody according to his merits,[13] merits being *meritum virtutis* or *meritum peccati*.[14] In the context of the Pelagian controversy, Augustine will emphasize that grace does not depend on our merits: it is given gratuitously. Time and again, Augustine will emphasize that grace precedes our merits and that our merits are the result of God's grace.[15] Good merits are only possible when done in love, which is the gift of grace.[16] These good merits can lead to eternal life, for they are done under grace, and confirm that faith without works is dead, as was held by James 2,17.[17] When our merits are God's gifts, God does not crown our merits as our own, but rather as his gifts.[18] However, Augustine emphasizes that we will not be justified without ourselves (cf. *Sermo* 169, 11.13), thus suggesting that we still have to act. Justification in Augustine's view changes the interiority of the sinner through the infusion of charity, a healing and renewing activity of God. Pouring out his love (cf. Rom 5:5), God changes our nature in the sense that from now on we direct our desires towards the divine good, no longer to the earthly good. We have to work on this day after day because the concupiscence of the flesh remains in us as long as we life on earth. Justification for Augustine is thus an internal process, in which people can grow. It is a process that changes the faithful in such a way that she or he, *sub gratia*, is able and willing to do what is required by God.[19]

3. Luther and Melanchton

After his discovery of the righteousness of God (around 1515),[20] Luther had stated that the human being is justified through faith and faith alone, thus stipulating that justification is the work of God and God alone. Since this discovery, Luther became aware that he himself was not able to realize or achieve his salvation. Luther experienced this insight as a liberation: that righteousness was not to be understood

---

12 With regard to merits in Augustine's work, see Drecoll: 2012, 1–5.
13 *De libero arbitrio* II,53. In passing, it should be said that Pelagius and Julian of Aeclanum will refer to this kind of texts when arguing that they hold the same positions as the early Augustine.
14 *De libero arbitrio* III,28.
15 *De gestis Pelagii* 14,35, *CSEL* 42, p. 91: "Redditur quidem meritis tuis corona sua, sed Dei dona sunt merita tua."
16 *De gratia Christi et de peccato originali* II,24,28.
17 *De fide et operibus* 17,32.
18 *De gratia et libero arbitrio* 6,15, *PL* 44, 891: "Si ergo Dei dona sunt bona merita tua, non Deus coronat merita tua tanquam merita, sed tanquam dona sua."
19 On this issue, see van Asselt: 2013, 1246f.
20 Before that period, Luther taught that God "gives grace without fail to whoever does what lies within him [quod in se est]"; quoted in McGrath: 1988, 71.

as a punishment (given men's incapacity to do what should be done in order to be saved), but as a gift of God to the sinner. God does not reward our works, but offers salvation through his mercifulness and grace. Repentance is the result of God's grace.[21] Luther insisted that God provides everything for our justification and the sinner passively will receive this: the justification of the sinner happens by grace through faith alone. All that is needed in the salvation process comes from God: faith, righteousness, justification. On this point, Luther, a former Augustinian, said farewell to Augustine.[22] Justification, for Luther, in opposition to Augustine,[23] did not result in an ontological change. Luther was so convinced of his sinfulness that he considered God's grace as something that was external to human nature, thus not renewing the human nature as was the case for Augustine.[24] God justifies, thus holding and declaring sinners to be righteous, if they believe. God justifies by giving justifying faith to the sinner; faith justifies insofar as it establishes a relation to God. Faith is understood as a trusting apprehension of the righteousness of Christ. It is a gift of the Holy Spirit. Sin(fulness) remains but is not imputed.[25] Needless to say that in such view, charity does not receive the role it had in Augustine, for whom faith must be informed by love in order to become saving faith. Luther limited his position to *fiducia* (confidence) in the mercy of God revealed in Christ. A similar position as the one of Luther was held by Melanchthon for whom the sinner is pronounced to be righteous, which is, quite evidently, not the same as being made righteous, position that was held by Augustine. However, Melanchthon considered Augustine's view on justification by faith as incomplete.[26]

---

21 McGrath: 1988, 73ff.
22 Luther: 1912, 347: "Principio Augustinum vorabam, non legabam, sed da mir in Paulo die thur auffgieng, da ich wusste, was iustificatio fidei ward, da ward es aus mit ihm". See also Schindler: 2007, 65–66.
23 Schindler: 2004-2010, 862: "Dass A. aber an eine Imputation denkt, wie man sie aus Luthers Rechtfertigungslehre kennt [...] ist zo gut wie ausgeschlossen."
24 See van Asselt: 2013, 1251. The author emphasizes that it is very difficult to give a precise account of Luther's doctrine.
25 See van Asselt: 2013, 1251.
26 Wengert: 2013, 1388.

4. The Tridentine Debate on Justification: Some Preliminary Observations[27]

In the debate on justification,[28] considered as the logical next step after the approval of the doctrine on original sin,[29] a debate that started on 21 June 1546, a great variety of positions was present, for it was, in a sense, a relatively new issue.[30] The discussion on the issue required much time and caused much confusion and dispute.[31] Theologians had their own views,[32] sometimes without showing expertise in the works of Augustine,[33] or thinking that ideas were fine and orthodox when disagreeing with Luther.[34] This also explains why the text would only be approved on January 13, 1547,[35] while initially this approval was scheduled for July 29, 1546. In the process, the discovery in 1546 of the statements of the Second Council of Orange (529) would be of help.[36] At the beginning of the discussion, the legates offered the theologians a series of questions to be answered. Theologians were asked to give answer to the questions: "What is justification?" Article 2 asked about the causes of justification: what is done by God, what is requested from man? How do we have to understand the sentence: "The human being is justified by faith" (article

---

27 The literature is overwhelming; see Susa: 2006, 34–55.
28 The issue was put on the 16th century theological debate agenda by Protestants, but the topic was also discussed by a good number of Catholic theologians, as is made clear by Jedin: 1959, 51–117. The first who systematically reflected on justification was Thomas de Vio Cajetanus (1469–1534); see his anti-Lutheran book *De fide et operibus* (1532), the title of which refers to a work of Augustine. Seripando had also reflected on the justification issue, having written a treatise on the relation between God's prescience and the human free will; see Cassaro (2010). He developed his view on justification on the basis of Augustine's *De fide et operibus* and *De spiritu et littera*. However, Luther would dominate the agenda. See Pfnür: 1970, 274–384; McGrath, 2020, 309ff. With regard to Trent's sources, see Leppin (2016, 167–183) with an excellent bibliography.
29 *Concilium Tridentinum* V (1911, 257–260).
30 See Martin-Palma: 1980, 53.
31 O'Malley: 2013, 109.
32 Between 22 and 28 June 1546, more than 30 theologians took the floor. See the survey as offered on June 25, 1546, in *Concilium Tridentinum* V (1911, 272ff). With regard to the "rich" diversity of their positions, see McGrath: 2020, 326–329.
33 Because of the fact that for most of the interventions of the theologians, only summaries are preserved, it is not always easy to grasp what they meant when appealing to Augustine. Only a few full texts are preserved; see the intervention of the Jesuit Salmeron; cf. *Concilium Tridentinum* V (1911, 265–272).
34 See the warnings of Cardinal Pole in *Concilium Tridentinum* I (1901, 82). Concilii Tridentini Diariorum. Pars prima. Herculis Severoli commentarius Angeli Massarelli diaria I-IV. Collegit edidit illustravit S. Merkle.
35 In this regard, Pesch (2000, 5) observed: "Les compromis y sont si nombreux que nous ne pouvons que nous étonner que finalement le texte du décret sur la justification ait abouti à une forme aussi achevée et cohérente."
36 See Evans: 1988, 264; cf. also McGrath: 1993, 90f; 1988, 69.

3). Article 4 was asking about the way in which works contribute to justification, before, during and after the justification. Article 5 invited to answer the question what precedes, accompanies and follows justification. Article 6 was asking for proofs in Scripture, Councils, the Church Fathers and the apostolic tradition that will be able to underpin the idea of justification.[37]

5. The Discussion among the Theologians

The summary of the debates (in six meetings, held between June 22 and June 28, 1546) was a summary of summaries and Augustine was seemingly not really present. However, in his very long intervention, Alfonso Salmeron,[38] theologian to Paul III, regularly appealed to Augustine and argued in favor of meritorious good works. Salmeron made clear that *iustitia* in the sense of righteousness is related to remission and renewal: an external and an internal effect. Through the new law of Christ human beings are just in the presence of God, free from sin and renewed in their spirit. Righteousness cannot be reached by human beings. It must be infused by God in order to take away sin and to help us to do the law of God.[39] Through the gift of justice, we are made just, as Augustine maintained.[40] Salmeron sharply criticized Melanchton who in his commentary on Romans had stated that we are not just, but considered as just. Salmeron, referring to Augustine who claimed that God's grace is only true "si hoc rebus exhibeat, quod verbis sonat",[41] was of the opinion that our justice corresponds to a reality. The justice of the Gospel, of God (Rom 1:17), *ex fide* (Phil 3:9), justification to life (Rom 5:18) is nothing else than love, as was abundantly said by Augustine.[42] According to Salmeron, love, grace and justice are identical for Augustine.[43] Love becomes famous (*nobilitare*) and exalts in the children of God, according to Augustine distinguishing them and

---

37 *Concilium Tridentinum* V (1911, 261).
38 On this humanist, see Kramp: 2015, 504–527; on his intervention, see Leppin: 2016, 177–180.
39 *Concilium Tridentinum* V (1911, 265f).
40 Salmeron quoted from *De spiritu et littera* 11,18 CSEL 60, 171: "Iustus ex fide vivit. Haec est iustitia Dei, quae in testamento vetere velata in novo revelatur; quae ideo iustitia Dei dicitur, quod impertiendo eam iustos facit."
41 *Contra Iulianum* V,11.
42 *Concilium Tridentinum* V (1911, 267). Quotes were taken from *De natura et gratia* 38,45; 42,49: 63,74; 70,84 and *De quaestionibus* 83, n. 63,4. For the possible Medieval background of this position, see Rückert: 1925, 123–124. However, see also the critique of Oberman 1964, 251–282; for the further discussion between the two, see Leppin: 2016, 168–169.
43 *Concilium Tridentinum* V (1911, 267).

those of the perdition.[44] In such context, it is clear that love transcends the classical concept of justice (*unicuique suum tribuere*), for love is the highest gift of justice.[45]

With regard to the second question, Salmeron argued that God is the actor of our entire justification (*totius nostrae iustificationis*), for God alone can forgive our sins, making us his heirs of the most happy vision. This is done on the basis of God's goodness and mercy through Christ, who takes away sins. In fact, through justification, God is forgiving our sins and infuses the habits of faith, hope and love. He further disposes us through his grace and vocation. However, this does not lead to complete passivity on our side.[46] At the end of his argumentation for 2, Salmeron concluded that this was the doctrine of Augustine, Bernard, and Thomas.[47] For nr. 3, Salmeron quoted Augustine's *De praedestinatione sanctorum* 2,6 in order to make clear that to believe is nothing else than reflecting with assent. Augustine was also his authority when Salmeron argued that faith without love does not help and that faith receives both remission of sins and the love of God.[48] For Salmeron it was clear that faith requires love in order to be fruitful. For nr. 4, Salmeron, when dealing with works done after grace is received, referred to *In epistola Ioannis tractatum* 5,4 where Augustine stated that love deserves to be augmented, and what is growing may deserve to become perfect.[49] Salmeron thus emphasized two points that will be characteristic for the decree: forgiveness and inner change.

6. The Debate among Bishops and Religious Superiors

In a next step, the discussion was continued by the bishops and the superiors of religious orders.[50] Several of the interveners were well informed, even those who did not belong to the schools of religious orders.[51] Some participants would explicitly refer to Augustine.[52] Bishops were aware that Councils such as Carthage, Milev,

---

44 See Augustine, *De Trinitate* 15,17,31–18,32
45 *Concilium Tridentinum* V (1911, 267).
46 *Concilium Tridentinum* V (1911, 267f).
47 *Concilium Tridentinum* V (1911, 268).
48 Salmeron appeals to *De Trinitate* 15,18,32, CCSL 50, p. 507: "Sine caritate quippe fides potest quidem esse sed non et prodesse." Cf. also *Enarrationes in Psalmos,* 31,2,6. The reference to *De gestis cum Emerito* seems to be wrong; I think that the correct reference is found in *Sermo ad Caesariensis Ecclesiae plebem* 3.
49 *Concilium Tridentinum* V (1911, 271).
50 For the summaries, see *Concilium Tridentinum* V (1911, 337–340; 379–383). In these summaries, Augustine is nowhere mentioned.
51 See the pertinent remarks of Jedin: 1957, 155.
52 See, e. g., the interventions of archbishop Saraceni of Matera; bishop Vigerio della Rovere of Sinigallia; bishop Cortesi of Vaison; the Dominican bishop of Mottola, Pasquali; the Dominican bishop of

Orange had stated that justification must be attributed to God's grace and not to our works. According to the Catholic faith people receive this grace in baptism. This grace enables us to do what would lead to our salvation, "Christo auxiliante et cooperante".[53] Augustine himself had made clear in *Ennarationes in psalmos* 145 that it is good for us that God honors us and that we honor God.[54] Archbishop Saraceni of Matera observed that our good works are both God's gifts and our works "quia nos fideliter [...] illa exercemus et sic fideliter exercendo et in illis ambulando habemus meritum ex promissione, quam nobis fecit Deus."[55] For the archbishop, the attribution of good works to us by no means is to be considered as a weakening of Christ's glory.[56] However, he insists that these good works are still *our* works.

No wonder that in such context, the statute of the human beings free will become a matter of debate. Pietro Bertano, bishop of Fano, in his intervention of July 8, referring to Augustine, *Sermo* 169,15: "Qui fecit te sine te, non te iustificat sine te. Ergo fecit nescientem, iustificat volentem", argued that the free will is not excluded, insisting on the crucial role of love, for "ergo non sola fide, sed fide viva et armata caritate, id est operibus, iustificamur".[57] In light of the debate with Luther and Melanchton, justification was understood as *per fidem* (through the mediation of faith), for faith will justify us when we receive Christ's justice through faith.[58] The Jesuit Claude Lejay, theological advisor of cardinal Truchsess von Waldbourg, bishop of Augsburg, and, like the cardinal very sensitive about the situation in Germany, seeking to avoid harming protestant feelings, distinguished between active justification (infusion of grace) and passive justification (liberation from sins and the justifying grace). He insisted that it is only after God's mercy that the human free will, helped by God, starts doing the good in his thoughts, believes in

---

Fano, Bertani; *Concilium Tridentinum* V (1911, 290, 293, 298, 304 (and 307), 310). Some bishops even attributed works to Augustine he had not written; see the intervention of bishop Campeggio of Feltre; *Concilium Tridentinum* V (1911, 298).

53 See *CCSL* 148A, 63: "Hoc etiam secundum fidem catholicam credimus, quod post acceptam per baptismum gratiam omnis baptizati Christo auxiliante et cooperante, quae ad salute animae pertinent, possint et debeant, si fideliter laborare uoluerint, adimplere."

54 *Enarrationes in psalmos* 145,11, *CCSL* 40, 2113 : "Tibi bonum est quod te colit Deus; tibi bonum est quod colis Deum."

55 *Concilium Tridentinum* V (1911, 290).

56 The idea that God is crowning his works in us, comes back time and again; see the intervention of the bishop of Senigallia, *Concilium Tridentinum* V (1911, 293), referring to Augustine, *Epistula* 194,5, *CSEL* 57, 190: "Cum Deus coronat merita nostra, nihil aliud coronet quem munera sua?" Cf. also *De gratia et libero arbitrio* 7,16.

57 *Concilium Tridentinum* V (1911, 310).

58 See also Cornelio Musso, bishop of Bitonto, July 9, 1546, *Concilium Tridentinum* V (1911, 318).

God and comes to baptism, clearly referring to Augustine,[59] for whom free will is restored and renewed through the gift of grace. Lejay thus made clear that works are necessary, and faith alone does not suffice, but at the same time he very much insisted on the fact that good works only will be done within the framework of faith and grace.

In such context, we will present the appeal to Augustine by two people. We focus first on bishop Tommasso Sanfelice of La Cava (South Italy). His incident with Dionisio de Zannettini, a Franciscan, bishop of Chironissa and Melopotamos in Crete[60] is often described with some pleasure by historians of the Council of Trent. While Sanfelice's first intervention on July 6 about the first state of justification had not caused turbulences,[61] his second, held on July 17, met with critique from Zannettini. Sanfelice had stated that Christian righteousness consisted of God's grace, the assent of human beings and the living faith. He had warned for human arrogance: without the constant help of the divine grace faith could not stand. No one could do any good without faith. The just must daily be watered by God's grace in order to do the works of justice. The faithful must be aware that they are sinners and must attribute all things to God's mercy and concede all things to God's glory, for He has changed our evil will into a good one, giving us the power to want and do the good. Sanfelice had underpinned his position not only with Biblical quotes and texts of the Council of Orange, but also had abundantly referred to texts of Augustine, making clear that God makes the unwilling willing (*Enchiridion* 32), that one must put his hope and glory "in praecedente et subsequente misericordia Dei, qua praeventus es peccator, ut salveris [...]" (*Sermo* 366,7, *PL* 39, 1650),[62] praying: "Opus tuum in me vide, non meum; nam meum si videris, damnas, tuum si videris, coronas", etc. (*Enarrationes in psalmos* 137,18, *CCSL* 40, p. 1989). Conversion was considered to be a gift of God (*De gratia et libero arbitrio* 5,10) and the faithful had to pray every day for forgiveness of sin, an argument very dear to Augustine

---

59 Lejay referred to Augustine, *Ad Bonifatium* (*Epistula* 98), and *De predestinatione sanctorum* 7,12. See his intervention on July 12, 1546, *Concilium Tridentinum* V (1911, 330).

60 On Zannettini, see Buschbell: 1910, 36–60.

61 For this intervention, see *Concilium Tridentinum* V (1911, 294ff). Sanfelice had spoken of *fides sola*, but in a context in which he not only said that one is justified by faith alone, but also that one is made from sinner faithful, thus loving God, putting his hope in God and committing himself to the divine faith in which the human being will find his salvation given and promised by God. He had quoted a very convincing text from *Enarrationes in psalmos* 55,8. On Sanfelice, see also Rückert: 1925: 162–167.

62 Already the Maurists had their doubts about the authenticity of this sermon; see *PL* 39, 1646f, note b. However, the ideas as expressed in this sermon and especially in the text quoted, cannot be considered as foreign to Augustine.

in his debates with the Pelagians.[63] In se, this was the position of a man who had well studied Augustine. It was also the position of a man who was aware of human beings' sinfulness, also under grace. However, as far as I can see, he never spoke of *servum arbitrium*.[64] When Zannettini called him either a knave or a fool, the incident ended in violence, Sanfelice grabbing Zanettini by his beard. Sanfelice had to leave the Council, partly because of Zannettini's provocation, partly because of his vehement reaction.[65]

Also the *votum* of Girolamo Seripando,[66] offered on July 13, 1546, was full of quotes from and references to Biblical texts and Augustine.[67] Seripando considered his presentation as a contribution to the life of the Church: for him the justification doctrine should be "clara et facilis, quia sapientibus et insipientibus exponenda est".[68] In passing, it should be said that several of Augustine's works were translated into Italian in the 16th century: *De spiritu et littera, De natura et gratia; De fide et operibus, De praedestinatione sanctorum*, a good indication that interest in Augustinian issues was not a privilege of theologians, but was considered as a topic that matters for faithful. Seripando, like many others, was well aware of the many meanings of justification but considered the following two important:

> "ex peccatore, impio, damnato, reo iustum, pium absolutum, reconciliatum effectum esse"
> Penitence "quae ex divina gratia provenit"

With regard to the first position, Seripando appeals to Augustine's commentaries on Psalm 32; 62, the letter to the Romans, the Gospel of John, and Letter 140, also entitled *De gratia novi testamenti*. Although Seripando made use of early works of Augustine, written before 396, most of his quotes and references were taken from the anti-Pelagian period or from the works as written in discussion with the monks of Hadrumetum and Marseille. Seripando insisted on the gratuitous character of grace, quoting quite evidently 1 Cor 4:7 (*Quid habes quod non accepisti*), John 8:36 (*when the son sets you free, you will truly be free*), but also abundantly from Augustine, *Enarrationes in Psalmos* 55,8; *De spiritu et littera* 30,52, CSEL 60,

---

63 Sanfelice also referred to Jerome, Ambrose, Cyprian, Cyrillus, Leo I and the Council of Orange, emphasizing that conversion is a gift of God. See *Concilium Tridentinum* V (1911, 352ff).
64 At contra, see Jedin: 1957 p. 159.
65 For the details, see *Concilium Tridentinum* V (1911, 396f); Jedin: 1957 pp. 160–163; O'Malley: 2013, 109.
66 The literature on Seripando is overwhelming but differs on the level of the evaluation of Seripando's contribution to the Tridentine theology; Stakemeier (1937); Forster (1963); Marranzini: 1997, 343–370.
67 July 13, 1546, *Concilium Tridentinum* V (1911, 332–336).
68 Evans: 1988, 264.

208: "Lex per fidem non evacutur,[69] sed statuitur"). Seripando insists that the power of grace "suaviter ex nolente facere volentem et libere quidem volentem", rightly referring to Augustine, *Contra duas epistulas pelagianorum* I,19,37, *CSEL* 60, 454: "Trahitur ergo miris modis, ut uelit, ab illo, qui nouit intus in ipsis hominum cordibus operari, non ut homines, quod fieri non potest, nolentes credant, sed ut uolentes ex nolentibus fiant."[70] Seripando emphasized that on the level of salvation, healing and the like, things can only happen with the help of grace: *Epistula* 217,4; *De gratia et libero arbitrio* 7,33; *Contra duas epistulas pelagianorum* I,3,7.

Also, with regard to penitence, Seripando appealed to the Bible and to Augustine, thus stating that penitence is coming from divine grace (cf. *Epistula* 265,7). In line with Augustine, Seripando maintained that remission is given to those who repent through the grace and mercy of God, not according to their merits.[71] With Augustine, Seripando argued that faith justifies both the just of the Old Testament and people today. This faith is faith in Jesus Christ, his suffering, cross, death and resurrection (*De natura et gratia* 44,51).

Seripando also spoke of another meaning of justification, namely living justly, obeying the divine mandates, which is properly speaking sanctification. On this level, the just is truly just because of God's love (*De natura et gratia* 38,45). Beginning love is beginning justice, progress in love is progress in justice, great love is great justice and perfect love is perfect justice. Seripando considered Augustine 's conclusion: "Sed caritas de corde puro et conscientia bona et fide non ficta, quae tunc maxima est in hac uita, quando pro illa ipsa contemnitur uita" (*De natura et gratia* 70,84, *CSEL* 60, 298) as an argument that justification is impetrated by faith, as was said by De *spiritu et littera* 29,51. Through justifying faith, people recognizing their weakness, will be able to fulfil the law and live according to the law.

It will be clear that for Seripando, as for Augustine, God's grace is prevenient and is not preceded by any human act. True human freedom *starts* once we are *sub gratia*. For both Augustine and the Augustinian Seripando, true human freedom is rooted in grace, is offered by God's pure goodness. It is only *sub gratia* that the free will can be healed and gradually overcome concupiscence. God's justice, understood as the divine will for salvation through the person Christ and his redemptive work, overcomes the human being who is now connected with Christ. An intimate relationship arises. Reconciled with God, human beings receive the *caritas* of God in order to be sanctified. This love goes hand in hand with faith and hope. This whole process of justification will be completed when we go over

---

69 Seripando uses the verb *destruitur*.
70 Seripando also refers to *Tractatus in Ioannis Evangelium* 26,4.
71 Augustine, *Epistula* 186, 9,32f.

from this life to eternal life, even although we are not sure about our final salvation. This final completion can be described as both merit and grace: the reward human beings receive is at the same time grace. In fact, our good works find their origin in the connection with the justice of Christ.

Both the intervention of Sanfelice and that of Seripando make clear that in the whole justification process God's grace takes precedence. Given our human sinfulness, this grace is needed during the whole process of justification and this up to the end. Because of the sinfulness of the faithful, his good works, meritorious as they are, do not suffice and all faithful have to put their hope in the mercy of God.

7. Towards a First Draft

While the debate on what should be present in the text continued,[72] through vote, four bishops were appointed to prepare a first draft: the Conventual Musso (40 votes), bishop Giacomelli of Belcastro (23 votes), archbishop Vauchop of Armagh (19 votes) and bishop de Nobili of Accia. After consultation of the Council theologians, the text was presented to the Council Fathers on July 23 and 24. In the first three paragraphs, the text positively explained what Catholics held. In the next 18 paragraphs, 18 positions were condemned. Given the fact that nobody was really happy with this draft and that meanwhile Seripando was already asked by Cervini to prepare a new text that was ready before the first draft became subject of discussion on August 13, we will not discuss this draft,[73] which showed that the bishops were still searching for a clear concept. The text was soon removed from the calendar on August 17.[74]

8. Seripando's August Draft

In the beginning of August, Seripando thus prepared a new draft (preliminary design A), which was ready on August 11, 1546.[75] The text consisted of an introduction and 5 chapters (chapter 5 consisting of 8 canones). This draft, very Biblical in tone, abundantly quoted from or referred to Augustine (45 times). In chapter 1, Seripando dealt with Adam and the fall. Explaining that our origins lay in Adam, the head of humanity and as it were our beginning, he referred to *Tractatus in Ioannis*

---

72 Jedin: 1957, 162.
73 For this draft, see *Concilium Tridentinum* V (1911, 384-391; for the discussion, see 402-417).
74 *Concilium Tridentinum* V (1911, 410).
75 For this text, see *Concilium Tridentinum* V (1911, 821-828).

evangelium 9,10. Describing the consequences of the fall, among others the perverse love, *De civitate Dei* 22,22 was invoked as testimony.[76] In chapter 2, Seripando discussed the duties of the law and the promises of Christ. Dealing with the contrast between the abundance of sin and the superabundance of grace, he referred to Augustine's *Enarrationes in psalmos* 102,15, where Augustine commented on verse 7 of that psalm. In chapter 3, Seripando discussed the incarnation of the Word, and commenting on John 1:14 (*the Word has become flesh*), he referred to *De vera religione* 16,30, *CCSL* 32, p. 205, where Augustine stated that Christ "totum hominem suscipere dignatus est." In chapter 4, Seripando searched for a definition of justification. Source of inspiration was Augustine's antithesis generation-regeneration, often present in Augustine's anti-Pelagian works but also in his other works and his sermons (see e. g., *Sermo* 111,2),[77] as became clear in Seripando's notes in the margin. Indeed, justification cannot be understood without reference to our being in Adam and our participation in his fall and its consequences. In Adam, we were confused. We must leave him and go to Christ in order to overcome our confusion (*Enarrationes in psalmos* 70,1,3).

Chapter 5 consisted of 8 well elaborated *canones*. The first dealt with the works of the unbelievers and the sins of the faithful. On the basis of *De spiritu et littera* 27,48, Seripando argued that good works, done by unbelievers, must not be criticized but even praised,[78] even although they do not contribute to a human beings' justification, as was stated in canon 14 of the Council of Orange. With Augustine (*Enarrationes in Psalmos* 31,2,2.4), Seripando held that God's grace alone through the human faith leads to the right intention. The theological-moral qualification of good depends on God's grace given to human being in order to do what is to be done (with a clear reference to Augustine, *Epistula* 164,4). Seripando concluded that the engagement of the faithful to convert sinning faithful or unfaithful will have an impact on the judgment of the latter, basing his argument on *De patientia* 26,23.[79]

Also in the canones (chapter 5), Augustine is abundantly present in Seripando's discussion of the preparation to justification (5 times),[80] the justification *ex sola*

---

[76] When speaking of prevarication and disobedience, he referred to *De ecclesiasticis dogmatibus* 21, attributing it to Augustine, because it was included in his works. Today, the authorship of Gennadius is generally accepted.

[77] In the most recent edition in *CCSL* 41Bb, p. 363, it is *Sermo* 167 appendix.

[78] With regard to the efforts made by these people, Seripando quotes from *Enarrationes in Psalmos* 31,2,4.

[79] In my view, the text mentioned in *Concilium Tridentinum* V (1911, 823), corresponds to *De patientia*, less to *De spiritu et littera* 27.

[80] Quotes are taken from early works such as the *Quaestiones*, anti-pelagian works such as *De peccatorum meritis et remissione*, *Contra duas epistulas pelagianorum* and *Contra Iulianum*, while also works written for the monks in Marseille, like *De praedestinatione sanctorum* are present.

fide (at least 14 quotes or references to Augustine, coming from works covering his whole oeuvre), the (absence of) certitude about predestination and perseverance to the end (7 quotes or references; several from his works written for the monks of Hadrumetum and Marseille), the possible observance of God's precepts (2 quotes or references), the loss of grace and righteousness through sin (4 quotes or references), the merits of the just and the crown of righteousness (2 quotes or references). Seripando did not offer a systematic study on Augustine, but Augustine clearly functioned as a source of inspiration.

On August 29, 1546 or some days before,[81] Seripando finished a kind of adapted text.[82] The canones were shortened, ending in anathema's (in the first version it was said that people should not say nor teach). In this shortened version of the canones, no reference to Augustine is present in the footnotes.[83] Given the fact that quite a good number of the texts, presented in Seripando A, returned in Seripando B, several of the references to Augustine in the first draft, are present in the second text, but are not indicated in footnotes!

Seripando made it very clear that justification is more than just the imputation of Christ's righteousness. It also has to do with righteousness diffused in our hearts.[84] If Christ's grace changes our inner life, we must be *capax gratiae* and thus actively willing to change our life.[85] At the same time, Seripando is well aware of the fact that our acts and deeds are imperfect and for that reason will time and again stress the importance of the mercy of God.[86]

9. The September Draft (Second Draft)

While Seripando's text would only partially become the basis for a next version, his method, putting "positive" theology first (with a theological statement in fifteen chapters, characterized by pastoral instructions), paved the way for an approach that will become standard for the following conciliar doctrinal decrees.[87] On September 23, the draft on justification was presented by Cervini in his own name, for the

---

81 The date is uncertain and we probably have to correct the date as given in *Concilium Tridentinum* V (1911, 828) (August 19) into August 29; see the arguments in Jedin: 1957 p. 485.
82 *Concilium Tridentinum* V (1911, 828–833).
83 Augustine is mentioned once, in the new canon 1, but the text is referring to Gennadius, not to Augustine; see *Concilium Tridentinum* V (1911, 832).
84 The idea was present in the text of August 11, and repeated in the text of August 29.
85 In this regard, Pas (1954, 7) rightly emphasizes that for Seripando in the final judgement not only our habitus but also our acts will be evaluated.
86 Pas: 1954, 8.
87 O'Malley: 2013, 111.

legates had refused to present it under their responsibility. Seripando was disappointed: "decretum … deformatum, ut illud neque agnoscerem neque probarem".[88] The changes were quite substantial, chapters 2–5 of Seripando's text being omitted. However, the drafters had found inspiration in Seripando's text for their introduction. Several texts of the September version resounded the texts as present in the canones 2–7 of Seripando A.[89] Indirectly, and although not mentioned in the version of September, Augustine remained present.[90] Explicit references to Augustine were reduced to only one in chapter 8 – the quote was already present in Seripando A[91] –, when it was said that God does not command what is impossible but commanding He is admonishing people to do what they can and to ask for what they cannot (*De natura et gratia* 43,50).[92] This quote would appear in all following versions up to the final text.

The number of canons had increased to 21. There are striking similarities between Seripando B, canon 4 and canon 7 of the September text. The two texts reject justification by faith alone. They also condemn those who deny that justice is diffused in our hearts and reduce justification to the remission of sin. Also, the idea about the certitude of remission of sins is condemned.[93] One of the titles for this canon in Seripando B was *iustitia duplex*, and although the September text did not offer titles for its canones, Seripando's idea was preserved, not the term *duplex iustitia*.[94] Also, Seripando B, canones 5 (on predestination and perseverance

---

88   See *Concilium Tridentinum* V (1911, 427, n. 2). See also Rückert: 1925, 97–98.
89   For the introduction, compare the September version, p. 421, ll. 5–8.8–12 with Seripando A, p.821, ll. 1–4; 7–11. 15f; for nr. 1, ll. 14–18 with Seripando A, p. 821 ll. 18–23 (although with some omissions); for nr. 6, p. 422, ll. 26–28.31–34; p. 423, ll.8–12 with Seripando, p. 824, canon 2, ll. 6–8.10–16.25–30; for nr. 7, p. 423–424, ll. 14–22.42 (p. 423)–4 (p. 424).12–19 with Seripando A, p. 824–825, canon 3, ll. 39 (p. 824)–5 (p. 825).ll. 22–26.27–28.31–36; for nr. 8, p. 424, ll. 33–37 with Seripando A, canon 4, ll. 11–16; for nr. 9, p. 425, ll. 22f, with Seripando, p. 826, canon 4, ll. 40f; for nr. 10, pp. 425f, ll. 30–42 (p. 425) and ll. 1–3.4–10 (p. 426) with Seripando A, p. 827, canon 6, ll. 15–24.29–29.31–38; for nr. 11, p. 426, ll. 14–22, with Seripando A, p. 828, ll. 14–22. Sometimes, the September text changed the order followed by Seripando, but the dependence is clear; see chapter 7, ll. 4–7 and Seripando A, p. 825, ll. 39–42. For all these texts, we follow *Concilium Tridentinum* V (1911).
90   For canon 3, Seripando several times referred to Augustine; chapter 7 of the September version took over Seripando's text, without explicitly mentioning these references. The same is true for chapter 10 and 11, where Seripando had Augustine in mind.
91   See *Concilium Tridentinum* V, (1911, 826, canon 5).
92   A reference is made to *De correptione et gratia* 15,46 when arguing that there is no certitude about one's the belonging to the number of the predestined.
93   Compare canon 7 of the September text (*Concilium Tridentinum* V, (1911, 427)) with Seripando B, canon 4 (*Concilium Tridentinum* V, (1911, 832)).
94   The September text explicitly says that there are not two justices and speaks of *una iustitia Dei per Iesum Christum*; see *Concilium Tridentinum* V, (1911, 423, l. 35). On this term and its context, see Rückert: 1925, 216–256

to the end), 6 (God's commands are not impossible), 7 (on the loss of the grace of justification), 8 (on the merits of good works, explicitly defended by Seripando) inspired the canones 8, 10, 16a and 21a in the September text.[95]

During a long debate, first among the theologians (September 27–29),[96] next among the bishops and superior generals (October 1–12),[97] the term *duplex iustitia* was rejected, although one cannot avoid the impression that both among the theologians and the Council fathers many did not worry about it.[98] During the debates, Augustine was not that often mentioned[99] and sometimes, when mentioned, the authors attributed works to him he in fact had not written.[100] Even worse, sometimes, they attributed ideas to Augustine that were in contradiction with what the bishop of Hippo held himself.[101]

But some interveners were very well familiar with Augustine. In his intervention, the general of the Conventuals appealed with agreement (among others) to Augustine, *De spiritu et littera* 9,15–10,16; 30,52;[102] 36,64. Augustine had argued that justification is gratuitous but that it does not happen *sine voluntate nostra*. In the text quoted, Augustine also argued that the law functions as a pedagogue, leading to grace, through which alone the law can be filled in. Augustine also emphasized that the good works are realized after we have received grace. Finally, the general of the Conventuals suggested that when Augustine may imply that it is impossible to implement all precepts, the bishop of Hippo had in mind the constant impediments that people continue to experience in this life.[103]

On October 8, Seripando took the floor. The idea of the *duplex iustitia*, too easily filled in as double justification,[104] was linked with positions held by the

---

95 Compare the September text (*Concilium Tridentinum* V, (1911, 427)) with the text in Seripando B, (*Concilium Tridentinum* V, (1911, 832–833)).
96 See *Concilium Tridentinum* V, pp. 431–442. We only have, for the most part, summaries at our disposal. As far as I can see, nobody extensively discussed Augustine.
97 For a summary of the interventions of the fathers, see *Concilium Tridentinum* V (1911, 500–509).
98 See the pertinent and detailed remarks of Pas: 1954, 20–23; see also McGrath: 2020, 332f.
99 Exceptions are della Rovere, asking to add at the end of chapter 11 Augustine's famous quote that God's gifts are our merits and that God crowns his gifts in our merits; cf. *De gratia et libero arbitrio* 6,15; see *Concilium Tridentinum* V (1911, 463).
100 See the intervention of bishop Filhol of Aix, arguing that God did not order impossible things. Filhol referred to a text which is no longer attributed to Augustine; see *Concilium Tridentinum* V (1911, 448). He, like bishop Lippomani of Verona, seemingly made use of compilations, based on works of Augustine; see p. 460.
101 See the appeal of bishop Roverella of Ascoli to *De civitate Dei* 18; *Concilium Tridentinum* V (1911, 464).
102 He rightly argued that this passage is even more convincing than the previous text; see *Concilium Tridentinum* V (1911, 483).
103 *Concilium Tridentinum* V (1911, 483f).
104 See McGrath: 2020, 312f.

Cologne theologian Johannes Gropper. Gropper attempted to build bridges between the *Catholica* and the Lutheran doctrine of justification.[105] It was taken over by Contarini – Contarini knew the work of Gropper that was translated in Italian –, who would speak during the diet of Regensburg of the *iustitia inhaerens*[106] and the *iustitia Christi* as two aspects of the justification.[107] Even although Contarini's definition of justification was not accepted by Luther and the pope, both Gropper and Contarini were respected as promoters of reform in the life of the Catholic Church. Both had attempted to bridge the gap between the Catholic Church and the Reformation. This explains why Seripando in his intervention in this debate (October 8, 1546), questioned the exclusion of these catholic theologians (like Pflug, Contarini[108] and Gropper, their doctrine being excluded in chapter 7 of the text).[109] Seripando defended these theologians because their view of double righteousness could do justice to both the human beings' attempts to live a good life and to the absolute priority of grace and Christ's *iustitia* in the justification process. Seripando insisted on the fact that Augustine and Bernard were their inspiration,[110] not Luther, Calvin, and Bucer. The *iustitia inhaerens*[111] was understood by Seripando as a justice, inhabiting in human beings as becomes clear in human beings' works, albeit that even under grace the good works of human beings are hindered and tempered by the still present and active concupiscence. Also, under grace, human beings continue to consider themselves as sinners/sinful. For Seripando, the last

---

105 See Braunisch (1974).
106 In passing, I observe that the term *iustitia inhaerens* is present in Trent's final version, in nr. 16.
107 For Contarini's view, see Hünermann: 1921, 1–22; Rückert: 1925, 158–162.
108 It is true that Contarini had to defend himself against accusations of unorthodoxy; cf. his *Epistola de iustificatione* (1541), but he remained a respected collaborator of Paul III. However, problems continued after his death; see Arnold: 2008.
109 Seripando would receive support from bishop Florimonte di Aquino: *Consilium Tridentinum* V (1911, 495): "[…] dixit […] quod nihil condamnetur nisi prius rationibus adversariorum examinatis, prout admonuit generalis Eremitarum, praesertim circa illas duas iustitias […]", referring to *Confessiones* V,9,17, where God's mercy receives a central place but also the merits of Monica, the mother of Augustine are praised and taken into account *coram Deo*. Florimonte suggested to leave out the *iustitia imputata*, holding "quod una sit iustitia tantum, qua iustificamur, videlicet nobis inhaerens." Whether Florimonte rightly understood Seripando, is another question; see *Concilium Tridentinum* V (1911, 496, note 1).
110 This claim has some validity; see Augustine, *Enarrationes in Psalmos* 142,10, CCSL 40, p. 2066: "Sed loquitur corpus, loquitur unusquisque illius gratia iustificatus, inhaerens illi in caritate, et deuota humilitate […]". In a written memorandum, Seripando also referred to Jacobus Perez, who indeed had written commentaries on the Psalms and who was considered to be one of those who promoted the doctrine of the *duplex iustitia*, just like Giles of Viterbo, somebody Seripando had known as the general of his order; for Jacobus Perez, see now François: 2020, 471–497.
111 Trent will never speak of the *gratia inhaerens*.

word in human beings' life and judgement is God's mercy in Christ. In the last judgment, the connectedness with Christ will be central.

With regard to the free will, Seripando appealed to Augustine, the latter making clear that grace does not destroy the free will but confirms it and that grace can only help the free will if it exists.[112] When discussing chapter 7 (being very critical to this chapter that insisted on one *iustitia*),[113] Seripando made use of Augustine to make clear that the law commands, while the righteousness of faith impetrates.[114] Explaining the difference between righteousness *ex fide* and righteousness *ex lege*, Seripando argued, on the basis of *Epistula* 186,8, written in the midst of the Pelagian controversy, that we are justified on the basis of our faith. Seripando thus rejected any righteousness *ex lege*.

At the end of the day, one has to admit that even although the term *duplex iustitia* was not accepted, the way Seripando made his case, very much resounded Augustine.[115]

10. Towards the November Draft

The topics of the imputed justice and the certitude of grace, both dealing with the impact of justice and human beings' weakness after baptism, would be subject of discussion among the theologians from October 15 to October 26 and this on the basis of a text proposed by Del Monte.[116] The majority of the theologians was of the opinion that the *iustitia inhaerens* sufficed and that there was no need for a new imputation of Christ's righteousness.[117] With regard to the certitude of grace, some

---

112 Augustine used this argument regularly in his debate with Julian of Aeclanum; see *Contra duas epistulas pelagianorum* II,10,22; III,7,20; IV,6,13.

113 With regard to the diversity of opinions, see *Concilium Tridentinum* V (1911, 504ff).

114 See *De spiritu et littera* 13,22; *Contra duas epistulas pelagianorum* IV,5,10; *De gratia et libero arbitrio* 16,32 etc.

115 Brunner (1966, 151) rightly observes that Seripando on this matter was less the looser than often suggested.

116 *Concilium Tridentinum* V (1911, 523–632). Pas (1954, 31f) makes very clear that the question about the imputed grace as formulated by Del Monte, did not do justice to the initial formulation of Seripando.

117 On the diversity of opinions among those who were opposed to the idea of *duplex iustitia*, see Pas (1954, 32–43). Generally speaking, one can say that the opponents of the *duplex iustitia* agreed that the deeds the justified do under grace are not perfect (the point of Seripando when arguing for the imputed justice), but this does not require the imputation of Christ's justice. (Pas, 1954, 44) emphasizes that most of the opponents to the idea speak very respectfully about Seripando. Already on October 29, Del Monte proposed not to condemn this doctrine, but only the protestant heresy, which was considered to argue that justification exclusively exists in the extrinsic imputation of Christ's merits, without interior grace; see (Pas, 1954, 45).

held that sometimes on the basis of faith, one could know that one was *sub gratia* (21), while an important minority was of the opinion that one could never know this (14). For two theologians, both positions did not need to be condemned.[118]

Gradually, it became clear that the text on justification needed more time and more body. Cervini would entrust the recasting of the September draft to Seripando,[119] who started his work on October 20, 1546. In his extensive work (taking into account the observations of theologians and bishops; the observations of the Roman theologians, arrived at Trent on October 24; the observations of cardinal Pole), he was helped by Massarelli, with whom he daily met.[120] This new version, ready on October 31,[121] was presented on November 5.[122] The text was, again, altered by cardinal Del Monte and Cornelio Musso, the Conventual bishop of Bitonto.[123] While Seripando's text consisted of 14 chapters and 32 canones, the text of November 5 counted 16 chapters and 31 canones. This change is somewhat misleading, for chapter 2-4 of the November text consisted of chapter 3 of the Seripando text. Furthermore, Seripando chapter 4 became chapters 5 and 6 in the November text. In comparison to the Seripando text, the chapters 1,[124] 2 (on Christ becoming man for our salvation), 6 (on the preparation of our justification),[125] 7 (on the gratuitous justification of the unfaithful through faith), 10 (on the increase

---

118 See *Concilium Tridentinum* V (1911, 632f); the dispute on this issue continued up to the closing session in January; see Buuck: 1951, 117; Schierse: 1951, 163f. McGrath (2020, 336) is of the opinion that Andrès de Navarra was opposed to the certainty of salvation and thus should be switched from the first to the second list. He thus questions Massarelli's list; however, it would not be the first time that fathers during votes support another position than the one defended during their intervention. Anyway, the crucial point remains the same: the division among the fathers.
119 I have the impression that McGrath (2020, 333) emphasizes too much that critique on imputed justice is indirectly directed against Seripando. If this were the case, I do not understand why Cervini is trusting him on this matter.
120 See *Concilium Tridentinum* I (1901, 581ff); *Concilium Tridentinum* V (1911, 436, note 1); Gutierrez: 1963, 66f.
121 For Seripando's text, see *Concilium Tridentinum* V (1911, 510–517). In comparison to the text of September, substantial changes had been made with regard to the chapter on the interior justification; for the details see Pas: 1954, 45f.
122 *Concilium Tridentinum* V (1911, 634–641).
123 For Seripando's text, see *Concilium Tridentinum* V (1911, 510–517). With regard to the work of Del Monte and Musso, see *Concilium Tridentinum* I (1901, 583).
124 Chapter 2 of the Seripando text, dealing with the consequences of the fall for the free will (ignorance and blindness) and the need to humbly confess one's sinfulness and the need to ask God's help, was partially taken up in chapter 1 of the November text.
125 The most important novelty in Seripando's text, the distinction in causes, will be preserved up to the final text. In this text, Seripando thus avoided to speak of a *duplex iustitia*, well aware of the sensitivity of this term. Seripando himself was speaking of "formalis iustitia una Dei" (*Concilium Tridentinum* V (1911, 512, l. 18f)), and this is taken over in the November text (*Concilium Tridentinum* V (1911, 636, l. 36f)). The best survey of this debate is Pas: 1954, 27–43.

of the received justification), 11 (on the need and possibility of the observation of God's commands), 14 (on the lapsed and their restoration) had undergone changes in comparison to Seripando's text. The sensitive nr. 14 (now 16) (on the fruits of justification) was a completely new text.[126]

This third project would be discussed from November 9 to December 1. In chapter 16, the text stipulated that the justified lack nothing and that they fully fulfil the divine law, sprinkled from all sides by the divine grace, and thus deserve (*promeruisse*) the eternal life.[127] Needless to say, Seripando was upset: these people either show their ignorance or their fear for Luther's doctrine. Seripando considered such attitude as a sign of lack of courage.[128] Seripando was indeed convinced that the exaltation of good works (in fact often absent in the life of Christians) was not needed, while we are scanty and thrifty with regard to the proclamation of God's grace, essential for our salvation, but often neglected by Catholics.[129]

Only three texts explicitly referred to Augustine, 2 in chapter 11, 1 in chapter 12. *De natura et gratia* 43,50 (about the observation of God's mandates) in chapter 11, was, like in the July and Seripando versions (chapters 8 and 10 respectively), still present. The whole context makes clear that human beings, "etiam quantumvis sancti et iusti" still are struggling with sinfulness and daily commit small and venial sins. Indeed, also the just truly and humbly pray: "Dimitte nobis debita nostra", a core argument in Augustine's argumentation against sinlessness.[130] *Sola fide* justification as such is only part of the truth: faith, working through love, invites and stimulates the human being to do good (though imperfect) works, but also hoping for God's mercy, but still good works.

A second reference in chapter 11 was to *De natura et gratia* 26,29 (already present in the first text of July and in the text of Seripando, nr. 8), stating that God does not leave people if people do not leave him. *De correptione et gratia* 13,40, dealing with the incertitude about those who will be predestined is present both in Seripando's text (nr. 8) and in the November text (chapter 12). In fact, this issue is extensively discussed by Augustine in *De correptione et gratia* 13,39-40, 14,43 and 15,46. Given the fact that in the final draft, reference will be made to *De correptione et gratia* 15,46, while the text remains for this part the same in Seripando's text and the version of November, I suggest that the whole context might be taken into account, and not only *De correptione et gratia* 13,40.

---

126 Seripando's attempt to make clear that the just still must put his trust in the divine mercy and the justice of Christ, because of the insufficiency of the human beings righteousness, is not accepted. See Pas: 1954, 46f. On Seripando's disappointment, see *Concilium Tridentinum* II (1911, 430f).
127 For the text, see *Concilium Tridentinum* V (1911, 639).
128 *Concilium Tridentinum* V (1911, 663, n. 2); Jedin: 1937, 413.
129 *Concilium Tridentinum* V (1911, 663, n. 2.); Jedin, *Geschichte des Konzils von Trient* II, 239.
130 See *Concilium Tridentinum* V (1911, 637).

In the November debate, the doctrine of the *duplex iustitia* recurred. Furthermore, the Council fathers did not that often refer to Augustine,[131] but when it happened, it was done in order to emphasize and confirm that no one can be sure that one is under grace through the certitude of faith.[132] Some bishops also insisted on the importance of God's mercy in the evaluation of human beings' life. This was the case for bishop Juan Fonseca of Castellamare di Stabia (Italy). Fonseca was asking for a better development of the idea that justified possess all to deserve eternal life. In his intervention, in which he refuted that the justified needed another application of Christ's passion than the one received in order to receive eternal life, he asked to answer the objections of the *auctoritates*. He invoked Augustine, *Confessiones* IX,13,34, where Augustine stated that even a praiseworthy life would be in danger, if God would examine it without mercy. The bishop also referred to *De perfectione iustitiae* 15,34 where again it is said that because of God's mercy the just will be fully purified. Fonseca thus recognized that after the justification in Christ, deficiency remained in the human person and that one had to expect God's mercy.[133] Musso, insisting on the fact that the justice, required by God, is the observance of the mandates of the law, added that no one is able to perfectly observe these mandates *sine peccato veniali*, but this imperfection does not make us damnable but humble, as was said by Augustine in his *De peccatorum meritis et remissione* II,16,23.[134]

On November 26, Seripando presented his intervention,[135] in which he explicitly protested against unfair critiques.[136] The content of his intervention is well known: he held a plea in defense of his orthodoxy and asked that trust in God's mercy for Christ's sake, besides our personal merit would be allowed.[137] At length, he

---

131 Sometimes, works were attributed to Augustine, which in fact were not written by him; cf. the reference to *De poenitentia*, made by Ambrosius Catharinus, bishop of Minori; *Concilium Tridentinum* V (1911, 656).

132 See, e. g., the intervention of the bishop of Aquino, Florimonte Galeazzo; bishop Antonio de la Cruz of Canary Islands; *Concilium Tridentinum* V (1911, 649.655). It is interesting to see that when the general of the Conventuals referred to Augustine in order to state that one can know "se esse in gratia" and that this is not presumptuous, in the footnote the commentator adds the references to sermons of Augustine, offering the following comment: "Sed semper (Augustinus) in sensu contrario, extollens sc. humilitatem publicani et diffidentiam in se ipsum, condemnans pharisaeum praesumptionem." In other words, one must be very careful when bishops appeal to Augustine; for the intervention, see *Concilium Tridentinum* V (1911, 662).

133 See his intervention in *Concilium Tridentinum* V (1911, 647).

134 *Concilium Tridentinum* V (1911, 648).

135 Both a summary by the secretary of the Council and Seripando's integral text are preserved; see *Concilium Tridentinum* V (1911, 663ff, 666–676).

136 *Concilium Tridentinum* V (1911, 666).

137 For a commentary, see Jedin: 1937, 418–421; *Geschichte des Konzils von Trient*, 241f.

explained his view on the *duplex iustitia*.[138] Seripando insisted on the fact that in the justification process something happens in us: through Christ's justice effects are caused in us, through which we are formally just. Seripando quoted at length Augustine, *De correptione et gratia* 13,40–41 (to which the text under discussion had already hinted) where the bishop of Hippo made clear that the holy predestined will be given perseverance to the end and that they will be preserved in absolute happiness "adhaerente sibi misericordia Salvatoris sui" (13,40, *PL* 44, 941). Augustine insisted in this context that also in the Kingdom of God for the predestined God's mercy is still necessary: the just will be judged with mercy, the unjust without mercy.[139] In this just judgement, Augustine continues, mercy is given "pro bonorum operum meritis" (13,41, *PL* 44, 941)[140] For Seripando, no one justified is sinless. He is aware that, theoretically speaking, Augustine admitted that those perfectly made just by God could be without sin, but immediately adds that Augustine stated that, except Christ, no one else ever succeeded in that.[141] The point for him is that no one should trust in the justice of his own works (as in opposition to the justice of Christ and the mercy of God),[142] but in the justice of Christ and the mercy of God. Seripando does not exclude that one puts trust in one's justice, but this should happen "propter illam (iustitiam) Christi."[143] Seripando rejected the idea that one should trust in Christ's justice alone (against Luther), but added that ours cannot be separated from it for ours depend on Christ's justice "in fieri, esse et conservari".[144] For Seripando, God's judgement is not an act of justice alone, but an act of justice and mercy. In this regard, Augustine's argumentation why he prayed for his mother, is used as an argument. Seripando, like Fonseca, thus quoted *Confessiones* IX,13,34, adding that Augustine said thanks for the good things his mother did, but implored

---

138 Seripando not only referred to Augustine but also to Thomas, when discussing the double justice; see *Concilium Tridentinum* V (1911, 669). Seripando insisted on the fact that he still held the doctrine as presented on October 8. For Seripando, it is matter of humility to recognize one's imperfection in light of the final judgement; see *Concilium Tridentinum* V (1911, 670).
139 All this is well underpinned by Augustine with a series of Scriptural quotes.
140 Seripando also refers to *Enarrationes in Psalmos* 31,2,1 where, again, Augustine emphasizes people need God's mercy and that the one who boasts on himself, will fail and fall.
141 See Augustine, *De spiritu et littera* 1; *Concilium Tridentinum* V (1911, 668).
142 Here, Seripando underpins his argument with quotes form Augustine, *Enarrationes in Psalmos* 142,2; 45,5,7, texts that make clear that one may think he is justified in his own view or that of other human beings, but not in the view of God, who may reprehend what is not seen by human beings.
143 *Concilium Tridentinum* V (1911, 663). In his elaborated votum, he argues that Christ himself, through his passion, death and resurrection, is God's justice. Again, this is elaborated with a series of references to *De spiritu et littera* 15.18 and the letters 157–178.
144 *Concilium Tridentinum* V (1911, 668f).

Christ's justice for the sins she had committed.[145] Seripando thus does not deny the validity of our good works, but considers them as insufficient when compared with God's commands.

At the end of the debate, in the general meeting of December 3, 1546, 9 issues were presented to the fathers: "Novem censurae seu capita dubitationum, quae graviora sunt ex censuris partum super decreto de iustificatione."[146] However, according to Jedin, the fathers were no longer willing to change too many things in the existing texts as became clear in the votes of December 6, 1546.[147] But there were still some pieces de résistances. Chapter 7, dealing with the question how the sinner can freely receive justification through faith was causing a series of problems. With regard to the role of faith in the justification process, several fathers insisted on faith's primacy. Both bishop Lippomani of Verona and Seripando appealed to Augustine, *De praedestinatione sanctorum* 7,12. Seripando also referred to *De fide et operibus* 14,21, where Augustine insisted that faith precedes good works.[148] Especially the intervention of Seripando is interesting. Indeed, during the meeting of December 17, 1546, Seripando intervened.[149] In his intervention, he argued that faith is not only a disposition but also the fundament and first part of righteousness. In this regard he referred to Augustine's position that faith as fundament of a building belongs to the building (*De praedestinatione sanctorum* 7,12). For Augustine, this fundament can only be Christ, who lives in our hearts through faith as was said by Paul (*De operibus et fide* 15,24; 16,27). Seripando mentioned explicitly Augustine's interpretation of Paul that human beings are justified on the basis of faith, not of their own works (Gal 2:6), because faith is given first, impetrating all other things by which one lives rightly. Seripando offered a long quote from *De fide et operibus* 14,21 in order to make clear that works of righteousness, never preceding faith, must not be contempt. He also quoted *Ad Simplicianum* I,2,2 where Augustine argues that through grace people start believing in God, being moved towards faith either by an internal or external admonition. Again appealing to Augustine, Seripando distinguished between *fides disponens* and *fides iustificans*. The first does not suffice for salvation, the second does. Referring to catechumens, Augustine argued that starting to believe is not enough. One must be incorporated in the Church through baptism in order to become a holy temple of God. Faith must not

---

145 Seripando also bases his arguments on the liturgy and refers to other interventions, like the one of bishop de Cruce of Canary Islands; *Concilium Tridentinum* V (1911, 671).
146 For the list, see *Concilium Tridentinum* V (1911, 686f); cf. also Jedin: 1957, 246f.
147 For the results, see *Concilium Tridentinum* V (1911, 691); see Jedin: 1957, 247. Cardinal de Monte wanted to speed up things; see his intervention on December 10, 1546; *Concilium Tridentinum* V (1911, 700); for the details, see also Jedin: 1957, 247.494.
148 Also Aquinas was invoked as holding such a position.
149 For the text of this intervention, see *Concilium Tridentinum* V (1911, 725f).

only be conceived, but one must also be born in order to reach eternal life. All this is only possible through the grace of mercy of God for good works come after grace is given, not before (*Ad Simplicianum* I,2,2).[150] Seripando thus made use of works written in about 396 (*Ad Simplicianum*), 413 (*De fide et operibus*), and a work written at the end of Augustine's life (*De praedestinatione sanctorum*), thus offering Augustine's doctrine as being coherent during his whole life.

Given the length of the debate, cardinal Cervini asked to examine the Church's position in her tradition with regard to Paul's statement that we are justified through faith.[151] Cervini also paid attention to the view of the Greek Church Fathers about justification though faith. While there was agreement that faith is the fundament of justification and that faith always precedes the good works, the specific role of human beings' nature in the justification process remained a problem. Fear to come too close to protestant positions clearly played a role in this matter.[152] Finally, an agreement would be found, the bishops-theologians accepting on December 21 a proposal made by Cervini: "Quia fides est humanae salutis initium, fundamentum[153] et radix omnis iustificationis. Nam sine fide impossibile est placere Deo et ad filiorum eius consortium pervenire."[154] It was this text that would find its way in the final draft, approved on January 13, 1547. The bishops and theologians discussed on December 22 the correct interpretation of Paul's view that justification is given *gratis*. It was again Cervini who made a proposal, later to be amended by Musso. After a vote, the following proposal was accepted: "gratis autem ideo iustificari dicamur quia nihil eorum quae iustificationem praecedunt vel fides vel opera, ipsam iustificationis gratiam merentur".[155] A comparison with *De spiritu et littera* 10,16, *CSEL* 60, 168: "per ipsam quippe iustificatur gratis, id est nullis suorum operum praecedentibus meritis – alioquin gratia iam non est gratia" and 26,45, *CSEL* 60, 199:

> neque enim contra se ipsum diceret, quod ait: factores legis iustificabuntur, tamquam per opera, non per gratiam iustificentur, cum dicat gratis iustificari hominem per fidem sine

---

150 The refence to *De fide et operibus* 14, 21 in *Concilium Tridentinum* V (1911, 726) is wrong. Seripando is abundantly quoting from *Ad Simplicianum*.
151 *Concilium Tridentinum* V (1911, 725). Cervini considered this more important than the positions of the bishops present at the Council.
152 *Concilium Tridentinum* V (1911, 729ff).
153 Cardinal Cervini had suggested in the meeting of December 18 that this was the view present among the Greek fathers; *Concilium Tridentinum* V (1911, 729). Bishop Fonseca observed in the meeting of the bishops-theologians of December 21 that the idea was also present in Augustine. He referred to *De spiritu et littera* 7,11. However, Augustine does not speak here of fundament, but he did so in *De praedestinatione sanctorum* 7, 12 as was already observed by Seripando.
154 For the text, see *Concilium Tridentinum* V (1911, 733).
155 See *Concilium Tridentinum* V (1911, 736f).

operibus legis nihilque aliud uelit intellegi in eo quod dicit gratis, nisi quia iustificationem opera non praecedunt,

reveals that Augustine's ideas about this matter are in the mind of the drafter. The chapter would finally become nr. 8.

A next point of debate worth to be mentioned was about the correct interpretation of Jas 2:24: "Videtis, quoniam ex operibus iustificatur homo et non ex fide tantum". In his intervention, Seripando appealed to Augustine (*Enarrationes in Psalmos* 31,2,3; *De diversis quaestionibus* 76,1 and *De fide et operibus* 14,23), when defending that the text was speaking about the first justification, not about the growth in love and justice.[156] For Seripando, James made clear that faith is followed by good works done through love and thus will lead to salvation. According to Seripando, there is no contradiction between Paul's stress on justification on the basis of faith and James' plea for works, because these works will come as a result of faith and the love given in faith.

The last chapter, discussed from 2 to 5 January, continued to cause problems, but Augustine seemingly was not used to solve them. Only one problem remained: nr. 9, dealing with the certainty of faith. Still on January 8, the bishops-theologians asked for extra time to reflect.[157] Finally, the fathers limited themselves to a condemnation of the Lutherans, without finding an agreement about the Catholic position. In the meeting of the bishops-theologians of January 9, both chapter 9[158] and canon 14 were approved: nobody can know with certainty that he himself is *in gratia Dei*.[159] On January 9 there was a last check of the changes made.[160] On January 11, the general congregation approved the decree which was promulgated on January 13, 1547 in the 6th session.

---

156 However, Augustine does not speak about the first justification, but states that James criticizes those who think that they will be justified on the basis of their faith and thus are not expected to do good works.
157 See *Concilium Tridentinum* V (1911, 764).
158 The phrase "Nemini tamen fiduciam et certitudinem remissionis peccatorum suorum iactanti […] remota fiducia" is, with a few linguistic differences, the same as in Seripando A; see *Concilium Tridentinum* V (1911, 825, ll. 31–34).
159 Here again, one must admit that the bishops follow the position of the minority among the theologians, doing justice to Augustine and to the one who appealed to Augustine, Seripando.
160 See *Concilium Tridentinum* V (1911, 776ff).

11. The Decree On Justification

In a period of about half a year, the Council was able to develop a more or less coherent view on justification. The decree on justification was a logical follow up of the decree on original sin. In that decree, both the damage caused by original sin for Adam and his progeny and the remedy by Christ were clearly stressed. Baptism was considered as mediating Christ's grace, forgiving truly our guilt. Left to our own vitiated nature, human beings are not able to restore their lives themselves. This can only happen through the grace of Christ as given in baptism. This position is repeated in the beginning of the decree on justification, thus making clear the bound between fall and justification. In this statement, it becomes immediately clear that for Trent, on the level of salvation, human beings' work does not suffice, for the free will, in no way extinct, is weakened. For this, God's grace through Christ is needed (chapter 1). All this is very much in line with Augustine. It creates space for human beings' good moral behavior *sub gratia*, as will be developed further in the decree. To live righteously, one needs to be enabled and empowered by the grace of God through Christ, which grace one receives in baptism. It is a transition from our being children of Adam to the state of grace and adoption as children of God, a transition which is only possible through regeneration (chapter 4).[161] The initiative is taken by God, calling human beings through Christ (*gratia praeveniens*)[162] without merits present in the human beings. The beginning of the process is that human beings hear God's word. Trent uses a vocabulary, present in Augustine,[163] insisting that it is God who excites and helps through his grace to convert and turn human beings towards their justification by giving free assent to and co-operate with this same grace. It is only within the context of this calling grace that human beings can convert or reject it, but without grace no one can move towards justice (chapter 5). The sinner is brought to hope by grace, confronted with the prospect of divine compassion, a central key concept in Augustine's theology of grace.[164] Hope then will lead to starting to love God, the source of all justice and thus to repent, in fact the next step needed in order to be baptized, thus beginning a new life, observing God's commandments (chapter 6). God, who created men without their active involvement, will not justify them without their free commitment.[165] Trent did

---

161 Regeneration is a key concept in Augustine's discussion of grace, especially during the Pelagian controversy; see Meconi: 2012–2018, 1107–1110.
162 This concept is very dear to Augustine, who will use it in this technical way more or less exclusively in the anti-Pelagian controversy and this from about 415 onwards; see, e. g., *Epistula* 186,15; 217,25.28; *Contra duas epistulas pelagianorum* IV,6,15.
163 See *Epistula* 186,39.
164 See Drecoll: 2012–2018a, 38f.
165 This text clearly resounds *Sermo* 169,14: "Qui ergo fecit te sine te, non te iustificat sine te."

not exclude the human engagement, but situated it within the context of the first initiative of God.[166]

In chapter 7, justification is described as forgiveness of sin and sanctification and renewal of the inward being by a willing acceptance of grace and gifts that make of the unjust a just, from an enemy a friend. Trent distinguishes here a series of causes, the final being the glory of God, Christ and eternal life. The efficient cause is God's mercy, for God gratuitously washes and sanctifies, places his seal and anoints with the promised Holy Spirit who is the guarantee of our inheritance (Eph 1:13-14).[167] The meritorious cause is Christ's suffering out of great love for us (Eph 2:4), while we were in enmity with him (Rom 5:10; Eph 2:4). Christ did satisfaction to God our father on our behalf. The instrumental cause is the sacrament of baptism, which is the sacrament of faith. The text here explicitly refers to Augustine, *Epistula* 98,9.[168] In the second part of that letter, Augustine insisted on the fact that baptism is the sacrament of faith and we thus can claim that a baptized infant had faith because of the sacrament of that reality. For Augustine, the sacrament makes the infant a believer, even although the infant cannot and does not assent to faith (*Epistula* 98,10). The Council makes clear that without baptism nobody can be justified, a point that, time and again was made by Augustine. Trent concludes this discussion stating that the one formal cause is God's justice: it is the cause by which he makes us just and endowed with it, we are renewed and we are not merely considered to be just but we are truly just (1 John 3:1), a very clear position in the debate with Luther. The sentence "Demum unica formalis causa est iustitia Dei non qua ipse iustus est sed qua nos iustos facit" is partially present in Augustine's *De trinitate* 14,12,25: "Sed quemadmodum dicitur etiam iustitia Dei non solum illa qua ipse iustus est sed quam dat homini cum iustificat impium",[169] again an indication that sometimes more Augustine is present in the decree than what is suggested in the critical apparatus.[170] We are declared and made righteous and thus really renewed. According to Trent, this justice will be personalized: each one of us will receive individually his own justice according to the measure the Holy Spirit apportions to each one as he wills (1 Cor 12:11) and in view of each one's dispositions and co-operation. Trent thus insists on the role of the faithful in the whole process of

---

166 Peter, *The Decree on Justification in the Council of Trent*, in H.G. Anderson, T.A. Murphy, and J.A. Burges, *Justification by Faith. Lutherans and Catholics in Dialogue VII*, Minneapolis: Augsburg Publishing House, 1985, 218-229, 223ff.
167 Peter (1985, 225) observes that Aristotelian terminology is used, but that this terminology is used in a very Biblical way, "in a way Aristotle never even imagined in his metaphysics".
168 The term *sacramentum fidei*, already present in the first draft (*Concilium Tridentinum* V (1911, 388, l. 28)), was now added again in the text during the December discussion.
169 See also *De spiritu et littera* 9,15; 11,18.
170 See the pertinent remarks of Grossi: 1997, 339.

justification and it will explicitly condemn in canon 32 the one who states that the good deeds of a justified person are the gifts of God and thus are not also the good merits of the one justified. At the same time, for Trent there is no justification apart from the merits of Christ's suffering: the love of God is poured out by the agency of the Holy Spirit in the hearts (Rom 5:5) of those who are being justified and abides in them. In this process of justification, faith, hope and love[171] are infused in us. The three must be kept together: faith, important as it is,[172] without hope and love will not unite the human being with Christ nor will make him a living member of Christ's body. In other words, Trent considers justification through faith alone as insufficient, for faith without works is dead and barren (Jas 2:17.20), for only faith working through love (Gal 6:6) will be effective.[173] It is interesting to see that Trent is making its point by referring to James' letter. As is known, the letter of James was qualified by Luther as a straw note. Trent insists that it is this faith that, from apostolic tradition, catechumens seek from the Church. Catechumens ask for a faith that gives eternal life, for which hope and charity are needed, for without these two, this is not possible. For Trent, justification overcomes people but does not exclude their own active involvement (cf. Matt 19:17). Thus receiving true and Christian justice in exchange for that which Adam by his disobedience had lost for himself and his progeny, the reborn are immediately ordered to preserve the justice 'freely' granted to them through Christ in a pure and spotless state like a best robe (cf. Augustine, *De Genesi ad litteram* VI,27,[174] so that they may carry it before the tribunal of our Lord Jesus Christ and possess eternal life (*Rituale Romanum, De administrando baptismo*).

After making clear that faith is the first stage of human salvation, foundation and root of all justification, Trent emphasizes that neither faith nor works cause the grace of justification (chapter 8) – in chapter 16, it will explicitly be said that it is Jesus Christ who continually (*iugiter*) gives his strength to the justified, strength that always (*semper*) precedes their good works and accompanies and follows them. Without that support, the justified will in no way be able to do any works meritorious and pleasing God.[175] In chapter 9, the protestants' claim that anyone's sins are or

---

171 On the crucial role of love in the justification process, see, next to nr.7, also chapter 16 and canon 11. Both in nr. 7 and canon 11 God's love is abiding in human beings.
172 Cf. chapter 8: faith is "fundamentum et radix omnis iustifcationis", but neither faith nor works merit the grace of justification.
173 For a similar view in Augustine, see *De gratia et libero arbitrio* 8,19.
174 The reference was already present in the September text, but only now the explicit link is made with Augustine.
175 Concilium Tridentinum, Sessio VI (13 jan. 1546), *Decretum de iustificatione* XVI: *De fructu iustificationis, hoc est, de merito bonorum operum, deque ipsius meriti ratione* (ed. Tanner, 678). Given the fact that these works are done *in Deo* and that they thus truly have deserved to gain eternal life in their time: " […]suo etiam tempore […] consequendam vere promeruisse censeantur." On the

have been forgiven simply because one has a proud assurance and certainty that they have been forgiven and relies solely on that, is criticized. It is considered an empty and ungodly position, preached today most controversially against the Catholic Church. Trent is of the opinion that no devout person ought to doubt the mercy of the Church and the power and efficacy of the sacraments, but it insists that our current state is not the perfect one. Justification quite evidently exists, but we are never sure, because of our weakness, reason why we are still anxious and fearful about our state of grace.

Trent thus rejects absolute certitude, but insists at the same time that the renewal happens from day to day (chapter 10). Everybody is able to make progress, by yielding themselves as instruments of righteousness for sanctification by observance of the commandments of God and of the Church. People grow and increase in justice, by faith united to good works (with again a quote from Jas 2:24). Trent also refers to the liturgy where people pray on the 13th Sunday after Pentecost: "Da nobis Domine fidei, spei et charitatis augmentum". The idea that renewal is not a static given, but a constant process, an idea present in Paul, 2 Cor 4:16, is regularly appreciated by Augustine, for whom perfection is only to be expected in the life to come.[176] However, one can diminish his sinfulness, thus making progress in the struggle against sinful desire. In fact, one is justified and is actively involved in the realization of this justification.

In chapter 11, the Council, referring to the Council of Orange (529), canon 25, rejects the idea that the commandments of God cannot be observed by those who are justified. Quoting from *De natura et gratia* 43,50 (a text already present in Seripando's version of August), Trent insists that we try as good as possible to keep the commandments, but exhorts us to pray for what we cannot do, in order that God gives his aid to enable us to do it. For Trent, the children of God love Christ and thus keep his words which they can keep in their deeds with the divine help. Trent insists that even holy and just people will sometimes fall into sin (meant are venial ones). Here it refers to Matt 6:12, so crucial for Augustine in the anti-Pelagian controversy.[177] The Our Father is the prayer of just, humble, and truthful people. Progress indeed means that one is not yet perfect and can make progress. God does not abandon those once justified by his grace, unless He is first deserted by them

---

discussion how to interpret *promereri*, see Leppin: 2016, 169–173. Leppin convincingly has shown that Trent opted for an "Ausgleichs- und Integrationspolitik"; see p. 173.

176 See, e. g., *De perfectione iustitiae hominis* 18,39; *De gratia Christi et de peccato originali* 11,12 (excluding perfection in this life); *De nuptiis et concupiscentia* I,18,20 (excluding perfection in this life).

177 See Vinel: 1987, 224–227.

(*De natura et gratia* 26,29, a text already present in the very first version).[178] Trent thus rejects the *sola fide*-doctrine because justification does not exclude pain and efforts. Moreover, it is against the orthodox teaching to claim that in every good work the just person sins at least venially.[179]

Trent warns for any presumption to hold for certain that one unquestionably belongs to the number of predestined, because sinlessness does not exist in this life, not even for the justified ones (chapter 12). Apart from a special revelation, nobody can know whom God has chosen for Himself. Here, Trent is referring to *De correptione et gratia* 15,46, where Augustine insists on our lack of certitude.[180] In fact, all have to place their hope in God's help and rest in it, working on their own salvation with fear and trembling "in works, watchings, almsgivings, prayers and offering, in fasting and chastity" (2 Cor 6:5–6). In this life people are reborn to the hope of glory, not to the glory itself and thus the struggle with the flesh remains, something that people can only overcome with the grace of God.[181] In the last 3 chapters (14–16), the decree deals with the restoration of the fallen, insisting that Christ had instituted the sacrament of penance for those who sin after baptism. The decree insists on the fact that people have to confess their sins, need absolution by a priest, and also satisfaction by fasting, almsgiving, prayer, and devout exercises of spiritual life. The idea of a sacrament of penance as such does not appear in Augustine's works,[182] and the way this sacrament is described in the decree, very much reminds of the practice in the 16th century.

After having stated that grace not faith is lost by every mortal sin (chapter 15), the decree abundantly deals in chapter 16 with the fruit of justification, namely the

---

178 To this reference is added: "Saepius in libris Augustini"; the idea that God and his love do not abandon his people/creation is indeed several times developed by Augustine in his sermons, but also in *Soliloquia* 1,1,6.
179 Cf. Bull *Exsurge Domine*, art. 31–32: In every good work the just man sins; a good work done very well is a venial sin; for Luther's positions as held at the Heidelberger Disputation, see Luther: 1883, WA 1, 353.356-359. Concilium Tridentinum, Sessio VI (13 jan. 1546), *Decretum de iustificatione* XI: *De observatone mandatorum deque illius necessitate et possibilitate* (ed. Tanner, 675f).
180 See *De correptione et gratia* 15,46: "Nescientes enim quis pertineat ad praedestinatorum numerum, quis non pertineat; sic affici debemus charitatis affectu, ut omnes velimus salvos fieri". This text, again, makes clear that predestination in a sense goes beyond our insights, but we still have to love in such a way that we all want to be saved. For the uncertainty about who will be predestined, see also 13,40. See our remarks *supra*.
181 Concilium Tridentinum, Sessio VI (13 jan. 1546), *Decretum de iustificatione* XIII: *De perseverantiae munere* (ed. Tanner, 676).
182 However, in case the author of a work on penitence is indeed bishop Victor of Cartenna in Mauretania, the concept is already known in Africa in the middle of the 5th century; see Mandouze: 1982, 1175.

merit resulting from good works and its nature.[183] According to Trent, for those who worked to the end and kept their trust in God – Trent will, up to the end, hold together grace and good works, resulting from the gift of grace –, eternal life is to be expected, both as a grace promised by God's mercy through Christ to the children of God and as a reward faithfully bestowed to these children for their good works and merits. Christ imparts strength to those justified. His strength always precedes, accompanies and follows the good work of the faithful. This strength is the prerequisite for any meritorious act. For Trent, nothing more is needed for the justified in order to gain eternal life. Our personal justice is not established on something that comes from us. Our justice is the same justice as the one of God. Good works exist (cf. Scripture), but no Christian should ever rely on or boast on oneself, but in the Lord, whose goodness toward all is so great that He desires his own gifts to be our merits.[184]

12. Concluding Observations

As we have observed several times, the decree on justification is very Biblical in tone: quotes from Scripture abound. It is hard to discover schools in the text.[185] The decree is the result of positive theology, chapter 7 on the causes being eventually an exception.[186] At the same time, chapter 7 is also the chapter that pays most attention to the crucial role of love in the justification process,[187] an idea very dear to Seripando.[188] According to Trent, in the justification process, there happen things on the objective level and on the subjective level. Justification changes our hearts and what we are expected to do *sub gratia* becomes (imperfectly) meritorious.

The most important patristic source is Augustine, and, as I have mentioned several times, he is more present in the final text than suggested in critical editions, while Thomas Aquinas, present in the interventions of the Council fathers, did

---

[183] Trent did not dwell into Scholastic subtleties, but opted radically for a series of Biblical texts; see Peter: 1985, 227.

[184] The text refers to Coelestinus, *Epistula* 22, 12,14, but the same idea is also present in e. g. Augustine's *De dono perseverantiae* 2,4: "[…] gratiam Dei non secundum merita nostra dari, quoniam Dei dona sunt."

[185] See the pertinent remarks of O'Malley: 2013, 114; Jedin: 1957, 151 is more hesitant; see also Leppin: 2016, 173. I am not convinced that one must appeal to Scotus; Rückert: 1925, 123–124 seems to neglect that justification and love are identical in Augustine, *De gratia Christi et de peccato originali* I,30,31 while the definition of justice as "reddere unicuique suum" present in Cicero, is taken over by Augustine in several of his works; see, e. g. *De consensus evangelistarum* II,55,111.

[186] Cf. McGrath: 2020, 340.

[187] Charity is mentioned 9 times in the final draft, 6 of which are found in chapter 7.

[188] See the pertinent remarks of Stakemeier: 1937, 162f.

not find his way in the footnotes of this decree. Augustine is used in order to underpin the positions of the Council, which is not the same as a systematic study of Augustine. Moreover, while most of the texts quoted or referred to are related to the anti-Pelagian period or to the discussion with the monks of Hadrumetum, the Council fathers also made use of works, written at the beginning of Augustine's career or at the eve of the Pelagian controversy. Augustine inspires them but a Conciliar decree can and does not want to offer a treatise on a Father of the Church.

My survey also makes clear that Augustine was well present in the interventions of several fathers, including Seripando. It has become clear that Augustine's work did not belong to the private domain of the Augustinians, but that he was also a source of inspiration for several theologians (cf. Salmeron) and bishops. A comparison of the full texts of some of these interventions with the summaries of Massarelli revealed that Augustine was more preponderantly present in the debates that one might think at first sight.

That the decree on justification was also directed against the protestants, is evident in chapter 9, this chapter – in the history of the decree one of the most debated issues – being the only place that speaks about heretics and schismatics.[189] However, Trent nowhere in this decree appealed to the anti-Donatist works when criticizing those causing a split in the Church. In fact, the decree did justice to the main ambition of Seripando: offering a text on justification that would be of help for all Catholic faithful. The disputes arising immediately after the promulgation made clear that people were not yet well prepared to fully grasp the richness of the Tridentine ideas, but that is another story.

Bibliography

ALBERIGO, GIUSEPPE/ROGGER, IGINIO (ed.) (1997), Il Concilio di Trento nella prospettiva del Terzo Millennio, Religione e Cultura 10, Brescia: Morcelliana.

ARNOLD, CLAUS (2008), Die römische Zensur der Werke Cajetanus und Contarinis (1588–1601), Grenzen der theologische Konfessionalisierung, Römische Inquisition und Indexkongregation 10, Paderborn: Schöningh.

ASSELT, WILLEM J. VAN (2013), Justification, in: Karla Pollmann (ed.), The Oxford Guide to the Historical Reception of Augustine, vol. 3, Oxford: Oxford University Press, 1246–1254.

BONNER, ALI (2018), The Myth of Pelagianism, Oxford: Oxford University Press.

BRAUNISCH, REINHARD (1974), Die Theologie der Rechtfertigung im 'Enchiridion' des Johannes Gropper, Sein kritischer Dialog mit Philipp Melanchton, Münster: Aschendorff.

---

189 The canones too are not intending to censure the protestant positions; see McGrath: 2020, 343.

BRUNNER, PETER (1966), Pro Ecclesia, Gesammelte Aufsätze zur dogmatischen Theologie, Berlin/Hamburg: Lutherisches Verlagshaus.

BURGER, CHRISTOPH (2020), Kenntnisreiche Distanz versus Inanspruchnahme, Erasmus' und Luthers Umgang mit Augustins Schriften, in: Anthony Dupont/Wim François/Johan Leemans (ed.), Nos sumus tempora, Studies on Augustine and his Reception offered to Mathijs Lamberigts, BETL 316, Leuven/Paris/Bristol: Peeters Publishers, 421–432.

BUSCHBELL, GOTTFRIED (1910), Reformation und Inquisition in Italien um die Mitte des XVI. Jahrhunderts, Paderborn: Schöningh.

BUUCK, FRIEDRICH (1951), Zum Rechtfertigungsdekret, Die Unterscheidung zwischen fehlbarem und unfelhlbarem Glauben in den vorbereitenden Verhandlungen, in: Georg Schreiber (ed.), Das Weltkonzil von Trient: Sein Werden und Wirken, vol. 1, Freiburg: Herder, 117–143.

CASSARO, GIUSEPPE C. (2010), Girolamo Seripando, La grazia e il metodo teologico, Rome: Università Pontificia Salesiana.

CONCILII TRIDENTINI ACTORUM (1901–1911), Pars altera. Acta post sessionem tertiam usque ad Concilium Bononiam translatum. Collegit edidit illustravit St. Ehses. Concilium Tridentinum. Diariorum, actorum, epsitularum, tractatuum. Nova Collectio V,2, Freiburg, Herder.

DRECOLL, VOLKER H. (2012), Article "Meritum", AL 4, 1/2, Basel: Schwabe Verlag, 2012, 1–5.

DRECOLL, VOLKER H. (2012–2018a), Article "Misericordia", AL 4, Basel: Schwabe Verlag, 2012–2018a, 34–40.

DRECOLL, VOLKER H. (2012–2018b), Article "Praedestinatio", AL 4, Basel: Schwabe Verlag, 2012–2018b, 826–837.

EVANS, GILLIAN R. (1988), Vis verborum: Scholastic Method and Finding Words in the Debates on Justification of the Council of Trent, in: Downside Review 106, 264–275.

FIORENTINO, FRANCESCO (2008), L'Agostinismo del secolo XIV, in: Revue d'études augustiniennes et patristiques 54, 135–151.

FORSTER, ANSELM (1963), Gesetz und Evangelium bei Girolamo Seripando, Paderborn: Bonifacius-Druckerei.

FRANÇOIS, WIM (2020), Jacob Perez of Valencia OESA (ca. 1408–1490) and his Commentaries on the Psalms. Biblical Hermeneutics and Augustinian Theology of Grace, in: Anthony Dupont/Wim François/Johan Leemans (ed.), Nos sumus tempora, Studies on Augustine and his Reception offered to Mathijs Lamberigts, BETL 316, Leuven/Paris/Bristol: Peeters Publishers, 471–497.

GAUMER, MATTHEW A. (2016), Augustine's Cyprian, Authority in Roman Africa, Brill's Series in Church History and Religious Culture 73, Leiden/Boston: Brill.

GROSSI, VITTORINO (1997), Agostino d'Ippona e il Concilio di Trento, in: Giuseppe Alberigo/Iginio Rogger (ed.), Il Concilio di Trento nella prospettiva del Terzo Millennio, Religione e Cultura 10, Brescia: Morcelliana, 313– 341.

Gutierrez, David (1963), Hieronymi Seripandi Diarium de vita sua (1513-1562), in: Analecta Augustiniana 26, 66-67.

Hünermann, Friedrich (1921), Die Rechtfertigungslehre des Kardinal Gasparo Contarini, in: Theologisches Quartalschrift 10, 1-22.

Janz, Denis. R. (1980), Towards a Definition of Late Medieval Augustinianism, in: Thomist 44, 117-127.

Janz, Denis. R. (1983) Luther and Late Medieval Thomism, A Study in Theological Anthropology, Waterloo: Wilfrid Laurier University Press.

Jedin, Hubert (1937), Girolamo Seripando, Sein Leben und Denken im Geisteskampf des 16. Jahrhunderts, vol 1., Werdezeit und erster Schaffenstag, Cassiciacum 2, Würzburg: Rita-Verlag.

Jedin, Hubert (1957), Geschichte des Konzils von Trient. Band II. Die erste Trienter Tagungsperiode 1545/1547, Freiburg: Herder

Jedin, Hubert (1959), Contarini und Camaldoli, in: Archivio Italiano per la storia della pietà 2, 51-117.

Kramp, Igna (2015), Der Jesuit Alfonso Salmeròn (1515-1585) als humanistischer Theologe, Ähnlichkeiten und Unterschiede zu Erasmus von Rotterdam, in Theologie und Philosophie 90, 504-527.

Lamberigts, Mathijs (2004), Augustine on Predestination: Some Quaestiones Disputatae Revisited, in: Augustiniana 54, 279-305.

Lamberigts, Mathijs (2016), Augustine and Augustinianism at Trent, in: Peter Walter/ Günther Wassilowsky (ed.), Das Konzil von Trient und die Katholische Konfessionskultur (1563-2013), Wissenschaftliches Symposium aus Anlass des 450. Jahrestages des Abschlusses des Konzils von Trient, Freiburg in Breisgau 18.-21. September 2013, Reformationsgeschichtliche Studien und Texte 163, Münster: Aschendorf, 141-166.

Lamberigts, Mathijs (2020), Review of Ali Bonner, The Myth of Pelagianism, Oxford, 2018, Journal of Anglican Studies 18, 1-5 (online).

Leppin, Volker (2016), Spätmittelalterliche Theologie und biblische Korrektur im Rechtfertigungsdekret van Trient, in Peter Walter/G. Wassilowsky (ed.), Das Konzil von Trient und die Katholische Konfessionskultur (1563-2013), Wissenschaftliches Symposium aus Anlass des 450. Jahrestages des Abschlusses des Konzils von Trient, Freiburg in Breisgau 18. -21. September 2013, Reformationsgeschichtliche Studien und Texte 163, Münster: Aschendorf, 167-183.

Lössl, Josef (2002), Augustine on Predestination: Consequences for the Reception, in: Augustiniana 52, 241-272.

Mandouze, André (1982), Prosopographie de l'Afrique chrétienne (303-533), Prosopographie chrétienne du Bas-Empire vol. 1, Paris: Centre National de la Recherche Scientifique.

Marranzini, Alfredo (1997), Girolamo Seripando dopo Hubert Jedin, in: Giuseppe Alberigo/Iginio Rogger (ed.), Il Concilio di Trento nella prospettiva del Terzo Millennio, Religione e Cultura 10, Brescia: Morcelliana, 343- 370.

MARTIN LUTHER (1883), D. Martin Luthers Werke: kritische Gesamtausgabe, WA 1, Weimar: Böhlau.
MARTIN LUTHER (1912), Tischreden 347, in: Tischreden, vol. 1, Weimar: Böhlau.
MARTIN-PALMA, JOSÉ (1980), Gnadenlehre, Von der Reformation bis zur Gegenwart, Handbuch der Dogmengeschichte III,5b, Freiburg/Basel/Wien: Herder.
MCGRATH, ALISTER E. (1981), Augustinianism? A Critical Assessment of the So-Called 'Medieval Augustinian Tradition' on Justification, in: Augustiniana 31, 247–267.
MCGRATH, ALISTER E. (1988), Reformation Thought, An Introduction, Oxford: Basil Blackwell.
MCGRATH, ALISTER E. (2020), Iustitia Dei, A History of the Christian Doctrine of Justification, 4th ed., Cambridge: Cambridge University Press.
MECONI, DAVID V. (2012–2018), Article "Regeneratio", in: AL 4, 2012–2018, Basel: Schwabe Verlag, 1107–1110.
OBERMAN, HEIKO AUGUSTINUS (1964), Das tridentinische Rechtfertigungsdekret im Lichte spätmittelalterlicher Theologie, in: Zeitschrift für Theologie und Kirche 61, 251–282.
O'MALLEY, JOHN W. (2013), Trent, What Happened at the Council, Cambridge: Belknap Press of Harvard University Press.
PAS, PAUL (1954), La doctrine de la double justice au Concile de Trente, in: ETL 30, 5–53.
PESCH, OTTO H. (2000), La réponse du Concile de Trente (1545–1563): Les decisions doctrinales contre la Réforme et les conséquences, in: Irénikon 73, 5–38.
PETER, CARL J. (1985), The Decree on Justification in the Council of Trent, in: H. George Anderson/T. Austin Murphy/Joseph A. Burges (ed.), Justification by Faith, Lutherans and Catholics in Dialogue VII, Minneapolis: Augsburg Publishing House, 218–229.
PFNÜR, VINZENZ (1970), Einig in der Rechtfertigungslehre? Die Rechtfertigungslehre der Confessio Augustina (1530) und die Stellungnahme der katholischen Kontroverstheologie zwischen 1530 und 1535, Veröffentlichungen des Instituts für Europäische Geschichte Mainz 60, Wiesbaden: Steiner, 274–384.
RÜCKERT, HANNS (1925), Die Rechtfertigungslehre auf dem Tridentinischen Konzil (Arbeiten zur Kirchengeschichte, 3), Bonn: A. Marcus und E. Weber's Verlag.
SCHIERSE, FRANZ J. (1951), Das Trienter Konzil um die Frage nach der christlichen Gewissheit, in: Georg Schreiber (ed.), Das Weltkonzil von Trient; Sein Werden und Wirken, Freiburg: Herder, 145–167.
SCHINDLER, ALFRED (2007), 'Rechtfertigung' bei Augustinus und im reformatorischen Streit, in: Cornelius Mayer-Andreas E.J. Grote-Christof Müller (eds.), Gnade-Freiheit-Rechtfertigung. Augustinische Topoi und ihre Wirkungsgeschichte. Internationales Kolloquium zum 1650. Geburtstag Augustinus vom 25. bis 27. November im Erbacher Hof zu Mainz, Akademie der Wissenschaften und der Literatur. Abhandlungen der Geistes- und sozialwissenschaftlichen Klasse, Mainz-Stuttgart: Akademie der Wissenschaften und der Literatur-Franz Steiner Verlag, 41–72.
SCHINDLER, ALFRED (2004–2010), Article "Iustificatio", in: AL 3, 2004–2010, Basel: Schwabe Verlag, 859–864.

STAKEMEIER, EDUARD (1937), Der Kampf um Augustin auf dem Tridentinum, Paderborn: Bonifacius.

SUSA, FILIP (2006), Neuere Studien zum Tridentinischen Rechtfertigungsdekret, Zum Verständnis der Gerechtighkeit, mit der Wir beschenkt wurden, in: Communio viatorum 48, 34–55.

VINEL, JEAN-ALBERT (1987), L'argument liturgique opposé par St. Augustin aux Pélagiens, in: Questions Liturgiques 68, 209–241.

WENGERT, TIMOTHY J. (2013), Melanchton, Philip, in: Karla Pollmann (ed.), The Oxford Guide to the Historical Reception of Augustine, vol. 3, Oxford: Oxford University Press, 1387–1389.

Wim François

Augustinus und die Löwener Kontroversen über Prädestination, Gnade und freien Willen

"Omnes nunc Augustiniani esse aut videri volumus"

Die Mitglieder der Theologischen Fakultät in Löwen, die 1432 innerhalb der dort sieben Jahre zuvor gegründeten Universität entstanden war, beteiligten sich intensiv an den Kontroversen über Gnade, freien Willen und Prädestination, die die theologische Agenda im sechzehnten und siebzehnten Jahrhundert beherrschten. In diesem Essay werde ich mehrere Phasen dieser Kontroversen beleuchten, wobei besondere Aufmerksamkeit (1) Jacob Latomus' Diskussion mit Martin Luther; (2) Michael Baius, dem Baianismus und den innerkatholischen Kontroversen mit Leonard Lessius und den Jesuiten; (3) Cornelius Jansenius und der jansenistischen Krise gilt. In jeder dieser Kontroversen ging es selbstverständlich um die richtige Auslegung des Augustinus, da sich alle beteiligten Parteien, unabhängig vom Inhalt ihrer Theologie, auf die Autorität dieses Kirchenvaters beriefen. In diesem Sinne schrieb Jansenius in seinem berühmten *Augustinus* über sich und seine (Löwener) Kollegen: "Wir alle wollen 'Augustinisten' sein oder wenigstens so erscheinen".[1] Wir werden nicht systematisch auf die Details einzelner Texte eingehen und untersuchen, welche Funktion konkrete Bezüge auf den Kirchenvater darin hatten, sondern einen Longue-Durée-Überblick skizzieren und dabei auch zeigen, dass Augustinus in verschiedenen und oft divergierenden theologischen Systemen an der Universität Löwen und ihrer Schwesteruniversität in Douai rezipiert wurde. Dieser Aufsatz basiert auf der historisch-theologischen Forschung zur Geschichte der "alten" theologischen Fakultät, die in den letzten Jahrzehnten von Wissenschaftlern wie Lucien Ceyssens, Jean Orcibal, Edmond van Eijl, Jan Roegiers, Marcel Gielis, Mathijs Lamberigts sowie dem Autor dieses Aufsatzes durchgeführt wurde. Während eine noch frühere Generation von Gelehrten besonders eifrig die doktrinären Abweichungen des Baianismus und Jansenismus anprangerte, lag den oben genannten Autoren ein solches Anliegen wesentlich ferner, einige von ihnen verlagerten sogar ihre Sympathien auf die ausgesprochen "augustinistischen" (und sogar jansenistischen) Fraktionen ("Philojansenismus"). Dieselbe Forschung wird von einer jüngeren Generation von Forschern fortgeführt, die sich für die Geistesgeschichte dieser

---

1 Jansenius: 1640, vol. 2, Kol. 52.

Episode interessieren, darunter Eleonora Rai, Antonio Gerace und Jarrik Van Der Biest.

1. Luther, die Löwener Theologen und das Konzil von Trient

Während die Löwener Theologen mit Erasmus eine Kontroverse über die theologische Methodik und damit über das Primat entweder einer biblischen Theologie oder einer scholastischen Systematisierung führten, hatten sie auch Meinungsverschiedenheiten über die Gnadenlehre. Sie verdächtigten den Humanisten angesichts seines Glaubens an die bleibenden Fähigkeiten des menschlichen Intellekts und Willens nach dem Sündenfall des Semipelagianismus. Die Löwener Theologen beriefen sich auf Augustinus, um die Verderbtheit der menschlichen Natur nach dem Sündenfall und die Notwendigkeit der Gnade für den Menschen zur Erlangung der Erlösung zu betonen. An dieser Debatte beteiligte sich besonders Johannes Driedo (1479/1480–1535), z. B. durch sein Buch *De gratia et libero arbitrio* (1537) und seine umfangreichen Verweise auf die antipelagianischen Werke des Augustinus.[2]

An einer anderen Front formulierten die Löwener Theologen auch eine Erwiderung auf Martin Luthers *Sola-Gratia*- und *Sola-Fide*-Lehre, als weitere Grundlage ihrer feierlichen Verdammung vom 7. November 1519. Berühmt ist die Debatte zwischen Jacob Latomus und Luther, wobei Luther im Nachhinein sogar bereit war, den Löwener Theologen als seinen ernsthaftesten Gegner anzuerkennen.[3] Latomus wollte eine der zentralsten Positionen Luthers widerlegen, nämlich, dass jedes "gute" Werk seinem Wesen nach sündig sei, auch das von Getauften und Heiligen.[4] Überzeugt vom überwältigenden Bedürfnis des gefallenen Menschen nach Gottes Gnade, argumentierte Luther, dass der Mensch in der Taufe den Glauben empfängt, den er als ein wirkliches inneres Gut, als *donum infusum*, das im Menschen wirkt, akzeptiert. Dennoch trägt der Mensch für den Rest seines Lebens die "Restsünde" der *concupiscentia* in sich, ein böses Verlangen in den Tiefen seiner Natur, das Luther als Sünde im wahrsten Sinne des Wortes ansah. Hier verwendet Luther seinen berühmten Begriff der "zugerechneten Gnade", in dem Sinne, dass Gott

---

2 Gielis: 2008, 197–214; 1994a, 19–32: Der erste Teil dieses Artikels basiert zum größten Teil auf der ausgezeichneten niederländischsprachigen Dissertation des Autors, Scholastiek en Humanisme. Außerdem: Rummel: 1989, vol. 2, 72–87.

3 Sehr berühmt ist sein Ausspruch, der in einem seiner Tischgespräche von Anfang 1533 festgehalten, wo er gesagt haben mag: "Einer nur, nämlich Latomus, ist sein Salz wert, er ist der Autor, der am besten wider mich geschrieben hat. Man beachte, dass allein Latomus wirklich gegen Luther geschrieben hat! Alle anderen, einschließlich Erasmus, waren nur quakende Frösche" ("*ranae coaxantes*"). Siehe WA. TR 1, Nr. 463, 202 l. 5–7.

4 Vind (2019); Grundmann (2012); Außerdem: Vercruysse: 1994, 7–18; 1983, 515–538.

den Sünder für gottgefällig erklärt, da ihm die Gerechtigkeit Christi gutgeschrieben wird, obwohl die in ihm verweilende Sünde wirkliche Sünde bleibt. Latomus verfasste 1521 sein berühmtes Werk *Articulorum doctrinae fratris Martini Lutheri per theologos Lovanienses damnatorum ratio ex sacris literis et veteribus tractatoribus* (oder *Begründung der Verurteilung der Lehrsätze des Bruders Martin Luther durch die Löwener Theologen aus den Heiligen Schriften und alten Autoren*). Dort räumte er ein, dass der Mensch, dessen Natur durch die Erbsünde verdorben ist, in der Taufe die heiligmachende Gnade empfängt, durch die seine Sünden vergeben werden, sowohl die Erbsünde als auch die persönlichen Sünden, und seine Natur von innen her mit der Liebe Christi neu geschaffen wird – im Sinne einer *gratia infusa* und einer *gratia inhaerens*. Dennoch neigt der Mensch zur Konkupiszenz: Sie ist jedoch keine Sünde im strengen Sinne des Wortes, sondern eine Folge der und zugleich Strafe für die Erbsünde, und sie ist der Anlass für das Auftreten der eigentlichen Sünde. Solange aber der Getaufte in seinem Willen den Verlockungen der Konkupiszenz nicht bewusst nachgibt, begeht er keine Sünde. Mit dem Beistand Gottes "helfender" Gnade ist der menschliche Wille zunehmend in der Lage, den Versuchungen der Sünde zu widerstehen und gute Werke zu tun, die Gott gefallen, und somit Verdienste zu erbringen, die zur ewigen Erlösung führen. Latomus betonte weiter, dass der Mensch, wenn er sündigt, aber echte Reue zeigt, im Sakrament der Beichte Vergebung der Sünden erfährt. Bei der Anfechtung von Luthers Thesen berief sich Latomus vor allem auf die Heilige Schrift und auf die Schriften der Kirchenväter als den wichtigsten Exegeten der Heiligen Schrift, wobei Augustinus und seine antipelagianischen Werke den Vorrang hatten. Anna Vind zählte rund 210 Verweise auf oder Zitate von Augustinus, die aus 46 Werken stammen.[5] Latomus akzeptierte jedoch, dass neuere scholastische Theologen die Heilige Schrift noch genauer, systematischer und vollständiger interpretiert hatten; Päpste und Konzilien definierten kanonisch, was Kirchenväter und scholastische Theologen auf Ebene der Lehre dargelegt hatten. Dies war ein Vorwurf an Luther, weil er sich weigerte, sich der Autorität der Kirche zu unterwerfen und seine eigene

---

5 Anna Vind konzentriert sich auf drei lange und ein kurzes Zitat aus den Werken des Augustinus, die Latomus als grundlegend für die Demonstration seines zentralen Punktes betrachtet, dass nicht jede gute Tat eine Sünde ist und dass der Mensch unter Gottes Gnade gute Werke im Hinblick auf die Erlösung tun kann. Diese Zitate sind entnommen aus Augustinus' De perfectione iustitiae hominis 21.44 (CSEL 42, 46–48); De spiritu et littera 36.65 (CSEL 60, 225–228); Contra duas epistolas pelagianorum 1.13.26–14.28 (CSEL 60, 445–447); und De bono coniugali (das kürzere) (siehe Vind: 2019, 93 und 99–103). Hannegreth Grundmann ihrerseits sieht zusätzlich eine zentrale Stelle in der Argumentation für, insbesondere, De peccatorum meritis et remissione 2.34.55 (CSEL 60, 124 l. 19–22); außerdem De libero arbitrio 3.20.56 (CChr.SL 29, 307–308) und 3.22.64 (CChr.SL 29, 312–313); Ep. 167.4.15 [29. Brief an Hieronymus] (CSEL 44, 602–603); Confessiones 9.13.34 (CChr.SL 27, 152); Retractationes 1.19.3 (CChr.SL 57, 56–57) (siehe Grundmann: 2012, 161ff, außerdem 128–133).

Auslegung der Schrift zur Norm machte. Latomus' Standpunkt, wonach die Lehre des Augustinus durch den scholastischen Interpretationsrahmen (die *Sentenzen* des Petrus Lombardus, in zunehmendem Maße aber auch die *Summa* des Thomas von Aquin) aufgefasst wurde und was ihn, so Anna Vind, nicht zu einem echten "Augustiner" (oder besser gesagt"Augustinist")[6] machte, war jedoch charakteristisch für die Hauptrichtung der Löwener Theologen jener Generation, von denen Ruard Tapper der Führende war.

Johannes Driedo seinerseits war pessimistischer hinsichtlich der Fähigkeiten des postlapsarischen Menschen, während er die Notwendigkeit der Gnade Gottes betonte, sodass er Luthers Ideen objektiv näherkam. In diesem Sinne kann Driedo als einer der Gründerväter einer Löwener "Schule" des katholischen antipelagianischen Augustinismus betrachtet werden. Am Rande sei bemerkt, dass in den frühen 1550er-Jahren zwei bedeutende, in Löwen tätige franziskanische Theologen, Nicholas Tacitus Zegers und Adam Sasbout, in ihren Werken Kenntnis der und Sympathie für die Lehre von der doppelten Gerechtigkeit zeigten, die sie mit Driedos Ansichten und Verweisen auf Augustinus verbanden. Die Lehre von der doppelten Gerechtigkeit wurde anlässlich des Regensburger Reichstages (1541) als Möglichkeit zur Versöhnung der lutherischen und katholischen Standpunkte ersonnen,[7] aber 1544–1545 in Löwen von Ruard Tapper abgelehnt. Obwohl sie auf dem Konzil von Trient ihre Verteidiger hatte, allen voran Girolamo Seripando, wurde die Lehre auch von den dort versammelten Vätern nicht angenommen. Dennoch war die Theologie unter den Franziskanern in Löwen noch in den 1550er-Jahren beliebt.[8]

In Trient wurde die katholische Lehre von der Erbsünde und der Rechtfertigung in den Sitzungen 5 und 6 der ersten Konzilsperiode, 1546 bzw. 1547, verkündet. Der endgültige Text war das Ergebnis langer Beratungen, bei denen alle möglichen Einflüsse eine Rolle spielten – nicht nur die augustinische Lehre. Es ist vielleicht nicht überflüssig, die wesentlichen Züge der Ideen des Konzils zu rekapitulieren. Bezüglich der Erbsünde argumentierte das Konzil, dass Adam durch den Sündenfall sowohl seine Heiligkeit als auch die Gerechtigkeit verlor, "in die er eingesetzt worden war" ("*in qua constitutus fuerat*"). Infolgedessen war er der Konkupiszenz des Fleisches, der körperlichen Verderbnis und dem Tod unterworfen. Die Sünde Adams und ihre Folgen wurden durch geschlechtliche Fortpflanzung von einer Generation auf die nächste übertragen und betreffen alle Mitglieder des Menschengeschlechts, an Leib und Seele.[9] Der Mensch im Stand der Erbsünde kann streng genommen kein einziges Werk aus eigener Kraft tun, um sich die Erlösung zu

---

6 Vind: 2019, 160–168, außerdem 123–135.
7 Hequet (2009); Beck: 2020, 135–157; Al Kalak: 2017, 267–286. Zur Lehre von der doppelten Gerechtigkeit, siehe McGrath: 2020, 293–300 und 313–316; Lane (2020).
8 Gerace/Gielis: 2018, 91–123.
9 O'Malley: 2013, 103.

verdienen, obwohl er *de iure* gut handeln kann. Denn die Fähigkeiten des Menschen waren geschwächt und ihrer Kräfte beraubt, aber keineswegs ausgelöscht. Hinsichtlich des Rechtfertigungsprozesses betonten die Konzilsväter das Primat der Gnade in allen Stufen. In der Taufe empfängt der Mensch durch die Verdienste Christi die Gnade Gottes, durch die seine Sünden vergeben werden, sowohl die Erbsünde als auch die persönlichen Sünden, und seine Seele wird erneuert, sodass in dem Wiedergeborenen nichts mehr ist, was Gott missfallen würde. Das Konzil bestätigte die scholastische Idee der *gratia inhaerens*, die besagt, dass Gottes "Gnade und Liebe, die durch den Heiligen Geist in die Herzen der Menschen ausgegossen wird", die Seele des Einzelnen von innen heraus zum Besseren verändert (*"renovatio interioris hominis"*). Die Rechtfertigung wird also nicht einfach der Person zugerechnet, eine klare Aussage nicht nur vor dem Hintergrund der Kontroverse mit den Lutheranern, sondern auch im Lichte künftiger Debatten unter katholischen Theologen.[10] Allerdings, so fuhren die Konzilsväter fort, muss der Mensch aus freien Stücken in die "Bewegung der Gnade" einwilligen, was sich darin äußert, dass er gute Werke tut, die ihm weitere Verdienste im Hinblick auf das ewige Heil eintragen. Das Konzil musste einräumen, dass die Konkupiszenz im Wiedergeborenen verbleibt, aber gegen die Lutheraner betonte es, dass sie keine Sünde im wahren und eigentlichen Sinne des Wortes ist, sondern eher die Folge der Sünde und eine Neigung zur eigentlichen Sünde. Sie wird erst dann zur eigentlichen Sünde, wenn der Mensch den Verlockungen der Sünde mit freier Willensentscheidung nachgibt. Das Konzil betonte daher, dass der Kampf des Menschen gegen die Sünde und sein Wollen und Vollbringen des von Gott gewollten Guten nur unter dem Anstoß und mit Hilfe der Gnade Gottes geschehen kann. Das Konzil vertrat jedoch den Standpunkt, dass der Mensch in Bezug auf Gottes Gnade *"posse dissentire si velit"*. Zur Prädestination äußerte sich das Konzil nur insofern, als es vor einer vorschnellen Anmaßung, zu den Prädestinierten zu gehören, warnte.[11] Die Dekrete des Konzils von Trient sollten zu den Referenztexten für katholische Theologen werden, die über das Thema Erbsünde, Gnade und freier Wille schreiben. Die Tatsache jedoch, dass sie in sich selbst Kompromisstexte waren und einen gewissen Raum für weitere Interpretationen ließen, sollte Anlass zu verschiedenen und oft gegensätzlichen Strömungen innerhalb der katholischen Kirche geben.

---

10 O'Malley: 2013, 115.
11 Den deutschen Text findet man bei Wohlmuth (2001) (Zitat *"posse dissentire si velit"*, siehe Kanon 4). Zum Konzil und zur Rechtfertigungslehre siehe O'Malley: 2013, 102–116; außerdem: Leppin: 2016, 167–183; McGrath: 2020, 307–321; Lehmann: 1989, 368–372.

2. Baius, Lessius und die Theologische Fakultät von Löwen

Während die führenden Professoren der theologischen Fakultät von Löwen unter der Leitung von Ruard Tapper am Konzil von Trient in den Jahren 1551–1552 teilnahmen, entwickelte der junge Professor Michael Baius, seit 1552 Inhaber des königlichen Lehrstuhls für die Heilige Schrift,[12] seine Ansichten, wobei er an die strenge antipelagianische augustinische Haltung seines viel bewunderten Meisters Johannes Driedo anknüpfte und diese sogar radikalisierte.[13] In den 1560er-Jahren konnte Baius eine Reihe von *opuscula* oder Traktaten veröffentlichen. Seine Bibelkommentare erschienen nie in gedruckter Form, obwohl aus den Aufzeichnungen der Universität hervorgeht, dass Baius mit Begeisterung die Heilige Schrift kommentierte und sogar einige handschriftliche Notizen der Studenten zu diesen Kursen erhalten sind. Die Tatsache, dass Baius Bibelkommentare nicht veröffentlicht wurden, mag auf die päpstliche Zensur seiner Ideen zurückzuführen sein.

In seinen Werken betonte Baius zunächst, dass der Zustand der unschuldigen Natur des Menschen (*natura integra* oder *natura sana*) zur natürlichen Schöpfungsordnung gehört, die ein Ergebnis der Einwohnung des Heiligen Geistes ist; der Theologe lehnt es ab, diese ursprüngliche Unschuld als ein unentgeltliches Gnadengeschenk zu bezeichnen, das der geschaffenen menschlichen Natur aufgesetzt wird.[14] Der Mensch sei in seiner unschuldigen Natur grundsätzlich in der Lage, Gottes Gebote zu befolgen, mit denen der Lohn (*merces*) des ewigen Lebens verbunden sei – so argumentierte der Löwener Theologe in seinem typisch legalistischen Ansatz. Zweitens betonte Baius, dass der Sündenfall zu einer Sündhaftigkeit führte, die den Menschen nicht nur völlig unfähig macht, den Verlockungen der Konkupiszenz zu widerstehen und den göttlichen Geboten zu gehorchen, sondern sogar in einer radikalen Verderbnis der menschlichen Natur (*natura viciata*) besteht – nicht nur im Verlust einer vermeintlich übernatürlichen Gnade. Laut Alfred Vanneste verzerrte Baius in seiner Radikalisierung Augustinus' Idee der *natura viciata*.[15] Drittens argumentierte Baius, dass die Gnade Gottes, die dem Menschen

---

12 Von 1549 bis 1552 war Baius Professor ad interim der scholastischen Theologie.
13 Van Der Biest: 2021, 193–221; Vanneste: 1994, 123–166; 1977, 327–350; außerdem: Schelkens/Gielis: 2007, 436–443; Quilliet: 2007, 315–334; Quilliets Buch fehlt leider ein brauchbarer Fußnotenapparat, obwohl seine Beschreibung der *causa Baii* und seine Darstellung der Theologie Baius im Allgemeinen zutreffend sind. Eine Zusammenfassung und weiterführende Literatur auch in François/Gerace: 2019, 17–23.
14 Baius: 1696, De prima hominis justitia, c. IV [1565], T.1, 55: "[…] haec fuerit naturalis ejus conditio, cujus semper necessario sit absentia malum, et non potius indebita quaedam humanae naturae exaltatio, quâ ex bona melior facta sit […]".
15 Vanneste weist auf die Zentralität von Augustinus' Idee vom Ursprung des Bösen hin, die er in seinem Enchiridion 3.11 (CChr.SL 46, 53–54) und anderen ähnlichen Texten in einem antimanichäischen Sinn entwickelt und die in Baius' Argumentation zur *natura viciata* eine wichtige Rolle spielt.

kraft des Todes und der Auferstehung Christi zuteil wird, "das wiederherstellt, was durch die Sünde in uns verloren gegangen ist", was der Löwener Theologe als eine wirkliche intrinsische Rechtfertigung betrachtete, es aber dennoch vorzog, sie als *animi motus* zu charakterisieren und nicht als einen *habitus infusa* oder eine echte ontologische Veränderung, wie es die Scholastiker und das Konzil von Trient betrachteten. Und weiter scheint Baius anzudeuten, dass die Konkupiszenz auch nach der Taufe eine echte Sünde bleibt: Die Argumentation ist hier, dass das, was aus der Sünde hervorgeht und zu ihr führt, auch eine Sünde an sich sein muss. Sie ist durch Gottes Gebot verboten: "*Non concupisces*". Diese Sichtweise, die in Richtung der protestantischen theologischen Intuitionen geht, wurde jedoch durch Baius Annahme ausgeglichen, dass der Christ nicht sündigt, wenn er den Verlockungen der Konkupiszenz nicht nachgibt.[16] Mit anderen Worten: Die Taufe hat die Schuld weggenommen, "und deshalb kann der technische Terminus von 'Sünde', *peccatum*, nicht verwendet werden"; es kann höchstens von einer "sündigen Bewegung" die Rede sein. Und obwohl Baius den Begriff der "Nichtanrechnung der Sünden"[17] sporadisch verwendete, verstand er ihn anders als ausgeprägte Protestanten. In jedem Fall befähigt Gottes Gnade den Menschen, sich für seine Gebote zu entscheiden und diese zu befolgen, was Gott im Gegenzug als Verdienst für das Jenseits anrechnet. Sogar für jede einzelne gute Tat ist der Mensch auf die Hilfe der Gnade Gottes angewiesen, so betonte Baius.[18]

Baius untermauerte seine Ansichten mit zahlreichen Verweisen auf die Bibel, insbesondere auf Paulus und Augustinus, wobei er eine Vorliebe für die antipelagianischen Werke des Letzteren zeigte – einer Erzählung aus dem siebzehnten

---

Vanneste ist jedoch überzeugt, dass Baius den Text des Augustinus nicht ganz richtig interpretierte, da er die Idee der *natura viciata* verhärtet und radikalisiert. Nach Augustinus, so argumentiert Vanneste, "ist das Böse keine Substanz, es ist nur die Verderbnis des Guten [...]" und deshalb "kann die Verderbnis niemals vollständig sein" und "das absolut Böse kann nicht existieren" (Dies ist der zentrale Punkt von Vanneste: 1977, 340–341 [Zitate; unsere Übersetzung]; cf. Van Der Biest: 2021, 196–198 und 217–219).

16 Baius: 1696, De peccato originis c. XVI [1566], T.1, 22: "Nam licet concupiscentia, quam peccatum vocat Apostolus, per baptismum sanctificata non sit, nec legis inobedientia esse desierit [...]"; Baius: 1569-1575, ms. 434, Fol. 31r°: "Peccatum: concupiscentia quae remanet post baptismum et quae ex suo genere est peccatum, licet mihi non sit peccatum quia ei non consentio"; cf. Van Der Biest: 2021, 215.

17 Van Der Biest: 2021, 215–216; Baius: 1696, De peccato originis c. XVII [1566], T.1, 22: "Cur illicitus concupiscentiae motus Christianis dissentientibus non imputetur".

18 Baius: 1696, De libero hominis arbitrio, c. X [1563], T.1, 83f: "[...] sed in singulis actibus, cogitationibus, motibus auxilio Dei indiget, non tantùm ad faciendum bonum quando nullà tentatione impugnatur, sed multò magis declinando à malo & quotidianis tentationibus resistendo; hoc est, homo lapsus, non tantùm in singulis operibus bonis quae nemine adversante facit, divino eget auxilio, sed etiam in singulis tentationibus superandis, quibus ad malum provocatur [...]".

Jahrhundert zufolge las er zu Lebzeiten neunmal das gesamte Werk des Augustinus.[19] An der Grenze zu den protestantischen Gebieten Europas lebend, hielten er und sein gleichgesinnter Freund und Kollege Johannes Hessels diese theologische Methode für die geeignetste, um die Auseinandersetzung mit den calvinistischen "Ketzern" aufzunehmen, wie Baius in einem oft zitierten Brief vom 16. März 1568 an den Kardinal Ludovico Simonetta erklärte.[20] Die Argumentation lautete auch, dass die Protestanten niemals durch Argumente aus der scholastischen Tradition überzeugt werden würden.

Baius Ansatz erregte Misstrauen unter seinen Löwener Kollegen, insbesondere Josse Ravesteijn alias Tiletanus (1506–1570), der sogar einen noch "augustinischeren" Standpunkt als sein alter Lehrmeister Ruard Tapper gewählt hatte.[21] Überzeugt, dass Baius von der heilsamen Lehre, wie sie in Trient definiert wurde, abwich, ließen Ravesteijn und seine gleichgesinnten Kollegen Baius' Werk von den theologischen Fakultäten von Alcalá und Salamanca prüfen, die 1565 und 1567 mehrere seiner Thesen zensierten. In der Folge richtete sich eine päpstliche Zensur, erlassen von Papst Pius V. (*Ex omnibus afflictionibus*, 1567), gegen mehrere Standpunkte von Baius. Pius ursprüngliche Bulle war nicht zur Veröffentlichung bestimmt, sondern wurde Baius in einer privaten Sitzung ausgehändigt, um die Unterwerfung des Theologen zu erreichen. Nach einer bestimmten Lesart der Geschichte bewirkte die bewusste (?) und zweideutige Platzierung eines Kommas in den Schlussfolgerungen der Bulle, das berühmte oder berüchtigte *comma pianum*, dafür, dass das Dokument entweder als leichte Ermahnung oder als strenge Verurteilung gelesen werden konnte – was ein Indiz dafür gewesen sein könnte, dass Rom den Fall nicht auf die Spitze treiben wollte.[22] Da Baius aber in Löwen, Rom und anderswo weiterhin für seine Lehrmeinung eintrat, erließ Papst Gregor XIII. 1580 eine neue Bulle *Provisionis Nostrae*, die in ihrer Verurteilung viel deutlicher war. Schließlich beugte sich Baius den anschließenden päpstlichen Zensuren seiner Positionen. Doch dieser Kniefall schadete seiner akademischen Laufbahn keineswegs: Baius wurde 1575 Dekan des Stifts St. Peter in Löwen und als solcher Vizekanzler der Universität.

---

19 Van Eijl: 1968, vol. 1: Text, 88, vol. 2: Fußnoten, 104 n. 99, mit Verweis auf Quellen aus dem siebzehnten Jahrhundert, die die Geschichte enthielten, aber offensichtlich auf die Leichenrede auf Baius zurückgingen, die von seinem Schüler Johann Bernaerts (oder Bernartius) gehalten wurde. Siehe Andreas: 1623, 610: "D. Augustinum nonies totum legisset, invenit tamen quod ruminaretur"; Sweertius: 1628, 565; und Vernulaeus: 1657, 151, neben anderen Autoren.

20 Baius: 1696, T.2: Baiana, 124f.

21 Orcibal: 1989, 26f. Orcibal eröffnet sein Buch über Cornelius Jansenius "von Ypern" mit einem sehr wertvollen Einführungskapitel über die Löwener "augustinistische" Tradition mit dem Titel: "Rome, Louvain et l'autorité de saint Augustin".

22 Quaghebeur: 2003, 61–79; van Eijl: 1955, 499–542; Orcibal: 1962, 115–139.

Augustinus zentrale Bedeutung in der Löwener Theologie ging Hand in Hand mit einer neuen Ausgabe von Augustinus Werken, die von Thomas Gozaeus (ca. 1515–1571) initiiert, von einer Gruppe von vierundsechzig fortgeschrittenen Studenten der Löwener Theologischen Fakultät vorbereitet und von einem Endredakteur, Johannes Molanus (1533–1585), betreut und zum Abschluss gebracht wurde. Der siebte und letzte Band, der die Werke des Kirchenvaters gegen die Donatisten und Pelagianer enthält, war von Henricus Gravius (1536–1591) herausgegeben worden, der damit wichtige Kenntnisse über diesen Teil der Werke des Augustinus erworben hatte. Die Löwener Ausgabe der Werke des Augustinus wurde 1576–1577 in Antwerpen von Christoph Plantin herausgegeben. Sie wurde im siebzehnten Jahrhundert in allen Richtungen des konfessionellen Spektrums verwendet.[23]

Als Reaktion auf Baius "Irrtümer" und die Krise, die seine Ideen ausgelöst hatten, verfasste der königliche Professor für scholastische Theologie Johannes Lensaeus (Jean de Lens; 1541–1593) 1586 eine sogenannte *Formula doctrinae*, in der er die "offizielle Lehre" der theologischen Fakultät von Löwen formulierte.[24] Verständlicherweise konzentriert sich das Dokument auf die Erbsünde und ihre Folgen: (1) Die ursprüngliche Gerechtigkeit des Menschen ist als übernatürliches Gnadengeschenk zu betrachten; (2) durch den Sündenfall hat der Mensch die ursprüngliche Gerechtigkeit verwirkt, aber seine natürlichen Fähigkeiten, Gutes zu tun, sind nicht völlig vernichtet; (3) die Rechtfertigung ist als eine innere Erneuerung der Seele des Menschen durch die ihm innewohnende Gnade zu sehen, sodass der Mensch die Gebote Gottes befolgen kann. Lensaeus berief sich wiederum auf die Autorität von Paulus und Augustinus; in der Tat war die richtige Auslegung des Kirchenvaters zweifellos eines der Ziele des Dokuments. Die *Formula doctrinae* sollte als erste wichtige Kodifizierung der "offiziellen" Löwener Lehre für die kommenden Jahre gelten, auf die einige Generationen einen Eid schwören mussten, während sie von den römischen Behörden begrüßt wurde.[25]

Ein Jahr später, im Jahr 1587, sah sich die theologische Fakultät von Löwen gezwungen, gegen einen Gegner an einer anderen Flanke vorzugehen. Die Jesuiten, die sich 1542 auf Einladung von Ruard Tapper in Löwen niedergelassen hatten, bemühten sich ab 1583, ihre philosophischen und theologischen Kurse für alle Studenten der Universität zu öffnen, mit dem damit einhergehenden Bestreben, akademische Grade zu verleihen. Abgesehen davon, dass die Universität ihr Bildungsmonopol bedroht sah, nahm die Fakultät auch Anstoß an den theologischen Ansichten, die zwei junge Jesuitenprofessoren, insbesondere Leonard Lessius (1554–1623), der von Johannes Hamelius (1554–1589) unterstützt wurde,

---

23 Visser: 2010, 86–106; Ceyssens: 1982b, 103–120.
24 Steyaert: 1742, vol. 1, 193–225.
25 Roegiers: 2003, 5–6; van Eijl: 1994, 215.

in ihrem Löwener Kolleg propagierten, Ansichten, die von der *Formula doctrinae* abwichen und eine Ablehnung der von Baius vertretenen Positionen enthielten.[26] Von dem Professor Jacobus Jansonius (1547–1625) denunziert und von der gesamten Fakultät mit den umstrittenen Positionen konfrontiert, verfasste Lessius eine umfangreiche Verteidigung, die den Titel *Conclusiones de praedestinatione et reprobatione* trägt und aus *vierunddreißig Thesen* besteht, ein Dokument, das er der Fakultät am 15. Mai 1587 vorlegte und das er auch an Bellarmine in Rom schickte – der von den Jahren 1569/1570 bis 1576 einen Studienaufenthalt in Löwen verbracht hatte. Diese Verteidigung beeindruckte die Fakultät nicht, sodass der bereits erwähnte Henricus Gravius im Namen der Fakultät eine *Censura* verfasste, die am 12. September 1587 dem Rektor der Jesuiten in Löwen übermittelt wurde. In der langen Einleitung stellt die Fakultät Augustinus als Bezugspunkt heraus, während sie Lessius vorwirft, die griechischen Väter gegen Augustinus auszuspielen – was eine falscher Schritt sei – und sich auf die Seite der "Semipelagianer" zu schlagen. Die eigentliche Kritik bezog sich auf vierunddreißig Propositionen, die Lessius verteidigt haben soll. Abgesehen von drei Rügen, die sich mit Lessius' Auffassung zur biblischen Inspiration befassten, betrafen einunddreißig Kritikpunkte Lessius' Betonung der Mitwirkung des Menschen in der Heilsökonomie, die die Theologen ausdrücklich als Abweichung von der echten Theologie des Augustinus und als des "Pelagianismus" und "Semipelagianismus" hochgradig verdächtig ansahen. Lessius argumentierte, dass Gott nach dem Sündenfall Adams Nachkommenschaft, also der gesamten Menschheit, gleichermaßen die hinreichenden Gnadenmittel gegen die Sünde und die Hilfsmittel zur Bekehrung und zum Streben nach ewigen Leben gegeben habe – eine Sichtweise zur *Gratia sufficiens*, die im Thomismus wurzelt. Woran die Löwener Theologen besonderen Anstoß nahmen, war Lessius Standpunkt, die Gnade werde nur dann wirksam (*efficax*), wenn der Mensch dieses Gnadenangebot durch eine freie Willensentscheidung und die Ausführung von verdienstvollen Handlungen annimmt – wozu es keiner zusätzlichen Gnade außer der begleitenden Gnade Gottes bedurfte –, was impliziert, dass der Mensch Gottes Angebot auch ablehnen kann.[27] Lessius akzeptierte, dass Gott einige Menschen dazu vorherbestimmt hatte, die Gnade zu empfangen, durch die sie zu einer positiven Reaktion angeregt wurden, und dass er dies auf der Grundlage seines bloßen

---

26 Jüngere Publikationen zu dieser Episode umfassen Eleonora Rai (2020) hier 118–128; Lamberigts: 2018, 32–46; Boute: 2010, 268–311; Außerdem: van Eijl: 1994, 209–224; Siehe auch die Zusammenfassung der Ereignisse in Roegiers: 2012, 159–161; 2003, 6–7.

27 Siehe auch in der *Responsio ad Censuram Facultatis Sacrae Theologiae Lovaniensis* von 1588 und veröffentlicht in (Apologiae: 1684, 36): "[…] potest homo libere credere vel non credere, converti vel non converti, prout voluerit: nec requiritur alia gratia praeveniens, quae faciat cum credere, sed tantum requiritur gratia concomitans seu concursus supernaturalis […] neque requirit praeter hoc aliam gratiam quandam quae infallibiliter faciat et operetur consensum".

souveränen Willens getan hatte. Der Jesuit beeilte sich jedoch immer zu behaupten, dass Gott in ein und demselben prädestinatorischen Akt den guten Gebrauch voraussah, den diese besonderen Menschen von den Gaben der göttlichen Gnade, die jedem gegeben sind, machen würden, wie auch die verdienstvollen Taten, die sie infolgedessen zu vollbringen imstande sein würden, was eine Grundlage für ihre Erwählung zur ewigen Herrlichkeit war. Diese Unterscheidung, die Lessius innerhalb des (einzigen) Prädestinationsdekrets Gottes zwischen der Prädestination zum Heil und der Prädestination zur ewigen Herrlichkeit machte, erhielt mehr Nachdruck, als er seine Position in späteren Dokumenten klärte, aber es kann kein Zweifel daran bestehen, dass seine Auffassung von der Prädestination zur ewigen Herrlichkeit *ex praevisis meritis*, im Kern seiner theologischen Intuition lag. Lessius war überzeugt, dass seine Standpunkte mit der Lehre der Kirchväter, insbesondere der Griechen, übereinstimmten, nicht ohne zu bemerken, dass "Augustinus in dieser Sache unklarer argumentierte".[28]

Die Löwener Theologen, die sich in ihrer Annahme einer lediglich hinreichenden und allen Menschen gegebenen Gnade zurückhaltend zeigten, fühlten sich auf sicherem Boden, als sie betonten, dass "Gottes Gnade an sich und aus sich selbst heraus wirksam" (*gratia divina ex se ab intrinseco efficax*) bei den allein Auserwählten sei. Es implizierte, dass Gottes Gnade so wirkmächtig in den Auserwählten war, dass sie nur das wollten und nur das taten, was Gott wollte, dass sie sich danach sehnten und es taten; in diesem Sinne kamen sie der Behauptung der Unwiderstehlichkeit der Gnade Gottes recht nahe. Es bedeutete auch, dass Gott die Auserwählten von Ewigkeit her auf der Grundlage seines absoluten souveränen Willens und ohne Berücksichtigung irgendwelcher vorhergesehener Verdienste ihrerseits vorherbestimmt hatte (*praedestinatio ante previsa merita*). Für diese Ansichten schöpfte die *Censura*, die die Theologen gegen Lessius erließen, auch aus den letzten Werken des Augustinus, darunter *De dono perseverantiae* und *De praedestinatione sanctorum* (428/429), denen Lessius und gleichgesinnte Jesuiten nur begrenzte Autorität zusprachen. Die an die Mönche von Hadrimetum gerichteten Werke beharrten auf der Prädestination der Auserwählten sowie auf der Idee, dass niemand seines

---

28 Die Angelegenheit wird in den *sechs Propositionen*, der Zusammenfassung seiner Standpunkte, die Lessius im Februar 1588 im Interesse des Erzbischofs von Mecheln schrieb, sehr deutlich herausgearbeitet: "Nos docemus homines non esse immediate et absoluta voluntate destinatos ad gloriam ante omnem praevisionem meritorum, quia hoc aperte docent omnes fere patres praeter Augustinum qui obscurius loquitur, quem tamen puto non dissentire: omnes tamen praedestinatos dicimus immediate esse electos ad gratiam per quam Deus sciebat illos perventuros ad gloriam, et consequenter seu mediate esse electos ad gloriam. Unde praedestinatio quidem non est ex praevisis meritis, quia est electio ad gratiam ad quam nemo eligitur ob sua merita, sed electio ad gloriam est ex praevisis meritis, quia Deus ab aeterno praeparavit gloriam iis quos praevidit sua gratia cum auxilio ipsius bene usuros". Zitiert auch in Rai (2020, 123) mit einem Verweis auf die fünfte der *sechs Propositionen*, in Le Bachelet: 1911, 194–198.

Heils sicher sein kann und dass gute Werke keine Garantie für eine zukünftige Erlösung geben. Am 20. Januar 1588 erließ die theologische Fakultät von Douai eine noch weitergehende und unverblümtere Rüge als Löwen, deren Hauptautor Willem Hessels van Est (1542-1613) war.[29] Lessius seinerseits verfasste eine Antwort an die Löwener Theologen mit dem Titel *Responsio ad Censuram Facultatis Sacrae Theologiae Lovaniensis*, die der Fakultät im Frühsommer 1588 übergeben wurde.[30] In dieser Arbeit äußerte sich Lessius "gegen eine selektive Lektüre von Augustinus, also gegen die Bevorzugung des antipelagianischen Augustinus gegenüber dem jungen Augustinus durch die Fakultät" und beschuldigte die Fakultät sogar, auf der gleichen Linie wie Calvin zu sein.[31] In derselben Kontroverse wurden weitere Schriften ausgetauscht und in Umlauf gebracht, darunter die *Antithesen*, eine Zusammenfassung in *sechs Propositionen*, die Lessius im Februar 1588 an die Adresse des Erzbischofs von Mecheln richtete, der es sich zur Aufgabe gemacht hatte, in diesem Konflikt zu vermitteln.[32]

Im Frühjahr 1588 war der gesamte Vorgang auch stückweise und von verschiedenen Seiten auf den Tisch des Papstes und des Heiligen Offiziums gelangt – und damit auch zu einer heiklen Mission für den päpstlichen Nuntius in Köln Ottavio Mirto Frangipani geworden. Während die Löwener Theologen auf eine römische Weihe ihrer Verurteilung Lessius hofften, konnte der Jesuit mit der Unterstützung mächtiger Verteidiger rechnen, darunter Roberto Bellarmino: Obwohl persönlich von einer "augustinistischen" *praedestinatio ante previsa merita* überzeugt, nahm Bellarmino Lessius in Schutz, vor allem weil er hinter der Löwener *Censura* den nachhaltigen Einfluss von Baius und seiner Theologie vermutete, den er um jeden Preis zurückdrängen wollte. Aufgrund der Intervention von Bellarmine und des Generaloberen des Jesuitenordens, Claudio Acquaviva, beurteilten die römischen Behörden beide Lehren – sowohl die von Lessius als auch die der Fakultät – als "sana doctrina". Der Nuntius Ottavio Mirto Frangipani kam persönlich nach Löwen, um am 10. Juli 1588 im Namen des Papstes zu verordnen, dass alle beteiligten Parteien die Kontroversen und vor allem die gegenseitigen Zensuren einstellen sollten, wobei er sie darauf hinwies, dass die Angelegenheit dem Papst vorbehalten sei. Dennoch erhielten die Löwener Theologen das Recht, die Gründe für ihre Einwände und die darauf folgenden Demarchen in Rom in einem Dokument darzulegen, das die

---

29 Wir verwendeten Censuræ: 1683, 3-51 (censura lovaniensis), 53-141 (censura duacensis). Eine Diskussion findet man in Stucco: 2014, 279-283; van Eijl: 1994, 217-223.
30 Eine ausführliche Analyse in Lamberigts: 2018, 38-46. Auch van Eijl: 1994, 224-245.
31 Lamberigts: 2018, 39 (unsere Übersetzung).
32 Eine Analyse der *sechs Propositionen* im Vergleich zu den *vierunddreißig Propositionen*, in Rai: 2020, 121-124. Auch van Eijl: 1994, 245-253.

Jesuiten am 10. September als *Justificatio seu Defensio censuræ* erreichte. Lessius Erwiderung folgte einen Monat später.[33]

Die oben skizzierte Kontroverse zeigt, dass das gemeinsame Ziel einer auf der Heiligen Schrift, Augustinus und Thomas basierenden Theologie sich als förderlich für divergierende Interpretationen erwiesen hatte. Dies wurde noch deutlicher im Werk von Thomas Stapleton (1535-1598). Er war ein englischer Exilierter, der sein Land unter Königin Elisabeth verlassen hatte, der zunächst in Löwen studiert hatte und 1571 Professor für Kontroverstheologie in Douai geworden war. Er entpuppte sich als Freund der Jesuiten und der von ihnen geförderten Theologie. Aufgrund seiner Opposition gegen die Rüge, die die Universität Douai Anfang 1588 gegen die oben genannten Thesen von Lessius und Hamelius ausgesprochen hatte, wurde er eine Zeit lang von allen Aktivitäten an seiner Fakultät ausgeschlossen. Es ist daher überraschend, dass ausgerechnet Stapleton von der Regierung König Philipps II. nach Löwen zurückgerufen wurde, um als Nachfolger des 1589 verstorbenen Michael Baius königlicher Professor für die Heilige Schriften zu werden. Am Ende seines Aufenthaltes in Douai und während seiner Amtszeit als Professor für die Heilige Schrift in Löwen veröffentlichte Stapleton eine Reihe von homiletischen Büchern und Akademischen Bibelkommentaren, die beide darauf abzielten, ein "Gegengift" oder "Antidot" zu den so genannten "giftigen" Auslegungen von Johannes Calvin, Theodore Beza und den anderen Reformatoren zu bieten. Daher erwies sich Stapletons Ansatz als sehr kontroverstheologisch. Merkwürdigerweise bezog sich Stapleton ausgiebig auf Augustinus, während er gleichzeitig den Kirchenvater durch ein stark thomistisches und sogar molinistisches Verständnis interpretierte. Dies veranlasste ihn z. B., das Zusammenwirken des freien Willens des Menschen mit der Heilsinitiative Gottes zu betonen, während er gleichzeitig mit den Auffassungen über die Prädestination auf der Grundlage des Vorwissens Gottes über die Verdienste des Menschen sympathisierte.[34]

Die Kontroversen in Löwen, aber auch die in Spanien zwischen Thomas Bañez und Luis de Molina, veranlassten Papst Clemens VIII. 1597, den katholischen Theologen zu verbieten, sich weiter auf solch hitzige Debatten einzulassen, und beauftragte eine römische Kommission mit der Organisation von Anhörungen, um die Angelegenheit auf der Grundlage der Lehre des Augustinus zu entscheiden, die so genannten *congregationes de auxiliis divinae gratiae*. Die Löwener Interessen wurden dort von Peter Lombard (1554-1625), einem Iren und Theologieprofessor, verteidigt, der 1601 Erzbischof von Armagh werden sollte (ohne sein Bistum in Besitz nehmen zu können). Obwohl Clemens VIII., unterstützt von den meisten

---

33 Zu den römischen Interventionen siehe insbesondere van Eijl: 1994, 255-276.
34 Seybold (1967); Leuridan (1898); Zu Stapletons Tätigkeit als königlicher Professor für Heilige Schriften siehe: Gerace: 2019, 160-175; François: 2009, 363-386; dieser Artikel sollte ergänzt werden durch (2010, 129-140). Verweise auf Stapletons Arbeit siehe dort.

Mitgliedern der Kommission, einschließlich Peter Lombard, zu einer Verurteilung Molinas und einer Akzeptanz der Standpunkte von Bañez tendierte, beendete sein Nachfolger Papst Paul V. schließlich 1607 die *congregationes de auxiliis*, indem er den beteiligten theologischen Strömungen erlaubte, ihre eigenen Positionen beizubehalten, sie aber ermahnte, sich von gegenseitigen Verurteilungen zurückzuhalten. Ein Dekret der Inquisition unter demselben Papst verbot 1611 die Veröffentlichung jedes Buches über die wirksame Gnade – ohne besondere Erlaubnis – bis der Heilige Stuhl die endgültige Entscheidung treffen würde, die sich auf die Theologie des Augustinus stützen sollte. Dieses Dekret wurde 1625 von Papst Urban VIII. bestätigt und in den nächsten Jahren und Jahrzehnten regelmäßig wiederholt, der Heilige Stuhl traf jedoch nie eine endgültige Entscheidung und manche katholische Theologen fühlten sich durch diese nachfolgenden Dekrete nicht besonders gebunden.[35]

3. Jesuiten, Jansenisten und die Theologische Fakultät von Löwen

Unmittelbar nachdem die *congregationes de auxiliis* ihre Tätigkeit beendet hatten, genauer gesagt im Jahr 1610, veröffentlichte Leonard Lessius sein Werk *De gratia efficaci*, gefolgt von einer zweiten Auflage im Jahr 1616. Mit dieser Veröffentlichung stellte sich Lessius gegen die politisch-theologische Richtung der *congregationes*, in denen die Jesuiten und insbesondere Molina nur knapp der Verurteilung entgangen waren. In seinem neuen Buch betonte Lessius noch stärker das Zusammenwirken des freien Willens des Menschen mit der Gnadeninitiative Gottes und ersetzte die Prädestination durch den Begriff des Vorherwissens, technisch die *praescientia conditionata*, die besagt, dass die Erwählung zum ewigen Leben auf der Vorauskenntnis der Verdienste des Menschen beruht, die zugleich als Gaben Gottes zu betrachten sind.[36] Es war nicht nur das Lessianische Äquivalent der molinistischen *scientia media*, denn Lessius ging noch einen Schritt weiter, indem er ein "Marktprinzip" oder gar "kontraktualistisches" Prinzip in die Heilsökonomie einführte: Wenn der Mensch das Gute tut, das Gott von ihm will, und ihm die dafür notwendige

---

35 Matava (2016), insbesondere 16–36; auch Stucco: 2014, 155–218. Zur Beteiligung der Löwener Theologen, insbesondere von Peter Lombard, siehe Boute: 2010, 316–390, insbesondere 375–390; eine Zusammenfassung in Roegiers: 2012, 164.

36 Lessius: 1610, 258: "Optime haec duo consistunt: Deus ad gloriam eligit absoluto decreto ex praevisis meritis, etc. et Deus non eligit ad gratiam ex praevisis meritis. Item Deus eligit ad gloriam ex praescientia operum, et ipsa opera sunt dona Dei [...]".

Gnade gewährt, darf der Mensch erwarten, dass Gott ihm das Heil nicht versagt.[37] In seiner Betonung der menschlichen Mitarbeit stärkte Lessius die Grundlagen seiner Lehre bei den griechischen Kirchenvätern, die sich vor Augustinus geäußert hatten, ohne den augustinischen Ansatz der Gnade, des freien Willens und der Prädestination gänzlich zu ignorieren.[38] Lessius' Position erregte nun den Zorn des Generaloberen Acquaviva, der mit Bellarmines Unterstützung sein *Decretum de uniformitate doctrinae, praesertim de gratiae efficacitate* (1613) veröffentlichte, um "seinen Orden vor äußeren Angriffen zu schützen und eine innere lehrmäßige Einheit herzustellen" ("mit einer Tendenz zum Thomismus, aber einschließlich einer gewissen Elastizität der Ansichten"). Bellarmine zog seine theologische Unterstützung für Lessius zurück, die er in einem früheren Stadium der Kontroverse zu geben bereit gewesen war. Auch die theologische Fakultät von Löwen distanzierte sich 1613 von Lessius' Veröffentlichung seiner verstärkten theologischen Positionen.[39]

In Douai war Willem Hessels van Est, kurz Estius (1542–1613), einer der Protagonisten der theologischen Fakultät in diesen Jahren. Estius war 1582 von Löwen nach Douai umgezogen, wo er zu den Hauptverfassern der oben erwähnten Rüge gegen Lessius und Hamelius gehörte und Stapleton wegen dessen Unterstützung für die Jesuiten und deren Theologie aus der Fakultät ausgeschlossen hatte. Als Professor der Kontroverstheologie kommentierte Estius ausführlich die *Sentenzen* des Peter Lombard – die er nach den Erkenntnissen des Thomas von Aquin erklärte. Sein vierbändiger Kommentar zu den *Sentenzen* des Peter Lombard, der 1615–1616 posthum veröffentlicht wurde, sollte sich als sehr wichtig erweisen. Seine einflussreichsten Werke waren jedoch seine *Kommentare zu den Paulusbriefen und zu den Katholischen Briefen* (erschienen 1614 und 1616) – das Ergebnis seiner Arbeit als Professor der Heiligen Schrift. Estius Kommentare wurden wegen ihres Reichtums und ihrer geschickten Herangehensweise bis zum Ende des neunzehnten Jahrhunderts mehrfach nachgedruckt. Estius galt oft als ein herausragender Vertreter der augustinisch-thomistischen Schule von Löwen und Douai mit ihrer antipelagianischen Tendenz. Estius verteidigte sogar die These, dass Christus nicht für alle

---

37 Siehe diesbezüglich insbesondere Decock: 2019, 169–196, insbesondere 187–195. Decock verweist auch auf Lessius' *De perfectionibus moribusque divinis*, veröffentlicht 1620, drei Jahre vor seinem Tod.

38 Lessius stützte seine Ansichten auf Augustinus, z. B. seine *Quaestio 2 ad Simplicianum*, eine Exegese zu Römer 9, verfasst in den Jahren 396/397, worin der Kirchenvater eine reife Reflexion über die Prädestination anstellte, wobei der Gnade die Hauptrolle zukommt, ohne den Wert der verdienstvollen Werke zu vernachlässigen (Orcibal: 1989, 46 n. 154; hier wird verwiesen auf Augustinus, Div. quaest. Simpl., I, q. 2, 4 [CChr.SL 44, 28–29]). Es war Augustinus' letzte Überlegung dieser Art vor der pelagianischen Kontroverse.

39 Rai: 2020, 131–141 (unsere Übersetzung).

Menschen gestorben sei – und leugnete damit die hinreichende Gnade (*gratia sufficiens*) – während er die Wirksamkeit der Gnade Gottes bei den allein Auserwählten betonte (*gratia efficax*). Gottes wirksame Gnade gewährte den Auserwählten nicht nur die Fähigkeit, gerettet zu werden, sondern prädeterminierte und "bewegte" sie auch effizient dazu, das Gute sowohl zu wollen als auch zu tun – die berühmte thomistisch-bañezianische Idee der *praedeterminatio* oder *praemotio physica*. Mehr denn je wurde die Frage aufgeworfen, ob die Gnade Gottes so unwiderstehlich sei, dass sie die Freiheit des menschlichen Willens beeinträchtige. Estius diesbezügliche Ideen kündigten bereits die hitzigen Debatten an, die in den kommenden Jahrzehnten die "jansenistische" Kontroverse beherrschen sollten. Nachdem der "Jansenismus" verurteilt worden war, zögerten Estius' Nachfolger in Douai nicht, auf einige berichtigungsbedürftige Thesen in seinem Werk hinzuweisen.[40]

Während Willem Estius in Douai eine auf die Heilige Schrift, Augustinus und Thomas gestützte Theologie entwickelt hatte, wurde der königliche Lehrstuhl für die Heilige Schrift in Löwen von oben genannten Jacobus Jansonius besetzt. Er teilte Estius theologische Vorlieben und seine Kommentare zeugen von seiner gründlichen antipelagianischen augustinischen Theologie, wobei er viel mehr betonte, dass die Gnade Gottes als eine innere geistige Kraft, Inspiration oder *delectatio* wirkt, die den Menschen nicht zwingt, sondern ein so starkes Verlangen und eine strahlende Liebe bewirkt, dass der Mensch tatsächlich in der Lage ist, über das widerstreitende Verlangen, das durch den Willen des Fleisches oder die Konkupiszenz repräsentiert wird, zu siegen. In diesem Sinne akzeptierte Jansonius, dass Gottes Gnade wirkmächtig ist, wobei er den Begriff *gratia efficax* nur widerwillig verwendete, und sicher nicht im Sinne einer *praedeterminatio* oder *praemotio physica*, wie Bañez, Estius und andere sie definiert hatten.[41] Jansonius erreichte nie die höchsten Stufen der akademischen Theologie, wurde aber tief in die akademische Politik seiner Zeit verstrickt und verteidigte u. a. das Monopol der Universität gegen die Bestrebungen der Jesuiten, ein vollständiges öffentliches Studium der Philosophie (und schließlich der Theologie) zu etablieren, sowie das damit verbundene Recht, akademische Grade ("*in ordine ad gradus*") zu verleihen.[42]

Einen neuen Höhepunkt in der Verbindung von augustinischer, antipelagianischer Theologie und Bibelkommentar in Löwen erreichte Cornelius Jansenius, genannt "von Ypern" (1585–1638). Jansenius wurde ab 1618 ordentlicher Professor an der theologischen Fakultät in Löwen und wurde 1630 auf den königlichen Lehrstuhl für Heilige Schriften berufen. Ab 1635/1636 Bischof von Ypern, erlag er

---

40 Ferrer (1960); Fleischmann (1940); Salembier (1913); Leuridan (1895). Zu Estius' biblischem Werk siehe u. a. François: 2014, 119–130. Siehe dort für Verweise auf Estius' Originalarbeit.
41 François: 2012, 343–344.
42 Boute: 2010, 463–486, 521–544, und 567–579; cf. Roegiers: 2012, 165–166.

schließlich 1638 der Pest und seine wichtigsten Werke wurden erst posthum veröffentlicht. Am bekanntesten ist sein *Augustinus* (1640), den er als eingehende Studie der Werke des Augustinus und der darin zu findenden Theologie der Gnade, des freien Willens und der Prädestination vorstellte, sodass sich seine Konzentration selbstverständlich auf die antipelagianischen Bücher des Kirchenvaters richtete.[43] Das Werk war ausdrücklich als Alternative zum scholastischen Ansatz gedacht, den Jansenius als eine verzerrte Interpretation ansah. In der Kurzbiographie, die dem Buch vorangestellt ist, lesen wir, dass Jansenius das Werk verfasste, nachdem er die Werke des Augustinus mehr als zehnmal, und seine Bücher gegen die Pelagianer leicht dreißigmal, von Anfang bis Ende gelesen hatte.[44] Nach Jansenius' Ansicht, die im letzten Teil des *Augustinus* zum Ausdruck kommt, waren die "neuen Pelagianer" seiner eigenen Zeit mit Lessius, Molina und den Jesuiten zu identifizieren.[45] Neben dem *Augustinus* wurden auch Jansenius' Bibelkommentare – das Ergebnis seiner Arbeit als königlicher Professor der Heiligen Schrift – veröffentlicht, nämlich sein *Tetrateuchus* oder *Kommentar zu den vier Evangelien* im Jahr 1639 und der *Pentateuchus* oder *Kommentar zu den fünf Büchern Mose* im Jahr 1641, wobei der *Tetrateuchus* der erfolgreichere von beiden war. In diesen Kommentaren, vor allem in denen zu den Evangelien, fühlte sich Jansenius vor allem dort heimisch, wo ihm die zu besprechende Bibelstelle Anlass gab, eine theologische, nämlich augustinische, Auslegung des Textes vorzunehmen. Im Gegensatz zu Estius zeigt Jansenius weit weniger Anfälligkeit für scholastische, d. h. thomistische, Einflüsse oder ihr Vokabular. Es ist nicht schwer, in Jansenius' Werken Aussagen zu finden, die leugnen, dass Gott allen Menschen seine hinreichenden Gnadenhilfen gegeben hat, um das Gesetz erfüllen zu können,[46] und gleichzeitig betonen, dass der Sohn Gottes, der für seine Herde gestorben ist, nur für diejenigen gestorben ist, die dazu vorherbestimmt sind, die damit verbundene Gnade zu empfangen.[47] Jansenius

---

43 Zu Jansenius und den Anfängen der "jansenistischen" Kontroverse, siehe insbesondere Ceyssens: 1977, 381–432. Wichtige Werke zur jansenistischen Kontroverse sind Orcibal (1989), außerdem Kolakowski: 1995, 3–25. Zu den Bibelkommentaren siehe François: 2014, 130–135; eine Zusammenfassung in François/Gerace: 2019, 32–38; Roegiers: 2003, 9–11. Weitere Literatur siehe dort.

44 "[…] se decies et amplius universa Opera Augustini, attentione acri, adnotatione diligenti, libros verò contra Pelagianos facile trigesies à capite ad calcem evolvisse". Siehe die "Synopsis vitæ auctoris", die Jansenius (1640) vorangestellt ist, vol. 1, S. [2]. Siehe auch Icard (2013).

45 Stanciu: 2011, 393–418.

46 Siehe Jansenius: 1640, vol. 3, Buch 3. "De gratia Christi salvatoris", Kap. 4, Kol. 262–263; Kap. 13, Kol. 324–337, mit dem Titel auf S. 262: "Ex natura gratiae Christi ostenditur, nullis dari sufficientem gratiam juxta sensum recentiorum". Siehe auch Kolakowski: 1995, 10.

47 Jansenius: 1639, Com. in Io 10:15: "ET ANIMAM MEAM PONO PRO OVIBUS MEIS, id est vitam ipsam pro eis liberandis profundo […]"; 10:16: "[…] Vocantur autem *Oves*, vel per anticipationem, quia oves erunt, vel potius ratione praedestinationis Dei […]"; 10:26: "[…] NON ESTIS EX OVIBUS MEIS, id est, ex praedestinatis ad vitam aeternam, sed potius ad interitum, prout exponit August."; 10:27:

betonte auch die Wirksamkeit der Gnade Gottes bei den allein Auserwählten und die (Quasi-)Unfähigkeit ihres Willens zum Widerstand. Für Jansenius wartet die Gnade Gottes nicht auf die Einwilligung des Menschen, sondern drängt sich dem Willen wirksam auf – *"quo fiat, ut velit"* – ein Punkt, auf dem Jansenius sowohl im *Augustinus*[48] als auch in seinen Bibelkommentaren[49] durchaus beharrt, der ihm aber auch Probleme bereiten sollte.

Aufgrund der Aktionen belgischer und französischer Jesuiten mit Unterstützung ihrer römischen Verbündeten erließ Papst Urban VIII. 1641/1643 die Bulle *In eminenti*, in der Jansenius *Augustinus* vorgeworfen wurde, einen Skandal verursacht zu haben sowie Propositionen zu enthalten, die bereits in Baius' Thesen verurteilt worden waren. An der theologischen Fakultät in Löwen reagierte man verblüfft, da man befürchtete, dass *In eminenti* tatsächlich die offizielle Lehre der Fakultät angriff, deren genuiner Bestandteil der Augustinismus war. Daraufhin reiste eine Löwener Delegation, bestehend aus dem Theologen John Sinnich und dem Kanonisten Corneille De Pape, im Herbst 1643 nach Rom, um Fragen zu stellen und Erklärungen abzugeben, und drang sogar bis zu Urban VIII. selbst vor. Dennoch wurde Jansenius unterstellte Leugnung der hinreichenden Gnade

---

"OVES MEAE, id est praedestinati, et mihi ad salvandum dati, VOCEM MEAM AUDIUNT, id est obediunt, credendo mihi". Siehe auch François: 2014, 132.

48 Jansenius: 1640, vol. 3, Buch 2. "De gratia Christi Salvatoris", Kap. 4, Kol. 97–102, esp. 99B-C: "Nimirum hoc isto adjutoriorum discrimine spectat Augustinus, ut sciamus adjutorium sanae voluntatis non fuisse talis conditionis, *quo* bonum opus fieret: hoc enim non conveniebat tàm robustae liberrimaeque voluntati, cum ipsa sufficeret, ut adjutorio quod sibi praesto aderat, si tantùm vellet, uteretur [...] Adjutorium verò infirmae captivaeque voluntatis vult esse tale, *quo fiat, ut velit*. Hoc est, esse hujusmodi ut simul ac datur, ipsum velle voluntati detur, et si non detur, nunquàm velit, quia sine illo nunc propter infirmitatem velle non potest"; weiter Kap. 24 und 25, Kol. 196–207: Kapitel 25 beginnt auf S. 202 mit dem Titel "[...] ejus [medicinalis gratiae] efficacissima natura declaratur, ex eo quod nulla prorsus effectu caret, sed eum in omnibus quibus datur, infallibiliter operatur" and concludes with the words in Kol. 207D: "Augustinus universim doceat, medicinalem Christi gratiam semper effectum suum inferre voluntati, cui eam Deus suâ benignitate largiatur". Eine Zusammenfassung siehe auch bei Stucco: 2014, 241; und Kolakowski: 1995, 14–15.

49 Jansenius: 1639, Com. in Io 6:37: "[...] AD ME VENIET, id est reipsâ indeclinabiliter mihi credet: quia quos Deus ab aeterno salvandos praedestinavit, hos sine dubio secundùm illud propositum suum vocabit [...]", mit einem offensichtlichen Verweis auf Augustinus, De dono perseverantiae 14.34–37 (PL 45, 1013–1015); Com. in Io 6:45: "Quantâ verò efficaciâ à Deo doceantur, consequenter aperit Christus: OMNIS QUI AUDIVIT A PATRE, ET DIDICIT; quae duo vel idem sunt, prout accipit August. De praedestinatione Sanctorum c. 8. vel certè *audire* ad informationem intellectus tantùm pertinet, *discere* ad tractum voluntatis. Omnis ergò talis non solùm potest venire ad me, quasi Deus tantùm tribuat per gratiam, posse si velit; sed VENIT AD ME, id est credit reipsa, ubi iam & possibilitatis profectus, & voluntatis affectus, & actionis effectus est, inquit August. De gratia Christi c. 14", mit Verweis auf Augustinus, De praedestinatione sanctorum 8.13–16 (PL 44, 970 l. 25 – 973 l. 6); und De gratia Christi et de peccato originali 1.14.15 (CSEL 42, 137 l. 23 – 138 l. 21); auch Jansenius: 1639, Com. in Matt 25:34–35. Siehe auch François: 2014, 134–135.

sowie der Unwiderstehlichkeit der wirksamen Gnade schließlich durch die von Papst Innozenz X. 1653 erlassene Bulle *Cum Occasione* verurteilt.[50] Die Fakultät unterwarf sich dieser und den folgenden päpstlichen Bullen gegen den Jansenismus, während sie gleichzeitig versuchte, die Linie der *Formula doctrinae* von 1586 und der *Censura* von 1587 fortzusetzen, mit ihrer strengen antipelagianischen augustinisch-thomistischen Lehre und ihrer Betonung der *gratia divina ex se ab intrinseco efficax*. Durch ein Breve vom 17. August 1660 ermutigte Papst Alexander VII. die Theologen, sich an "*Augustini et Thomae Aquinatis inconcussa tutissimaque dogmata*" zu halten.[51] In den folgenden Jahrzehnten bekräftigte Rom weiterhin seine Unterstützung für die theologische Linie Löwens.

Jansenius gleichgesinnter Freund, Libertus Fromondus (1587–1653), war der (Mit-)Herausgeber seiner Bücher sowie sein Nachfolger auf dem königlichen Lehrstuhl für die Heiligen Schriften. Und obwohl Fromondus zugegebenermaßen der "jansenistischen" Fraktion angehörte, zeigt ein genaueres Studium seiner *Kommentare zu den Briefen des Paulus und den Katholischen Briefen*, dass seine Ansichten bezüglich der Gnade und des freien Willens im Einklang mit einer orthodoxeren katholischen Position stehen. Fromondus mag ein Löwener Vertreter einer Entwicklung gewesen sein, die Sylvio Hermann De Franceschi für Frankreich skizzierte, nämlich dass einige "Jansenisten" schon vor 1653 von den umstrittensten Punkten ihrer Lehre von Gnade, freiem Willen und Prädestination, abrückten, um zumindest auf einer theoretischen Ebene den Begriff der hinreichenden Gnade zu akzeptieren, wie er von den Thomisten verstanden wurde.[52]

Mehr noch: Bei Fromondus sehen wir, wie sich die "Jansenisten" zunehmend für innere, mystische Erfahrungen (sowie die damit einhergehenden Wunder und andere übernatürliche Ereignisse) interessierten. Denn das einzige biblische Werk, das Fromondus zu seinen Lebzeiten veröffentlichen ließ, war sein *Kommentar zum Hohelied* (1653). Dem fügte er bewusst die *Divisio animae ac spiritus* hinzu, ein Werk des mystisch begabten Kapuzinerpaters Johannes Evangelista von 's Hertogenbosch (ca. 1588–1635), der im Kloster Löwen lebte und mit Fromondus in regem Kontakt stand.[53] Nach dem Tod von Fromondus wurde der Lehrstuhl für die Heilige Schrift in Löwen an Nicolas Du Bois vergeben, einen Anti-Jansenisten, der aus kirchenpolitischen Gründen ernannt wurde und als Theologe und Bibelkommentator völlig inkompetent war.

---

50 Eine genaue Untersuchung des Vorhandenseins solcher Aussagen in Jansenius' *Augustinus* und im Werk des Kirchenvaters sowie der Gerechtigkeit der Verurteilung, siehe Ceyssens: 1980, 368–424; 1982a, 39–53.
51 Strayer: 2008, 59–61 und 67–69; Quilliet: 2007, 435–453; Kolakowski: 1995, 3–25; Roegiers: 2003, 10–12. Siehe dort für weitere Literaturhinweise, darunter Ceyssens: 1942–1943, 31–111.
52 François: 2014, 136–142; Franceschi: 2009, 64–82.
53 Ceyssens: 1963, 1–46.

Ab derselben Zeit unterstützten "jansenistisch" gesinnte Löwener Theologen mehrere belgische Bischöfe in ihrer Auseinandersetzung mit den Jesuiten und gleichgesinnten Theologen, denen man ihre (angeblich) laxistischen moralischen Überzeugungen und Praktiken sowie ihren Attritionismus vorwarf, die sich in ihren Schriften und ihrer Beichtpraxis zeigten. Die Löwener Theologen, die einer rigoristischeren Moralauffassung sowie dem Kontritionismus anhingen, verurteilten den Laxismus ebenso wie den Probabilismus, der als Quelle moralischer Lockerheit angesehen wurde – eine Phase im belgischen Jansenismus, die mit den Diskussionen in Frankreich vergleichbar ist. Solche Ideen waren in Gommarus Huygens' (1631–1702) *Methodus remittendi et retinendi peccata* von 1674 enthalten. Einer nach Rom entsandten Löwener Delegation, bestehend aus Christian Lupus, Francis van Vianen und Martin Steyaert (1677–1679), gelang es schließlich, den Papst dazu zu bringen, mehrere laxistische Propositionen zu verurteilen, die größtenteils aus jesuitischen Publikationen stammten, darunter die von Lessius und Molina. Außerdem konnten sie vom Heiligen Offizium der Inquisition "die Zusicherung erhalten, dass die *Censuræ* von Löwen und Douai (zu denen sie die *Defensio* von Löwen hinzugefügt hatten) 'eine gesunde Lehre sind, die nie einen Tadel erfahren hat, die ohne jedes Risiko gelehrt, gelesen und sogar gedruckt werden kann.'" Das Heilige Offizium war jedoch nicht bereit, diese Zusicherung in einem offiziellen Schriftstück beglaubigen zu lassen.[54] Die Jesuiten ihrerseits sowie eine unter ihrer Leitung in Löwen heimlich gegründete antijansenistische Gesellschaft bezeichneten die an der Fakultät vertretenen Thesen, insbesondere von Gommarus Huygens, als rigoristisch. Lange Auszüge wurden nach Rom geschickt, wo einige von ihnen schließlich 1690 von Papst Alexander VIII. verurteilt wurden.[55]

Mit anderen Worten, was als antipelagianische, augustinisch-thomistische Ansicht über Gnade, freien Willen und Prädestination begonnen hatte, hatte sich in mehrere Richtungen aufgefächert, nämlich mit Augenmerk auf eine innere mystische Haltung (und sogar übernatürliche Ereignisse, wie Heilungen und Wunder), rigoristische moralische Ansichten und die Forderung nach wahrer Reue, ganz zu schweigen von einer Zurückhaltung gegenüber Ansprüchen auf päpstliche "Unfehlbarkeit" und römische Interventionen in lokale kirchliche Angelegenheiten, angesichts der (angeblichen) faktischen Fehler, die Rom in der "jansenistischen" Angelegenheit gemacht hatte. Dies ist ein Hinweis darauf, dass es sich beim "Jansenismus" um ein vielschichtiges Phänomen handelt, bei dem "ausgehend von einem anfänglichen Konflikt zu den bestehenden Streitpunkten ständig neue Streitigkeiten

---

54 Orcibal: 1989, 38 (Zitat; unsere Übersetzung) und 53; Roegiers: 2003, 9 und 13–14; und 2012, 171. Weitere Literatur siehe dort, darunter Ceyssens: 1950a, 167–253.

55 Roegiers: 2003, 14–15; und 2012, 172. Weitere Literatur siehe dort, darunter Ceyssens: 1950b, 343–397; 1953, 193–229.

oder neue Kampffelder hinzukommen, ohne dass diese früheren Streitpunkte verschwinden", wie Jan Roegiers festgestellt hat.[56]

4. Fazit

Cornelius Jansenius Beobachtung "Wir alle wollen 'Augustinisten' sein oder wenigstens so erscheinen" galt sicherlich für das Löwener theologische Milieu, dessen "Augustinismus" berüchtigt geworden ist. Diese Ausführungen machen jedoch deutlich, dass dieses theologische Milieu keineswegs ein monolithischer Block war, sondern mehrere "Augustinismen" umfasste. Während der augustinisch geprägte Thomismus der führenden Theologen des frühen 16. Jahrhunderts, vor allem Jacobus Latomus und Ruard Tapper, unter ihren Nachfolgern im späteren Verlauf des Jahrhunderts deutlichere antipelagianische Züge annahm, musste sich die von ihnen entwickelte "offizielle" Löwener Lehre gegen Abweichungen in mehreren Bereichen behaupten. Während Michael Baius eine noch radikalere antipelagianische Variante pflegte, waren Leonard Lessius und die Jesuiten darauf bedacht, das Zusammenwirken des menschlichen Willens mit der Gnadeninitiative Gottes zu betonen, wobei beide Varianten letztlich der römischen Sorge um die katholische Lehreinheit unterlagen, in einem Bereich, in dem der Protestantismus eine wichtige Herausforderung darstellte. Nachdem die römischen *congregationes de auxiliis* ohne klaren Abschluss endeten, blieb Löwen weiterhin das Forum theologischer Kontroversen, mit Lessius und vor allem Cornelius Jansenius als Protagonisten, Letzterer durch die posthume Veröffentlichung seines *Augustinus*. Obwohl Jansenius radikaler antipelagianischer Augustinismus oft als eine Wiederbelebung des zensierten Baianismus angesehen wurde, waren seine Hauptanliegen tatsächlich nicht dieselben, wobei seine (Quasi-)Leugnung der hinreichenden Gnade und seine Formulierung der Unwiderstehlichkeit der wirksamen Gnade schließlich einer geradlinigen Verurteilung unterzogen wurden. Alle oben erwähnten "Augustinismen" beriefen sich in gleicher Weise auf den *doctor gratiae* zur Untermauerung ihrer Standpunkte, wobei sowohl der "erste" Augustinus, der sich eher geneigt zeigte, einen Beitrag der menschlichen Willensfreiheit zu akzeptieren, als auch der "zweite" Augustinus, der in seiner Kontroverse mit den Pelagianern die überwältigende Notwendigkeit der Gnade Gottes in der Heilsökonomie betonte und sich in seinen letzten Werken *De praedestinatione sanctorum* und *De dono perseverantiae* sogar expliziter über die Prädestination geäußert hatte, berücksichtigt wurden. Lessius und die Jesuiten nahmen allmählich eine kritische Distanz zu den Positionen des Augustinus ein, besonders zu denen, die in den letzten Werken zum Ausdruck

---

56 Roegiers: 2003, 2 (unsere Übersetzung), mit Verweis auf Hersche: 1977, 25–43.

kamen, und bemühten sich, seine Theologie mit der der griechischen Väter ins Gleichgewicht zu bringen, die den Beitrag des Menschen in der Heilsökonomie viel stärker akzeptieren wollten.

Quellen und Literatur

Ungedruckte Quellen

BAIUS, MICHAEL (1569–1575), Comment. in epistolas D. Pauli et canonicas, et in apocalypsin, Utrecht University Library, (ms. 434 (ms. 5 E 16)).

Gedruckte Quellen

ANDREAS, VALERIUS (1623), Bibliotheca Belgica, in qua Belgicae seu Germaniae inferioris provinciae, urbesq. Viri item in Belgio vitâ scriptisque clari & librorum nomenclatura, Leuven: Henricus Hastenius.

APOLOGIAE (1684), Apologiae patrum societatis contra censuram Lovaniensem & Duacensem conscriptae circa annum 1588, Martinus Steyaert (ed.), Liège: Henricus Hoyoux.

BAIUS, MICHAEL (1696), Opera: Cum Bullis Pontificum et aliis ipsius causam spectantibus [...] opuscula aucta, [Gabriel Gerberon (ed.),] 2 T. 1 vol., Köln, Balthasarus ab Egmond et Socii.

CENSURÆ (1683), Censuræ facultatum sacræ theologiæ Lovaniensis ac Duacensis super quibusdam articulis de Sacra Scriptura, gratia & praedestinatione, Paris: s.n.

JANSENIUS, CORNELIUS (1639), Tetratevchvs, sive Commentarivs in sancta Iesv Christi evangelia, 2 vol., Leuven: Jacobus Zegerus.

JANSENIUS, CORNELIUS (1640), Augustinus: seu S. Augustini de humanae naturae sanitate, aegritudine, medicina adversus Pelagianos et Massilienses, 3 vol., Leuven: Jacobus Zegerus.

LE BACHELET, XAVIER-MARIE (1911), Bellarmin avant son Cardinalat. 1542-1598. Correspondance et documents, Paris: Gabriel Beauchesne.

LESSIUS, LEONARDUS (1610), De gratia efficaci decretis divinis libertate arbitrii et præscientia Dei conditionata disputatio apologetica, Antwerpen: ex officina Plantiniana/Ioannes Moretus.

STEYAERT, MARTINUS (1742), Opuscula, 6 vol., Leuven: Martinus van Overbeke.

SWEERTIUS, FRANCISCUS (1628), Athenæ Belgicæ sive Nomenclator infer. Germaniæ scriptorum, qui disciplinas philologicas, philosophicas, theologicas, iuridicas, medicas et musicas illustrarunt, Antwerpen: Gulielmus a Tungris.

VERNULAEUS, NICOLAUS (1657), Academia Lovaniensis. Ejus origo, incrementum, forma, magistratus, facultates, privilegia, scholæ, collegia, viri illustres, res gestæ, Christian van Langendonck (ed.), Leuven: Petrus Sassenus.

Wohlmuth, Josef (ed.) (2001), Dekrete der ökumenischen Konzilien/Conciliorum Oecumenicorum Decreta (COD). vol. 3: Konzilien der Neuzeit, Paderborn: Ferdinand Schöningh.

Forschungsliteratur

Al Kalak, Matteo (2017), Trento Ratisbona? Irenismo e istanze di conciliazione all'ombra di Gasparo Contarini, in: Michela Catto/Adriano Prosperi (ed.), Trent and Beyond: The Council, Other Powers, Other Cultures, Mediterranean nexus 1100-1700: Conflict, influence and inspiration in the Mediterranean area 4, Turnhout: Brepols, 267-286.

Boute, Bruno (2010), Academic Interests and Catholic Confessionalisation: The Louvain Privileges of Nomination to Ecclesiastical Benefices, Education and Society in the Middle Ages and Renaissance 35, Leiden: Brill, 268-311.

Beck, Andreas J. (2020), Doing Justice to Justification: Historical Reflections on a Decisive Controversy of the Reformation, in: Peter De Mey/Wim François (ed.), Ecclesia semper reformanda: Renewal and Reform Beyond Polemics, BEThL 306, Leuven: Peeters Publishers, 135-157.

Ceyssens, Lucien (1942-1943), Verslag over de eerste Jansenistische deputatie van Leuven te Rome (1643-1645), BIHBR 22, 31-111.

Ceyssens, Lucien (1950a), De Leuvense deputatie te Rome (1677-1679), in: Lucien Ceyssens (ed.), Jansenistica, Studiën in verband met de geschiedenis van het Jansenisme, vol. 1, Mechelen: St. Franciscus-Drukkerij, 167-253.

Ceyssens, Lucien (1950b), Een geheim genootschap ter bestrijding van het jansenisme in België, in: Lucien Ceyssens (ed.), Jansenistica, Studiën in verband met de geschiedenis van het Jansenisme, vol. 1, Mechelen: St. Franciscus-Drukkerij, 343-397.

Ceyssens, Lucien (1953), Gommarus Huygens in de verwikkelingen van de strijd tussen Kerk en Staat (1678-1687)," in: Lucien Ceyssens (ed.), Jansenistica, Studiën in verband met de geschiedenis van het Jansenisme, vol. 2, Mechelen: St. Franciscus-Drukkerij, 193-229.

Ceyssens, Lucien (1963), Le janséniste Libert Froidmont (1587-1653), Bulletin de la Société d'Art et d'Histoire du Diocèse de Liège 43, 1-46.

Ceyssens, Lucien (1977), Les débuts du jansénisme et de l'antijansénisme à Louvain, in: Edmond J.M. van Eijl (ed.), Facultas S. Theologiae Lovaniensis, 381-432.

Ceyssens, Lucien (1980), L'authenticité des cinq propositions condamnées de Jansénius, Antonianum 55, 368-424.

Ceyssens, Lucien (1982a), La cinquième des propositions condamnées de Jansénius: sa portée théologique, in: Jan van Bavel/Martijn Schrama (ed.), Jansénius et le Jansénisme dans les Pays-Bas. Mélanges Lucien Ceyssens, BEThL 56, Leuven: Peeters Publishers, 39-53.

Ceyssens, Lucien (1982b), Le "Saint Augustin" du XVIIe siècle: L'édition de Louvain (1577), XVIIe Siècle 34, 103-120.

DECOCK, WIM (2019), Le marché du mérite: Penser le droit et l'économie avec Léonard Lessius, Brüssel: Zones Sensibles.
FERRER, XAVERIO (1960), Pecado original y justificacion en la doctrina de Guillermo Estio (Diss. doct. Pontificia Universitas Gregoriana. Facultas Theologiae), Madrid.
FLEISCHMANN, ALFONS (1940), Die Gnadenlehre des Wilhelm Estius und ihre Stellung zum Bajanismus. Eine dogmengeschichtliche Untersuchung zu den Gnadenstreitigkeiten des ausgehenden 16. Jahrhunderts (Diss. doct. Ludwig-Maximilians-Universitat München. Theologische Fakultät), Kallmunz/Regensburg.
FRANCESCHI, SYLVIO HERMANN DE (2009), Entre saint Augustin et saint Thomas. Les jansénistes et le refuge thomiste (1653–1663): à propos des 1re, 2e et 18e Provinciales, Univers Port-Royal, Paris: Nolin, 64–82.
FRANÇOIS, WIM (2009), *Augustinus sanior interpres Apostoli*. Thomas Stapleton and the Louvain Augustinian School's Reception of Paul, in: Ward Holder (ed.), A Companion to Paul in the Reformation, Brill's companions to the Christian tradition 15, Leiden/Boston: Brill, 363–386.
FRANÇOIS, WIM (2010), Thomas Stapleton (1535–1598) sobre la caída de Adán y las consecuencias de ella para su descendencia. ¿Exégesis agustiniana o cripto-jesuítica?, Augustinus 55, 129–140.
FRANÇOIS, WIM (2012), Bible Exegesis in Early Seventeenth Century Louvain: The Case of Jacob Janssonius' Digression on John 12,39–40, in: Wim François/August A. den Hollander (ed.), "Wading Lambs and Swimming Elephants": The Bible for the Laity and Theologians in Late Medieval and Early Modern Era, BEThL 257, Leuven: Peeters Publishers, 323–345.
FRANÇOIS, WIM (2014), Efficacious Grace and Predestination in the Bible Commentaries of Estius, Jansenius and Fromondus, in: Dominik Burkard/Tanja Thanner (ed.), Der Jansenismus – eine 'katholische Häresie'? Das Ringen um Gnade, Rechtfertigung und die Autorität Augustins in der frühen Neuzeit, RGST 159, Münster: Aschendorff Verlag, 117–143.
FRANÇOIS, WIM/GERACE, ANTONIO (2019), The Doctrine of Justification and the Rise of Pluralism in the Post-Tridentine Catholic Church, in: Karla Boersma/Herman J. Selderhuis (ed.), More than Luther: The Reformation and the Rise of Pluralism in Europe, Refo500 Academic Studies 55, Göttingen: Vandenhoeck & Ruprecht, 15–44.
GERACE, ANTONIO (2019), Biblical Scholarship in Louvain in the 'Golden' Sixteenth Century, Refo500 Academic Studies 60, Göttingen: Vandenhoeck & Ruprecht.
GERACE, ANTONIO/GIELIS, GERT (2018), The Ambiguous Reception of the Doctrine of the Duplex Iustitia in Leuven (1544–1556), Aug(L) 68, 91–123.
GIELIS, MARCEL (2008), Leuven Theologians as Opponents of Erasmus and of Humanistic Theology, in: Erika Rummel (ed.), Biblical Humanism and Scholasticism in the Age of Erasmus, Brill's Companions to the Christian Tradition 9, Leiden/Boston: Brill, 197–214.
GIELIS, MARCEL (1994a), L'augustinisme anti-érasmien des premiers controversistes de Louvain Jacques Latomus et Jean Driedo, in: Mathijs Lamberigts/Leo Kenis (ed.), L'augustinisme à l'ancienne Faculté de Théologie de Louvain, 19–61.

GIELIS, MARCEL (1994b), Scholastiek en Humanisme: De kritiek van de Leuvense theoloog Jacobus Latomus op de Erasmiaanse theologiehervorming, TFT-Studies 23, Tilburg: Tilburg University Press.

GRUNDMANN, HANNEGRETH (2012), Gratia Christi: Die theologische Begründung des Ablasses durch Jacobus Latomus in der Kontroverse mit Martin Luther, Arbeiten zur historischen und systematischen Theologie 17, Berlin: LIT Verlag.

HEQUET, SUZANNE (2009), The 1541 Colloquy at Regensburg: In Pursuit of Church Unity, Saarbrücken: VDM Verlag.

HERSCHE, PETER (1977), Der Spätjansenismus in Österreich, Österreichische Akademie der Wissenschaften. Veröffentlichungen der Kommission für Geschichte Österreichs 7/Schriften des Ddr. Franz Josef Mayer-Gunthof-Fonds 11, Wien: Verlag der Österreichischen Akademie der Wissenschaften, 25–43.

ICARD, SIMON (2013), Jansénius lecteur de saint Augustin. Autour des cinq propositions condamnées, Annuaire de l'École pratique des hautes études (EPHE), Section des sciences religieuses [En ligne], 120, online gestellt am 2. Juli 2013, zuletzt eingesehen am 15. Januar 2021, http://journals.openedition.org/asr/1173, doi:https://doi.org/10.4000/asr.1173.

KOLAKOWSKI, LESZEK (1995), God Owes us Nothing: A Brief Remark on Pascal's Religion and on the Spirit of Jansenism, Chicago/London: University of Chicago Press.

LAMBERIGTS, MATHIJS (2018), The Dispute between the Louvain Faculty of Theology and the Jesuits (1587–1588): *Solus Augustinus* versus Thomist Positions, in: Benjamin Dahlke/Bernhard Korn (ed.), Eine Autorität für die Dogmatik? Thomas von Aquin in der Neuzeit (FS Leonhard Hell), Freiburg/Basel/Wien: Herder, 32–46.

LAMBERIGTS, MATHIJS/KENIS, LEO (ed.) (1994), L'augustinisme à l'ancienne Faculté de théologie de Louvain, BEThL 111, Leuven: Peeters/Leuven University Press.

LANE, ANTHONY N.S. (2020), Regensburg Article 5 on Justification: Inconsistent Patchwork or Substance of True Doctrine?, New York: Oxford University Press.

LEHMANN, KARL (1989), Das Dekret des Konzils von Trient über die Rechtfertigung: Historisches Verständnis und theologische Bedeutung in ökumenischer Sicht. Bibliographie, in: Karl Lehman (ed.), Lehrverurteilungen-kirchentrennend?, vol. 2: Materialen zu den Lehrverurteilungen und zur Theologie der Rechtfertigung, Dialog der Kirchen 5, Freiburg i. Br./Göttingen: Herder, 368–372.

LEPPIN, VOLKER (2016), Spätmittelalterliche Theologie und biblische Korrektur im Rechtfertigungsdekret von Trient, in: Peter Walter/Günther Wassilowsky (ed.), Das Konzil von Trient und die katholische Konfessionskultur (1563–2013), Wissenschaftliches Symposium aus Anlass des 450, Jahrestages des Abschlusses des Konzils von Trient, Freiburg i. Br. 18. – 21. September 2013, RGST 163, Münster: Aschendorff Verlag, 167–183.

LEURIDAN, THÉODORE (1895), Les théologiens de Douai, vol. 5: Guillaume Estius, Amiens: Rousseau-Leroy.

LEURIDAN, THÉODORE (1898), Les théologiens de Douai, vol. 6: Thomas Stapleton, Lille: H. Morel.

MATAVA, ROBERT JOSEPH (2016), Divine Causality and Human Free Choice: Domingo Báñez, Physical Premotion and the Controversy de Auxiliis Revisited, Brill's Studies in Intellectual History 252, Leiden/Boston: Brill.

MCGRATH, ALISTER (2020), *Iustitia Dei*: A History of the Christian Doctrine of Justification, Cambridge: Cambridge University Press.

O'MALLEY, JOHN W. (2013), Trent: What Happened at the Council, Cambridge: The Belknap Press of Harvard University Press.

ORCIBAL, JEAN (1962), De Baius à Jansénius: le "Comma Pianum", Revue des Sciences Religieuses 36, 115–139.

ORCIBAL, JEAN (1989), Jansénius d'Ypres (1585–1638), Études augustiniennes. Série Moyen Age et Temps modernes, 22 Paris: Études Augustiniennes.

QUAGHEBEUR, TOON (2003), "Sed illud intactum reliquerit", une virgule mal biffée: le Comma pianum, la bulle *Ex omnibus afflictionibus* du St-Office et la lecture du Cardinal de Lugo, RHE 98, 61–79.

QUILLIET, BERNARD (2007), L'acharnement théologique. Histoire de la grâce en Occident. Paris: Fayard.

RAI, ELEONORA (2020), *Ex Meritis Praevisis*: Predestination, Grace, and Free Will in Intra-Jesuit Controversies (1587–1613), JEMC 7, 111–150.

ROEGIERS, JAN (2003), Le Jansénisme de Louvain à la fin du XVIIe siècle, in: Guido Cooman/ Maurice van Stiphout/Bart Wauters (ed.), Zeger-Bernard van Espen at the Crossroads of Canon Law, History, Theology and Church-State Relations, BEThL 170, Leuven: Peeters/ Leuven University Press, 1–17.

ROEGIERS, JAN (2012), Awkward Neighbours: The Leuven Faculty of Theology and the Jesuit College (1542–1773), in: Rob Faesen/Leo Kenis (ed.), The Jesuits of the Low Countries: Identity and Impact (1540–1773), Proceedings of the International Congress at the Faculty of Theology and Religious Studies, KU Leuven (3–5 December 2009), BEThL 251, Leuven: Peeters Publishers, 153–175.

RUMMEL, ERIKA (1989), Erasmus and his Catholic Critics, BHRef 45, 2 vol., Nieuwkoop: De Graaf.

SALEMBIER, LOUIS (1913), Art. Estius, DThC 5, 871–878.

SCHELKENS, KARIM/GIELIS, MARCEL (2007), From Driedo to Bellarmine. The Concept of Pure Nature in the 16th Century, Aug(L) 57, 425–448.

SEYBOLD, MICHAEL (1967), Glaube und Rechtfertigung bei Thomas Stapleton, KKTS 21, Paderborn: Bonifatius-Verlag.

STANCIU, DIANA (2011), The Feelings of the Master as Articles of Faith or Medicine against Heresy? Jansenius' Polemics against the "New Pelagians", ETL 87, 393–418.

STRAYER, BRIAN E. (2008), Suffering Saints: Jansensists and Convulsionnaires in France, 1640–1799, Eastbourne: Sussex Academic Press.

STUCCO, GUIDO (2014), The Catholic Doctrine of Predestination from Luther to Jansenius, Bloomington: Xlibris.

Van Der Biest, Jarrik (2021), Teaching Romans 7 after Trent: Michael Baius on Concupiscence and Original Sin to his Students in Early Modern Louvain (1552–1589), JEMC 8, 193–221.

van Eijl, Edmond J.M. (1955), L'interprétation de la bulle de Pie V portant condamnation de Baius, RHE 50, 499–542.

van Eijl, Edmond J.M. (1968), Michael Baius 1513–1589. Studie over zijn leven. I: Tot aan de veroordeling door Rome in 1567, 2 vol. (Diss. doct. Katholieke Universiteit Leuven. Faculteit Letteren en Wijsbegeerte), Leuven.

van Eijl, Edmond J.M. (ed.) (1977), Facultas S. Theologiae Lovaniensis 1432–1797: Bijdragen tot haar geschiedenis/Contributions to its History/Contributions à son histoire, BEThL 45, Leuven: Leuven University Press.

van Eijl, Edmond J.M. (1994), La controverse louvaniste autour de la grâce et du libre arbitre à la fin du XVIe siècle, in: Mathijs Lamberigts/Leo Kenis (ed.), L'augustinisme à l'ancienne Faculté de Théologie de Louvain, 207–282.

Vanneste, Alfred (1977), Nature et grâce dans la théologie de Baius, in: Edmond J.M. van Eijl (ed.), Facultas S. Theologiae Lovaniensis, 327–350.

Vanneste, Alfred (1994), Le "De prima hominis justitia" de M. Baius: une relecture critique, in: Mathijs Lamberigts/Leo Kenis (ed.), L'augustinisme à l'ancienne Faculté de Théologie de Louvain, 123–166.

Vercruysse, Jos E. (1994), Die Stellung Augustins in Jacobus Latomus' Auseinandersetzung mit Luther, in: Mathijs Lamberigts/Leo Kenis (ed.), L'augustinisme à l'ancienne Faculté de Théologie de Louvain, 7–18.

Vercruysse, Jos E. (1983), Jacobus Latomus und Martin Luther: Einführendes zu einer Kontroverse, Gregorianum 64, 515–538.

Vind, Anna (2019), Latomus and Luther. The Debate: Is Every Good Deed a Sin?, Refo500 Academic Studies 26, Göttingen: Vandenhoeck & Ruprecht.

Visser, Arnoud (2010), How Catholic was Augustine? Confessional Patristics and the Survival of Erasmus in the Counter-Reformation, JEH 61, 86–106.

Jakub Koryl

Common Bond of Thinking

Saint Augustine and the Socinian Metaphysics of Presence

1. Introduction: onward to the margin and back

This study is intended as an experiment in Western metaphysics. It is designed to set off in quest of the common bond of thinking. For that particular reason the Socinian system of thinking about a being will be discussed against the general background of metaphysics developed by Plato, Aristotle and Saint Augustine. While Plato and Aristotle are rather obvious figures when Western metaphysics is taken into consideration, the part of Augustine requires here an explanation. Acclaimed as the doctor of grace and advocate of Trinitarian dogma, Augustine seems to be a chief opponent of Socinianism. Since doctrinal priorities of Socinians stand in stark contrast to those of Augustine, such juxtaposition will actually stretch the whole Christian doctrine to its outermost limits. Well, that's precisely my point. For only then will it be possible to reveal what happens in the center of this encounter and, so to say, against everything what makes the feuding parties different. I decided, therefore, to bring Augustine into action as the said experiment and hence to direct my attention to the margins of the encounter between the spokesman of Trinity and its opposer. As the place where Socinians neither wanted to get nor got there deliberately, the margin can be equally instructive and innovative. For in the margins everything will appear 'against': against the Socinian priorities they openly manifested and most of all against our habit of thinking about the Socinianism and its part in the Christian history. Margin is a baffling place: it ignores author's presumed intent, but it does not violate the meaning of his words. Let's see what we can get out of it.

There are three basic questions I would like to discuss here. First of all, the so-called metaphysics of presence which laid down the principles underlying Western thought. Secondly, Aristotelian notion of "now" (τὸ νῦν) as the timepoint of presence. And thirdly, what I call the Augustinian semiotics of presence as a metaphysical enquiry into high-profile relationship between the being by itself unintelligible and its disclosing sign. In both cases it is Augustine, more than anyone else, who will provide us with a powerful blueprint for comprehending the Socinian metaphysics. Indeed, I want to discuss Socinianism as a companion of Augustine. I say this most emphatically: companion, not a competitor. As it was already mentioned, doctrinal differences between Augustine and Socinians regarding the Trinity, original sin, grace, predestination, free will and salvation are more than obvious to everyone familiar with the basic issues of Christian history. That's not all. Everyone familiar with Socinian writings knows that Polish antitrinitarians followed the common path of Western metaphysics, they approvingly used exactly the same vocabulary as the Western classics like Plato, Aristotle or Augustine. As a matter of fact, with this observation nothing is gained as long as it remains disclosed to what extent genealogy of Western thought gave shape to Socinian metaphysics. The full scale of this impact cannot be measured until the metaphysics of presence have been revealed and examined, namely the fundamental way of experiencing every being as 'something present'. However, certain directions of influence and reception or, in general, intellectual interchange, do not affect the point at issue here. The system of thinking that Western metaphysics entails is the matter in hand for now. For that reason, I am not interested in comparing doxographical matter of Augustine and Socinian writings, not at all.[1] Instead, I would like to discuss the way such doctrinal matter was determined. In other words, this study sets out to examine the system of thinking, instead of matter of thinking. For if we will take into account merely the fundamental and irreducible modes of thinking, the affinity between Augustine and Socinianism can no longer be considered perverse or ridiculous. Such system of thinking about reality, either divine or human, constitute the subject matter of this study. In the long run, its aim is twofold: to let us reconsider the place Socinianism occupies in the history of Christianity and to reveal a common feature of Christian thought which cannot be suppressed by any doxographical and doctrinal differences.

Why Socinians? Did Socinian metaphysics reveal anything new or groundbreaking in the history of Western thinking? Was Socinianism a challenge to metaphysics of presence? As we know, the founding gesture of antitrinitarian theology (at least one of its grand gestures) was breaking off with Platonism.[2] It was not, however, an

---

[1] The most comprehensive discussion on the Socinian doxography, philosophical and theological in particular, can be found in recent studies by Ogonowski (2015); Salatowsky (2015) and Daugirdas (2016).

[2] Among the large number of anti-Platonic statements at least two are of particular importance, because both were concerned with the impact of Platonism upon the Trinitarian dogma. Such statements were given by Johann Ludwig von Wolzogen in his commentary on the Johannine Prologue and by Samuel Przypkowski in his famous treatise on peace and concord. See Wolzogen: 1668, 706b: "quoddam commentum, quod Veteres Patres primitus ex Ethnica Platonis schola in religionem Christianam introduxerunt, quodque hodie etiam plerisque Interpretibus Sacrae Scripturae supra modum placet: nimirum ajunt, Dominum Jesum ideo dici Verbum, quia est Dei naturale atque essentiale Verbum, quod Deus per elocutionem intellectus sui ab aeterno genuit ac produxit." Przypkowski: 1981, 84: "magnus quidam vir [Justus Lipsius in the *Manuductio ad Stoicam Philosophiam*, I, 3] nostra aetate scripsit: multos tum ita externa professione Christum induisse, ut animo Platonem non exuerent. Proinde nec abs re suspicati sunt in permultis doctrinae capitibus simplicia verba in alienos ac

expression of some preference given for one standpoint or source over another; for instance, the Bible in preference to Plato. The history of Christianity knows plenty of such decisions which were taken either in favor or against the particular books and their authors. Antitrinitarian determination to break off with Platonic metaphysics was not one of these well-known changes. As the founding gesture, the departure from Platonism was undertaken deliberately in order to shake foundations of Christian doctrine and Western thought. Socinian investigation into ontological status of the λόγος divinity, being either the *nomen proprium* or merely the *nomen appelativum*, forces us to think over the Socinian discovery of appellative nature of Christ's divinity.[3] Namely, whether divinely fixed and thus immutable constitution of reality could resist the destabilizing impact of such discovery. Therefore, a series of difficult yet complementary questions arises: if λόγος ultimately lost its divine nature, was it possible to preserve universal order of things in its self-contained form which was originally not capable of being derived from its protean names? If the divinity of λόγος became a matter of convention and consisted in function rather than in substance, was it a case of necessity to loosen or even to break off the universal covenant of things and names? Did antitrinitarian departure from Platonism exert a transformative effect on Western thought and as such could help to foster one of the very few genuine revolutions of thinking in Western history? Namely, was it possible to overcome the metaphysics of presence by means of the Socinian anti-Platonism? Or was it actually an empty gesture in terms of metaphysics of presence, and consequently no considerable change took place? It's time to start for good.

---

philosophicos sensus detorta, cum mysteria philosophiae suae verbo divino ingeniosis commentis assuerent, ne frustra didicisse viderentur. Quorsum enim pertineret - aiunt illi - quod de recepta Sacrosanctae Trinitatis explicatione Plato et Trismegistus clarius loquantur quam Sacra Scriptura, aut quid erat in causa, ut Scripturae tam sanctum mysterium timidius atque obscurius traderent quam supradicti philosophi?" All these objections were raised and discussed in detail as early as 1531 in *De Trinitatis erroribus* by Michael Servetus. See Servetus: 1932, 73–83.

3 Socinus: 1668, 79b: "nomen Deus, non est nomen substantiae cujusdam proprium vel personae, sed auctoritatis, potentiae ac benevolentiae, et (ut grammatici loquuntur) non est nomen proprium, sed appellativum." Smalcius: 1608, 69f: "Est igitur ista vox [Deus – J. K.] non propria, sed, ut vocant, appellativa, et primum significat illum, qui a seipso dominatur, et ita omnium est autor, ut neminem superiorem habeat, vel ab eo pendeat." Wolzogen: 1668, 708a: "eos qui hoc loco ex solo Dei nomine argumentantur et inferunt, Dominum Jesum esse Deum Altissimum, non considerare, neque attendere, quod nomen Dei commune sit et appellativum, quod in Sacris Literis pluribus attribuatur." See also Domański: 1974, 80; Bietenholz: 2005, 15f; Daugirdas: 2016, 62.

2. Metaphysics of presence

As a notion, metaphysics of presence was coined by phenomenology and then elaborated by deconstruction in the second half of the 20th century.[4] From the very beginning it was used as a descriptive tool to disclose a basic way of experiencing every single being as something present. Metaphysics of presence stands here for the attitude prevalent in Western tradition according to which every single thing or being remains always a part of a larger whole. Consequently, every single thing remains deep-rooted in the transcendent order which is self-reliant and has the power to give particular existence to something. There is a sacred covenant, justified religiously or by logical means, a covenant between the enduring substance and ever-changing qualities. For the idea of rootedness, otherwise extremely distinctive for the metaphysics of presence, ultimately entails that there is always something essential in things, something which cannot be derived from the way these things are recognized and used. On the other hand, the way one thing is either used or recognized does not deprive it of its whatness or quiddity. A table, to take a simple example, will never lose its tableness as a matter of principle. This means eventually that tableness is permanently present, no matter how the tables are recognized and used, including – as we will see – even their identification as something non-being.

The established conceptual equivalent of presence, albeit thoroughly inadequate, is substance. Latin *substantia*, as well as the countless vernacular substances, traces back itself to the Greek noun οὐσία which stands for a present participle of the verb εἰμί. Literary speaking, οὐσία means 'being now' or 'being present'. Being present stands therefore for what we use to call 'substance' or 'essence'. Augustine and Socinians prove this linguistic consideration correct. In Latin speaking word οὐσία was rendered either as the *substantia* or *essentia*. In his study *On Trinity* Augustine not only discussed which of these two could be properly applied to God, but also tried to explain what does the Greek οὐσία actually mean. First of all, Augustine noticed a pivotal difference between the *substantia* and *essentia*: "just as essence receives its name from being [*esse*], so substance is derived from subsisting [*subsistere*]". Then he drew a following conclusion of such observation:

> If, indeed, it is fitting to speak of God as subsisting! For to subsist is rightly applied to those things to which the qualities, which need another being in order to be able to be, cling for support, as the color or form of the body. [...] if God subsists, so that He may be properly called a substance, then there is something in Him as it were in a subject, and He is no longer simple; His being, accordingly, would not be one and the same with

---

4 See Heidegger (1996); Heidegger (1998a); Heidegger (1998c); Derrida (1982); Derrida (1967); Fuchs (1976).

the other qualities that are predicated of Him in respect to Himself, as for example, to be great, omnipotent, good, and any other attributes of this kind that are not unfittingly said of God. But it is wrong to assert that God subsists and is the subject of His own goodness, and that goodness is not a substance, or rather not an essence, that God Himself is not His own goodness, and that it inheres in Him as in its subject. It is, therefore, obvious that God is improperly called a substance. The more usual name is essence, which He is truly and properly called, so that perhaps God alone should be called essence. For he is truly alone.[5]

Although Augustine was not well-versed in Greek, his theological intuition did not fail him. He favored the use of *essentia* over *substantia*. Most of all he argued that when it comes to basic way of experiencing the entity, including the supreme one like God, being (or *esse*) and not the subject (that is *subiectum*) must be taken into account. "Essence is so called from being. […] Being is in the highest and truest sense of the term proper to Him from whom being derives its name", as one may read in the fifth book of *De Trinitate*.[6] If there is one privileged entity in terms of *essentia*, it follows inevitably that other entities partake in such presence on the basis of analogy. *Essentia* or presence stands therefore for the basic rule that governs the universal order, either by means of giving being or by making such given being intelligible. Samuel Przypkowski, leading Socinian thinker, in his later work *Hyperaspistes* repeated almost word for word that Augustinian argument about a hierarchized web of interdependence with God as its anchorage:

> Essence is a generic notion to the extent that it can not be denied even in relation to the innermost of beings, although by far more perfect and sublime way it is relevant to the highest being. […] we read nevertheless that God took his name from "being the being" (when the abundance of things forces the poverty of language to supply itself with the new expressions). Since the reason itself indicates that He is the most eminent being, because both the essence and nature are the notions most suitable for him, who obviously neither was born nor received his nature at birth. Moreover, without an essence being is unable to be, and therefore the better being is, the better essence it must have. Consequently, they do no wrong who attribute the notion of essence to God.[7]

---

5 Augustine of Hippo: 1963, 234f. See also Augustine of Hippo: 1952, 248: "This noun, 'being,' is derived from the verb 'to be' just as 'wisdom' from the verb 'to be wise.' In Latin, essentia, being, is a new word, not used by ancient writers, recently adopted in order to find an equivalent of the Greek, οὐσία, of which essentia is the exact translation." Cf. Anderson: 1965, 72–76.
6 Augustine of Hippo: 1963, 177.
7 Przypkowski: 1692, 458a: "Vox essentiae ita generalis est, ut etiam intimis entium negari nequeat: quamvis nobilissimo enti, longe perfectius et excellentius competat. […] legimus tamen Deum, ab essendo (ubi rerum copia poscit paupertas linguae novis vocibus supplenda est) sibi nomen adoptasse.

That's not all however. Socinian system of thinking reaches further and deeper than to Augustinian tradition. For when Przypkowski admitted that in the truest sense of the term *essentia* is proper only to the supreme being, namely to God who took his name *ab essendo*, he got through actually to the foundations of Western thought. Over there οὐσία is a synonym either for εἶναι or τὸ ὄν. Obviously, it was no other than Plato who drew up that formative rule for the metaphysics of presence: "οὐσία bears its name from ὃ ἔστιν", or simply "the essence bears its name from *what is*".[8] By no means οὐσία could be separated from εἶναι, that is from something 'being present'. This principle axiomatizes, therefore, as constitutive the concept of presence which makes well-founded the claim that being *is* and, as we shall see in a little while, that language never refers to itself exclusively. Thereby Socinians, whether they like it or not, declared themselves thoroughly Platonists. Step by step a supposed gap between the Socinianism and Platonism as well as the anti-Platonic mystification of Socinians should be taken to pieces.

The predominance of οὐσία implies necessarily that there *is always* 'there' there, to invert a witty remark of Gertrude Stein.[9] Consequently, the principle of presence non only supports but also axiomatizes the claim that reality is a complex yet coherent structure which was once fixed and arranged according to a particular pattern. The idea of orderliness, therefore, became inevitable and as such entailed an urgent necessity to discover and explain the universal principles behind every single phenomenon. Metaphysics, at least in the form which set the tone of western way of thinking, recognized and answered that call. For what makes the Good of Plato and the Aristotelian substance similar is the belief in something that persists in reality through its change and consequently provides beings with an everlasting basis. In his early work *De ordine*, Augustine explicitly shared such belief by employing the Platonic notion of goodness.[10] Socinian metaphysics did actually the same by devoting itself entirely to tracing the origin of universal order of beings. In his major work *Religio rationalis*, Andrzej Wiszowaty catalogued eighty-two axioms which

---

Et cum ipsa ratio ostendat, eum esse Ens eminentissimum, essentiae quam natura vox, longe aptius ipsi tribuitur, quippe qui nunquam natus sit, aut nascendo naturam acceperit. Ens autem absque essentia et quo potius est, eo absque potiori essentia, esse nequeat. Nihil igitur peccant, qui essentiae vocem Deo tribuunt."

8 Plato: 1900, 92d: "ἡ οὐσία ἔχουσα τὴν ἐπωνυμίαν τὴν τοῦ 'ὃ ἔστιν'."
9 Cf. Steiner: 2010, 139.
10 Augustine of Hippo: 2007, 81: "evil could not come out of order, if order began after evil came into being. Order, however, was always with God. As to this non-entity [nihil] we call evil, it either always was, or it began at some stage. And since order itself is either good or proceeds from good, there was never anything outside order nor will there ever be. Although something may happen, and afterwards escape my mind as usual, I would still accept that this very phenomenon would have happened because of a certain order: a reason of its own, perhaps, or its being a necessary step in life, or being part of the order of life itself."

were supposed to govern understanding of divine and human reality in its entirety. "Reason – as seen by Wiszowaty – observes certain principles and common notions or ideas that are universally and generally true."[11] It is particularly significant that these fundamental prepositions were by no means internalized. Without exception the *axiomata* were considered self-reliant and thus discovered as the guiding force of reality rather than made or established by the creative force of reason or ideation. Contemplation merely made them discernible as the manifestation of presence. Every form of interpretation of reality, metaphysical in particular, was determined then to stick as closely as possible to the principles previously discovered by reason. Accordingly, Joachim Stegmann was keen to mark out that such principles provided cognition with the set of normative rules.[12] Axioms stood then for the proof of predominant οὐσία, they led pure reasoning to its foundations.

If we continue this quest for the common bond of thinking, the example of axioms becomes twice as instructive and reliable for accomplishing this task. In doxographical terms the *axiomata* make clear the distinctiveness of Socinianism. These natural and normative rules provided Socinian hermeneutics with an indispensable tool for understanding the Word of God. On that account, the Bible and the principles of truth established together a pattern (*norma*) for faith. Such claim, as much as the antitrinitarian doctrine, caused offence to numerous Christian denominations and made Socinianism extremely distinctive stance. Whereas in metaphysical terms the *axiomata* reveal a common ground for the standpoints that otherwise differed from each other. It should be emphasized that by offering a basic framework *axiom* determined not the subject matter of thinking but first and foremost set up a common system for it. Such system could be applied to miscellaneous objects, but regardless of its matter thinking was always conducted in the same way. This common mode always had at its disposal the strict criteria for evaluating its pronouncements, since essentialist thinking was concerned primarily with the whatness of beings. If such mode of thinking proclaimed and supported the sovereignty of οὐσία, all the acquired knowledge was based first on empirical experience and then on pure reasoning about the reality whose elements and features were noticed and comprehended according to the permanent and thus all-pervasive *axiomata*. Wiszowaty put that long and involved process in a

---

11 Wiszowaty: 1960, 20: "A ratione observata axiomata quaedam universalia atque communes notiones seu notitae sunt omnino universaliter verae."
12 Stegmann: 1633, 30, 33: "solas sacras literas pro norma fidei ponant, ut principia veritatis, sive natura nota, sive e rerum aliarum consideratione deducta, philosophica vocant, inde excludant. […] Caeterum ad sacrarum literarum auctoritatem et genuinam mentem dignoscendam, principia etiam illa, quae philosophica appellant, advocanda esse. […] Haec et similia, quae nemini sano ignota sunt, statuendum est, esse fundamenta cognitionis nostrae, quoad auctoritatem sacrarum literarum, et quoad verum earum sensum."

nutshell: *a ratione observata axiomata*. Augustine made the same: order should be comprehended and followed. Reality, therefore, must have been recognized as a structure marked by a great deal of variety but at the same time orderly arranged by the principle of οὐσία.[13] For that particular reason Plato, Augustine and Socinians were actually forced to conclude that man either observed such order or took part in it. By no means was it governed or constructed according to man-made laws. Individual sets of axioms could and usually did differ significantly between the different doctrinal standpoints, but the very idea of axiom – as evidenced by *De ordine* of Augustine – axiomatized in general terms the claim that there was always 'there' there.

Plato, Augustine and Socinians agreed upon that *essentia* remains the measure of presence and thus the sign of disposition of things in relation to each other according to a general principle of presence. They all enable us therefore to reinforce the previous consideration that οὐσία refers either to 'being present' (as God alone), or 'being made present' (as God's creation). In both cases presence means being, either in absolute or relative way. Every single entity is either present or was made that way, since "without an essence being is unable to be", as Przypkowski openly admitted. For that reason, he argued, in the same way as Augustine, that *essentia* and *substantia* should not be applied interchangeably:

> Notions of substance and essence certainly should not be confused, because the former signifies something concrete, while the latter something abstract. Moreover, the notion of essence has a wider meaning, since the things which are not self-existent have some essence as well.[14]

In other words, principle of *essentia* gives grounds for the universal order of reality, while *substantia* refers to its particular components. What does God, man or stone have in common? They all *are*, although in a lower or higher degree of being present. Because of that Augustine, could name God as the *summa essentia* and *summe esse*

---

13 Augustine of Hippo: 2007, 3, 19: "There is an order to be found, within things and between them, which binds and directs this world. To attain and retain that order, Zenobius, to open one's eyes and other people's to it, it is difficult and very uncommon. Even one who has the ability for it will not necessarily succeed. One needs to find worthy listeners with an ordered lifestyle and an ordered mind to grasp such divine but obscure realities. […] Everything is related to everything else, each thing impelled to its appointed effects by a series of fixed laws. There are so many and act in so many fashions as to force us to speak of them endlessly."

14 Przypkowski: 1692, 459a: "Non sunt quidem confundere substantiae et essentiae voces; quia illa concretum, haec abstractum significat. Praererea vox essentiae latius patet, cum et eorum quae per se non subsistunt, sit aliqua essentia." The notion *per se subsistens* refers clearly to Aristotle and Aquinas and – to put it simply – it means substance.

since it is God alone who provides his creation with more or less of *esse*. "To some things He gave more of being and to others less" as one may read in *De civitate Dei*.[15] Exactly the same statement Augustine made in his early work *De vera religione*.[16] Interestingly enough, the paragraph in question had to be, according to young Luther, strongly reminiscent of *Parmenides* of Plato and his idea of the One.[17] It is indeed.

Johannes Crell whose *Liber de Deo et ejus attributis* provided Socinians with the most comprehensive study on God's ontology, followed up that clue. Detailed observation of the impact God exerts variously upon creation made Crell confident about so-called "grades of divine presence" (*praesentiae divinae gradus*). He arrived therefore at an inevitable conclusion which makes us think of the Platonic μέθεξις or the participation of beings in the supreme one which reveals itself through the former:

> God is said to be present everywhere and to fill up everything with his divine will. [...] God is said to be closest to those things He favors, sustains, and helps. Hence these different grades of divine presence were made visible and are explained to a common man by those who discuss God. For through his global providence He is present in everything he has created.[18]

---

15 Augustine of Hippo: 1952, 248.
16 Augustine of Hippo: 2006, 241f: "Why do they become defective? Because they are mutable. Why are they mutable? Because they have not supreme existence [non summe sunt]. And why so? Because they are inferior to him who made them. Who made them? He who supremely is [summe est]. Who is he? God, the immutable Trinity, made them through his supreme wisdom and preserves them by his supreme loving-kindness. Why did he make them? In order that they might exist [ut essent]. Existence [esse] as such is good, and supreme existence [summe esse] is the chief good."
17 Luther: 1983, 426, l. 3–10: "Secunda pars patet ex Platone in Parmenide, ubi pulcherrima disputatione primum exuit illud unum et ideam, donec Omnia ei auferat et ipsum nihil esse relinquat. Rursum illud idem induit omnibus, donec nihil reliquitur, in quo non sit ilud unum, et nihil sit, quod non inposito uno sit. Et sic est extra Omnia et tamen intra Omnia, quomodo et beatus Augustinus libro 1 De vera religione disputat. Ista autem participatio et separatio unius seu ideae magis potest intelligi quam dici, imo numeri intelligi quam vere est."
18 Crell: 1668, 91a: "ubique praesens, omniaque numine suo complere dicitur. [...] Maxime autem illis adesse rebus dicitur Deus, quas fovet, sustentat, ac juvat. Hinc orti sunt diversi illi praesentiae divinae gradus, qui etiam vulgo ab iis explicantur, qui de Deo agunt. Nam generali sua providentia omnibus adest rebus a se creatis." Plato regularly uses the notion of *μέθεξις* and *μετέχω* in a number of his dialogues, for instance *Phaedo* 100c and *Symposium* 211a-b. See Plato: 2005, 345: "if anything is beautiful besides absolute beauty it is beautiful for no other reason than because it partakes [μετέχει] of absolute beauty; and this applies to everything". Plato: 2008a, 49: "Nor, again, will the beautiful appear to him as a face is beautiful or hands or any other part of the body, nor like a discourse or a branch of knowledge or anything that exists in some other thing, whether in a living creature or in the earth or the sky or anything else. It exists on its own, single in substance and everlasting. All

If creation, through its being, exhibits the presence of its creator, it *is* for no other reason than it takes part in the one who makes everything present. In this way Crell was not only following in the footsteps of Augustine who in exactly the same manner spoke of divinely established *essentiarum gradus*,[19] but most of all he called the diverse intensity with which the divine will reveals itself in time. The *praesentiae gradus* concept eventually leaves no doubt that in terms of Western metaphysics it doesn't matter that Socinians recognized the divinity of λόγος as merely the sign of Christ's godlike dignity and power (instead of his nature). For if the divinity of λόγος had been recognized substantially, not functionally, it would have made actually no difference. In both cases, the grades of divine presence were taken for granted. The difference between them comes down to nothing but a distinction between similarity of paternal and filial οὐσία on the one hand and their essential identity on the other. If μετέχω stands actually for εἰμί, there is no other form of existing available for every single entity, including the supreme one like God, than being a lower or higher, always specified grade within the established framework of presence. God's *ubique praesens* together with its various disclosures made longing for presence the major concern of metaphysics. That's not all. In the long run it forced Crell and other metaphysicians of presence to design and run a system of opposites, like presence and absence, identity and difference, and most of all being and nothingness, where one term was always favored at the expense of its counterpart.

Metaphysics of presence comes out into the open as the system of thinking about the way every single being is or exists. This particular approach assumes a privileged fixed entity at which all beings are anchored. In this view 'to be' means 'to belong', 'to partake' and 'to resemble', or, to cut a long story short, *being* is *presence*, because belonging, partaking and resembling refer to a whole which is not only larger than its components but prior to and independent of them. To participate in beingness, in the Greek οὐσία, means therefore being-present, or being in the presence of the present. For that reason, Crell was keen to employ *esse* and *praesentia* interchangeably (at least when God was taken into consideration). In relation to a divine realm, to speak of being and presence, or simply 'to be' and 'to be present' was virtually the same. Crell admits openly: "What makes everything constantly

---

other beautiful things partake [μετέχοντα] of it, but in such a way that when they come into being or die the beautiful itself does not become greater or less in any respect, or undergo any change."

19 Augustine of Hippo: 1952, 248: "Since God is supreme being [summa essentia], that is, since He supremely is and, therefore, is immutable, it follows that He gave 'being' [esse] to all that He created out of nothing; not, however, absolute being [summe esse]. To some things He gave more of being and to others less and, in this way, arranged an order of natures in a hierarchy of being [naturas essentiarum gradibus ordinauit]."

present to God, it makes also that all these things basically *are*. Things are present to God for no other reason than that they actually *are*."[20]

To be sure, it was not a matter of linguistic usage Crell used to follow. For metaphysics of presence does not know any other way of being, namely the way beyond or without οὐσία. The answer of metaphysics of presence to the basic question of metaphysics, namely 'what is being?', is more than distinctive. In this case, our everyday language is reliable enough for understanding that distinctiveness. Since every answer consists in giving a statement – for instance 'being is', or simply 'table is', 'man is', 'God is', etc. – the copular verb *is* already gives us the basic answer to this question. What is being then? *Being is*. That's the essence of being: *to be*, and *is* means presence, as witnessed by the Greek οὐσία or present participle of εἶναι / εἰμί. The meaning of such concepts like being, the present, the now, substance and essence, always refers back to the same source, namely to the form of the present participle and the third person presence of the indicative, it relates directly to οὐσία and ἐστί. To say, therefore, that something *is present* would be a tautology. It is enough to say that *being is*. All these linguistic deliberations were ultimately justified by Aristotelian interpretation of time.

3. "Now" as the timepoint of presence

Aristotle was the first who provided Western tradition with a detailed, highly influential explanation of the phenomenon of time. In the fourth book of his *Physics* he established the unity between being and presence and as such laid the groundwork for what has been already said about the metaphysics of presence. Aristotle declares in an explicit manner: "time is both everywhere and present alike to all things."[21] It is essential for my line of argument that Aristotle gave a preference to what remains at hand and at disposal, namely to "now" (τὸ νῦν) of time. For Aristotelian concept of time is founded upon the assumption which privileges presence over absence, being over nothingness, and such a privilege is never put into question. Aristotle advocates a concept of time consisting of a succession of "nows" (τὰ νῦν). For that reason, absence can be comprehended merely as a modalization of presence. The past and the future are always experienced as present from the past or as present from the future. In other words, the present is present, the past was present, and the future will be present. Aristotelian definition of time

---

20 Crell: 1668, 69b–70a: "Quod autem effecit, ut omnia Deo ab aeterno essent praesentia, effecit etiam, ut ea simpliciter essent. Cum non aliam ob causam Deo res sint praesentes, quam quia revera sint".
21 Aristotle: 1999, 102.

becomes quite clear: "a number of change in respect of before and after" because "when we notice before and after, then we say that there is time".[22]

Time is considered then as that in which every being *is* or *begins to be* and *ceases to be*. Obviously, *beginning to be* and *ceasing to be* have nothing to do with nothingness as something devoid of its οὐσία. In no way it undermines the predominance of presence. The concepts of beginning and end are still understood by Aristotle with regard to modes of time, namely before and after. With regard to every possible modality of being presence remains inevitable and irreducible. Aristotle declares:

> The point is that to be in time is to be measured by time, and time is a measure of change and rest. Clearly, then, not everything that does not exist is in time either; I am thinking, for example, of things which cannot be [...] all those things whose existence time measures will exist in a state of rest or a state of change. [...] all those things which time does not contain in any manner neither were nor are nor will be.[23]

Aristotle speaks of "being in time" (ἐν χρόνῳ εἶναι) as the basic form of being. According to him such being means "being in existence when time is in existence [...] it is a necessary consequence of something's being in time that a time should exist when it does".[24] Being in time becomes here a criterion for separating the being from nothingness. Domination of presence involves as a necessary consequence that it is impossible to go beyond the οὐσία. Nothingness is neither comprehensible nor capable of being expressed in words, expressed on its own terms. As the basic form of being, "being in time" forces us to consider nothingness as something that *is* such and such, it always forces us to recognize nothingness as nothing but a mutable form of presence. Thing which is not now is neither absent nor nothing. It was present or it will be present. Martin Heidegger, who was particularly interested in Aristotelian interpretation of time, noticed that the arbitrary fixed "now" or τὸ νῦν of time made it impossible for the state of "before" and "after" (or becoming and ceasing) to remain something absolute, undetermined and self-reliant.[25] Consequently, nothingness or lack of οὐσία turned out to be a major

---

22 Aristotle: 1999, 106.
23 Aristotle: 1999, 111f.
24 Aristotle: 1999, 110.
25 Heidegger: 1992, 4f, 17: "Time is something in which a now-point may be arbitrarily fixed, such that, with respect to two different timepoints, one is earlier and the other later. And yet no now-point of time is privileged over any other. As 'now', any now-point of time is the possible earlier of a later; as 'later', it is the later of an earlier. This time is thoroughly uniform, homogeneous. Only in so far as time is constituted as homogeneous is it measurable. Time is thus an unfurling whose stages stand in a relation of earlier and later to one another. Each earlier and later can be determined in terms of a now which, however, is itself arbitrary. [...] If the attempt is made to derive from the time of nature what time is, then the νῦν [now] is the μέτρον [measure] of past and future. Then time

stumbling block for metaphysics of presence. It could be removed solely in wholly inadequate manner, namely only insofar as nothingness was comprehended as its opposite, namely as something which either *is* not yet or *is* no longer. For to say that being *is* not, does not mean that it lacks its οὐσία. At the very beginning of Western thought Plato spotted what was wrong with these efforts and found it impermissible to consider the absolute nothingness or non-being in and by itself (τὸ μὴ ὂν αὐτὸ καθ' αὑτό) as something available for thinking and speaking.[26] Such attempts were made nevertheless, by Augustine and Socinians among others, but no one managed to go beyond the way Plato utterly rejected. Metaphysics of presence could not free itself from the domination of οὐσία. There is always something inherently present in what we say or think of.

That conclusion of the idea of "being in time" was fundamental for Socinians, who followed Aristotelian concept of time or more specifically his preference for the presence over absence. To my knowledge the only separate piece Socinians wrote about the concept of time is chapter four of the *Metaphysica repurgata*, a treatise penned by Christopher Stegmann in 1635.[27] Those who are acquainted with the Aristotelian ἐν χρόνῳ εἶναι will find this chapter familiar. For Stegmann never ceases to be a spokesman of presence, clearly prioritizing it over the absence. Stegmann was interested in the metaphysical, as he called it, meaning of time. In this sense, he defined time as a point and therefore as a presence or now-point. That being so, it is clear that Stegmann confirmed Aristotelian unity of being and time. For it is only time or its "now" (τo νῦν) that enables us to perceive that being is present, was present, or will be present. On the basis of Aristotelian τo νῦν Stegmann spoke of three forms of duration of every singe being: past duration, present duration and future duration. Consequently, before and after do not exist on their own as the separate entities. Before and after are nothing but modalities of the present: "by nature they are actually not entities. The past ceased to be, while the future is not yet" as one may read in the *Metaphysica repurgata*.[28] This way being was fundamentally bound with the presence. Although without any further explication Crell took up this stance as well and explicitly spoke of time as *diuturnitas* and

---

is already interpreted as present, past is interpreted as no-longer present, future as indeterminate not-yet-present: past is irretrievable, future indeterminate."
26 Plato: 2015, 131, 162 (238c, 258e): "So do you see that it's impossible, correctly, to express or to say or to think what is not in and by itself [τὸ μὴ ὂν αὐτὸ καθ' αὑτό]; it's unthinkable, unsayable, inexpressible, and unaccountable [...] let no one accuse us of having the temerity to declare that what is not is the opposite of being and then say that it is." See also Barney: 2001, 182.
27 Stegmann: 1991, 543ff.
28 Stegmann: 1991, 543.

duratio: "time is nothing but duration".[29] Metaphysical concept of time described by Stegmann remains at the basic level thoroughly Aristotelian, and in the long run Augustinian as well. This concept becomes, as will be shown in a short time, particularly important for understanding the Socinian metaphysics of presence and the deliberate attempts they made to put nothingness into words or maintain the non-being in language.

4. Saint Augustine and the semiotics of presence

The presence to which I am constantly referring is οὐσία associated with the highest authority in complementary terms of being and signifying, namely with the one which gives an existence and makes it meaningful. For that reason, now I would like to identify semiotic implications of the discussed problem. From Plato onwards, meaning has never been brought out otherwise than by dint of presence and as a presence. The concept of meaning was guided by a hierarchical system of relationships, so every time a question of meaning was posed it was posed within the particular idea of being. Augustine was well aware that every attempt to free the problem of meaning from metaphysics was doomed to failure. In his search for God and himself, Augustine was not only accompanied by the Platonic idea of presence as belonging, partaking and resembling, but also the first Christian thinker who elaborated on the inalienable metaphysical foundation of meaning:

> I considered the other things below you, and I saw that neither can they be said absolutely to be or absolutely not to be. They are because they come from you. But they are not because they are not what you are. That which truly is is that which unchangeably abides. But 'it is good for me to stick fast to God' (Ps 72:28); for if I do not abide in him, I can do nothing (John 15:5). But he 'abiding in himself makes all things new' (Wis 7:27).[30]

This well-known fragment of book seven of his *Confessions*, where Augustine gives an account of his initiation into Platonism, can be considered as a perfect exemplification of metaphysics of presence. It mentions all the elements that together make up the discussed standpoint, including its general assumption that every single being draws its meaningful presence from the realm existing prior to it and independent of it. No one exists by himself nor for himself alone. Everyone remains a place where such realm makes itself present. Augustine, however, was not only a

---

29 Crell: 1668, 17b: "Etsi enim temporis diuturnitas, sine mutatione aliqua non sentitur: tempus tamen etiam sine mutatione est. Tempus enim nil alius, quam duratio est".
30 Augustine of Hippo: 2008, 124. See also Anderson: 1965, 61–65; Dobell: 2009, 138–182.

follower of Platonic metaphysics. In his latter years, he gave a well-thought-out and methodical shape to the idea which I would call the semiotics of presence.[31]

It is essential for our line of argument that Augustinian idea of presence was founded upon a distinction between *res* and *signum* which Augustine introduced and carefully discussed in *De doctrina christiana*, book one and two. From the outset and throughout the treatise it is put straight and clear that *res-signum* distinction should not be reduced to a sermocinal or, more precisely, to a logical difference. At the basic level, where it is no longer possible to decompose it into some other primary constituents, *res-signum* stands for the ontological difference, namely for the different ways of experiencing the presence, like being present, making present and marking present. That's the area of discussion Augustinian semiotics was particularly interested in:

> All teaching is teaching of either things or signs, but things are learnt through signs. What I now call things in the strict sense are things such as logs, stones, sheep, and so on, which are not employed to signify something; [...] These are things, but they are at the same time signs of other things. There are other signs whose whole function consists in signifying. Words, for example: nobody uses words except in order to signify something. From this it may be understood what I mean by signs: those things which are employed to signify something. [...] And we must be careful to remember that what is under consideration at this stage is the fact that things exist, not that they signify something else besides themselves.[32]

In ontological terms the difference between things and words had merely a functional significance, which means that according to Augustine there was no substantial contrast between language and reality. It had a considerable importance for the semiotics of presence. Augustine advocated most emphatically the semiotic covenant of things and words. Basic difference between them consists in nothing but the modes of experiencing the presence, namely *esse* and *significare*. In *De doctrina christiana* Augustine argued constantly that there is a privileged fixed point at which every meaning is anchored. There are at least two basic forms of such semantic anchorage. One remaining on the surface, Augustine used to call it on many occasions the *intentio scriptoris*; and the second under the surface, namely the presence of a non-linguistic thing. Neither such thing nor linguistic sign could remain self-reliant. Although beings are and do not signify, they need signs to

---

31 On Augustine's theory of language and sign see Gramigna (2020); King (2014); Burton (2012); Clarke: 1990, 23–28.
32 Augustine of Hippo: 1995, 13ff.

signify their presence. Even in its figurative use sign could not refer only to another sign.

Antitrinitarian discovery of λόγος divinity as nothing but the *nomen appelativum* or *nomen auctoritatis, potentiae et beneficientiae* (instead of trinitarian *nomen proprium* or *essentiae*) by no means could affect that semiotic anchorage. Przypkowski gave particular emphasis to a point that figurative use could not be practiced ad infinitum, it always had to reduce itself to a non-linguistic thing. There is no metaphor which is the metaphor of another metaphor, Augustinian semiotics of presence makes it impossible. Although the sign signifies and refers to, it also exists, and everything that is, is a thing. Accordingly, the road became wide open for Socinians to attribute not only a meaning but also an existence to every sign. "There is absolutely nothing in metaphor that could be called nothingness or non-being. [...] It cannot be said that non-being is similar to something, because it lacks any quality",[33] Przypkowski concludes. If it were otherwise, sign would signify solely another sign. However, *stat rosa pristina non sola nomine*, as one may invert a mediaeval dictum once made famous by Umberto Eco.

Socinians stuck to that principle of presence and as a matter of fact were impelled to use the notion of likeness or image which presupposed a specific stance towards the relationship of the thing to its sign. It was first made and taken by Plato who interpreted the difference between the παράδειγμα or pattern and its image in explicitly metaphysical terms. At the basic level παράδειγμα and εἰκών were recognized as two different forms of being present. In order to tell and explore this important but fluid difference, Plato drew a clear-cut distinction, namely between the οὐσία and γένεσις. Accordingly, as the image is to pattern, so is becoming present (γένεσις) to being present (οὐσία).[34] By that means it became possible to eventually bridge the ontological gap between the image and real thing. Plato made himself clear that the images – as far as their own form of being present was concerned – were determined to take part in things they imitate, since they appeared to lack a separate οὐσία, and thus were unable to be by themselves:

---

33 Przypkowski: 1692, 454b–455a: "Et sensus improprius semper supponit, cum a quo ducitur esse proprium; nec ulla metaphora metaphorae esse solet. [...] Nullum enim Metaphoricum, dici potest nihil aut non ens uti et metaphorice dictum. Nam cujus vox, a propria significatione alterius rei, translata est, ad impropriam alterius illud certe esse in rerum natura necesse est, [...] Non ens autem nulli rei simile dici potest, cujus nullae sunt affectiones."

34 Plato: 2008b, 17f (29a-v): "The craftsman of this universe, then, took as his model that which is grasped by reason and intelligence and is consistent, and it necessarily follows from these premisses that this world of ours is an image [εἰκόνα] of something. [...] statements about things that are in fact images, because they've been made in the likeness of an original, are no more than likely, and merely correspond to the first kind of statement: as being is to becoming." See also Patterson: 1985, 25–62; Gerson (1996).

since even the conditions of an image's occurrence lie outside the image itself — since it is an ever-moving apparition of something else — it has to occur in something other than itself (and so somehow or other to cling on to existence), or else it would be nothing at all.[35]

The difference consisted then in varying modes of being real, either in an unconditional or conditional manner. The εἰκών is just like a shadow which is real-like but cannot cast itself. As such εἰκών was supposed to indicate not the signified thing, or, at least, not only it, but a particular grade of presence more than anything else. In other words, εἰκών stood for a thing which remained in a lower degree of being present. This means, therefore, that παράδειγμα and εἰκών, just like the signified thing and its sign, were bound by the principle of presence. Timothy Baxter gives a concise and clear explanation of it: "what the name truly means is nothing other than that essence, since names are so related to their nominata that examination of the former is tantamount to investigation of the latter."[36] Only when such principle began to underlie Western system of thinking, were Socinians able to arrive at the said conclusion that no metaphor could be the metaphor of another metaphor.

When Przypkowski discussed the biblical notion of likeness (εἰκὼν τοῦ θεοῦ), he did it in the same manner as Plato. For in his interpretation considerable emphasis was placed on the belonging of *imago* to the order of substance and presence. If the Bible – Przypkowski argued – calls Christ the accurate image of invisible God (as witnessed by Col 1:15 and 2 Cor 4:4), it follows that Christ is called the mark of God's substance.[37] Quotation from Heb 1:3 did not prevent Przypkowski from putting a philosophical interpretation on Paul's phrase χαρακτὴρ τῆς ὑποστάσεως, even though only a genuine biblical meaning of ὑπόστασις (as the *qualitas rei* and condition or way of being rather than its *quidditas*) would have supported his argument.[38] He did not take pains to go through it. Instead, Przypkowski considered whether the essence given to Christ at birth could be separated from his subjectness or not, and then arrived at the conclusion that ὑπόστασις should be taken as something which always carries the essence and provides essence with the base. Moreover, relative to Christ the notion of substance by no means could belong

---

35 Plato: 2008b, 45 (52c).
36 Baxter: 1992, 74.
37 Przypkowski: 1692, 454b: "Quanto magis id faciendum, cum eum Sacrae Scripturae filium Dei proprium, eumque Unigenitum et expressam invisibilis Dei imaginem et substantiae ejus characterem, appellet, ut ab aliis filiis improprie aut analogice sic dictis, discernatur."
38 Already young Luther emphasized that philosophical renderings of ὑπόστασις as *essentia* or *quidditas* were improper for the biblical usages of this term. For in the Bible *substantia* stood for something external and was concerned with a way of being rather than being itself. See Luther: 1885, 419–20, l. 25–38, 1ff.

to the order of accidental qualities.[39] *Imago Dei*, therefore, could not be the empty gesture or display solely another image. Quite the opposite – every single image had to be reduced to the presence itself. Another Socinian, Jonas Schlichting made one step further and in his commentary on the difference between ὁ λόγος τοῦ θεοῦ and ὁ θεός he dispelled any doubts as to the non-biblical, thoroughly metaphysical meaning of the substance. Schlichting used to employ the semiotic category of *imago* as well. He was, however, keen enough to explicitly and approvingly recognize its Platonic meaning by calling Philo of Alexandria as the reliable witness, thereby making no attempt to conceal his intentions to use Platonism in support of his line of argument:

> Greek-speaking Jews used to call messengers of God the λόγους or speeches, as can be clearly seen in Philo's writings among others. Moreover, in his writings the only and preeminent Son of God was called the λόγος in the full sense of this word. According to Philo, who was educated in the Platonic school, λόγος is the idea shaped by man and that image of God according to which man was created. Angels, however, were called the speeches of God metaphorically, because as the immediate translators they explained the will of God which constitutes also the proper meaning of the phrase "speech of God". For no one is perfect except Jesus alone. As the immediate translator he not only revealed to us all the mysteries of divine will towards our salvation, but he followed them to the grave. Accordingly, the Evangelist embellished him with this name in the full sense of the word.[40]

---

39 Przypkowski: 1692, 454a: "Filius Dei, ob generationem suam proprie dictam proprie dictus et ipse censendus est, quia generatio ejus fuit substantialis. Vox autem generationis ad substantias pertinet proprie, ut Alternationis ad accidentia; et ea generatio ex qua substantia producitur ut substantialis, ita propere dicta sit oportet, qualis est Filii Dei. Alia est ratio, generationis impropriae dictae, per quam Christiani regeneratio, ex Dei nascuntur; quae potius Alteratio est, uti et natura aut potius qualitas per eam producta; accidentalis est; quae adesse et abesse potest, absque corruptione subjecti. [...] Non ita se habet Christi generatio, qui semel natus Dei filius; filius Dei esse desinere non potest. Substantialis enim ejus generatio est: ideo essentia per eam producta, a supposito suo, avelli non potest." See above footnote 14.

40 Schlichting: 1665, 3a–b: "Solebant Judaei Graecizantes Angelos Dei appellare λόγους, id est, sermones, ut ex Philone inter caeteros patet, apud quem etiam unus est insignis et κατ' ἐξοχήν dictus λόγος Dei Filius, quem is in Platonica edoctus Schola, ideam hominis putat, et imaginem illam Dei, ad quam homo conditus sit. Vocabantur autem Angeli Sermones Dei per metaphoram, quod tanquam immediati interpretes voluntatem Dei declararent, et effectui darent, quae eadem sermonis Dei proprie dicti vis est. Quod quia Jesu nemo perfectius fecit, qui nobis omnia divinae voluntatis de salute nostra, tanquam immediatus interpres, exposuit arcana, eademque et exequitur, merito eum Euangelista hoc titulo κατ' ἐξοχήν exornavit." Similar statement about Christ as "the most excellent translator of God's will" was made by Wolzogen. See Wolzogen: 1668, 714b: "Hunc igitur hominem Jesum vocat Johannes Sermonem, seu Verbum, non tantum simpliciter ideo, quia Deus per eum, tanquam primum ac perfecitissimum Interpretem, suam voluntatem de salute hominis revelavit."

Deliberately or not, yet to the detriment of coherence of its reasoning, antitrinitarian theology turned biblical notion of εἰκών or *imago* back to its Platonic roots.

Augustinian idea of presence enables us, therefore, to consider the *signum* as both distinct from and essential to the thing it represent. Since the difference between *esse* and *siginificare* had no substantial importance, only functional, we cannot treat *signum* as not necessarily bound up with a thing. Reality does exist outside the sign, but it is only the *signum* which makes the being of reality intelligible, because reality is not capable of accomplishing anything besides being (*esse*). For that reason, another Socinian, Thomas Pisecki described the word as *nota rerum*, that is the sign which makes a thing noted.[41] Przypkowski went further: "There is no other way to speak or discuss the things and persons than by means of words and expressions. Consequently, every single mistake made in language affects the thing itself which is signified by the language."[42]

If *signum* signifies something other that the sign itself, if it always refers to something other, it is reasonable to assume that sign only represents the present in its absence. And this obviously does not mean that we put sign in the place of the thing itself. For Augustine and Socinians were, as a matter of principle, extremely sensitive to every attempt to make *res* or *signum* self-reliant and self-sufficient. Such attempt would abolish the semiotics of presence. In the book two of his *De doctrina christiana* Augustine made this correlation an indispensable condition. Without its sign beingness would become undiscernible, while a sign devoid of its signified thing would be struck dumb:

> When I was writing about things I began with the warning that attention should be paid solely to the fact that they existed, and not to anything besides themselves that they might signify. Now that I am discussing signs, I must say, conversely, that attention should not be paid to the fact that they exist, but rather to the fact that they are signs, or, in other

---

Regarding Philo of Alexandria see his *De opificio mundi*, 25, 69, 139; *Legum allegoriae*, III, 96; and *De confusione linguarum*, 63, 146. All these fragments, otherwise not as unambiguous as suggested by Schlichting, can give a good insight into the issues in question (namely ἀρχέτυπον, παράδειγμα, ἀπεικόνισμα, θεοειδής or εἰκών). On the pre-Erasmian translations of λόγος as *sermo* see O'Rourke Boyle (1977).

41 Pisecki: 1654, 81: "Nam res, quam oratione complectimur, ex verbis constat, verba ex literis. Quamobrem si res in sacris literis est inclusa, verba eandem rem loquantur oportet. Mitto Trinitatis, Essentiae, et aliorum terminorum vocabula, quae rerum sunt notae."

42 Przypkowski: 1692, 454b–455a: "Quod si quis ex eo, quia metaphora, non in rebus sed in vocibus tantum propria sedes sit, arguat nos de ei litigare quod vox est tantum, praetereaque nihil; huic in mentem revocandum est, nos de rebus aut personis, nisi per verba et voces loqui aut differere non posse, ideoque in gratiam rerum aut personarum, quoties illis absurde, ineptae, aut incompetentes voces tribuuntur, eo necessitatis adigi, ut voces quoque ad res et personas intelligendas excutiamus. Nam quicquid in vocibus peccatur, res ipsas quarum sunt signa afficit."

words, that they signify. For a sign is a thing which of itself makes some other thing come to mind.[43]

When the presence of things becomes discernible through a sign, we are getting back then to a place occupied and governed by the metaphysics of Plato. Again, the relationship between *significare* and *esse* is not just a matter for the sermocinal theory of signification but first and foremost for the metaphysical enquiry into the incomprehensibleness of being and the sign which gives it the ability to be comprehended. That's the crux of the matter here. For not only the sign takes the same measures as a sun, which – according to a famous metaphor Plato employed in the *Republic* – makes everything visible by shining light on it, but also it supplements and supports every entity in its variation, just as through its shining sun sustains and stimulates the growth of everything. In other words, every sign remains converged with the being of signified entity. Plato made it clear that being known (τὸ γιγνώσκεσθαι), being as such (τὸ εἶναί) and being present (οὐσία) are inseparable, because the only object each eye can see is the existing thing.[44] Presence means nothing but the constant disclosure of being. Platonism, therefore, enabled Augustine and Socinians to consider sign not only as a tool for signification but most of all as a revealing source of being. It is the sign which makes a being something noted. Accordingly, sermocinal principles did not apply to the *signum-res* correlation, at least on its basic level, since such relationship was justified on the ontological ground and for ontological purposes more than for anything else.

The road became wide open and, as evidenced by Augustine's remark on speaking the unspeakable, his semiotics of presence went all the way. If metaphysics of Plato tended to restrict the feature of language to signification – since "words are never going to be more than images and representations of things"[45] – Augustinian semiotics constitutes a considerable step forward beyond the Platonism. Augustine points out carefully that "every sign is also a thing, since what is not a thing does not exist."[46] Signs not only signify but also they exist. They belong to metaphysics and are governed by its rules, most of all by the principle of presence which gives no permission to go beyond the οὐσία. If in its metaphysical aspect language *is* when it *signifies*, language eventually bears witness and testifies the being. It means,

---

43 Augustine of Hippo: 1995, 57.
44 Plato: 1998, 236 (509b): "the ability to be seen is not the only gift the sun gives to the things we see. It is also the source of their generation, growth, and nourishment, although it isn't actually the process of generation. […] it isn't only the known-ness of the things we know which is conferred upon them by goodness, but also their reality and their being, although goodness isn't actually the state of being, but surpasses being in majesty and might."
45 Plato: 2008b, 104 (107b). See also Anderson: 1965, 69.
46 Augustine of Hippo: 1995, 15.

therefore, that it is impossible to convey in words the absence or nothingness. Augustine was acute enough to recognize that paradox of speaking the unspeakable:

> God should not even be called unspeakable, because even when this word is spoken, something is spoken. There is a kind of conflict between words here: if what cannot be spoken is unspeakable, then it is not unspeakable, because it can actually be said to be unspeakable.[47]

It should be noticed that the unspeakable does not stand here for something unutterable. It actually means nothingness, since "every sign – according to Augustine – is also a thing". Now the fundamental problem arises.

Such signification implies presence; what cannot be spoken, does not exist. The reverse holds true as well, yet it leaves no room for confusion with the Wittgensteinian logic: what does not exist, cannot be spoken. This general principle was formulated as early as by Plato who in the *Sophist* made a radical demand: "Speech, when there is speech, must necessarily say something *of* something; it's impossible for it to say something of nothing."[48] Language perforce requires something (τι) as its object. If only a non-object had been available, there would have been no language. For that reason, speaking, with no exception whatsoever, conveys or speaks τὸ ὄν or the being, either in ontological or logical way, as explicitly stated in the *Cratylus*.[49] When language seeks to signify nothingness, it inevitably turns signified nothingness (μηδέν, οὐδέν, *non ens, nihil*) into its opposite, that is into being. Augustine and Socinians leave no doubt that in such cases language deprives itself of its own object. Consequently, in the most challenging confrontation with nothingness semiotics of presence violated both rules formulated by Plato: the sovereignty of absolute non-being and the covenant between the real thing and its real-like image. This conclusion can be regarded as a semiotic sequel to the principle of presence: if signification is a mode of being, language must turn non-being into being. It becomes clear now that sign not only signifies being or presence in its absence, but also it makes thing present. Semiotics of presence insures then the

---

47 Augustine of Hippo: 1995, 17.
48 Plato: 2015, 168 (262e). Similar statement Plato made in his *Theaetetus* (189b). See Plato: 2015, 66: "it's not possible to believe what is not [τε τὸ μὴ ὄν], whether about the things that are, or what is not itself by itself [τῶν ὄντων οὔτε αὐτὸ καθ' αὑτό]."
49 Plato: 1977, 155, 159 (429d, 430d): "Why, Socrates, how could anyone who says that which he says, say that which is not [μὴ τὸ ὄν]? Is not falsehood saying that which is not [μὴ τὰ ὄντα]? […] I call that kind of assignment in the case of both imitations paintings and names – correct, and in the case of names not only correct, but true; and the other kind, which gives and applies the unlike imitation, I call incorrect and, in the case of names, false." Regarding this whole paragraph see also Patterson: 1985, 110–113; Baxter: 1992, 13; Barney: 2001, 173, 185f; Sedley: 2003, 132ff.

plenitude of every sign, but at the same time this standpoint knows nothing about nothingness.

Socinians tried hard to solve the problem of nothingness, but eventually the principle of presence forced all of them to move back to a place where the semiotics of Augustine stopped. Chief dogmatists of Socinianism, like Johannes Völkel and Johannes Crell, strived to find a gap in the Western metaphysics where they would get a permission for putting nothingness into words that maintains it in its original state, namely as the non-being in and by itself. For this reason, Völkel and Crell used the scholastic distinction between the *nihil privativum* and *nihil negativum*. If there is any accessible object for signification, it would be only the *nihil privativum*, namely the matter without a form.[50] There is no need to say that it was a very clever trick. No solution, however, was found for maintaining the *nihil negativum* (which stood for the Platonic τὸ μὴ ὂν αὐτὸ καθ' αὑτό) or the absolute non-being in language. For Socinians still took the view that the task of cognition was determined by the rules of presence. Both Crell and Joachim Stegmann took it for granted that intelligibility of the thing depended on its presence, since *nihil negativum* have nothing to comprehend. Only within such limits, cognition would take effect. It would not, if reason was either pointing out something that did not exist or denying what did exist[51]. Consequently, every attempt to convey non-being in words will turn nothingness into its opposite, that is being. The only method available then for grasping a non-being involved juxtaposition of opposites. Crell insisted that every time language gives the floor to nothingness, it perforce speaks about the reverse side of being, just like darkness can be seen only in contrast to daylight. For according to the principle of presence and Aristotelian notion of now (τὸ νῦν) there is no other way to comprehend nothingness than as the temporary lack of being:

> Knowable things are those that have so-called beingness, whether with respect to the past, or with respect to the now or finally with respect to the future. Although we are accustomed also to speaking about non-being and hereafter even to comprehending it in one way or another, by itself and as such it nevertheless cannot be known more than

---

50 Völkel: 1630, 6: "Quam ad rem pertinet illa Scholasticorum distinctio, qui nihilum aliud faciunt privativum, aliud negativum. Privativum appellant materiam forma ea carentem, quae in eam est introducenda. Negativum illud dicunt, quod nihil prorsus est." Crell: 1668, 10a: "Itaque etiamsi tandem constaret, creationem non nisi ex nihilo, quod negativum vocant, esse posse; non liceret tamen eo argumento adversus mundi creationem niti."

51 Stegmann: 1963, 58: "Nimirum sufficit ad veritatem cognitionis eiusmodi conceptuum nostrorum cum re ipsa convenientia, qua nihil intellectui repraesentetur, quod in re ipsa non sit, nihilque, quod insit, negetur. […] Ille demum conceptus falsus est, qui ita est alius, ut vel aliquid ponat, quod rei non insit, vel tollat aut neget, quod insit".

the darkness seen. For non-being, especially in the absolute meaning of the word, is absolutely nothing. As such, mind loses entirely sight of it and, consequently, it is not the object of knowledge. It is recognized, however, and considered in a certain manner from its opposite, namely through the thing which *is*, just as the darkness is recognized and considered through the daylight. […] Entities *are*: some only in a potential manner (for instance somehow future things), the other in actual manner; among the latter we include not only the present, but also the past ones. Each one is recognized by God insofar as it has beingness. For God grasps a thing as it actually *is*.[52]

Indeed, Crell showed his hands here. For alleged nothingness of *non ens* was clearly reduced to merely *nihil privativum*. Whereas *enititas* or beingness Crell confirmed and even reinforced as the only basis for every attempt to grasp the order of reality ranging from the lack of being through to the plenitude of being. As such, the *entitas* left no room whatsoever for its opposite. Accordingly, the relationship between language and non-linguistic reality fired some serious ontological questions at Crell from all angles (just as it shot Augustine before), first of all why language perforce turns nothingness into being. In the end Socinianism, deliberately or not, approved the Augustinian semiotics of presence and took up his stance towards speaking the unspeakable. "The greatest puzzle about the whole matter", as Plato called the issue of nothingness, remained without any satisfactory solution. As if all that weren't enough, Socinians confirmed his fears that every attempt to challenge such puzzlement will inevitably force thinking to contradict itself.[53] Nothingness, therefore, brought thinking to crisis point, it really pushed Western metaphysics to the limit and eventually put thinking off its stroke.

Essentia remained the prerequisite of being and speaking. Consequently, it enabled metaphysics to design and run the system of opposites where being was deified at the expense of nothingness. Such stance towards being and nothingness did not transgress the basic principle of Platonism that without a signified thing images would turn themselves into nothingness. Despite the strong pressure put on

---

52 Crell: 1668, 67a: "Scibilia autem sunt, quae entitatem, ut loquuntur, habent, sive respectu praeteriti temporis, sive rspectu praesentis, sive denique respectu futuri. Etsi enim etiam de non ente loqui soleamus, et porro etiam illud aliquo modo intelligere: id tamen per se ac qua tale est, non magis intelligi potest, quam tenebrae videri. Cum enim non ens, praesertim simpliciter ita dictum, nihil prorsus sit; omnem mentis obtutum, qua tale est, effugit, et sub cognitionem non cadit. Cognoscitur tamen et aestimatur quodammodo ex suo opposito, hoc est, ex eo, quod est: quemadmodum tenebrae ex lumine. […] Iam vero entia alia sunt potentia tantum, ut res qualicunque modo futurae; vel actu; in quorum posteriorum numero non praesentia tantum, sed et praeterita hic ponimus. Horum quodlibet, prout entitatem habet, a Deo cognoscitur. Deus enim ita concipit, ut revera est."
53 Plato: 2015, 131 (238d): "I wonder that you didn't notice from the very things we've been saying that what is not reduces even a would-be challenger to puzzlement, to the extent that if ever he tries to challenge it he is forced to contradict himself on the subject."

the Christian doctrine, no considerable change took place in terms of the modes of thinking. The idea of universal order of things remained untouched, while the covenant of things and names managed to preserve itself in the pre-Socinian form.

5. Conclusion: common bond of thinking

Example of Socinianism convincingly proves that Christianity needed Platonism to retain its metaphysical orientation. Contrary to the founding gesture of antitrinitarian theology, the Socinians were unable to free themselves from the shackles of Platonism. It is clearly shown by the Platonic nomenclature Schlichting or Przypkowski used to include deliberately and approvingly in their Christology, and most of all by the fact that Socinian idea of being was shaped by the principle of presence. None of them have ever called this principle into question. Quite the opposite, each one used to observe that rule. Much talked-about at the time remark of Justus Lipsius about those who "outwardly clothed themselves with Christ but did not remove Plato from their mind" can be, in a sense, appropriate to Socinians as well.[54]

That being so it remains not yet resolved whether it was possible to build any metaphysics in support for the antitrinitarian dogma. For Socinian antitrinitarianism turns out to be extremely incoherent standpoint in terms of metaphysics, especially when its doctrinal priorities are taken into account. In fact, Socinian metaphysics gives grounds for the same thing which their doctrine otherwise denies. Socinianism replaced essential divinity of λόγος with the functional meaning of being a godlike entity which was, however, still able to exercise its chief influence upon the entities lower in rank. Except for converting time-honored meaning of divinity as the supreme essence, actually nothing essential happened. The very idea of hierarchy of beings, their rootedness and durable participation – otherwise constitutive for the metaphysics of presence – was then fully accepted but put into a slightly different action. *Essentia* however remained irreplaceable as a driving force of *ens*. Notions of *esse, essentia, praesentia, entitas*, and last but not least substance and function, were all taken by Socinians according to long-established meanings. Every single change introduced by the Socinian doctrine was merely cosmetic from the metaphysical point of view, because none of these changes was possible beyond the principles underlying Western thought. Even in their most radical moves, Socinians only replaced elements that still belonged to the same, larger whole. Whether interested in it or not, Socinianism was not capable of overcoming

---

54 See above footnote 2.

the metaphysics of presence. For "the reversal of a metaphysical statement remains – as Heidegger soberly observed – a metaphysical statement."[55]

Jean Delumeau noticed that "European culture saw itself in Augustine and to some extent pushed him to the foreground"[56]. Socinians did actually the same, even though none of them was keen to acknowledge it. For that reason, we need to get to margins to know what happens in the center. Over there it becomes clear that Socinian metaphysics did not overcome the structures developed by Plato, Aristotle and reinforced by Augustinian semiotics of presence. Despite all the differences implicit in their views on the Trinity, original sin, grace, predestination, free will and salvation, ontological position of Socinianism remains at the basic level thoroughly common with Augustine. As seen from the margin, Socinianism eventually ceases to be the grand enemy of Platonism and its Christian ramifications. Whereas Socinian Aristotelianism, as a well-known theorem, discloses its unknown, yet basic implications and features. On this account, we are able to reach the common bond which links and therefore determines every single form of Christian theology and philosophy, at least until the twentieth century. Such bond is the being (and non-being as well) constantly experienced as οὐσία.

Bibliography

Sources

ARISTOTLE (1999), Physics, translated by Robin Waterfield, with an introduction and notes by David Bostock, Oxford: Oxford University Press.
AUGUSTINE OF HIPPO (1952), The City of God, Books VIII-XVI, Gerald G. Walsh/Grace Monahan (trans.) Washington: The Catholic University of America Press.
AUGUSTINE OF HIPPO (1963), The Trinity, Stephen McKenna (trans.), Washington: Westminster John Knox Press.
AUGUSTINE OF HIPPO (1995), De Doctrina Christiana, R. P. H. Green (ed.) (trans.), Oxford: Clarendon Press.
AUGUSTINE OF HIPPO (2006), Of True Religion, in: Augustine, Earlier Writings, John H.S. Burleigh (ed.) (trans.), Louisville: Westminster John Knox Press, 225–283.
AUGUSTINE OF HIPPO (2007), On Order (De Ordine), Silvano Borruso (trans.), South Bend: St. Augustine Press.
AUGUSTINE OF HIPPO (2008), Confessions, Henry Chadwick (trans.), Oxford: Oxford University Press.

---

55 Heidegger: 1998b, 250.
56 Delumeau: 1991, 265.

Derrida, Jacques (1967), La voix et le phénomène. Introduction au problème du signe dans la phénoménologie de Husserl, Paris: Presses Universitaires de France.

Derrida, Jacques (1982), Ousia and Grammè. Note on a Note from Being and Time, in: Jacques Derrida, Margins of Philosophy, Alan Bass (trans.), Chicago: University of Chicago Press, 29–67.

Faustus Socinus (1668), Explicatio Primae partis primi capitis Euangelistae Johannis Scripta a Fausto Socino Senense, in: Fausti Socini Senensis Opera omnia in Duos Tomos distincta. Quorum prior continet ejus Opera Exegetica et didactica posterior Opera ejusdem Polemica comprehendit. Accesserunt quaedam hactenus inedita, T. 1, Irenopoli, 75–85.

Heidegger, Martin (1992), The Concept of Time, translated by William McNeill, Oxford: Wiley-Blackwell.

Heidegger, Martin (1996), Being and Time. A Translation of Sein und Zeit, translated by Joan Stambaugh, Albany: State University of New York Press.

Heidegger, Martin (1998a), Introduction to "What Is Metaphysics?", Walter Kaufmann (trans.), in: Martin Heidegger, Pathmarks, William McNeill (ed.), Cambridge: Cambridge University Press, 277–290.

Heidegger, Martin (1998b), Letter on "Humanism", Frank A. Capuzzi (trans.), in: Martin Heidegger, Pathmarks, William McNeill (ed.), Cambridge: Cambridge University Press, 239–276.

Heidegger, Martin (1998c), What Is Metaphysics?, David Farrell Krell (trans.), in: Martin Heidegger, Pathmarks, William McNeill (ed.), Cambridge: Cambridge University Press, 82–96.

Joachim Stegmann (1633), Brevis disquisitio, An & quomodo vulgo dicti Evangelici Pontificios, ac nominatim Val. Magni de Acatholicorum credendi regula judicium, solide atque evidenter refutare queant, Eleutheropoli, Apud Godfridum Philalethium.

Joachim Stegmann (1963), Ioachimi Stegmanni De iudice et norma controversiarum fidei, ediderunt Iulius Domański et Sbigneus Ogonowski, Warszawa: Państwowe Wydawnictwo Naukowe.

Johann Ludwig von Wolzogen (1668), Commentarius in Euangelium Johannis, in: Ludovici Wolzogenii Opera Omnia, Exegetica, Didactica et Polemica, Irenopoli, 697–1038.

Johannes Crell (1668), Liber de Deo et ejus attributis, in: Johannis Crellii Franci Operum tomus quartus. scripta ejusdem didactica et polemica complectens. Accesserunt nonnulla antehac inedita, Irenopoli, 1–116.

Johannes Völkel (1630), Iohannis Volkelii Misnici De vera religione Libri uinque: Quibus praefixus est Iohannis Crellii Franci Liber De Deo et ejus Attributis, ita ut unum cum illis opus constituat, Racoviae, Typis Sebastiani Sternacii.

Jonas Schlichting (1665), Jonae Slichtyngii à Bukowiec Equitis Poloni Commentarius In Euangelium Joannis Apostoli, in: Jonae Slichtyngii de Bukowiec Commentaria posthuma in plerosque Novi Testamenti Libros Cuncta hactenus inedita. In duos Tomos distincta, T. 1, Irenopol, Sumptibus Irenici Philalethii, 1–151.

Martin Luther (1885), Dictata super Psalterium 1513–1516, in: D. Martin Luthers Werke, kritische Gesamtausgabe, vol. 3, Weimar: Hermann Böhlau.

Martin Luther (1983), Die philosophischen Thesen der Heidelberger Disputation, in: D. Martin Luthers Werke, kritische Gesamtausgabe, vol. 59, Weimar: Hermann Böhlaus Nachfolger, 409–426.

Michael Servetus, (1932), On the Errors of the Trinity. Seven Books by Michael Serveto, in: The Two Treatises of Servetus on the Trinity, translated into English by Earl Morse Wilbur, Cambridge Mass.: Harvard University Press, 3–184.

Plato (1900), Phaedo, in: Platonis Opera, recognovit brevique adnotatione critica instruxit Ioannes Burnet, T. 1, Oxford: Clarendon Press.

Plato (1977), Cratylus, in: Plato, Cratylus, Parmenides, Greater Hippias, Lesser Hippias, Harold North Fowler (trans.), Cambridge Mass.: Harvard University Press.

Plato (1998), Republic, Robin Waterfield (trans.), Oxford: Oxford University Press.

Plato (2005), Phaedo, in: Plato, Euthyphro, Apology, Crito, Phaedo, Phaedrus, Harold North Fowler (trans.), Cambridge Mass.: Harvard University Press.

Plato (2008a), The Symposium, Frisbee C. C. Sheffield/ Margaret C. Howatson (ed.) (trans.), Cambridge: Cambridge University Press.

Plato (2008b), Timaeus and Critias, Robin Waterfield (trans.), Oxford: Oxford University Press.

Plato (2015), Theaetetus and Sophist, Christopher Rowe (ed.) (trans.), Cambridge: Cambridge University Press.

Samuel Przypkowski (1692), Hyperaspistes seu defensio Apologiae ab afflictis nuper in Polonia et extorribus Ecclesiae in Prussia periclitantibus Serenissimo ac potentissimo Principi ac Domino D. Friderico Wilhelmo electori Brandenburgico oblatae et Illustrissimis Ducatus Prussiae ordinibus traditae. anno Domini, 1666, in: Samuelis Prizipcovii Equitis Poloni et Consiliarii Electoris Brandenburgici Cogitationes sacrae ad initium Euangelii Matthaei et omnes Epistolas Apostolicas. Nec non tractatus varii argumenti, Praecipue De jure christiani magistratus. Quorum Catalogus post praefationem exhibetur, Eleutheropoli, 451–474.

Samuel Przypkowski (1981), Samuelis Przipcovii Dissertatio de pace et concordia ecclesiae, recensuit, in linguam Polonam vertit Miecislaus Brożek, praefatione instruxit, versionem Polonam recognovit Sbigneus Ogonowski, Warszawa: Państwowe Wydawnictwo Naukowe.

Tomasz Pisecki (1654), An Doctrina Trinitatis sit Mysterium, in: Fausti, et Laelii Socini, item Ernesti Sonneri Tractatus aliquot Theologici, nunquam antehac in lucem editi. Quorum Catalogum sequens pagina indicabit, Eleutheropoli. Typis Godfridi Philadelphi, 71–96.

Valentinus Smalcius, (1608), De divinitate Jesu Christi, Liber editus, a Valentino Smalcio Gothano, Coetus Racoviensis Minsitro, Racoviae: Typis Sebastiani Sternacii.

Wiszowaty, Andrzej (1960), Andreae Wissowati Religio rationalis seu de ratione iudicio in controversiis etiam theologicis ac religiosis adhibendo tractatus, editio tertia revisa et adnotata, recensuerunt Lodovicus Chmaj, Daniela Gromska, Victor Wąsik, Warszawa: Państwowe Wydawnictwo Naukowe.

Secondary Literature

Anderson, James F. (1965), St. Augustine and Being, A Metaphysical Essay, The Hague: Martinus Nijhoff.

Barney, Rachel (2001), Names and Nature in Plato's Cratylus, New York: Routledge.

Baxter, Timothy M.S. (1992), The Cratylus. Plato's Critique of Naming, Leiden: Brill.

Bietenholz, Peter (2005), Fausto Sozzini and the New Testament Scholarship of Erasmus, in: Lech Szczucki (ed.), Faustus Socinus and His Heritage, Kraków: PAU, 11–28.

Burton, Philip (2012), Augustine and Language, in: Mark Vessey/Shelley Reid (ed.), A Companion to Augustine, Malden: Wiley-Blackwell, 113–124.

Clarke, David S. (1990), Sources of Semiotic. Readings with Commentary from Antiquity to the Present, Carbondale: Southern Illinois University Press.

Daugirdas, Kestutis (2016), Die Anfänge des Sozinianismus. Genese und Eindringen des historisch-ethischen Religionsmodells in den universitären Diskurs der Evangelischen in Europa, Göttingen: Vandenhoeck & Ruprecht.

Delumeau, Jean (1991), Sin and Fear. The Emergence of a Western Guilt Culture. 13th-18th Centuries, Eric Nicholson (trans.), New York: St. Martin Press.

Dobell, Brian (2009), Augustine's Intellectual Conversion. The Journey from Platonism to Christianity, Cambridge: Cambridge University Press.

Domański, Juliusz (1974), „Explicatio primae partis primi capitis" de Fauste Socin et l' exégèse d'Érasme, in: Movimenti ereticali in Italia e Polonia nei secoli XVI-XVII. Atti del convegno italo-polacco, Firenze: Instituto Nazionale di Studi sul Rinascimento, 77–102.

Fuchs, Wolfgang Walter (1976), Phenomenology and the Metaphysics of Presence. An Essay in the Philosophy of Edmund Husserl, The Hague: Martinus Nijhoff.

Gerson, Lloyd P. (1996), Imagery and Demiurgic Activity in Plato's Timaeus, Journal of Neoplatonic Studies 4, 1–32.

Gramigna, Remo (2020), Augustine's Theory of Signs, Signification, and Lying, Berlin: Walter de Gruyter.

King, Peter (2014), Augustine on Language, in: David Vincent Meconi/Eleonore Stump (ed.), The Cambridge Companion to Augustine, Cambridge: Cambridge University Press, 292–310.

Ogonowski, Zbigniew (2015), Socynianizm. Dzieje, poglądy, oddziaływanie, Warszawa: PAN.

O'Rourke Boyle, Marjorie (1977), Sermo. Reopening the Conversation on Translating JN 1,1, Vigiliae Christianae 31, 161–168.

Patterson, Richard (1985), Image and Reality in Plato's Metaphysics, Indianapolis: Hackett.

SALATOWSKY, SASCHA (2015), Die Philosophie der Sozinianer. Transformationen zwischen Renaissance-Aristotelismus und Fruhaufklarung, Stuttgart: Frommann-Holzboog.
SEDLEY, DAVID (2003), Plato's Cratylus, Cambridge: Cambridge University Press.
STEGMANN, KRZYSZTOF (1991), Metafizyka oczyszczona, translated by Tadeusz Włodarczyk, in: Zbigniew Ogonowski (ed.), Myśl ariańska w Polsce XVII wieku. Antologia tekstów, Wrocław: Ossolineum, 538–551.
STEINER, GEORGE (2010), Real Presences. Is There Anything in What We Say?, London: Faber and Faber.

Hartmut Rudolph

Der Rekurs auf Augustinus in G. W. Leibniz' ökumenischer Argumentation

Mit vielen seiner intellektuellen Zeitgenossen teilte Leibniz ein hochgradiges Interesse an Augustinus.[1] Dem Kirchenvater räumte er eine nahezu einzigartige Stellung unter den christlichen Schriftstellern der Antike ein. Augustinus, so argumentiert er gegenüber dem damals führenden Theologen des Gallikanismus, Bischof Jacques-Bénigne Bossuet, zähle zusammen mit Hieronymus zu den einzigen lateinischen Kirchenvätern, die "par son erudition" (Hieronymus) oder "par son esprit penetrant" (Augustinus) eine Ausnahme von der allen übrigen geltenden Regel bilden, bloße Kopisten der griechischen Autoren zu sein.[2] Zu Leibniz' Lebzeiten findet die Edition der großen Maurinerausgabe statt (Paris 1679–1700), deren Entstehen in der mit der europäischen Gelehrtenwelt eng vernetzten Leibniz-Korrespondenz immer wieder Spuren hinterlassen hat. Schon 1672 wusste Leibniz von dem Vorhaben der französischen Benediktiner,[3] bereits 1677 wird ihm aus Paris das baldige Erscheinen der *Opera Sancti Augustini omnia* angekündigt,[4] Ende Mai 1679 zeigt ihm der Utrechter Rhetorikprofessor Johann Georg Graevius das Erscheinen des ersten Bandes der Ausgabe an, von der man berichte, dass sie "alle vorhergehenden in den Schatten stellen werde";[5] 1687 erhält er Gelegenheit, in Würzburg die ersten Bände einzusehen.[6] In den 1690er Jahren wird er von Paul Pellisson-Fontanier, dem Juristen, Priester, Gelehrten und Konvertiten im Dienste Ludwig XIV., für die Lösung einzelner textkritischer Probleme in Anspruch genommen.[7] Im März 1700 informiert der französische Parlamentsadvokat François

---

1 Cf. hierzu Arbeiten von Nourrisson: 1866, 265–274; Trepte (1889); Hugon (1921); Rudolph (2009) und Backus (2016).
2 Leibniz am 14. Mai 1700 an Bossuet; Leibniz: 1923, I,18 638 (im Folgenden zitiert als A, [römische Ziffer für die Reihe], [arabische Ziffer für den Band, gegebenenfalls Großbuchstabe für den Teilband] [Seitenzahl]). – Gerade der Briefwechsel mit Bossuet, konzentriert auf die durch das Tridentinum virulent gewordene Frage des biblischen Kanons, belegt bei beiden einen außergewöhnlich hohen Respekt vor dem Kirchenlehrer und dessen Autorität.
3 Leibniz am 27. Februar 1672 an Gottlieb Spitzel; A I,1 193.
4 Friedrich Adolf Hansen am 13. August 1677 an Leibniz; A I,2 289.
5 Am 20./30. Mai an Leibniz; A I,2 481 – bei den deutschen Leibniz-Zitaten handelt es sich, ohne dass darauf im Folgenden gesondert hingewiesen würde, um Übersetzungen des Verfassers.
6 Cf. Reise-Journal 1687, Bl. 4; A I,5 429, Erläuterung zu Z. 27.
7 Am 16. Juni 1691 an Leibniz; A I,6 N. 94 und Leibniz' Antwort vom Juli 1691, A I,6 N. 98.

Pinsson Leibniz vom bevorstehenden Abschluß des Unternehmens, der letzte von den elf Bänden sei in den Druck gegangen.[8] Die durch die Ausgabe provozierte Kontroverse zwischen Benediktinern und Jesuiten wird von Leibniz aufmerksam verfolgt und in seiner Korrespondenz mehrfach thematisiert. So überrascht es nicht, dass seine Korrespondenz und seine Gutachten, sein ganzes Schrifttum eine Fülle von Augustinus-Referenzen aufweisen. Wenn es im Folgenden um diese Augustinus-Bezüge bei Leibniz gehen wird, bleiben die Hinweise auf den Bereich seines Werkes beschränkt, in dem es um die Überwindung der konfessionellen Spaltung der Christenheit in Europa geht. Lange Zeit und der nur äußerst eingeschränkten Kenntnis des Gesamtwerkes einer der großen Gelehrtengestalten im Europa des ausgehenden 17. und frühen 18. Jhs. geschuldet, galt Leibniz', wie man es gerne nannte, "irenisches" Engagement als ein eher marginaler Bereich, als ein Wirken, das zudem nur wenig Spuren in der Geschichte der Kirche, namentlich der Ökumene hinterlassen habe. Unbestritten waren die Positionen nach Leibniz' Tod kaum weniger hart gegeneinander gerichtet, die konfessionellen Grenzen kaum weniger deutlich markiert als vorher, und das, obwohl die ersten Jahrzehnte seines lebenslangen Wirkens für die Annäherung der getrennten Kirchen noch vom Abscheu vor den barbarischen Auswüchsen des 30jährigen Krieges geprägt waren und dieser Krieg vielen als ein fanatisch geführter Kampf christlicher Konfessionen erschien. Erst der Fortgang der Leibniz-Akademieausgabe in den letzten zwei Jahrzehnten erlaubt uns eine neue Bewertung des Ökumenikers Leibniz und der Bedeutung, die seinem umfangreichen Bemühen um die Einheit der Christen für seine eigene Lebensplanung, seine gelehrten und politischen Ambitionen und Tätigkeiten zugemessen werden muss. Zunehmend deutlich tritt dabei eine in der Kirchengeschichte, namentlich der Geschichte der Irenik und Ökumene, vielleicht singuläre Position zutage. Sah doch Leibniz eine nachhaltige Annäherung und Versöhnung der kontroversen Positionen an Voraussetzungen geknüpft und in derartig universelle Zusammenhänge gestellt, wie sie von seinen Korrespondenten nicht begriffen oder nicht akzeptiert werden konnten. Dies sei hier zunächst kurz erläutert, um danach an seinem Umgang mit Augustinus in seiner ökumenischen Argumentation vorzuführen, an welche Methode Leibniz seine Erwartung eines ökumenischen Fortschritts geknüpft hat.

1. Die Bedeutung der *Demonstrationes catholicae* (1668/1669)

Es gehört zu den bemerkenswerten Erscheinungen des zweifellos genialen Gelehrten, dass sich bei ihm schon in relativ jungen Jahren all das abgezeichnet hat, was

---

[8] F. Pinsson am 19. März 1700; A I,18 464; cf. auch ders. am 28. Juni 1700 an Leibniz, A I,18 730f.

seit dem 18. bis noch weit in das 21. Jahrhundert an wissenschaftlicher Leistung und philosophischen Alleinstellungsmerkmalen in seinem Gesamtwerk zutage gefördert wurde und noch werden wird. Dies gilt auch für die Originalität seiner irenisch-ökumenischen Bemühungen. Als 21jähriger war Leibniz bereits *doctor utriusque juris*, veröffentlichte eine umfangreiche juristische Reformschrift und trat in den Dienst des politisch im Reich einflußreichen Johann Philipp von Schönborn am Mainzer Hof, wohin ihn sein Förderer Johann Christian von Boineburg vermittelt hatte. Der irenisch gesonnene Boineburg, ursprünglich Calixtinischer Lutheraner, dann zum Katholizismus konvertiert, war enger Vertrauter des Mainzer Erzbischofs. In Mainz nun entwarf Leibniz einen *Demonstrationum catholicarum conspectus*, was man mit "Zusammenschau alles umfassender Beweise" übersetzen sollte, einen universellen Plan. Dieser enthielt bereits nahezu alles, dem sich Leibniz als Logiker, Metaphysiker, Mathematiker und eben auch als Ökumeniker in den darauf folgenden fünf Jahrzehnten zuwenden wird, und der auf nichts weniger abzielte, als die Erlangung des Glücks für die ganze Menschheit und zwar schon hier auf Erden[9] (keineswegs darf aber wegen dieser Zielsetzung Leibniz ein Utopiker genannt werden[10]). Der Plan enthielt einen klar gegliederten kirchenpolitischen Kernbereich, denn unverzichtbare Voraussetzung für die Erlangung dieses Ziels war für Leibniz die Aufhebung der Kirchenspaltungen, die Einheit der Christenheit. Um dem Ziel näherzukommen, seien folgende Aufgaben zu erledigen: ein Beweis der Existenz Gottes, der Unsterblichkeit der Seele und der vor der Vernunft zu legitimierenden Möglichkeit der suprarationalen christlichen Mysterien, Trinität, Inkarnation, Realpräsenz Christi in der Eucharistie und leibliche Auferstehung. Einen aktuellen Anlass, den Plan Boineburg vorzulegen, der ihn sehr positiv aufnahm, bildete die bevorstehende Reise von Schönborns nach Rom, weil sich daran die Hoffnung knüpfte, dass Leibniz' Entwurf der Kurie zur Kenntnis gebracht werden könne.

Das gewiss gewaltige Programm erfordert, wie schon der junge Leibniz erkannt hatte, eine andere Metaphysik als die aristotelische, als die atomistische und auch und vor allem eine andere als die neue Philosophie Descartes. Voraussetzung für diese andere Metaphysik bilden für ihn die Entwicklung der Elemente wahrer Philosophie, klare Begriffe von Gott, von der Seele, der Substanz etc., subtilere Begriffe der Physik und eine neue Logik für dies alles. Schon als junger Jurist hatte Leibniz sich gegen die *methodus divisiva* des Ramismus gewandt, weil die fortwährende Teilung der Begriffe zu einem leeren Sammelsurium unverstandener Begriffe führe, und gegen den Lullismus die euklidische "methodus demonstrativa"

---

9 Ich halte mich im Folgenden im Wesentlichen an Heinrich Schepers grundlegenden Aufsatz (2011, 6–10).
10 Cf. A VI,4 Nr. 207; und bereits aus der Mainzer Zeit, A IV,1 536.

oder "scientifica" propagiert, eine Verknüpfung von Aussagen durch rationale Beweise.

Es ist erstaunlich, wie sehr dieses Vorhaben der *Demonstrationes catholicae* in den vielfältigen Bereichen des Schaffens und in den alle Disziplinen umfassenden Themen der Schriften von Leibniz einen gemeinsamen inneren Bezug erkennbar werden lässt und wie weitgehend in der Abfolge und in den Schwerpunkten seiner Aktivitäten die Konsequenz sichtbar wird, mit der Leibniz versucht hat, seinen Lebensplan zu realisieren. Ebenso klar ist, dass Leibniz vieles, auch vieles Grundlegende, gerade auch im Bereich der Logik und der *Characteristica universalis*[11] in seinem Leben nicht hat vollenden können. Und eines wird daran deutlich: Man muss Leibniz' politische Bestrebungen und allem voran seine Kirchenreunions- und Unionsbemühungen im Zusammenhang dieses Programms verstehen und sollte sie keinesfalls als separate, neben der Mathematik, neben der Substanzmetaphysik, neben der übrigen natürlichen Theologie, neben seiner Dynamik, neben seiner Wahrscheinlichkeitslogik etc. verrichtete Tätigkeiten sehen – wie auch umgekehrt Leibniz auf diesen zuletzt genannten Wissenschaftsfeldern gewirkt hat, weil ihm dies für seine politische Zielsetzung sinnvoll und notwendig erschien. "Das überhaupt kennzeichnet L.' Rationalismus, daß er um der Theologie willen Mathematiker geworden ist". Mit dieser Feststellung schließt der von Heinrich Schepers verfasste Artikel über Leibniz in der 3. Auflage der RGG (Band IV, Sp. 293), und aus jenem konzeptionellen und lebensgeschichtlichen Zusammenhang lässt sich auch Leibniz' Auseinandersetzung mit Augustinus begreifen, um die es nun, wenn auch fragmentarisch, gehen soll.

2. Augustinus in Leibniz' ökumenischer Argumentation

2.1 Zur Bedeutung von *caritas* und *amor dei*

Eines der grundlegenden Kennzeichen des Leibnizschen Ökumenismus ist die Liebe als *caritas* (Leibniz übersetzt es einmal mit "brüderlicher Liebe")[12] und als *amor dei*. In beidem beruft er sich schon in den ersten Jahren seiner konkreten Bemühungen um eine Annäherung mit der katholischen Kirche auf Augustinus, vor allem in seiner Korrespondenz mit dem befreundeten zum Katholizismus konvertierten Landgrafen Ernst von Hessen-Rheinfels, zunächst in dem einfachen Sinn, dass die Liebe unverzichtbare Voraussetzung für die Einheit der Kirche ist

---

11 Cf. etwa Leibniz im Februar und am 30. März 1679 an Herzog Johann Friedrich, wo dieses universale Projekt ausführlich beschrieben wird; A I,2 N. 110, N. 127; A II,²1 N. 197a, 204a.
12 A VI,4C, 2806.

und die Kirchenspaltungen sich allemal auf einen Mangel an dieser Liebe zurückführen lassen: "Non habent DEI caritatem, qui Ecclesiae non diligunt unitatem", und ein ganzes Florilegium ähnlicher Aussagen bietet Leibniz in seiner ersten großen Reunionsschrift 1683 aus den Schriften des Kirchenvaters an.[13] Er steht darin in der Tradition nahezu aller vom Humanismus geprägten Gestalten der vortridentinischen Zeit, gleich auf welcher Seite sie in den Religionsgesprächen des 16. Jhs. fochten. Martin Bucer, Philipp Melanchthon und natürlich Erasmus von Rotterdam sind schon dem 21jährigen Vorbilder, wenn es um die *conciliatio* der getrennten Kirchen geht.[14] Doch Leibniz' Verhältnis zu Augustinus ist an diesem Punkt ein noch innigeres, als es jenes eine Zitat erkennen lässt. In Leibniz' Verständnis der Liebe, wie er sie als Voraussetzung für die Einheit der Kirche sieht oder als Voraussetzung der Kontrahenten, um dieser Einheit näher zu kommen, spiegelt sich, was Augustinus in *De doctrina*, in *De libero arbitrio* oder in *De civitate dei* über den *ordo dilectionis*, bzw. über den Unterschied zwischen *uti* und *frui*, bzw. über die beiden Weisen zu lieben, bzw. über die Art, wie Menschen gemeinhin lieben, und die Art der Liebe unter christlichen Brüdern sagt. Als Beispiel sei nur auf eine Stelle in *Contra Faustum Manicheum* XXII, c. 78 verwiesen, die Leibniz auch zitiert hat: "[...] propter DEUM amat amicum, qui DEI amorem amat in amico".[15] Es ist keine utilitaristische Liebe,[16] sondern sie bedeutet einfach Glück, Glückseligkeit, *dilectio*, *felicitas*, als Liebe der göttlichen Vollkommenheiten; sie bewirkt die Freude am Glück des anderen und an dem Grad der Vollkommenheit, den der andere erlangt hat. Die Stelle verdient in unserem Zusammenhang deshalb besondere Beachtung, weil Augustinus hier, wie auch an anderen Orten, den engen Bezug zur Gerechtigkeit herstellt, um die es Augustinus in dem genannten Kapitel eigentlich geht.

> Ein Mensch ist gerecht, wenn er die Dinge um des Zweckes willen nutzt, den Gott an sie geknüpft hat und wenn er seine Freude in Gott als dem Ziel aller Dinge findet, während er sich seiner selbst und seines Freundes in Gott und um Gottes willen erfreut (*c. Faustum* XXII, 78).

Dass diese Art zu lieben jedoch keineswegs den Verzicht auf das eigene Wohl des so Liebenden bedeutet, hat Leibniz seit den 1690er Jahren in seiner Kritik am Quietismus, besonders an Molinos und Fénelon betont,[17] für welche die reine

---

13 Cf. z. B. A IV,3 284.
14 A VI,1 323.
15 A IV,3 285.
16 Cf. hierzu v. a. Riley: 1996, 160ff.
17 Cf. hierzu Riley: 1996, 144–152; und ders., "Monadology":2014, passim.

Liebe zur Gleichgültigkeit dem eigenen Wohl gegenüber und zur Selbstaufgabe und Annihilation der eigenen Seele (leibnizisch gesprochen: der individuellen Substanz) und so zum Rückzug aus der sozialen Welt führen sollte:

> Wie kann man Gott über alle Dinge und frei von jeder Berechnung lieben und gleichwohl, der Eigentümlichkeit der menschlichen Natur folgend, das eigene Wohl berücksichtigen? Lieben bedeutet nichts anderes als davon getragen zu werden, seine Freude im Glück und in der Vervollkommnung des anderen zu finden. Und diese Definition lässt es einsichtig werden, dass die Abtrennung der Liebe des anderen vom eigenen Wohl bedeutet, eine Chimäre zu schmieden. Ich habe mich hundertemal darüber gewundert, dass man so über die reine Liebe disputiert hat ohne eine verstandesmäßig einsichtige Definition von Liebe zu liefern.

Die Autoren, die sich dazu üblicherweise äußerten, erklärten das eine Unverständliche durch ein gleichfalls Unverständliches.[18] Deshalb habe er immer große Sorgfalt auf die Definitionen gelegt.[19]

2.2 Gerechtigkeit als der Weisheit ebenförmige Liebe

Am Beginn der innerprotestantischen Unionsverhandlungen zwischen den Kurfürstentümern von Brandenburg und Hannover 1697 übermittelt Leibniz der hannoverschen Kurfürstin die folgende Definitionenkette:

---

18 Schon der junge Leibniz hat die von den Ramisten geübte *methodus divisiva* als eine Anhäufung unbegriffener Begriffe kritisiert (A VI,1 295f.) und demgegenüber einen vernunftgeleiteten Umgang mit den Prinzipien aller Wissenschaften, d. h. die im euklidischen Sinne vorzunehmende mathematisch-logische Verknüpfung von Aussagen auf der Grundlage klarer Definitionen der Begriffe, gefordert; cf. etwa am 11. / 21. Dezember an Philipp Jakob Spener; A I,1 108; Antognazza: 2009, 39–44.

19 Leibniz am 4. Juli 1706 an Pierre Coste; A II,4 448: Dort geht es um das Problem, "comment on peut aimer Dieu sur toutes choses et d'un Amour non mercenaire, et rapporter tout cependant à son propre bien, suivant la proprieté de la Nature humaine. C'est qu' A i m e r n'est autre chose qu'estre porté à trouver son plaisir dans la felicité ou perfection d'autruy, et cette definition fait voir, que separer l'amour d'autruy de son bien propre, c'est forger une chimere. Je me suis aussi etonné cent fois, qu'on a tant disputé sur l'amour pur sans donner une definition intelligible de l'Amour. Car en considerant ce qu'en disent les auteurs ordinairement, on trouve qu'ils expliquent *obscurum per aeque obscurum*. C'est à quoy j'ay cherché de remedier et j'ay tousjours eu grand soin de donner des Definitions. J'y fais voir après cela, qu'entre les veues mercenaires et l'amour veritable qu'on peut appeller pur, lorsqu'il a pour fondement le bien de l'objet aimé, il y a autant de difference qu'il y en a entre l' Utile, et l'Agreable, c'est à dire entre ce qui est un bien seulement par le bon effect qu'il contribue à faire produire, et entre ce qui est un bien de soy même; entre Uti et frui, comme S. Augustin le distingue fort bien dans sa Cité de Dieu, lib. XI. c. 25 et ailleurs; et que l'Honneste n'est autre chose que l'Agreable de la Raison." – Cf. hierzu auch Riley: 1996, 163.

Die Gerechtigkeit ist eine der Weisheit ebenförmige Liebe.
Die Weisheit ist die Wissenschaft der Glückseligkeit.
Liebe ist universelles Wohlwollen.
Das Wohlwollen ist eine Weise zu lieben.
Lieben heißt, seine Freude am Wohl, an der Vervollkommnung und am Glück des anderen zu finden.[20]

Eben diese Weise zu lieben, die als *benevolentia universalis* auch für Leibniz den Inhalt der Gerechtigkeit bildete, war für ihn Voraussetzung nachhaltiger ökumenischer Verhandlungen. Und im Blick auf frühere wie auf die bevorstehenden Ausgleichsverhandlungen geißelt er den *amour mercenaire*, den *amor mercenarius*, den auch Augustinus bereits dem *amor dei* im eben dargelegten Sinn gegenübergestellt hatte und der sich für Leibniz im halsstarrigen Festhalten an den eigenen Positionen (*opiniâtreté*)[21] und in der rigiden Verteidigung der eigenen kirchlichen Machtverhältnisse äußert.[22] Doch bei aller Nähe zum Kirchenvater zeigt sich nun die für Leibniz wesentliche Weiterentwicklung des augustinischen heilsgeschichtlichen Konstrukts der beiden "*amores*, die zwei *civitates* bewirken":[23] Leibniz definiert die *civitas dei* als "eine moralische Welt in der natürlichen", sie ist die "assemblage des Esprits" qui "doit composer la Cité de Dieu".[24] Jeder Geist – und das heißt bei Leibniz, jede vernunftbegabte individuelle Substanz – ist nicht nur wie überhaupt jede Monade ein lebendiger Spiegel des Universums, sondern die Geister besitzen einen höheren Grad der Vollkommenheit, sie sind zusätzlich "images de la Divinité" und als solche fähig, "eine Art Gemeinschaft mit Gott einzugehen" (M § 83f.). Sie bilden die "Cité divine des Esprits" unter Gott, der als Monarch dieser *civitas* betrachtet wird ("Dieu consideré comme Monarqve de la Cité divine des Esprits"; M § 87). Dies macht es auch verständlich, warum Leibniz trotz sich immer wieder einstellender Mißerfolge seine Bemühungen nicht aufgegeben hat. Seine rationale Metaphysik, gleichbedeutend mit der natürlichen Theologie, gab ihm das Vertrauen in die göttliche Providenz, die alles zum Guten, zur Vervollkommnung führen wird, auch wenn die Geister als Kreaturen nicht über eine so ungetrübte Einsicht in die Vollkommenheit des Ganzen verfügen können, dass sie die auch dem Scheitern zugrunde liegende Harmonie[25] zu erkennen vermöchten (M § 90).

---

20 An Kurfürstin Sophie im August 1697; A I,14 58.
21 Am 16. Juli 1691 an Madame de Brinon; A I,6 235.
22 Am 19./20. November 1697 an Madame de Brinon; A I,14 744.
23 "Fecerunt itaque ciuitates duas amores duo, terrenam scilicet amor sui usque ad contemptum dei, caelestem uero amor dei usque ad contemptum sui. denique illa in se ipsa, haec in domino gloriatur"; *de civ* XIV,28.
24 *Monadologie* (1714, im Folgenden: M), § 85f.
25 Hierauf wird weiter unten näher eingegangen werden.

Wohl aber führt der Vernunftgebrauch die Geister zu der Erkenntnis, dass Gott, der universelle Monarch, als das Wesen der vollkommensten Vernunft, der vollkommensten Gerechtigkeit, der vollkommensten Güte alles in vollkommenster Weise der Vernunft, Gerechtigkeit und Güte richten wird.

2.3 Die Bedeutung der Vernunft

Dieser Kerngedanke der Leibnizschen Metaphysik wird zum entscheidenden Argument etwa im Zusammenhang der zwischen den Konfessionen kontrovers behandelten Erwählungslehre, wenn Leibniz die unterschiedlichen calvinistischen Positionen und den lutherischen Universalismus einander anzunähern versucht.[26] Aber er bestimmt auch Leibniz' ökumenisches Engagement generell, denn daraus ergibt sich ein zweites Merkmal der ökumenischen Methodik, ohne das dem Erfordernis des *amour non-mercenaire*, einer Liebe, die ihre Freude an der Vervollkommnung des anderen findet, nicht entsprochen werden kann. Leibniz hat es auf verschiedene Weise immer wieder zu definieren versucht, sowohl grundsätzlich als auch in der Praxis der Verhandlungen, an denen er beteiligt war. Ausgehend von Augustins Unterscheidung des *uti* und *frui*, etwa in *De civ* XI, c. 25, wobei nur letzteres die wahre Liebe kennzeichnet, die ihr Gutes im Guten selbst findet und nicht in dem, was an Effekt aus dem Guten besitz- und greifbar wird, also ausgehend hiervon nennt Leibniz die *fruitio*, wir könnten sie übersetzen als den der wahren Liebe innewohnenden Genuss, das "Agréable", das Anmutig-Freundliche, und paraphrasiert Augustinus, indem er von *l'Honneste*, dem Ehrenhaften, spricht,[27] das nichts anderes sei, als das "Agréable de la Raison", das Anmutig-Angenehme der Vernunft. Dass Leibniz hier den Begriff "honneste" verwendet, führt uns in seine Auslegung der Prinzipien des Naturrechts, wie sie der römische Jurist Ulpian im 3. Jahrhundert n. Chr. in so genannten *Digesten*, d. h. einer Zusammenstellung des römischen Zivilrechts, formuliert hatte: "Die Vorschriften des Rechts sind die Folgenden: Ehrenvoll leben, niemanden verletzen und jedem das Seine zuteil werden lassen" (*Juris praecepta sunt haec: honeste vivere, alterum non laedere, suum cuique tribuere*).[28] Dies aufnehmend nennt Leibniz nun drei Prinzipien oder auch Stufen (*gradus*) des Naturrechts,[29] deren erste (*alterum non laedere*) für ihn das Recht im strikten Sinne (*jus strictum*), deren zweite und höhere Stufe für ihn die Billigkeit (*aequitas*), und deren dritte und höchste Stufe, das "ehrenhaft leben" (*honeste vivere*)

---

26 Leibniz' Position in dieser Frage hat sich die theologische Forschung auf Grund durch die Akademieausgabe neu erschlossener Quellen gerade in den letzten Jahren zugewandt; cf. besonders Backus: 2016, 57–151, darunter Leibniz und Augustinus 126–151; Link (2017) und Rols (2017).
27 s. oben, Anm. 19.
28 *Digesten* 1,1,10 § 1.
29 A VI,1 343, § 73.

die *pietas* bildet, was wir gemeinhin als Frömmigkeit übersetzen, womit aber die leibnizsche Bedeutung keineswegs ausgeschöpft wäre. *Pietas* ist bei ihm dasjenige Verhalten, das auf die Vervollkommnung und Wirksamkeit der anderen genannten Stufen abzielt.[30] Für Leibniz ist das Naturrecht, wenn es von der *pietas* zur Wirkung gebracht wird, auf das Allgemeinwohl, das *bonum commune*, ausgerichtet. Wieder zurück zu Leibniz' Paraphrase der augustinischen *fruitio* können wir von der *pietas* als dem "Anmutig-Angenehmen der Vernunft"[31] oder noch mehr zugespitzt von der *pietas* der Vernunft sprechen.

Bei Augustinus gibt es in dem Zusammenhang ein anderes Element der Vernunft, wenn er seine Vorstellung der "geordneten Liebe" (*dilectio ordinata*) entfaltet, etwa in *De doctr.* I,[32] wo derjenige, welcher in Gerechtigkeit und Frömmigkeit lebt (es ist damit dasselbe angesprochen, was Leibniz im Zitat eben als *l'Honneste*, das Ehrenhafte, meistens aber die *pietas*, die recht gelebte Frömmigkeit, bezeichnete), ein *rerum integer aestimator* genannt wird. Das ist einer, der redlich die Dinge einzuschätzten weiß, so dass er nicht etwas mehr liebt, das weniger Liebe erheischt, sondern der das Liebenswerte um Gottes willen liebt und von dem Gott um seiner selbst willen geliebt wird. Letzteres ist bei Augustinus wie bei Leibniz gleichbedeutend mit der Freude an den göttlichen Vollkommenheiten; denn Vernunft, Gerechtigkeit und Güte sind keine Eigenschaften Gottes oder eines menschlichen Individuums, sie sind die ewigen Wahrheiten, denen gemäß Gott in höchster Vollkommenheit wirkt und an denen wir in unterschiedlichen Graden der Unvollkommenheit partizipieren. Diese ursprünglich platonische Erkenntnis bildet eine entscheidende Grundlage der Leibnizschen Metaphysik, von der aus er auch sein ökumenisches Konzept entwickelt hat und so weitgehend wie möglich in die Praxis umzusetzen versuchte. Schon allein diese universelle Grundlage gibt uns die Berechtigung, Leibniz einen Ökumeniker zu nennen, weil er nicht nur sehr konkrete Vorstellungen für eine Verbesserung der Lage der Menschheit mit Hilfe eines intensiven Austausches zwischen Europa und China entwickelt und publiziert hat, sondern gerade auch weil seine Kirchenunionsbemühungen Teil

---

30 Zu Leibniz' Interpretation dieser drei Prinzipien cf. ausführlich Busche (2003).
31 s. oben, Anm. 19.
32 "Ille autem iuste et sancte vivit, qui rerum integer aestimator est. Ipse est autem qui ordinatam habet dilectionem, ne aut diligat quod non est diligendum, aut non diligat quod diligendum est, aut amplius diligat quod minus diligendum est, aut aeque diligat quod vel minus vel amplius diligendum est. Omnis peccator in quantum peccator est, non est diligendus, et omnis homo in quantum homo est, diligendus est propter Deum, Deus vero propter seipsum. Et si Deus omni homine amplius diligendus est, amplius quisque Deum debet diligere quam seipsum. Item amplius alius homo diligendus est quam corpus nostrum, quia propter Deum omnia ista diligenda sunt et potest nobiscum alius homo Deo perfrui, quod non potest corpus, quia corpus per animam vivit qua fruimur Deo" (De doctr. I, c. 27. 28).

eines wirklich die ganze Menschheit umfassenden Plans sind und auch die praktischen Ansätze über das Christentum des Westens, also die römisch-katholische Kirche, die protestantischen Konfessionen und die anglikanische Kirche hinaus das orthodoxe Christentum einbezogen und schließlich, weil er zumindest mit seiner Idee eines Weltkonzils unter der Patronage des russischen Zaren[33] seiner Zeit so weit voraus war, dass wir ihn zu Recht mit einem erst im späteren 19. Jahrhundert aufgekommenen Begriff einen Ökumeniker nennen können.[34]

2.4 Zur Umsetzung in der Praxis

Einige wenige Bemerkungen seien erlaubt, um zu beschreiben, wie Leibniz dies alles in die Praxis der Verhandlungen umzusetzen gedachte. Gerade im Vergleich zur Argumentationsweise seines langjährigen Korrespondenzpartners, des französischen Bischofs und Hauptes des Gallikanismus, Jacques-Bénigne Bossuet, verzichtet er darauf, die Einheit erzwingen zu wollen, indem man die eigene (lutherische) Position auf Kosten derjenigen des Gegenübers als die einzig wahre behauptet, was im Falle der Reunionsverhandlungen mit der katholischen Seite, so auch in der Argumentation Bossuets, letztlich auf eine Rückkehrunion hinausliefe. Stattdessen finden sich bei Leibniz Beispiele für das, was der um unsere Kenntnis des Leibnizschen Ökumenismus hoch verdiente Pallotinerpater Paul Eisenkopf in seinem bis heute unüberholten Buch *Leibniz und die Einigung der Christenheit* 1975 unter dem zeitgenössischen Begriff der συγκατάβασις oder der *condescendance* ausführlich erörtert hat.[35] Bei Leibniz bedeutet dies nicht den Versuch, durch ein liebevolles Hinwegsehen über die Sachunterschiede, über eine Angleichung der kontroversen Positionen durch verbal geschickte Formulierungen oder durch Reduktion der Lehrgrundlagen auf ein Minimum (den vermeintlichen und von Leibniz äußerst kritisch bewerteten *consensus quinquesecularis* z. B.)[36] zu einer vermeintlichen Einigung zu gelangen. Für Leibniz – und die Erfahrungen mit den Religionsgesprächen des 17. Jahrhunderts gaben ihm darin Recht – konnte es auf diesem Weg nie zu einer nachhaltigen Einigung kommen, er sprach einmal davon, dass so der Krieg nur umso mehr befestigt werde, aber vom Frieden sei man noch allzu weit entfernt.[37]

---

33 Cf. Li (2012).
34 Zur Charakterisierung der Leibnizschen Ökumenik cf. zuletzt Rudolph (2019) – Hingewiesen sei aber auch auf Arbeiten, die nach dem 2. Vatikanum im Geist der konziliaren Theologie entstanden sind: Henrici (1968); Werling (1977) (eine von Henrici betreute Dissertation) und besonders Eisenkopf (1975) (aus einer von Heinrich Fries betreuten Dissertation hervorgegangen). Als Beispiele für frühere Arbeiten seien Jordan (1927) (Anglikaner); Benz (1945–1950) und Schmidt (1963) genannt.
35 Eisenkopf: 1975, 119–123.
36 Cf. etwa A I,9 181.
37 Leibniz im September (2. Hälfte) 1698 an Daniel Ernst Jablonski; A I,15 834.

Seine Bereitschaft zur *condescendance* betraf vielmehr die Praxis der Kirchenleitung, die äußere Gestalt und Gestaltung des kirchlichen Lebens. Hier war ihm der Apostel Paulus das Vorbild, der seinen jüdischen Brüdern in Jerusalem anbot, den Griechen Timotheus beschneiden zu lassen (Apg 16,3).[38] Doch er findet auch bei Augustinus Beispiele, etwa, wenn dieser aus seiner, wie Leibniz sagt, *prudentia* und *sanctitas* heraus in *c. Faustum* zur Unterscheidung dessen rät, was "wir lehren, und dem, was wir in der Kirche bloß dulden, was wir verbessern müssen und was wir, bis es verbessert worden ist, ertragen müssen".[39] So kann Leibniz auch dem Tridentinum zustimmen, sofern es die Ansicht anathematisiert, ein von einem in Todsünde befindlichen Diener gespendetes Sakrament sei unwirksam,[40] und zur Bestärkung dessen auf Augustinus' *De baptismo* verweisen.[41] Desgleichen kann er sich aus Gründen der Einheit der Kirche für die eucharistische Anbetung aussprechen, hier wiederum neben anderem die Autorität des Kirchenvaters bemühend.[42] Ähnliches gilt für den Opfergedanken des Altar-Sakraments.[43] Um die Einheit der Kirche zu erlangen, ist Leibniz zur *condescendance* bereit, d. h., wo nur irgend möglich, auf die eigene Position zugunsten der anderen Seite zu verzichten. Die Berufung auf den Kirchenvater dient in solchen Fällen dann dazu, die so getroffenen Entscheidungen gegenüber der eigenen Partei der Protestanten rechtfertigen zu können. Nicht zu den Beispielen der *condescendance* zählt dagegen Leibniz' erfolgreicher Versuch 1698, die Helmstedter theologische Fakultät zu einem Gutachten zu bewegen,[44] in welchem der Primat des Papstes über die *ecclesia universalis* nicht bloß, wie etwa von Melanchthon und Bucer geschehen,[45] *jure humano*, sondern *jure divino*, also göttlichen Rechts, konstatiert wurde, eine Lehrmeinung, die für Georg Calixt noch zu den katholischen *errores intolerabiles* zählte. In Leibniz' Argumentation ging es nicht, wie bei den eben genannten Beispielen um ein aus Gründen der brüderlichen Liebe der katholischen Partei entgegengebrachtes Zugeständnis, sondern der Papstprimat ergab sich für ihn aus den Vernunftgründen des Naturrechts und war damit, weil deshalb *jure divino* begründet, auch dem Ermessensspielraum kontingenter Entscheidungen der Kirchenleitungen entzogen.

---

38 A IV,4 339; A I,19 208; A IV,8 263 u. ö.
39 VI,4 2407 (= Augustinus, *Contra Faustum* XX,21 – diese und die folgenden Referenzen finden sich im historischen Apparat von A zur jeweiligen Stelle).
40 Cc. Tridentinum, sess. VII, Decretum de sacramento vom 3. März 1547; DS N. 1612.
41 A VI,4 2415 (= Augustinus, *De baptismo* VII,52f.).
42 A VI,4 2429 (= Augustinus, *Ennaratio in psalm.* 98[99], 9).
43 A VI,4 2433 (= Augustinus, *Sermones*, sermo 221).
44 Cf. Utermöhlen (1995) sowie Einleitung zu A I,15 XII-XIV und Rudolph (1999a).
45 BSLK 463[10]–464[4]; zu Martin Bucer cf. Pollet: 1962, 488–518; zum lutherischen und reformierten Bekenntnisstand cf. Rudolph: 1999a, 76f.

2.5 Die eine Wahrheit

Im Blick auf die erwähnten Beispiele der *condescendance* gab es gute Gründe, Leibniz als einen Ireniker in der Nachfolge des von ihm durchaus geschätzten Helmstedter Lutheraners Georg Calixt zu sehen. Die vorhin beschriebene wahre Liebe sah er jedoch auf andere Weise wirksam werden als die Ireniker seiner Zeit, nämlich indem er sich dem Anliegen der gegenüberstehenden Partei öffnete, nach der Wahrheit in der Wahrheit der anderen suchte und die anderen in die eigene Wahrheit einbeziehen und so zu der einen Wahrheit gelangen wollte, denn für Leibniz,[46] wie schon für Aristoteles und auch für einen so großen Ireniker wie Martin Bucer[47] ist die Wahrheit immer nur eine: "Omne verum vero consonat" bzw. "verum vero non dissonat" zitieren beide die *Nikomachische Ethik* (A 8, 1098 b 10–11). Um die Kontrahenten der lutherischen Konfession, sei es die tridentinische Theologie oder seien es die reformierten Parteien zu jener Einheit bringen zu können, dies war Leibniz' feste Überzeugung, bedurfte es der Klärung der Ursachen für die verfestigten kontroversen Positionen. Diese Ursachen sah Leibniz nicht in der Theologie, sondern im jeweiligen philosophischen Vorverständnis, welches die Kontrahenten daran hinderte, gemeinsam zu der einen Wahrheit des Christenglaubens zu finden.[48] Deshalb entstand seine Metaphysik, die gewiss keine einfache war.[49] Aber sie sollte zum Beispiel die "Irrtümer" der aristotelischen Unterscheidung von Substanz und Akzidenz wie auch des cartesischen Verständnisses der Substanz als einer *res extensa* aufhellen, welches der zeitgenössischen reformierten Theologie die Zustimmung zur lutherischen Realpräsenzvorstellung unmöglich machte. Das bedeutet, dass Leibniz sein Argument in beide Richtungen einbringen

---

46 Am 8. / 18. April 1698 an Thomas Burnett of Kemney; A I,15 489; cf. auch bereits Pichler: 1869–1870, I, 221.

47 Bucer: 1536, Bl. 5r/v.

48 Besonders scharf tritt diese Position in dem von Leibniz gemeinsam mit Molanus 1698/1699 verfassten Gutachten *Unvorgreiffliches Bedencken über eine Schrifft genandt Kurtze Vorstellung der einigkeit und des unterscheids im Glauben beeder protestirenden Kirchen* (A I,7 N. 79) hervor, mit dem die beiden Hannoveraner auf die ihnen vom brandenburgischen Hofprediger Daniel Ernst Jablonski zugesandte Unionsschrift *Kurtze Vorstellung der Einigkeit und des Unterscheides, im Glauben beyder Evangelischen so genandten Lutherischen und Reformirten Kirchen* (ediert in Rudolph: 1999b, 128–166) antworteten.

49 Cf. Leibniz' eigenes Urteil über seine Methode im Vergleich zu den Irenikern: "[...] car ils promettent tousjours des methodes tres aisées, par le moyen des quelles ils esperent de convaincre leurs adversaires en peu de temps; au lieu que je declare, que la methode que j'entreprends est tres difficile, et qu'elle a besoin d'une grande application et de beaucoup de temps. De sorte qu'il y a autant de difference entre leurs promesses et les miennes, qu'il y en a entre un Lulliste, qui pretend de nous apprendre la Pansophie en peu de temps, et entre un Geometre, qui entend la vraye analyse et qui nous avertira, qu'il faut un peu plus de soin pour parvenir à une connoissance solide"; A IV,3 205 – cf. dazu auch oben, Anm. 18.

konnte, ob es um die Frage der Realpräsenz Christi in der Eucharistie ging oder um die Frage der Soteriologie und Erwählungslehre.[50]

Im innerprotestantischen Ausgleichsbemühen, an dem er in führender Position in den Jahren 1697 bis 1716 mitgewirkt hat, versuchte Leibniz, als "Moderator"[51] mit Hilfe der auf strenger Logik basierten und einander zugeordneten Definitionen seiner Metaphysik die kontroversen Lehraussagen der Reformierten und Lutheraner dauerhaft aneinander anzugleichen, so dass keine Partei die Lehraussagen der anderen länger als häretisch und kirchentrennend ansehen müsste.

2.6 Vernunft und Offenbarung – Ein Beispiel kritischer Augustinusrezeption

Es ist kaum möglich, im Rahmen dieses Beitrags die Vielfalt der Augustinusreferenzen in Leibniz' jahrelanger Arbeit als Moderator zu dokumentieren. So soll hier nur auf seine Auseinandersetzung mit Augustinus eingegangen werden, soweit es dabei um die Rolle der Vernunft, die Definition ihrer Grenzen und ihrer Zuordnung zur göttlichen Offenbarung geht – eine Fragestellung, die uns zu den Grundlagen und Kernaussagen der Leibnizschen Metaphysik führt und seine doch auch zu konstatierende kritische Distanz gegenüber Augustinus verständlich werden lässt. Wie schon mehrfach angedeutet, hatte Leibniz eine strenge Methode des Vernunftgebrauchs entwickelt, wozu auch bereits die Bedingungen des Denkens, eine von ihm entwickelte ontologisch fundierte Logik zählen, die von der Isomorphie von Denken und Sein[52] ausgeht. Seine Definitionen und Beweise, seine gesamte Argumentation hatten aus der *rigeur exacte du raisonnement*[53] zu erfolgen. In einem Plan für die *scientia generalis* Mitte der 1680er Jahre zieht er Augustins spöttische Aussage *contra academicos* II,3 heran: "Ihr wollt nicht glauben, dass ihr die Wahrheit in der Philosophie nicht erkannt hättet, wenn ihr nicht gelernt hättet, was ihr ja nun zum mindesten wisst, dass eins, zwei, drei, vier in der Summe zehn macht".[54] Doch wird mit diesem eher polemischen Rekurs auf Augustinus Leibniz' Bestimmung der Rolle der Vernunft im Zusammenhang der Theologie natürlich noch nicht angemessen erfasst.

---

50 Cf. hierzu Backus: 2016, 9–54 (Eucharistie) und oben, Anm. 26 (Prädestination).
51 " […] je pretends en un mot d'ecrire des controverses en sorte, que le lecteur ne puisse point juger quel party l' auteur peut avoir épousé. Si j'en viens à bout, de quoy me pourrat-on accuser et comment puis je estre exposé la colere de qui que [ce] soit? On sera obligé de reconnoistre que la forme de mon dessein m'obligeoit à la moderation, et que je n'aurois pu me deguiser sans addoucir les choses, et sans garder une certaine égalité partout"; A IV,3 206.
52 Cf. Schepers: 1999, XLIII, LXV.
53 "Les Geometres ont trop de moyens de decouvrir les moindres erreurs, si par mégarde il[s] leur en echappoient. C'est dans la philosophie qu'il faudroit employer principalement cette rigeur exacte du raisonnement parce que les autres moyens de s'asseurer y manquent le plus souvent"; A VI,4A 705.
54 wie vorhergehende Anm.

"Gegen die Vernunft würde kein nüchterner Mensch urteilen, gegen die Schrift kein Christ, gegen die Kirche kein Friedensstifter".[55] Gerne zitiert Leibniz diesen Satz aus dem 4. Buch *De trinitate* (c. 6). Seiner großen Reunionsschrift *Apologia fidei catholicae ex recta ratione* (1683) dient das Zitat sogar als einleitendes Motto (A IV,3 226). Blickt man auf die Interpretation dieses Mottos, so zeigen sich trotz mancher verbaler Übereinstimmungen[56] doch letztlich grundlegende Differenzen des rationalistischen Metaphysikers zu dem aus den gleichen philosophischen Quellen wie dieser schöpfenden Kirchenvater, der der Vernunft gewiss einen hohen Rang einräumt, ihr aber in der theologischen Erkenntnis, wie ja auch *Confessio Augustana* XVIII eine nur eingeschränkte Funktion zugesteht und ihr die Fähigkeit abspricht, einen Menschen zum Glauben an Christus zu bringen.[57] Leibniz beginnt anscheinend auch in Augustins Richtung zu argumentieren: "Das unserem Glauben innewohnende Prinzip ist nicht die Vernunft, sondern die Autorität des sich offenbarenden GOTTES", doch fährt er fort:

> Indessen, es gäbe keine Pflicht zu glauben, wenn nicht GOTT selbst, indem er durch die Vernunft in uns spricht, uns reichlich mit Kennzeichen (*nota*) versehen hätte, mittels deren das Wort GOTTES von dem Wort eines Betrügers unterschieden werden kann. Doch ist es, nachdem das WORT GOTTES einmal gestiftet worden war, für gewiss und bewiesen zu erachten, dass, was in ihm enthalten ist, wahr ist, wie sehr die Vernunft auch dagegen zu stehen scheint – nicht, weil, wie es einst gewisse Leute, anscheinend um die Religion zu verspotten, zu lehren wagten, das Wahre dem Wahren widerstreiten könne (denn, abgesehen davon, dass sowas per se völlig absurd ist, würde es ja bedeuten, dass sich GOTT an sich selbst vergeht, dessen Wohltat nicht weniger die Vernunft als die Offenbarung ist).[58]

---

55 A VI,4 2298.
56 Gerade auch im Blick auf den homo sapiens in Augustinus' *De utilitate credendi*.
57 Dort heißt es unter Berufung auf Pseudo-Augustinus' *Hypomnesticon contra Pelagianos* etc. von der *voluntas humana*, "non habet vim sine spiritu sancto efficiendae iustitiae Dei seu iustitiae spiritualis, quia animalis homo non percipit ea, quae sunt spiritus Dei"; BSLK, 73.
58 "Principium fidei nostrae domesticum non rationem, sed autoritatem esse constat revelantis DEI. Quanquam enim nulla esset obligatio credendi, nisi DEUS ipse per rationem in nobis loquens, notas suppeditasset, quibus Verbum DEI a verbo impostoris discerni posset […]; constituto tamen semel VERBO DEI, pro certo ac demonstrato habendum est, quicquid in eo continetur verum esse, quamvis ratio repugnare videatur; non quod verum vero pugnare possit, quemadmodum aliqui olim eludendae ut videtur religionis causa docere sunt ausi (id enim praeterquam quod est per se absurdissimum, esset DEUM ipsum sibi committere cujus beneficium non minus ratio est, quam revelatio)"; A IV,3 226.

Hier widerspricht Leibniz dem Averroismus, wie er etwa 1513 durch das 5. Lateranum in Gestalt des Pietro Pomponazzi verworfen wurde (DS N. 1440f.). "Aber", so fährt Leibniz fort,

> weil die Finsternis unseres Geistes so groß ist, dass wir dem, was die Vernunft weithin hervorbringt, kaum vertrauen können, es sei denn, der Verlauf der [auf solche Weise gezogenen] Schlussfolgerungen wird von anderswoher, nämlich durch gewisse Prüfungen oder durch Erfahrungen a posteriori und durch andere Zeichen einer Übereinstimmung mit der Wahrheit befestigt.[59]

Hier deutet sich trotz des erkennbaren Versuchs, so nahe wie möglich an Augustinus zu bleiben, der ja durchaus auch, etwa in *de trinitate* XV, c. 2, von einer Bewegung vom Glauben zum Erkennen weiß und einräumt, dass auch für ihn die Glaubenswahrheiten weitgehend einer "richtig gelenkten" ratio zugänglich werden können,[60] doch schon eine schließlich bedeutende Differenz der beiden großen christlichen Platoniker an. Wenn Augustinus in *De utilitate credendi* unter Hinweis allein schon auf die Alltagserfahrung die Autorität der katholischen Kirche als Grundlage des Glaubens hervorhebt, so kann dies für Leibniz nicht den Dispens der Vernunft hinsichtlich der Prüfung der offenbarten Glaubenswahrheiten bedeuten.[61] Wie sollte man sonst die wahre christliche Religion von einer falschen unterscheiden

---

59 "sed quia tanta est caligo mentis nostrae ut rationibus in longum productis fidere vix possimus, nisi successus conclusionum aliunde per examina quaedam aut experimenta a posteriori aliosve consensus veritatis indices, confirmetur."; A IV,3 226.
60 Cf. Schindler: 1979, 664f.
61 Cf. z. B. am 27. September 1702 an den Hildesheimer Domkapitular Johann Sigismund Wilhelm von Reuschenberg; (Hinweis auf diesen Brief schon bei Baruzi: 1907, 283): "J'ay soin de repondre aux raisons ou aux passages qui sont decisifs, et tiennent lieu de raisons. Mais j'avoue, que je ne m'arreste pas beaucoup ordinairement à quelque passage d'un Pere, quand il ne s'agit pas des faits de son temps; à moins que ce Pere n'allegue des bonnes preuves luy meme. On trouve une infinité de passages contraires entre eux, et outrés chez les Peres. Ainsi j'avoue de n'avoir point fait trop d'attention à ces deux passages de S. Augustin, que vous avés allegué, Monsieur; et dont vous me faites souvenir. Il est vray que je ne me souviens que d'un seul, n'ayant pas à la main vos lettres precedentes, qui dit qu'il faudroit estre insolent jusqu'à la fureur (insolentissimae insaniae est) pour s'opposer à toute l'Eglise. Cependant quelque forte que soit l'expression de ce Pere, je ne crois point qu'elle soit exacte. Quand toute l'Eglise se seroit soulevée ou se souleveroit contre Copernic ou Galilei, elle auroit tort. Un homme exact, qui fait des recherches avec soin est plus croyable que tout un monde d'ignorans ou de gens qui ne traitent que superficiellement des matieres difficiles. Et si quelqu'un repond que la question du systeme de Copernic n'est pas du ressort de l'Eglise, je repliqueray qu'une infinité d'autres questions qu'on veut faire decider à l'Eglise ne sont gueres moins philosophiques et de fait historiques, et par consequent non sujettes à de telles decisions où l'on puisse asseurer que l'Eglise soit privilegiée. S. Augustin estoit un grand homme sans doute[,] mais il se laissoit emporter bien

können, fragt er. An anderer Stelle weist Leibniz auf den Zirkelschluss hin, soweit es um die Autorität der Hl. Schrift und der Kirche geht:

> Woher wissen wir, dass wir der Kirche unser Vertrauen schenken müssen, wenn nicht aus der Hl. Schrift? Dass wir andererseits der Schrift zu glauben haben, sagt uns die Kirche – hier wird offenbar, dass wir uns in einem Zirkel bewegen.[62]

Augustinus verweist in *De utilitate* (c. 29) als Antwort hierauf: Es sei gemäß der Lehre der katholischen Kirche der Glaube, dessen alle, die sich der Religion annähern, zuvor überzeugt sein müssen. Leibniz jedoch glaubt diesen Zirkel auflösen zu können. Im *Dialogus inter Theologum et Misosophum* (1678/1679) hält ihm der Misosoph vor, dass wir [auch] ohne Logik gerettet werden können. Leibniz als Theologe stimmt ihm zunächst zu: Wir können ohne Vernunftgründe gerettet werden und können diese auch ohne Syllogismen anwenden (*ratiocinari*). Jedoch können wir bei sehr schwierigen Fragen die Wahrheit nicht so leicht herausbekommen oder einen, der sie hartnäckig bestreitet, ohne die Künste der Logik nicht überzeugen. Und etwas später formuliert er den von Augustinus beschriebenen Zirkel noch simpler: "Ich glaube, weil die Kirche glaubt, [und] die Kirche glaubt, weil ich glaube", um dann fortzufahren, notwendig sei es zusätzlich, die Kirche mit Hilfe fester Vernunftgründe zu "stabilisieren".[63] Das führt m. E. nun zum entscheidenden Differenzpunkt der theologischen Erkenntnislehre und Anthropologie, schließlich auch der Frage der Prädestination, also der Soteriologie, der hier noch kurz skizziert werden soll.

Für Leibniz bildet die Vernunft das Gott und den ihn nachahmenden Geistern gemeinsame Band. Gott vermag alles in vollkommenster Weise in seinem Verstand, d. h. ohne jede Erfahrung, "adäquat" zu erkennen, die vernunftbegabten Geister als seine Geschöpfe dagegen *vix ulla*, kaum etwas, *adaequate, pauca a priori*. Zu

---

souvent par la chaleur de la declamation ou de la dispute. Cependant les Protestans ne s'opposent point à toute l'Eglise, ainsi ce passage ne les regarde point. Au contraire on peut dire que Trente en decidant sur le Canon s'est opposé à toute l'Eglise ancienne"; A I,21 479f.

62 "At vero inquies unde scimus Ecclesiae esse fidendum, nisi hoc Scriptura doceret? Quod si vicissim scripturae credendum est, ob Ecclesiam, manifestum erit nos in circulum revolvi"; A IV,3 276; cf. hierzu detaillierter Rudolph (2008).

63 "Fateor nam possumus etiam salvari sine rationibus et possumus ratiocinari sine syllogismis: non tamen possumus fidei fundamenta tenere ac tueri sine rationibus; nec in rebus valde difficilibus facile eruere veritatem, aut convincere pertinacem adversarium, sine logicis artibus. [...]
M[isosophus]. Tutissimum est simpliciter credere, quod Ecclesia credit. Nosti historiolam illam Bellarmini de eo qui in agone cum diabolo disputabat.
T[heologus]. Jocaris opinor, nam historiola illa ridicula est. Nec puto te eodem quo ille circulo usurum: credo quod Ecclesia credit, et Ecclesia credit quod ego. Necesse est praeterea Ecclesiam stabilire firmis rationibus"; A VI,4C 2217 f.

diesem "wenigen" zählt bei näherem Zusehen doch sehr viel, nämlich die einer strengen Logik folgende Metaphysik oder natürliche Theologie, also das Wissen um Gott, um uns als von einem vollkommenen Wesen erschaffene mit Geist begabte Menschen, das Wissen um das Universum und sein Ziel. Dies alles und nicht zuletzt der Nachweis, dass die christlichen Mysterien vor dem Gerichtshof der Vernunft zwar nicht als wahrscheinlich, wohl aber als möglich beurteilt werden und dass diese Possibilia nicht widervernünftig, sondern übervernünftig (suprarational) sind,[64] verdanken ihre Erkenntnis einzig der Vernunft *a priori*.[65]

Grundlegend und eine *necessitas metaphysica*, d. h. *a priori* sich erschließend, ist für Leibniz das *unde malum* des antimanichäischen Augustinus,[66] auf das er sich immer und immer wieder bezieht.[67] Bei Augustinus ist das Böse die Folge der aus eigenem Hochmut getroffenen Willensentscheidung des ersten Menschen gegen Gott. Das Böse sei, so interpretiert Leibniz Augustinus, eine "privation de l'être",[68] dem Bösen kommt keine *realitas* zu, denn diese ist als Schöpfung des in höchstem Maße guten Gottes bei Augustinus wie bei Leibniz notwendigerweise gut. Das Böse ist vielmehr eine *privatio*, der Mangel an Gutem, aus dieser *privatio* erwächst die Sünde, die zur Ursache der weiteren Sünden und des Todes der Menschen und für Augustinus auch die Ursache für die *caligo mentis*, die Finsternis des menschlichen Geistes, geworden ist. Die schöpfungsmäßige Freiheit des Willens hat der Mensch durch die Sünde, wie Augustinus im *Enchiridion ad Laurentium* sagt, gegen die Freiheit eines Sklaven eintauschen müssen, er ist zum Untertanen

---

64 Cf. hierzu vor allem Gerhardt: 1875–1890, VI, 49–101.
65 "Quo modo omnia intelliguntur a Deo a priori et per modum aeternae veritatis, quia ipse experimento non indiget; et quidem ab illo omnia adaequate, a nobis vix ulla adaequate, pauca a priori, pleraque experimento cognoscuntur, in quibus postremis alia principia aliaque criteria sunt adhibenda. In rebus ergo facti sive contingentibus quae non a ratione sed observatione sive experimento pendent, primae veritates (quoad nos) sunt, quaecunque immediate intra nos percipimus seu quorum nobis de nobis conscii sumus, haec enim per alia experimenta nobis propiora magisque intrinseca probari impossibile est. Percipio autem intra me, non tantum me ipsum qui cogito, sed et multas in cogitationibus meis differentias, ex quibus alia praeter me esse colligo, et sensibus paulatim fidem concilio, Scepticisque occurro, nam in talibus, quae non sunt metaphysicae necessitatis, pro veritate habendus est nobis consensus phaenomenorum inter se, qui temere non fiet, sed causam habebit, certe nec somnium a vigilia, nisi hoc phaenomenorum consensu distinguimus, nec cras solem oriturum praedicimus, nisi quia toties fidem implevit. Huc facit magna vis autoritatis et testimonii publici, cum plures ad fallendum conspirare credibile non est, quibus addi possunt quae S. Augustinus De utilitate credendi dixit"; A VI,4 543f.
66 Augustinus, *Enchiridion ad Laurentium sive de fide, spe et caritate liber unus*, cap. 11 u. 23.
67 Cf. etwa A VI,4B, 1577; *Essais de théodicée*, § 29 und öfter, im 3. Teil, § 377 verweist Leibniz bei diesem Gedanken neben Augustinus schon auf Basilius von Caesaraea (gest. 379) und dessen *2. Homilie zum Hexaemeron*; Gerhardt: 1875–1890, VI, 119, 340 – cf. hierzu Rateau (2008) (grundlegend).
68 *Essais de théodicée*, 1. Teil, § 29.

der Sünde geworden.[69] Doch diese Sichtweise erfährt durch Leibniz schon in der Mainzer Zeit[70] und dann in den 40 Jahre später publizierten *Essais de théodicée* eine entscheidende Modifizierung – hier modifiziert Leibniz auch die augustinische Idee des Sünders, der lediglich die Freiheit eines Sklaven besitze: Zwar entsprechen unsere Leidenschaften den Fesseln und Zwängen eines Sklaven, und unsere Sinne vermitteln uns verworrene Gedanken, dagegen stehe aber die Möglichkeit klarer Erkenntnis:

> Unsere Erkenntnis ist zweifacher Natur [. . .]. Die klare, deutliche Erkenntnis oder die Intelligenz findet im wahren Vernunftgebrauch statt; die Sinne aber liefern uns nur verworrene, konfuse Gedanken. Und wie wir sagen können, sind wir so weit der Sklaverei enthoben, wie wir aus klarer Erkenntnis heraus handeln. Aber wir sind den Leidenschaften unterworfen, und in so weit sind unsere Wahrnehmungen konfus.

In diesem Sinne, dass wir nicht über die völlige Freiheit des Geistes verfügen, wie sie wünschenswert wäre, kann Leibniz dann mit Augustinus sagen, "wir seien der Sünde unterworfen und verfügen über die Freiheit eines Sklaven". Gleichwohl hört ein Sklave, "ganz Sklave, der er ist", keinesfalls auf, dem Zustand entsprechend, in dem er sich befindet, über die Wahlfreiheit zu verfügen, auch wenn er sich meistens der harten Notwendigkeit ausgesetzt sieht, nur zwischen zwei Übeln wählen zu können, weil eine höhere Gewalt ihn nicht zu den Gütern gelangen lässt, die er anstrebt. Es sind diese Bindungen und Zwänge, die aus uns Sklaven machen, und das geschieht durch die Leidenschaften, deren Macht süß, aber darum nicht weniger verderblich ist. Dennoch hindert uns unser Sklavenzustand trotz aller seiner Einschränkungen nicht daran, eine freie Wahl dessen zu treffen, was uns unserem Vermögen und unseren Erkenntnissen gemäß als das uns Gefälligere erscheint. Die äußeren Eindrücke bringen uns häufig davon ab, aus einer Spontaneität heraus zu handeln, deren wir teilhaftig sind, soweit es um das Prinzip unserer Handlungen geht, das in uns selbst ist, unbeeinflusst von allen äußeren Eindrücken. Dies darzulegen, gesteht Leibniz, könne nicht mit alltags- und umgangssprachlichen Mitteln gelingen, ohne der Wahrheit Gewalt anzutun, es bedürfe vielmehr der "rigeur philosophique", und das bedeutet in diesem Fall seiner Kritik an Augustinus wiederum, wie schon auf dem ganz anderen Feld der Sakramentstheologie,[71] den Rückgriff auf die Metaphysik, genauer gesagt, die Substanzmetaphysik. Wir teilen die Spontaneität als Voraussetzung eines freien Willens mit der Wahlmöglichkeit zum Guten mit allen einfachen intelligenten Substanzen. In seiner Metaphysik hat

---

69 *Enchiridion ad Laurentium*, cap. 103.
70 Leibniz im Mai 1671 an Magnus Wedderkopf; A II,1² 186.
71 s. oben, Anm. 50.

Leibniz die Beziehung der Substanzen untereinander, zu Gott und dem Universum sowie zwischen der Seele und dem durch die Substanz repräsentierten Körper auf exakte Weise erläutert.[72] Aus dem, was Leibniz in einer Vielzahl von Schriften und Briefen über die Jahrzehnte und auch an dieser Stelle der Theodizee *cum rigore metaphysico* entwickelt hat, zieht er im Blick auf die Spontaneität des Individuums den Schluss, "dass die Seele in sich selbst eine vollkommene Spontaneität besitzt der Art, dass sie in ihren Handlungen nur von Gott und von sich selbst abhängig ist".[73] So hat der Mensch durch die Sünde auch nicht die Freiheit des Willens zum Guten verloren und ist in der Lage, sich aus den Fesseln der Sklaverei zu lösen.

Für Leibniz ist das *malum* folgerichtig auch kein gottwidriger Einbruch in Gottes gute Schöpfung, kein gottwidriger Akt eines sich hochmütig gegen Gott auflehnenden Geschöpfs, sondern eine *necessitas metaphysica*. Nicht Adams Sündenfall ist für ihn die Ursache, sondern die Unvollkommenheit der Schöpfung gewissermaßen als ein metaphysisches Übel. Wäre die Schöpfung vollkommen, würde sie ja in derselben Weise wie Gott zu definieren sein, der alles, das Vernünftige, Gute und das Gerechte, in vollkommenster Weise ist. Aber Gott hat aus der unendlichen Zahl möglibler Welten, die als Ideen in seinem Verstand waren, diejenige ausgewählt, von der er "voraussah, dass ihre Existenz am meisten seiner Weisheit entsprechen" werde,[74] und das heißt, dass sie den höchstmöglichen Grad an Vollkommenheit bzw. den niedrigstmöglichen Grad an Unvollkommenheit haben werde. Zu dieser besten aller möglichen Welten gehören auch Adam und Judas, die in freier Willensentscheidung handeln werden. Das Üble ihrer Handlungen gehört zur universellen

---

72 *Essais de théodicée,* § 289ff.; Gerhardt: 1875–1890, VI, 288ff. – Aus der uferlosen Literatur zu diesem Thema sei hier nur auf neuere Beiträge von Mugnai (2018a); (2018b); Schepers (2017) und Poser: 2016, 149–159, 174–201 und 218–227 hingewiesen.
73 "Nostre connoissance est de deux sortes, distincte, ou confuse. La connoissance distincte ou l'intelligence a lieu dans le veritable usage de la Raison; mais les sens nous fournissent des pensées confuses. Et nous pouvons dire que nous sommes exemts d'esclavage, entant que nous agissons avec une connoissance distincte; mais que nous sommes asservis aux passions, entant que nos perceptions sont confuses. C'est dans ce sens que nous n'avons pas toute la liberté d'esprit qui seroit à souhaiter, et que nous pouvons dire avec S. Augustin, qu'étant assujettis au peché, nous avons la liberté d'un esclave. il faut savoir, qu'une spontaneité exacte nous est commune avec toutes les substances simples, et que dans la substance intelligente ou libre, elle devient un Empire sur ses actions. Ce qui ne peut être mieux expliqué, que par le systeme de l'harmonie préetablie [...] J'y fais voir, que naturellement chaque substance simple a de la perception, et que son individualité consiste naturellement les unes des autres, pour representer le corps qui luy est assigné, et par son moyen l'univers entier, suivant le point de veue propre à cette substance simple, sans qu'elle ait besoin de recevoir aucune influence physique du corps: comme le corps aussi de son côté s'accommode aux volontés de l'ame par ses propres loix, et par consequent ne luy obeit, qu'autant que ces loix le portent. D'où il s'ensuit, que l'ame a donc en elle même une parfaite spontaneité, en sorte qu'elle ne depend que de Dieu et d'elle même dans ses actions." (*Essais de théodicée,* §§ 289ff.; Gerhardt: 1875–1890, VI, 288ff.).
74 Gerhardt: 1875–1890, IV, 476 [1695], siehe hierzu Schepers: 2017, 11f. (Übersetzung ebenda).

Harmonie, denn "Nulla enim nisi ex contrariis harmonia est", eine Harmonie entsteht aus Gegensätzlichem.[75] Insofern kann er die Sünden einmal sogar zu den Gütern zählen, weil sie als Sünde dank ihrer Tilgung Teil der Harmonie sei.[76]

Als Schöpfung Gottes muss sich das Universum immer stärker der Vervollkommnung annähern, was die Güte, die Gerechtigkeit und den Gebrauch der Vernunft betrifft. Gott hasst deshalb die Sünde, er will das Heil für jeden Menschen. Und in dem Maße, wie der einzelne Mensch nach der klaren Erkenntnis der Vernunft handelt, wird er keine Sünde begehen, sondern ohne Nötigung dem Motiv des Guten folgen, das der Verstand erkennt.[77] Dies gilt für Gott wie für die von ihm in die Existenz gerufenen Geister, als die mit Vernunft begabten individuellen Substanzen, die unter seiner Monarchie die *civitas dei* bilden und an der Vervollkommnung der Welt mitwirken. Entsprechend wortkarg bleibt Leibniz' Theologie hinsichtlich des Erlösungswerkes Christi durch den Tod am Kreuz.

Es widerspricht dieser Metaphysik, dass Gott in freier Willensentscheidung gegen die Vernunft handeln könnte, gewissermaßen als Tyrann. Entsprechend lehnt Leibniz das auf Gottes freien Ratschluss bezogene Motto der Voluntaristen ab, "stat voluntas pro ratione",[78] das den Partikularisten eine Begründung für die Lehre der doppelten Prädestination liefern sollte. Unter der Voraussetzung einer solchen Ablehnung kann er Augustinus zustimmen, alles sei auf die reine Gnade zurückzuführen.[79] Aber deshalb hält Leibniz in seinem ökumenischen Argument auch den Gedanken für widervernünftig, Gott wähle unter den Menschen welche aus zur Verdammnis. Und deshalb lehnt er entschieden Augustins Lehre der Verdammnis der ungetauften Kinder ab, aber auch solcher, die wegen ihres Alters oder wegen geistigen Unvermögens nicht des Vernunftgebrauchs mächtig waren. Diese Lehre werde weder von der Vernunft noch von der Hl. Schrift ausreichend gestützt, sie sei vielmehr von "erschreckender Grausamkeit".[80] Die Unbegreiflichkeit seiner Gerichte und das Unerforschliche der Wege Gottes (Rö 11:33) gründen nicht in göttlicher Willkür, sondern in der uns als Geschöpfen eigenen Unvollkommenheit in der Erkenntnis der specialia der universellen Harmonie, welche Paulus mit dem βάθος πλούτου καὶ σοφίας καὶ γνώσεως θεοῦ in Rö 11:33 gerühmt habe, während

---

75 wie Anm. 70.
76 Zu Leibniz' Deutung des *peccatum originale* cf. Rudolph: 2017, 538ff.
77 *Essais de théodicée*, § 288; Gerhardt: 1875–1890, VI, 288.
78 Cf. Leibniz am 1. April 1696 an Detlev Markus Friese; A I,12 N. 346a.
79 Augustinus, *De dono perseverantiae*, c. 14, § 35.
80 *Essais de théodicée*, §§ 92ff.; Gerhardt: 1875–1890, VI, 153f. Leibniz' Widersprüche zu Augustinus waren im Wesentlichen bereits 1866 von Nourisson (1866, 269ff) aufgezählt worden.

wir um die generalia jener Harmonie dank unserer Vernunft sehr wohl wissen können.[81]

Leider konnte im Rahmen eines solchen Beitrags dies alles nicht mehr dem ökumenischen Diskurs im einzelnen zugeordnet werden. Aus dem hier Skizzierten mag man jedoch ungefähr ermessen, welche Position Leibniz gegenüber dem Jansenismus, gegenüber den Jesuiten, gegenüber den Reformierten der unterschiedlichen Lager, aber auch gegenüber großen Geistern seiner Zeit, vor allem John Locke und Thomas Hobbes, eingenommen haben muss.

Quellen und Literatur

ANTOGNAZZA, MARIA ROSA (2009), Leibniz: An Intellectual Biography, Cambridge: Cambridge University Press.

BACKUS, IRENA (2016), Leibniz: Protestant Theologian, Oxford: Oxford University Press.

BARUZI, JEAN (1907), Leibniz et l'organisation religieuse de la terre d'après des documents inédits, Paris: F. Alcan.

BENZ, ERNST (1949–1950), Leibniz und die Wiedervereinigung der christlichen Kirchen, in: Zeitschrift für Religions- und Geistesgeschichte, 2. Jg., 97–113.

BUSCHE, HUBERTUS (2003), Gottfried Wilhelm Leibniz, Frühe Schriften zum Naturrecht, Hamburg: Meiner.

DENZINGER, HEINRICH / SCHÖNMETZER, ADOLF S.J. (ed.) (1965): Echiridion symbolorum, definitionum et declarationum de rebus fidei et morum, editio XXXIII, Freiburg/Br.: Herder.

DINGEL, IRENE (ed.) (1982), Die Bekenntnisschriften der evangelisch-lutherischen Kirche, Göttingen: Vandenhoeck & Ruprecht.

---

81 "Ainsi il faut tenir pour asseuré qu'il y a des raisons qui ont porté Dieu à dispenser ses graces de telle façon qu'elles ont eu un plein effect dans les uns, et non pas dans les autres. Mais ces raisons ne doivent point estre cherchées dans nos bonnes qualités (soit foy ou oeuvres) qui sont elles mêmes des presens de Dieu, mais dans l'harmonie de l'univers ou dans cette altitudo divitiarum, dont parle S. Paul. Il suffit que nous sçachions en general que Dieu choisit le meilleur, conformement à ce que demande la perfection de l'univers; bien que le détail nous soit incomprehensible dans cette vie"; A I,12 N. 346. – Ähnlich an anderer Stelle: "Es sind demnach rationes die gott bewegen einem seine gnaden auff solche weise zu geben, daß sie nicht ermanglen bey ihm anzuschlagen dem andern aber nicht also. Aber die rationes muß man nicht in unsern guthen qvalitäten suchen (es sey gleich fides oder merita) als welche selbst gaben gottes, sondern in harmonia universi, oder altitudine divitiarum davon Paulus redet. Und ist gnug daß wir in genere wißen gott habe das beste erwehlet, so die perfectio universi erfordert, ob schohn specialia davon zu begreiffen in diesem leben ohnmüglich"; Leibniz am 1. April 1696 an Detlev Markus Friese; A I,12 536f.

EISENKOPF, PAUL (1975), Leibniz und die Einigung der Christenheit, Überlegungen zur Reunion der evangelischen und katholischen Kirche, Beiträge zur ökumenischen Theologie 11, München/Paderborn/Wien: Ferdinand Schöningh.

GERHARDT, CARL IMMANUEL (ed.) (1875–1890), Leibniz, Gottfried Wilhelm, Die philosophischen Schriften, vol. 1–7, Berlin: Weidmann [Neudr. Hildesheim 1960–1961].

HENRICI, PIERRE, S.J. (1968), Herméneutique, oecuménisme et religion, Le cas Leibniz, in: L'Herméneutique de la Liberté Religieuse. Actes du colloque organisé par le Centre international d'Etudes Humanistes et par l'Institut d'Etudes Philosophiques de Rome, Rome, 7–12 Janvier, 553–561.

HUGON, JOSEPH (1921), Concept leibnizien de la liberté et théodicée augustinienne, Recherches de schiences religieuses 11, 380–383.

JORDAN, GEORGE JEFFERIS (1927), The reunion of the churches, A study of G. W. Leibnitz and his great attempt, London: Constable & Co.

LEIBNIZ, GOTTFRIED WILHELM (1923), Sämtliche Schriften und Briefe, Darmstadt/Berlin: O. Reichl.

LI, WENCHAO (2012), "Le point de ps. 10.14.21.32.", – Leibnizens Projekt eines Weltkonzils unter Peter dem Großen, in: Wenchao Li/Hans Poser/Hartmut Rudolph (ed.), Leibniz und die Ökumene, Studia Leibnitiana, Sonderhefte 41, Stuttgart: Franz Steiner Verlag, 87–94.

LINK, CHRISTIAN (2017), Leibniz' Auseinandersetzung mit der reformierten Konfession, in: Wenchao Li/Hartmut Rudolph (ed.), Leibniz im Lichte der Theologien, Studia Leibnitiana, Supplementa 40, Stuttgart: Franz Steiner Verlag, 209–226.

MARTIN BUCER (1536) Metaphrases et enarrationes perpetuae Epistolarum D. Pauli Apostoli. Tomus primus, Continens metaphrasim et enarrationem in Epistolam ad Romanos [= Römerbrief-Kommentar], Straßburg: Wendelin Rihel.

MUGNAI, MASSIMO (2018a), Essences, Ideas, and Truths in God's Mind and in the Human Mind, in: Maria Rosa Antognazza (ed.), The Oxford Handbook of Leibniz, New York: Oxford University Press, 11–26.

MUGNAI, MASSIMO (2018b), Theory of Relations and Universal Harmony, in: Maria Rosa Antognazza (ed.), The Oxford Handbook of Leibniz, New York: Oxford University Press, 27–44.

POSER, HANS (2016), Leibniz' Philosophie, Über die Einheit von Metaphysik und Wissenschaft, Wenchao Li (ed.), Hamburg: Meiner.

NOURRISSON, JEAN-FÉLIX (1866), La philosophie de Saint-Augustin 2, Paris : Didier et cie., (Nachdruck Minerva 1968).

PICHLER, ALOYS (1869–1870), Die Theologie des Leibniz aus sämtlichen gedruckten und vielen noch ungedruckten Quellen, 2 vol., München (Nachdruck Hildesheim: Verlag Georg Olms, 1965).

POLLET, JACQUES V. (1962), Martin Bucer: Etudes sur la correspondance avec de nombreux textes inédits 2, Paris: Presses Universitaires de Frances.

Rateau, Paul (2008), La question du mal chez Leibniz. Fondements et élaboration de la Théodicée, Paris: Honore Champion.

Riley, Patrick (1996), Leibniz's Universal Jurisprudence: Justice as the Charity of the Wise. Cambridge/MA: Harvard University Press.

Riley, Patrick (2014), Leibniz' "Monadologie" 1714-2014, in: Leibniz Review 24, 1-27.

Riley, Patrick (2017), Leibniz' Monadologie als Theorie der Gerechtigkeit, Hefte der Leibniz-Stiftungsprofessur 30, Hannover: Wehrhahn Verlag.

Rols, Jan (2017), Leibniz und der lutherisch-reformierte Prädestinationsstreit, in: Li, Wenchao/Rudolph, Hartmut (ed), Leibniz im Lichte der Theologien, Studia Leibnitiana, Supplementa 40, Stuttgart: Franz Steiner Verlag, 185-208.

Rudolph, Hartmut (1999a), Kirchenbegriff und päpstlicher Primat bei Leibniz, in: Herbert Breger/Friedrich Niewöhner (ed.), Leibniz und Niedersachsen, Studia Leibnitiana, Sonderheft 28, Stuttgart: Franz Steiner Verlag, 76-86.

Rudolph, Hartmut (1999b), Zum Nutzen von Politik und Philosophie für die Kirchenunion. Die Aufnahme der innerprotestantischen Ausgleichsverhandlungen am Ende des 17. Jahrhunderts, in: Martin Fontius/Hartmut Rudolph/Gary Smith (ed.): Labora diligenter, Studia Leibnitiana, Sonderheft 29, Stuttgart: Franz Steiner Verlag, 108-166.

Rudolph, Hartmut (2008), The Authority of the Bible and the Authority of Reason in Leibniz's Ecumenical Argument, in: Marcelo Dascal (ed.): Leibniz: What Kind of Rationalist?, Logic, Epistemology, and the Unity of Science 13, Leiden: Springer, 441-447.

Rudolph, Hartmut (2009), "Je suis du sentiment de S. Augustin ... ", Leibniz' (1646-1716) Nähe und Distanz zu Augustinus, in: Norbert Fischer (ed.), Augustinus, Spuren und Spiegelungen seines Denkens, Vol. 2: Von Descartes bis in die Gegenwart, Hamburg: Meiner, 59-87.

Rudolph, Hartmut (2017), Leibniz's References to St. Paul, in: Maria-Cristina Pitassi/Daniela Solfaroli Camillocci/Arthur Huiban (ed.), Crossing Traditions, Essays on the Reformation and Intellectual History, In Honour of Irena Backus, Studies in Medieval and Reformation Traditions 212, Leiden: Brill, 532-550.

Rudolph, Hartmut (2019), Liebe und Vernunft, Gottfried Wilhelm Leibniz' Weg zur Wiedervereinigung der Kirchen, in: Wichmann-Jahrbuch des Diözesangeschichtsvereins Berlin, NF 15. 58.-59. Jg., 95-112.

Schepers, Heinrich (1999), Einleitung, in: A VI,4, Berlin, XLV-XCI.

Schepers, Heinrich (2011), Demonstrationes Catholicae – Leibniz' großer Plan, Ein rationales Friedensprojekt für Europa, in: Friedrich Beiderbeck/Stephan Waldhoff (ed.), Pluralität der Perspektiven und Einheit der Wahrheit im Werk von G. W. Leibniz, Beiträge zu seinem philosophischen, theologischen und politischen Denken, Berlin: Akademie Verlag, 3-14.

Schepers, Heinrich (2017), Iter rationis. Reise der Vernunft in Leibniz' Welt der Monaden, in: Studia Leibnitiana 49 Heft 1, Wiesbaden: Franz Steiner Verlag, 2-27.

Schindler, Alfred (1979), Artikel Augustin, in: Theologische Realenzyklopädie 4, Berlin/New York: De Gruyter, 645-698.

SCHMIDT, MARTIN (1963), Die ökumenische Bewegung auf dem europäischen Festlande im 17. und 18. Jahrhundert, in: Ruth Rouse/Stephen Charles Neill (ed.), Geschichte der ökumenischen Bewegung 1517–1948, Vol. 1, Göttingen: Vandenhoeck & Ruprecht, 100–166; über Leibniz 128–132 und 152–158 (zuvor schon in Englisch: Dieselben [ed.], A History of the Ecumenical Movement 1517–1948, London 73–120.

TREPTE, ADOLF (1889), Die metaphysische Unvollkommenheit der Creatur und das moralische Uebel bei Augustin und Leibniz, Halle a/S: Gundlach & Eggers.

UTERMÖHLEN, GERDA (1995), Die irenische Politik der Welfenhöfe und Leibniz' Schlichtungsversuch der Kontroverse um den päpstlichen Primat, in: Dieter Breuer (ed.), Religion und Religiosität im Zeitalter des Barock, vol. I, Wolfenbütteler Arbeiten zur Barockforschung 25, Wiesbaden: Harrassowitz, 191–200.

WERLING, HANS FRIEDRICH (1977), Die weltanschaulichen Grundlagen der Reunionsbemühungen von Leibniz im Briefwechsel mit Bossuet und Pellisson, Europäische Hochschulschriften reihe 20, vol. 30, Frankfurt a. M./Bern/Las Vegas: Peter Lang AG, Internationaler Verlag der Wissenschaften.

Register

Personenregister

A

Abbott, George 142
Acquaviva, Claudio 200, 203
Adam 33, 65, 68, 154, 164, 165, 178, 180, 192, 265
Aeclanum, Julian of 155, 170
Alber, Matthaeus 80
Ambrose, s. a. Ambrosius 48, 49, 52, 107, 141, 162
Amerbach, Johann, s. a. Amerbach, Johannes 10, 15, 31, 45, 49, 78, 79, 91, 98
Anselm 63, 69
Aquin, Thomas v., s. a. Aquinas, Thomas 44, 61, 66, 99, 110, 139, 147, 159, 174, 175, 183, 192, 201, 203, 204, 224
Aristoteles, s. a. Aristotle 25, 29–31, 217, 218, 224, 227, 228, 241, 258
Arminius 142
Atreus 67

B

Bachmann, Claus 61, 67
Backus, Irena 34
Baius, Michael 189, 194–198, 200, 201, 206, 209
Bañez, Thomas 201, 202, 204
Basilius von Caesaraea 263
Bavinck, Herman 122
Baxter, Timothy 233
Bellarmine, s. a. Bellarmino, Roberto, Bellarminus 137, 140, 198, 200, 203
Benedikt von Nursia, s. a. Benedictum 11
Berkhof 127

Bernaerts, Johann, s. a. Bernartius 196
Bernhardi, Bartholäus, s. a. Bernhardi v. Feldkirch, Bartholomäus 30, 45
Bertano, Pietro, s. a. Bertani 160
Beza, Theodore 139, 142, 147, 201
Biel, Gabriel 29
Biest, Jarrik van der 190
Billick, Eberhard 107
Billikan, Theobald 90
Boineburg, Johann Christian v. 249
Bonaventura 29, 67
Bonifatius 103
Bossuet, Jacques-Bénigne 247, 256
Bradwardine, Thomas 16, 17, 25
Brakel, Theodorus à 145
Brenz, Johannes 83, 84
Brutus 66
Bucer, Martin 97–111, 169, 251, 257, 258
Buckwalter, Stephen 98
Bullinger 124
Burnett, Thomas 258

C

Calixt, Georg 257, 258
Calvin, Johannes, s. a. Calvin, John 61, 62, 115, 119, 121–130, 135, 136, 138, 142, 146–148, 169, 200, 201
Catalina 67
Catharinus, Ambrosius 173
Cato 66
Cervini 164, 166, 171, 176
Ceyssens, Lucien 189
Chrysostom, Chrysostomus 53, 98, 105, 107, 135

Cicero   145, 183
Clairvaux, Bernard v., s. a. Bernhard, Bernardum, St. Bernardus   11, 49, 52, 139, 147
Coccejus, Johannes   143
Contarini   169
Cortesi   159
Coste, Pierre   252
Cranmer   124
Crell, Johannes   225–227, 229, 238, 239
Cruz, Antonio de la, s. a. de Cruce   173, 175
Cyprian   49, 98, 107, 127, 141, 154, 162
Cyril, s. a. Cyrillus   89, 127, 162

D

Daňhelka, Jiří   20
Dardanus   81, 88
David   65
De Ionge, Dirck Vlack   146, 147
De Nobili   164
De Pape, Corneille   206
Del Monte   170, 171
Delumeau, Jean   241
Dienst, Tobias   97
Donatus   116
Driedo, Johannes   190, 192, 194
Du Bois, Nicolas   207

E

Eck, Johann, s. a. Eck, Johannes   16, 20, 21, 43, 51–54, 56, 62
Eco, Umberto   232
Eijl, Edmond v.   189
Eisenkopf, Paul   256
Erasmus v. Rotterdam   27, 49, 56, 71, 79, 80, 91, 99, 100, 110, 190, 251
Est, Willem Hessels v., s. a. Estius, Willem   200, 203–205
Evangelista v. 's Hertogenbosch, Johannes   207

Evodius   81
Exalto, John   144

F

Farel   124
Fenacolius, Johannes Lenaertsz   146
Fénelon   251
Filhol   168
Fonseca, Juan   173, 174, 176
Fraenkel, Peter   72, 73
Franceschi, Sylvio Hermann de   207
Frangipani, Ottavio Mirto   200
Frederick the Wise   53
Friedrich, Johann   104, 250
Friese, Detlev Markus   266, 267
Froben, Johann, s. a. Froben, Johannes   33, 79, 91, 98, 141
Fromondus, Libertus   207
Fulgentius v. Ruspe   15, 87, 88, 106

G

Galeazzo, Florimonte   173
Gennadius   165, 166
Gennep, Jaspar v.   107
Gerace, Antonio   190
Gerson, Jean   13, 18
Giacomelli   164
Gielis, Marcel   189
Gomarus, Francis   142
Goudriaan, Aza   142, 143
Gozaeus, Thomas   197
Graevius, Johann Georg   247
Gratian   11, 45, 79, 88
Gravius, Henricus   197, 198
Graybill, Gregory   70
Gregor von Rimini   16, 21, 25
Gregory the Great   49
Greving, Joseph   51
Gropper, Johannes   97, 100, 103, 104, 107–111, 169
Grundmann, Hannegreth   35, 191

H

Haar, J. van der 146
Hamelius, Johannes 197, 201, 203
Hamm, Berndt 26
Hansen, Friedrich Adolf 247
Heidegger, Martin 228, 241
Henrich of Ghent 44
Herder, Adriaan de 146
Herodot 66
Hessels, Johannes 196
Hessen-Rheinfels, Ernst v. 250
Hieronymus, s. a. Jerome 15, 26, 33, 34, 48, 49, 53, 54, 61, 105, 107, 141, 162, 247
Hilary 89
Hobbes, Thomas 267
Hof, Willem J. op 't 144
Hoornbeeck, Johannes 145
Huber, Samuel 139, 140
Hus, Jan, s. a. Hus, Johannes 9–22
Huygens, Gommarus 208

I

Ignatius 127

J

Jablonski, Daniel Ernst 256, 258
James 177, 180
Jansenius, Cornelius, s. a. Ypern, v. 189, 196, 204–207, 209
Jansonius, Jacobus 198, 204
Januarius 83, 86, 88
Jedin, Hubert 175
John 80
Jung, Martin H. 70
Junghans, Helmar 15

K

Kain 65, 67
Karlstadt, Andreas, s. a. Bodenstein v. Karlstadt, Andreas 16, 22, 27, 30–32, 43–57
Kaufmann, Thomas 43
Kimmedoncius, Jacob 138
Klug, Joseph 64
Köhler, Walter 33
König Philipps II 201
Königin Elisabeth, s. a. Queen Elisabeth of England 201
Kruse, Jens-Martin 31

L

Lamberigts, Mathijs 189
Lang, Johannes 30, 31, 45, 47
Latomus, Jacob, s. a. Latomus, Jacobus 35–38, 189–192, 209
Lehr Evans, Alyssa 43
Leibniz 247–267
Lejay, Claude 160, 161
Lens, Jean de, s. a. Lensaeus, Johannes 197
Leo I 162
Lessius, Leonard, s. a. Lessius, Leonardus 189, 194, 197–203, 205, 208, 209
Leydecker, Melchior 143, 144
Lippomani 168, 175
Lipsius, Justus 240
Locke, John 267
Loewenich, Walter v. 25
Lombard, Peter, s. a. Lombardus, Peter, Lombardus, Petrus 14, 33, 44, 45, 79, 85, 88, 99, 137, 192, 201–203
Ludwig XIV 247
Lupinus, Petrus 48
Lupus, Christian 208
Luther, Martin 10, 13–15, 17–22, 26–33, 35–38, 44–48, 51, 61, 64, 72, 86–89, 99, 101, 102, 104, 111, 126, 138–140, 145, 146, 153, 155–157, 160, 169, 172, 174, 179, 180, 182, 189–192, 225, 233

M

Madame de Brinon 253
Markschies, Christoph 38
Masenius, James 143

Massarelli 171, 184
Matthias, Markus 31
Maurer, Wilhelm 72
Medea 67
Melanchton, Phillip 153, 155, 158, 160
Molanus, Johannes 197, 258
Molina, Luis de 201, 202, 205, 208
Molinos 251
Monetarius, Thomas 66
Monica 169
Musculus, Wolfgang 103, 139
Musso, Cornelio 160, 164, 171, 173, 176

N
Navarra, Andrès de 171
Noordmans 127

O
Obermans, Heiko A. 12
Ockham, Wilhelm v. 25
Oecolampadius, Johannes 78, 79, 81–87, 89–91
Oort, Johannes v. 141
Orcibal, Jean 189, 196
Origenes 33, 61, 63, 68, 69
Osiander, Andreas 61, 65, 67–69, 73

P
Páleč, Stephan 16
Papst Alexander VII 207
Papst Alexander VIII 208
Papst Clemens VIII 201
Papst Gregor XIII 196
Papst Innozenz X 207
Papst Paul III 158, 169
Papst Paul V 202
Papst Pius V 196
Papst Urban VIII 202, 206
Pasquali 159
Paulus, s. a. Paul 18, 28, 61–65, 69, 71, 100, 175–177, 181, 195, 197, 233, 257, 266

Pelagius 15, 107, 117, 155
Pellisson-Fontanier, Paul 247
Perez, Jacobus 169
Petri, Johannes 98
Petrus 21
Pflug 169
Philipp of Hesse 88
Philo of Alexandria 234
Pico della Mirandola, Giovanni 44
Pinsson, François 248
Pirckheimer, Willibald 78, 83–86, 90, 91
Pisecki, Thomas 235
Pitiscus, Bartholomew 136
Plantin, Christoph 197
Plato 217–219, 222, 224, 225, 229, 230, 232, 233, 236, 237, 239–241
Pole 157, 171
Pompeius 66
Pomponazzi, Pietro 261
Przypkowski, Samuel 218, 221, 222, 224, 232, 233, 235, 240
Pseudo-Augustinus, s. a. Pseudo-Augustine 146, 260
Pseudo-Dionysius 63

R
Rai, Eleonora 190
Ravesteijn, Josse, s. a. Tiletanus 196
Raynolds, Johannes, s. a. Reinoldus, Johannes 142
Rennecherus, Herman 138, 139
Reuschenberg, Johann Sigismund Wilhelm 261
Rhagus, Johannes 48
Ridderus, Francis 146
Roegiers, Jan 189, 209
Roverella 168

S
Sadolet 125, 126
Saldenus, Guiljelmus 145

Salmeron, Alfonso   158, 159, 184
Salomo   71
Samosata, Paul von   68
Sanfelice, Tommasso   161, 162, 164
Saraceni   159, 160
Sasbout, Adam   192
Schepers, Heinrich   250
Schindler, Alfred   32, 33
Schlichting, Jonas   234, 235, 240
Schönborn, Johann Philipp v.   249
Scipio   66
Scotus   66, 183
Scultetus, Abraham   97, 136–138
Seneca   145
Seripando, Girolamo   157, 162–177, 181, 183, 184, 192
Servetus, Michael   219
Sinnich, John   206
Smytegelt, Bernardus   144
Sohn, Georg   138, 139
Spalatin   26, 47
Spener, Philipp Jakob   252
Spitzel, Gottlieb   247
Staphorstius, Caspar   146
Stapleton, Thomas   201, 203
Staupitz, Johann v.   27, 28, 30, 31, 45, 47, 48
Stegmann, Christopher   229, 230
Stegmann, Joachim   223, 238
Stein, Gertrude   222
Steyaert, Martin   208

T
Tapper, Ruard   192, 194, 196, 197, 209
Teellinck, Willem   144
Tertullian   80
Thyestes   67
Timotheus   257
Tossanus, Daniel   136, 138, 139

Treger, Konrad   99, 100
Trigland, Jacobus   142
Truchsess von Waldbourg   160

U
Udemans, Godfrey   145, 146

V
Vanneste, Alfred   194
Vauchop   164
Venatorius, Thomas   85
Vianen, Francis v.   208
Victor of Cartenna   182
Vigerio della Rovere   159, 168
Vind, Anna   38, 191, 192
Vio Cajetanus, Thomas de   157
Visser, Arnoud   78
Voetius, Gisbertus   141–143
Völkel, Johannes   238
Vooght, Paul de   9

W
Wedderkopf, Magnus   264
Wegener, Lydia   28
Wengert, Timothy   72
Westphal, Joachim   126
Wied, Hermann v.   104, 106
Wiszowaty, Andrzej   222, 223
Wtenbogaert   142
Wyclif, John   10, 13, 16, 17, 61

Z
Zannettini, Dionisio de   161, 162
Zegers, Nicholas Tacitus   192
Zenobius   224
Znaim, Stanislaus v.   16
Zwingli, Huldrych   32–34, 78–84, 87, 90, 101, 102

Sachregister

A
Abendmahl, s. a. Last Supper, Lord's Supper 77, 79-81, 88, 89, 100-102, 124, 137
Abendmahlslehre 100, 101, 109, 111
Alten Kirche, s. a. Early Church 11, 77, 99, 105, 106, 109, 123, 126-128, 130, 136, 137, 143, 147
Anrufung der Heiligen, s. a. cult of saints, Heiligenverehrung 50, 105, 109
Anthropologie 25, 32, 35, 66, 67, 262
Antitrinitarianism 218, 219, 223, 232, 235, 240
Aristotelianism 87, 217, 222, 227-230, 238, 241
Auferstehung Christi, s. a. resurrection of Christ 70, 128, 163, 195, 249
Augustinismus, s. a. Augustinianism 11, 14-16, 27-29, 32, 35, 135, 192, 206, 209

B
Baianismus 189, 209
Barmherzigkeit Gottes, s. a. mercy of God 36, 48, 62, 65, 68, 141, 156, 159-161, 163, 164, 166, 170, 172-174, 176, 179, 183
Bibel, s. a. Bible 11, 25, 30, 48, 50, 53-56, 110, 138, 140, 143-146, 163, 195, 219, 223, 233
Body of Christ 80-90, 118, 119, 122, 123, 125, 128, 129, 180
Buchdruck 10, 11, 97
Buße, s. a. penance 35, 66, 182

C
Calvinists 138, 140
Christentum, s. a. Christenheit, Christianity 19, 97, 106, 107, 116, 218, 219, 240, 248, 249, 256
Christologie, s. a. christology 68, 137, 240
Council of Nicea 136

Council of Orange 157, 160, 161, 165, 181
Creed 117, 118, 121-123, 127

D
Donatismus, s. a. Donatism 18, 116
Donatisten, s. a. Donatists 18, 107, 115-117, 119, 120, 129, 130, 154, 184, 197

E
Ekklesiologie, s. a. ecclesiology 70, 128-130, 154
Erastianismus 103
Erbsünde, s. a. original sin 36, 64, 66, 69, 157, 178, 191-193, 197, 217, 241
Errettung, s. a. Erlösung, salvation 63, 68, 70, 118, 119, 123, 139, 146, 154-156, 160, 163, 164, 171, 172, 175, 177, 178, 180, 182, 190-192, 200, 218, 234, 241, 266
Erwählung, s. a. election 64, 70, 120-124, 128-130, 139, 199, 202, 254, 259
Eucharistic controversy 77, 79, 89-91
Eucharistie, s. a. Eucharist 78, 79, 81, 82, 88-90, 249, 259
Ewig Leben, s. a. eternal life 66, 68, 69, 101, 117, 121, 123, 155, 164, 172, 173, 176, 179, 180, 183, 194, 198, 202
Exegese, s.a exegesis 56, 71, 82, 123, 125, 135

F
Fall der Sünde, s. a. fall of Adam 65, 66, 68, 69, 154, 164, 165, 178, 181, 190, 192, 194, 197, 198, 265
Frömmigkeit, s. a. devotion, godliness, piety 50, 62, 100, 136, 141, 147, 154, 255
Further Reformation, s. a. Nadere Reformatie 136, 144-147

G

Gallikanismus 247, 256

Gebote Gottes, s. a. commandments of God, command of God, Gesetz Gottes, law of God 36, 37, 66, 69, 143, 158, 163, 165, 168, 170, 172, 173, 175, 178, 181, 194, 195, 197, 205

Gerechtigkeit, s. a. righteousness 48, 64, 67, 69, 70, 72, 73, 155, 156, 158, 161, 166, 169, 170, 175, 181, 191, 192, 197, 251–255, 266

Gesetz und Evangelium, s. a. law and gospel 46, 48, 64, 72, 128

Glaube, s. a. faith 12, 14, 20, 56, 62, 63, 66, 69, 70, 73, 85, 88, 117, 118, 120–123, 125, 126, 129, 138, 139, 141, 146, 153, 155, 156, 159–161, 163, 165, 170–173, 175–177, 179–182, 190, 223, 258, 260–262

Glaubenslehre 12, 19

Gnade, s. a. grace 16, 19, 22, 27, 30, 32, 34, 46, 48, 52–54, 61, 63, 68, 69, 86, 126, 142, 147, 154–156, 158–166, 168–170, 172, 173, 175, 176, 178–183, 189–195, 197–199, 202–209, 217, 218, 241, 266

Gnadenlehre, s. a. doctrine of grace 18, 43, 44, 46–53, 55, 57, 104, 190

Gute Werke, s. a. good works 22, 35, 36, 52, 53, 69, 154, 158, 160, 161, 164, 165, 168, 169, 172, 175–177, 180–183, 190, 191, 193, 200

H

Häretiker, s. a. heresy, Irrlehre, Kerzerei 12, 15, 18–20, 29, 68, 79, 107, 123, 125, 153

Heidelberger Disputation 29

Heilige Schrift, s. a. Holy Scripture 10–12, 14, 17, 33, 46–57, 62, 63, 68, 77, 82, 83, 100, 105–109, 111, 116, 120, 124, 137, 139, 140, 143, 158, 183, 191, 194, 201, 203–205, 207, 262, 266

Heilsökonomie 198, 202, 209, 210

Hermeneutik, s. a. hermeneutics 25, 32, 50, 223

Humanismus, s. a. humanism 11, 90, 251

Humanist 72, 78, 83, 90, 91, 190

Hussiten 10, 12, 13, 18

Hussitentum 9, 10, 16

I

Inkarnation, s. a. incarnation 165, 249

Inquisition 202, 208

J

Jansenismus 189, 204, 207, 208, 267

Jansenist 202, 207

Jesuiten, s. a. Jesuits 97, 143, 160, 189, 197–206, 208, 209, 248, 267

K

Katholizismus, s. a. Catholicity 25, 115, 116, 118–122, 126–130, 249, 250

Ketzer, s. a. heretic 100, 120, 184, 196

Kirche, s. a. Church 12, 16, 21, 34, 55–57, 62–64, 66, 68, 99, 100, 102, 103, 105, 108, 115–130, 136, 137, 140, 142, 143, 146, 147, 153, 162, 169, 175, 176, 180, 181, 184, 191, 193, 248, 250, 251, 256, 257, 260–262

Kirchenvater, s. a. Church Father 15, 25–27, 34, 37, 38, 44–46, 48, 49, 52–55, 77, 78, 80–83, 85–88, 90, 98, 100, 106, 116, 118–120, 129, 135–138, 140, 141, 143–147, 158, 176, 189, 197, 201, 205, 247, 251, 253, 257, 260

Kölner Reformation 97, 103, 106, 107, 111

Konfession, s. a. confession 7, 97, 104, 121, 124, 126, 248, 254, 256, 258

Konzil von Trient, s. a. Council of Trent 124, 153, 161, 178–184, 190, 192–195
Konzil, s. a. council 14, 21, 54, 56, 57, 107, 108, 124, 153, 158, 159, 162, 164, 168, 173, 178, 179, 181, 184, 191

L

Leipziger Disputation, s. a. Leipzig Debate, Leipzig Dispute 16, 20, 35, 43, 50–55, 57
Logik 11, 61, 249, 250, 259, 262, 263
Lord's Supper, s. a. Abendmahl, Last Supper 77
Löwener Theologie 197
Lutheraner, s. a. Lutherans 89, 138–140, 169, 177, 193, 249, 258, 259

M

Manichäern 107, 109
Marburg Colloquy 78, 87, 88
Metaphysics of presence 217–220, 222, 226, 227, 229, 230, 240, 241
Metaphysik, s. a. metaphysics 47, 217–219, 222, 223, 226, 230, 231, 236, 238–241, 249, 250, 253–255, 258, 259, 263, 264, 266
Mittelalter, s. a. Middle Ages 25, 26, 115, 122, 125, 126, 128

N

Natürlichen Theologie 250, 253
Naturrecht 66, 254, 255, 257
Neoplatonismus 67, 87
Nominalism 87
Nominalisten 16, 17

O

Offenbarung, s. a. revelation 48, 123, 182, 259, 260
Ökumenismus 250, 256
Opfer, s. a. Messopferlehre 68, 105, 106, 110, 111, 257

P

Päpst, s. a. pope 12, 54, 56, 128, 140, 169, 191
Patristic quotations, s. a. patristic sources, patristic texts 45, 46, 48–50, 53, 136, 137, 183
Pelagianismus, s. a. anti-Pelagian, Pelagian, Semipelagianismus, semi-pelagian 14, 16, 18, 22, 25, 43–46, 48, 50–53, 67, 99, 140, 142, 154, 155, 162, 165, 170, 181, 184, 190, 197, 198, 205, 209
Perseverance of the saints 142, 146, 166, 167, 174
Philosophen 16, 25, 65
Platonism 218, 219, 222, 230, 234, 236, 239–241
Pneumatology 120
Prädestination, s. a. double predestination, predestination 27, 46, 70, 117, 124, 128, 138, 139, 142, 146, 147, 154, 166, 167, 189, 193, 199, 201–203, 205, 207–209, 218, 241, 262, 266
Prädestinationslehre, s. a. doctrine of predestination 28, 138, 154
Priestertums, s. a. priesthood 13, 154
Protestant 78, 122, 124, 135–138, 144, 148, 153, 195, 196, 257
Protestantismus, s. a. Protestantism 10, 13, 29, 97, 103, 111, 144, 209
Providenz, s. a. providence 128, 225, 253

R

Rationalismus 250
Realism 87

Realisten 17
Realpräsenz Christi, s. a. presence of Christ's body 79, 83, 84, 87, 88, 101, 111, 249, 258, 259
Rechtfertigung aus Glauben, s. a. justification by faith, justification of works 66, 124, 126, 156, 157, 163, 167, 171
Rechtfertigung, s. a. justification 20, 27, 69, 73, 110, 126, 128, 129, 153–169, 171–184, 192, 193, 195, 197
Rechtfertigungslehre, s. a. Rechtfertigungstheologie 18, 26, 27, 33, 35, 65, 104, 110, 111
Reformation 10, 14, 15, 18, 19, 25, 26, 35, 43, 46, 97, 98, 100, 102, 104, 111, 115, 122, 123, 127, 128, 137, 138, 142, 144, 169
Reformator, s. a. reformer 10, 13, 14, 17, 21, 36, 61, 77–84, 86, 87, 89, 90, 100, 126, 127, 129, 135, 146, 153, 201
Reformed Orthodoxy 136, 141, 142
Remonstrants, s. a. Counter-Remonstrants 142, 146, 147

S

Sakrament der Beichte, s. a. confession 117, 191
Sakrament, s. a. sacrament 20, 77–90, 101, 117, 120, 122, 126, 128, 145, 179, 181, 182, 257
Sakramentslehre, s. a. Sakramentstheologie, sacramental theology 77, 78, 80, 90, 99, 264
Sanctification 128, 129, 154, 163, 179, 181
Scholastik, s. a. scholasticism, scholastic tradition 25, 44, 47, 48, 57, 143, 195
Schöpfung, s. a. creation 116, 128, 154, 194, 224–226, 263, 265, 266
Semiotics of presence 217, 230–232, 235–237, 239, 241
Socinianism 217, 218, 222, 223, 238–241

Soteriologie, s. a. soteriology 61, 128, 259, 262
Spaltung, s. a. schism 97, 123, 125, 126, 248, 249, 251
Spiritualisten 102
Sünde, s. a. sins 29, 35–38, 48, 52, 54, 63, 64, 68, 69, 72, 73, 104, 109, 110, 117, 120, 142, 147, 158–160, 165, 166, 172, 174, 175, 180, 182, 190, 191, 193, 195, 198, 257, 263–266
Sündenlehre 109
Supralapsarism 142
Synod of Dordrecht 142, 145–147

T

Taufe, s. a. baptism 35, 38, 83, 109, 116–118, 120, 145, 160, 161, 170, 175, 178, 179, 182, 190, 191, 193, 195
Täufern, s. a. Anabaptists 102, 125
Tauflehre 109
Theodizee 265
Thomismus 18, 198, 203, 209
Transubstantiation 82, 90
Trinität, s. a. Trinity 118, 119, 128, 217, 241, 249

U

Universalienstreit 17
Universalismus 254

V

Verdammnis, s. a. reprobation 70, 124, 266
Vergebung von Sünden, s. a. forgiveness of sins, remission of sins 19, 20, 36, 37, 48, 66, 73, 117, 118, 120, 122, 130, 143, 154, 158, 159, 161, 163, 167, 179, 191
Vernunft, s. a. reason 12, 13, 56, 63, 71, 223, 249, 254, 255, 257, 259–264, 266, 267
Voluntaristen 266

W

Wahrheit, s. a. truth   17, 19, 47–49, 53–57, 66–68, 81, 82, 86, 87, 129, 130, 140, 172, 223, 255, 258, 259, 261, 262, 264

Willensentscheidung   17, 22, 193, 198, 263, 265, 266

Willensfreiheit, s. a. free will, Freie Wille   27–29, 32, 46, 52–54, 57, 70, 124, 160, 161, 163, 170, 178, 189, 193, 201–203, 205, 207–209, 218, 241, 263–265

Wittenberger Bewegung, s. a. Wittenberg Reformation   25, 30, 43

Wort Gottes, s. a. Word of God   19, 20, 64, 117, 118, 125, 126, 128–130, 140, 165, 178, 223, 260